Anonymous

Radical Rule - Military Outrage in Georgia

Arrest of Columbus prisoners - with facts connected with their imprisonment and release

Anonymous

Radical Rule - Military Outrage in Georgia
Arrest of Columbus prisoners - with facts connected with their imprisonment and release

ISBN/EAN: 9783337118068

Printed in Europe, USA, Canada, Australia, Japan

Cover: Foto ©ninafisch / pixelio.de

More available books at **www.hansebooks.com**

MILITARY OUTRAGE IN GEORGIA.

ARREST OF COLUMBUS PRISONERS:

WITH

FACTS CONNECTED WITH THEIR IMPRISONMENT AND RELEASE.

LOUISVILLE, KY:
PRINTED BY JOHN P. MORTON AND COMPANY, 156 Main Street.
1868.

PREFACE.

IF a proper conception of the Military Despotism which has oppressed the South is conveyed to the Northern mind through these pages, their object will have been accomplished.

MILITARY OUTRAGE IN GEORGIA.

GEORGE W. ASHBURN.

The death of this man was the pretense upon which Gen. Grant, Gen. George G. Meade, and the Radical party based the infamous outrage upon the personal liberty of citizens of Georgia, the details of which this work will contain.

Ashburn made his appearance in Columbus, Georgia, immediately after the war, in the capacity of a Government spy in search of property belonging to the late Confederate States. Here he might have lived and died without a thought from the public of his antecedents, but his ardent, intense love for the colored people soon brought to light and into general comment the fact that before the war his usual occupation was that of an overseer remarkable only for his cruelty to the slaves placed under his control by the gentlemen who owned them. This vicious trait of his character rendered it difficult for him to retain his position of overseer very long on the same plantation, and he made other shifts for a maintenance. He was at one time steward or waiter in the Oglethorpe Hotel, in Columbus, Ga., and while there was well caned for his insolence by a boarder, a young man still a resident of that city. It is not the writer's desire or intention to exonerate his murderers upon the plea of his low instincts and habits. His assassination was a crime. His death in a negro brothel of the lowest order renders comment upon his life unnecessary; but whatever his character might have been, until accused of crime as directed by the law, and convicted to death by a jury of his peers, no human being had a right to take his life. This man was politically odious and morally infamous to the respectable portion of the community in which he lived; but that his death was the result of political differences, as claimed by the Radical press throughout the country, is not sustained by facts. He was a thorn in the side of his own party and not considered as formidable by his opponents. That there are bad men in the Columbus community, as in others, there is not the least doubt. Ashburn was killed at the dead hour of night, and doubtless by men who did not dare meet a foe in open day. There are good reasons for believing, too, that the assassins were Radicals, black and white, to whom he was a stumbling-block in the road to office. In proof of the correctness of this suspicion are produced the following facts.

Previous to the election of delegates to the Constitutional Convention of Georgia, and in the temporary absence of Ashburn from Columbus, a hand-bill was issued signed by fifteen or twenty Radicals—the entire white element of the party in the city—calling a meeting to appoint delegates to a nominating Convention at Cusseta. The leader in the movement avowed uncompromising hostility to Ashburn, and expressed a determination that Ashburn should no longer control the party. Ashburn returned before the day for the meeting, went in and took possession of it, and appointed delegates to his liking, himself among the number.

So hostile had the feeling become between Ashburn and two leading Federal office-holders in Columbus, that he threatened to have them removed. Time sped on. The nominating Convention assembled at Cusseta and put out candidates for the senatorial district suited to the taste of Ashburn—himself among the number, from Muscogee county. Ashburn, having the ear and confidence of the negroes and full control of the Loyal Leagues, whipped in the fight, and proved himself master of the situation. His ticket was elected. The Convention met, did its work, and adjourned. Ashburn returned to Columbus, avowed his intention to be elected by the Legislature to the Senate of the United States, and set to work to organize his colored friends and secure the election of such members from his senatorial district as would support his senatorial pretensions.

On the Saturday before he was killed, through his influence, a large number of negroes assembled in the Court-house square and were harangued by him, and a ticket was nominated for the House and Senate, composed, for the House, of one of the delegates to the Convention and a negro, and the head of the Freedmen's Bureau, a known friend of Ashburn's, for the Senate. What part, if any, his former Radical opponents took in this meeting, or whether they were present at all, the writer can not say.

On the Monday night succeeding the meeting referred to, the career of Ashburn was brought to a close. Between dark and the time of his death the President of the Loyal League, named Bennett, handed Ashburn a letter from one Costin, a negro of Talbot county and representative elect from that county to the Georgia Legislature. Ashburn threw this letter into Bennett's face. Afterward, while a prisoner for obtaining goods under false pretenses, Bennett gave it to the Sheriff. It was written upon paper furnished the Constitutional Convention, of which Costin was a member. He abused Ashburn in unmeasured terms as a pensioner upon his party, and reminded him that he (Costin) had raised the embargo placed on his baggage by a hotel-keeper in Talbatton. He closed by offering to bet two hundred and fifty dollars that he would never represent Georgia in the United States Senate, and two hundred and fifty dollars more that he would not receive fifteen votes upon joint ballot.

Bennett declared, the day after his death, that he would have killed him if the mob had not. Woodfield, another Radical, who disappeared immediately after the murder, had stated that Ashburn must settle a debt he owed him or he would kill him.

After he was dead, and had come to his death, too, at the hands of assassins, what was the conduct of the Columbus Radicals? If they had felt any pangs of grief or indignation at this outrageous act, is it not reasonable to suppose they would have interested themselves so much, at least, as to have called to see the corpse and given some assistance toward the final disposition of his remains. Not one of the white members of his party did his remains even the honor of a call. Being a pauper, the expenses of his funeral were borne by the city. His remains were attended to the depot for shipment to Macon by only two white men—his son and a Radical Jew named Coleman.

The above facts are sent forth to the world for what they are worth. Many other things could be told to show the hostility of feeling which existed between leading Radicals of this city and Ashburn, but their relation would spin out the subject to too great a length.

Between the citizens of Columbus and Ashburn there existed no feeling of antagonism. They looked upon his course as mischievous in its tendency. They knew, however, that he was no worse in his intentions than other men of Radical proclivities in Columbus, and that to destroy him would accomplish nothing. Having more sense than half a dozen of the others, and having aspirations, he was looked upon as less dangerous than the herd that were pursuing him. The citizens outside of the Radical ranks did not come in contact with him in any shape, and had no more reason to desire the destruction of his life than those of others of less sense. Aside from this, the people had all the time used every precaution against permitting anything to be done that could, in the remotest degree, give capital for Radical rule to feed upon.

REIGN OF TERROR.

Ashburn's death was succeeded by a period of deep excitement. Negroes openly avowed their intention to avenge his death, and threats were made upon the streets to burn Columbus.

On Wednesday night following his murder, a meeting of the Young Men's Democratic Club was startled by a message from Mayor Wilkins, that intelligence had reached him that an attempt to fire the city would be made that night. If such an intention existed it was defeated by prompt action. On the 6th day of April, the Monday after the assassination, the excitement was raised to fever heat by the military arrest of nine white and three colored citizens. W. D. Chipley, Doc. E. J. Kirksey, Columbus C. Bedell, Wm. R.

Bedell, James W. Barber, Alva C. Roper, Thos. W. Grimes, Robert Ennis, and Wm. L. Cash, white; and John Wells, John Stapler, and Jim McHenry, colored; were arrested by Capt. Mills, commanding post, and confined in the Court-house. All were men of respectability and character, and the negroes stood well in their sphere, though unpopular with their race because they were Democrats. The next day one Wade Stephens, a low rowdy, was added to the party, as the sequel will show, in the capacity of a spy, though he may not have known it at the time. No cause was assigned for the arrest, and the repeated and untiring efforts of the prisoners, their friends and their counsel, failed to arrive at any. The men arrested were so far above any suspicion of complicity in Ashburn's murder that it was difficult to associate the two events; yet following each other so closely, with no other alleged cause, an occasional surmise would rest in that direction. This conclusion would never have been reached by any one but for their knowledge of the malice of certain Radicals toward these men as Democrats, and especially Chipley and Kirksey, who were working men in their party.

Before these arrests were made it was positively known that a man holding civil position by military appointment had offered bribes for affidavits against Mr. Columbus Bedell, and it was not unnatural for persons knowing these facts to surmise that the arrests were made upon suborned evidence. The manner in which the charge and names of the accusers were withheld, and the absence of all investigation, strengthened this belief, and occasioned a general feeling of uneasiness.

Capt. Mills stated that he did not know the cause of the arrests, which nobody believed, and it is only mentioned here to show how arbitrary the arrests were and the weakness of the case. After four days and nights in durance vile, Capt. Mills informed the prisoners that their most gracious Majesty Gen. Meade had concluded to release them under bond of twenty-five hundred dollars each to appear whenever Gen. George G. Meade, commanding Third Military District, or his successor, should desire it. There was a general feeling among the prisoners to decline this offer and test the legality of their arrest; but older heads thought the bond would be the last of it, and advised them to accept the terms and return to their families and business. A general bond was then prepared, a copy of which is given in Appendix, together with its signers. The names exceed four hundred, and would have reached three times that number had the citizens been allowed sufficient time to sign it. Nothing more occurred in this connection until the 14th of May, when James W. Barber, and the fellow Wade Stephens and two negroes—John Wells and John Stapler—were re-arrested and hurried off to Fort Pulaski. Mr. Barber was not even permitted to see his wife.

On the 18th May, W. D. Chipley, indignant at his illegal and unwarranted arrest, and being unable to secure an investigation in any other way, sought one through Congress. His letter to Hon. James B. Beck, of Kentucky, and action of the House on Mr. Beck's resolution, are given in Appendix. The action of the House was significant, and shows that the Radical plotters at Washington were afraid of an investigation.

On the 23d May, Mr. R. H. Daniel, a gentleman, and George F. Betz, a dissipated loafer, were arrested and sent to the Government bastile at Savannah. Very soon Bennett and a courtezan of the lowest stripe, called Amanda Patterson, followed. These two, like Stephens, it was understood, were to be suborned. Betz, at that time (though a man of no character), was thought to be above swearing a man's life away for gain or safety.

On the 2d June, W. D. Chipley, E. J. Kirksey, Clifford B. Grimes, and Columbus Bedell were arrested, and on the 3d sent to Atlanta and confined at McPherson Barracks.

On the 16th June, Isaac Marks, Jacob Marks, Alva C. Roper, Robert A. Wood, James L. Wiggins, Drew W. Lawrence, and Wm. L. Cash were taken into custody by the omnipotent Mills and forwarded to Meade's Hotel, at Atlanta. Sergeant Chas. Marshall, of Mill's company, was also sent along, for the purpose developed by the trial. On the 19th June, Robert C. Huddson and James Lawrence were started, preceding Wm. A. Dukes some five days. The charges against these men were still mere matters of conjecture. From the best information that could be gathered, the parties had been arrested upon negro testimony, much of it forced, whilst with others bribery had been the instrument used. In addition to $500 offered by the city of Columbus, Gen. Meade's military Governor of Georgia, through his proclamation, announced a reward of $2,000 for the first and $1,000 for each additional party connected with the assassination, with proof to convict. This was a large sum of money, in the eyes of a bad negro, as an inducement to bear false witness. With such inducements no citizen of Columbus, however exemplary his walk in life, felt that he was exempt from arrest. No one knew where the arrests would end, and what number of citizens would be incarcerated, under the influence of such testimony—no one could conjecture. As arrest after arrest succeeded each other, the best citizens would exclaim: " 'Tis but an accident that I am left!" and they extended their sympathy to the unfortunate men with a consciousness that it was but a chance that placed the prisoners there instead of themselves.

TREATMENT OF PRISONERS.

The treatment of the Columbus prisoners will ever remain a blot upon the fame of American soldiers. These men, arrested at a moment's notice, were carried from family, friends and business, and without an opportunity being given them to prove their innocence, were thrown into cells which law and humanity dictated as only proper for the confinement of condemned criminals. The murder occurred during the night, between the 30th and 31st of March. The first arrests were made on 6th April; they were renewed through May and June. Yet, in this great and free country, no charges were delivered to the prisoners until the 27th day of June. Their trial was set for 29th of the same month. The enormity of the proceedings in this connection may possibly be appreciated, when it is stated that the intervening day between the reception of a copy of charges brought against them and the day set for their trial was Sunday. The Holy Sabbath day was given them upon which to prepare their defense against the charge of "MURDER," and that too when removed 140 miles from the scene of the crime and the residence of their witnesses. This outrage upon the personal liberty of these men should make boil the blood of every freeman who reads these pages. But to return to their physical treatment.

This was barbarous in the extreme. Those who were carried to Fort Pulaski were confined in cells four feet by seven feet. There was no ventilation whatever, and a greater portion of the time the small hole which admitted light was closed and the cell left in darkness. These dungeons were their sole habitation. Calls of nature were attended to in a vessel that was removed once in twenty-four hours. Their rations consisted of a slice of bread, and coffee (if they had a cup) in the morning; another piece of bread and soup in the same cup in which coffee was served at breakfast, with an occasional ration of fat pork, constituted their dinner. For supper, bread alone was issued. Yet the friends of these prisoners would have been glad and did offer to furnish them any comforts they might desire. Will the world not say they were entitled to different treatment, until their guilt had been established, or at least until something besides ex parte testimony had been produced? In these horrid holes, borne down by the heat of the climate, and driven almost to madness by the myriads of mosquitoes, these men were detained day after day, denied the privilege of visits from friends or counsel, and not even allowed to write to or receive letters from their families. Humanity must have suggested an exception to this rule in the case of one of the prisoners, whose wife was expecting to be confined, but if so the whispers were not heeded by the "genial and popular commander of Fort Pulaski." He added another laurel to the wreath that marks his victories. "The gallant Cook," with heroic fortitude, saw that no word of love and sympathy reached the young wife in her trying hour. It may be well for the reader to remember just here, that the witnesses for the prosecution stated on their examination that they were told that if they did not make disclosures they would be kept in prison—as Bennett expressed it, would have to "rot there." On the other hand, by making disclosures they would secure their liberty, and protection from "harm" from the Government. The removal of the Pulaski prisoners to McPherson Barracks, Atlanta, was an improvement in climate and some other respects. They were permitted to correspond with their friends, but all letters, although only breathing the affection and sympathy of a wife, were submitted to rigid inspection. How disgraceful in the representatives of a great government! Chipley, Kirksey, Grimes and Bedell reached the barracks on the 3d day of June, having no suspicion of imprisonment. They were unprovided with bedding. It was three days and four nights before bed or blanket was furnished. Friends were not allowed to visit them nor counsel to see them. On the 8th these four men were placed under bond in comfortable quarters. When Daniel arrived from Fort Pulaski he was placed in the house with them, and there he and Grimes remained until released. On the 12th Bedell was returned to the cells. On the 15th Chipley and Kirksey followed. On the 19th the last two were returned again to quarters outside of the guard-house, and next morning Bedell joined them. On 22d he and Kirksey were returned to cells, and Roper was placed with Chipley. The other prisoners were in cells. This status was continued until the 14th July, when Chipley was offered bail with the liberty of Atlanta, which he declined. On the 16th, the entire party were removed to comfortable quarters, where they remained until released. The cells up to the 16th June were five feet ten in width by ten feet long. The window, two feet by one foot six inches, was eight feet high from the floor, and in addition to bars was so slatted as to prevent the inmate of the cell from seeing either heaven or earth. There was no other means of ventilation, and with the door closed (which was always the case, except when the guard was humane enough to transcend his orders,) a gale might blow outside without sending one puff of fresh air to relieve the distended bursting veins of the prisoner, although the opening of the cell door would create a draft that was often objectionable. The prison sink, just at the end of the hall upon which the cells opened, emitted such a stench as to render the risk of suffocation preferable to the horrid odor. But all this was not sufficiently horrible. With twenty vacant houses that might have been used, the military commenced on the 16th June to make more prison room by dividing the cells, reducing them in width to exactly two feet ten inches. Will an indignant public believe this? A positive, horrible truth. Not until the memorials of Dr. Chipley and Col. Lamar to Congress had elicited a deep and earnest protest from the press of the whole country, did the treatment of the prisoners change. On the 19th June some of them were allowed to see counsel, although in the absence of charges, it was impossible to plan any definite line of defense. Soon after the remainder saw counsel, and *a few* friends were permitted to pay short visits and send delicacies to the prison. The embargo on certain newspapers was also raised. On the 22d June C. B. Grimes and R. A. Daniel were released, and a week later the Messrs. Lawrence, the Messrs. Marks, and W. L. Cash. No evidence whatever has been produced against either one of these gentlemen, and the only explanation that is given them for the torture they were subjected to is, that it was a mistake. At no time was the private correspondence of the prisoners relieved from inspection.

CAUSE OF THE ARRESTS.

On the 6th of April, ten white and three colored men were arrested and placed in confinement in court-house at Columbus. On the trial the prosecution rested their case upon evidence which did not claim that any disclosures were made to the military, or other authorities, before the last week in May, except by the witness Bennett. This creature professed to have made statements to Capt. Mills the day after the occurrence, implicating five men. These men were all accessible, yet in the list of thirteen arrested in April, the name of but one of Bennett's five can be found. Another one, Marshall, was in the room several times during their incarceration, but as a visitor. How improbable it must appear to every reader that Bennett charged Marshall with being one of the murderers before his Captain, as that officer, twenty-five days later, allowed him to leave his company on a thirty days' furlough. The question very naturally arises, why were the first arrests made? The mystery was easily solved, and its solution does not involve a midnight murder. A general apathy had pervaded the Democratic party in regard to registering and voting. The policy of inaction had governed the party, but the result in Alabama occasioned new acts of Congress that rendered this policy no longer available, and an active canvass was inaugurated. Mr. Chipley, as Chairman of the Executive

Committee, had prepared complete printed lists of the voters in the county who could and had not registered, and was, through sub-committees, urging all such to do their duty. Messrs. Grimes and Barber were candidates on the Democratic ticket. All the remainder except the spy, Stephens, were known to be earnest Democrats. It was a common boast among the Radical negroes of the city, that John Wells's Democratic principles had gotten him into jail.

But one comment is necessary. The party was arrested the day registration commenced, and released the day it closed. Mr. Chipley's second arrest followed close upon the presentation of his letter by Mr. Beck to Congress—in fact, as soon as the proceedings in that connection could reach General Meade's headquarters. Another coincidence in dates occurred when Dr. Chipley's memorial was presented to the Senate. It was telegraphed to Atlanta, and Mr. Chipley was returned to a cell. If there was any other reason for this renewal of torture in Chipley's case, it has never been developed. In the evidence for the prosecution, the date of their disclosures is placed by the witnesses themselves, subsequent to the arrest of a majority of the persons. Then upon what foundation were the arrests based? The whole object was for political purposes.

No attention was paid to the death of Ashburn in Columbus at the time it occurred. It was known that this victim of assassination was a wretched outcast from society, and one forced to seek a home in a negro brothel. Yet when the report of Ashburn's death reached Washington, party machinery was set in motion to manufacture out of it political capital. An opportunity was offered to prove a southern barbarity which would justify Radical tyranny and outrage. General Meade was appealed to to have the matter investigated, and he dispatched to Columbus Major Smythe, a member of his staff, to examine into and report the facts; at the same time offering a large reward for the apprehension of the murderers. The Major caused the arrest of a large number of citizens, but failing to obtain any clue to the perpetrators of the deed, abandoned the game as not worth the chase. The Washington directory, however, were not so easily satisfied. The services of a detective who had been in Washington under the pay of the War Department, to "work up" the impeachment matter, was detailed by General Howard, acting under orders from General Grant, to proceed to Atlanta, and report to General Meade for orders. The detective having reported according to instructions, General Meade referred him to Major Smythe, who told him of the examination already had, and its barren results. In the mean time General Howard telegraphed to Kansas for one Major Whitley, who had figured prominently in the services of the War Department in connection with General Baker. Upon these two worthies had Stanton and Holt devolved the duty of getting the testimony on the trial of Mrs. Surratt, and now Whitley was to be appealed to in the Georgia trials. He arrived in Washington in obedience to General Howard's telegram, and was hurried off to his new field of labor under the incentive of $40,000 reward. How well he has succeeded in his work of manipulating witnesses, has been shown in the published testimony taken before the Commission.

Can the people of the North imagine that men of unimpeachable character could be subjected to the barbarous treatment detailed in these pages, upon suborned ex parte evidence, which when produced in court broke down of its own weight? Yet it can not be denied. A brief account of his action in the N. E. Thomas murder, will show that General Meade was influenced by political prejudice in the case of the Columbus prisoners.

One Joshua Morse, a renegade Alabamian, elected on the negro ticket to the position of Solicitor for his circuit, together with a man named Gilmore, in cold blood murdered N. E. Thomas, editor of the Choctow (Ala.) Herald. Morse, in a letter to the Marengo Recorder, of date June 29th, 1868, gives a version of the difficulty and closes thus: "I have been refused bail. The Justice of the Peace has prejudged the case, and my political enemies declare I ought to be hung. We have been forced to apply to the commanding General for protection.

"Very truly yours,

[Signed.] "JOSHUA MORSE."

This murderer flies to General Meade for bail, while gentlemen against whom no charge has been made, are detained in loathsome cells for months, under circumstances without parallel in a free country.

Then what explanation can General Meade offer an indignant people for the outrage upon R. A. Daniel, Cliff B. Grimes, Wm. L. Cash, James Lawrence, Drew Lawrence, Isaac Marks, Jacob Marks, John Stapler, and John Wells? These men were placed in cells, and the affidavits in Appendix will show how cruelly they were treated. Yet they were released without trial, condition, or explanation. The witnesses altered their affidavits time and again, under the direction of Joe Brown, Whitley, and Smythe. For instance, General Meade stated positively that he had sufficient evidence to hang every prisoner. A distinguished gentleman and friend of Meade's in the old army, replied that he could swear that Mr. Grimes was at his house, three miles from town. The result was the release of Grimes. As proof of their innocence was discovered by the detectives, eight others were released. The father of one witness for the prosecution, openly stated that his son was at home dead drunk at the time of the murder, and was unworthy of belief. The early adjournment of the Commission alone prevented this evidence from being produced. Betz owned he went into the affair for fifty dollars. Stephens was impeached by his mother and aunt before the Superior Court of Muscogee county. His mother, a white woman, lives in open adultery with a negro man. Bennett and Amanda Patterson lived in a *negro* brothel, and both swore to one thing on the inquest and another on the trial. Charles Marshall, the soldier, acknowledged that he was *persuaded* to commit murder by associates, and all said that their disclosures were made under promises of protection if they would, and threats of imprisonment if they refused, to give evidence. The trial commenced a few days before the Georgia Legislature was convened. The prosecution expected to place their suborned evidence on record before the country and then turn the case over to the civil authorities upon the adoption of the fourteenth amendment. They were disgusted with their own case and saw no other chance to influence public opinion. Fortunately the Legislature hung fire, and several *alibis* were proven, among others, Duke's, the best ever produced in any court, before the amendment was passed. Duke was arrested but four days before the trial commenced. Had he been taken into custody sooner the detectives would have found out that he was forty miles from town on the night of the murder, (as indiscreet friends always hastened to tell all they knew) and he would have been released, as Grimes, Cash, Daniel, and others were. When the prosecution had fallen through of its own weight, the suborner Smythe hurried off with the poor creatures he had used. Could there be a more severe comment upon the prosecution? Why were the perjured wretches taken out of the State upon the eve of Georgia's mock return to the Union? General Meade unblushingly shields perjury.

HUMANITY IN HIGH PLACES.

While the love of liberty and republican institutions is held dear in the hearts of the people of the United States, just so long will the memory of George G. Meade be abhorred and detested. A new era is dawning, and soon this pliant minion of power will only be remembered as a poor, unreasoning satrap, whose highest ambition was to hold place by pandering to his Radical masters at Washington.

Gen. Meade, upon his return from Philadelphia, was accompanied by an officer sent out by the President to investigate the arrests, when the partitions in the cells were knocked out, thereby making their width five feet ten inches, instead of *two feet ten inches*, as they were before. He also remarked to Mr. Chipley, in the presence of his mother-in-law and wife, that it had not been his intention to confine men so who could give guaranties for their appearance. This was after the whole country had, in thundering tones, denounced his despicable cruelty. His sincerity (?) even then was evinced by the fact that men were continued in cells for weeks afterward who could have given bond to any amount. It is not an unusual practice for generals of limited renown to inflict censure upon subordinates; but Gen. Meade must stand square to the rack this time and receive the verdict of an outraged and indignant public.

When Mr. Chipley left Columbus for Atlanta he was accompanied by a friend who had known Meade intimately in the old army, and during the war served on Gen. Lee's staff. He sought at once and found him (Gen. Meade) on the eve of his departure from Atlanta. In a short interview which followed, he told this gentleman that he had left full instructions with Gen. Sibley as to the disposition of the Columbus prisoners. Upon application this gentleman received a promise from Gen. Sibley that he should send the prisoners some comforts. When morning came and the proper permit was applied for, Gen. Sibley informed him that on re-examining *his instructions* he found it impossible to make good his pledge. Gen. Meade had already said that these instructions were left by his order, and it was these instructions that deprived men at that time, not even accused of any crime, of liberty, of visits from friends or counsel, of comforts to which they were accustomed, and even of the free air of heaven. This duplicity and cruelty may secure his family claim, now before Congress, but it will forever damn the name of George G. Meade.

GENERAL GRANT.

In a few months the country will be called upon to decide whether or not this man shall be placed at the head of the Government. Will not every thinking man pause and reflect? The crime upon the Columbus prisoners followed close upon the Etawaw outrage. The recurrence of such affairs as that these pages describe presses home the questions: How long are the denizens of our Southern States to be made the victims of military misrule? Must the people of that region forever be made the shuttlecocks of military power? Will not the people enforce some rule whereby peaceable, industrious, order-loving citizens can prosecute their business without momentary dread of being incarcerated upon charges trumped up by political or personal foes? More than three years have elapsed since the late civil war terminated. The condition of the Southern people is worse than during the war. In the field they met open enemies only. Now they suffer everything from the machinations of pretended friends—adventurers of all sorts through the southern portion of our republic. The military, who ought to be their safeguard and protection, are turned into an engine of opprsssion. Call their localities States, Territories, or what you will, there is no excuse for so great a Government as our own withholding prompt, speedy, exact justice through the civil tribunals of the localities wherein crimes are alleged to have been committed.

A few more cases like that of the incarceration of the Columbus prisoners will open the eyes of the people to the necessity of providing for the trial of accused persons through the civil courts. The military have been, now are, and always will be an unsafe depository of the legal relations of citizens. The power which they exert in the field is arbitrary and, to a great extent, irresponsible. Their province is to command, not to give reasons for their orders. Not so with the civilian. When sitting as a judge he is confined to precedents, and is making precedents in every decision which he announces. With the latter, the property, the liberty, the life of the citizen is comparatively safe. The military act upon emergencies, and the rapidity of their action precludes the due consideration which justice to accused persons demands. The courts, on the other hand, are calm, careful, deliberate. Their rules of evidence allow everything which can be brought before the court in exculpation of the accused. Military law seizes only a few salient points and on these a judgment is rendered. The people owe it to themselves and the nation speedily to abolish military rule. Its effect is evil, and only evil. During the progress of a war there may be some necessity for its exercise. But in times of peace, when there is no armed force against the Government, and no hostility manifested by the citizens against the laws, military rule becomes a constant source of irritation, which disturbs the social relations, deranges business, and keeps whole communities in a state of inquietude. None are benefited by such a state of things save the gang of unscrupulous adventurers who are ready to do anything which will fill their coffers, regardless of the effects thereof upon the people among whom they may temporarily reside. The South is well-nigh paralyzed by the military parasites which it is compelled to support. Let these parasites be withdrawn and peace, order, and prosperity will again prevail throughout the sunny side of our republic.

One word from Gen. Meade would have put an end to all these wrongs inflicted upon the Columbus prisoners; yet he withheld that word. One line from the pen of Gen. Grant would have checked the mad career of Gen. Meade, restored justice

MILITARY OUTRAGE IN GEORGIA. 11

to the seat from which she had been rudely thrust, and established civil liberty throughout the blighted regions of the South. But that line remained unwritten, and the rude tyranny of brute force held high revelry in the prisons of Georgia.

Is the man who thus abuses power throughout ten States of the Union a suitable depository of the destinies and the liberties of the people of the United States? As the tree is judged by its fruit, so must the fitness of Gen. Grant for preserving the liberties of the citizen be judged by the manner in which he sustains the subversion of the Constitution wherever his authority extends.

CONFESSION OF ONE OF THE SUBORNERS.

Affidavit of Wm. H. Reed, Government Detective.

WASHINGTON, D. C.,
July 3, 1868.

Personally appeared before me, a Justice of the Peace for the District of Columbia, Wm. H. Reed, who, being duly sworn, deposeth and sayeth: I was telegraphed to by H. C. Whitley, a Government detective, to come to Washington from Boston, Mass. In answer to that dispatch I arrived in Washington on the 6th of March, 1868. I joined H. C. Whitley; he took me to Chipman & Hosmer's office on 14th street, and they told me they wanted to employ me as a United States Government detective in the impeachment of the President of the United States. Hosmer took me upstairs, in the same building with his office, to a one-legged man's room they called Doctor. Hosmer told me to go around the hotels and make my report every day to the Doctor. In a few days Hosmer sent me to Gen. O. O. Howard, commanding Freedmen's Bureau. The General told me to make my report to Maj. Mann. I did so with several other detectives, including a number of negroes, to the 14th or 15th of April, and was paid by the Doctor and Maj. Mann $300. General O. O. Howard then ordered me to go to Atlanta Georgia, and report to Gen. Meade, to work up the Ashburn murder case. He, Gen. Howard, says, you go there by the order of Gen. Grant. He, Howard, sent me to Maj. Mann, who paid me one hundred dollars. Gen. Howard gave me a letter to Gen. Meade, in Atlanta, Ga., stating that I came as a Government detective, and he, Gen. Meade, to pay my expenses. I arrived there about the 18th of April. General Meade referred me to Maj. Smythe, that he, Smythe, knew about the Ashburn murder case. Before I arrived in Atlanta there had been several arrests made in Columbus, Ga., and Maj. Smythe informed me that he had discharged them for the want of evidence to implicate them with the murder of Ashburn. He told me I could not make anything by going to Columbus, but hoped I could make up a case. General Meade ordered me to go to Columbus. I stayed there two or three weeks. In this time I felt it was necessary for me to arrest several parties. H. C. Whitley having been sent for by Gen. Meade at my request. Gen. Meade desired I should not make any arrests until the arrival of Whitley. Gen. Meade telegraphed to Washington to have the Government telegraph to Whitley, who was then in Kansas, for him to come immediately to Georgia. He arrived in a few days. Whitley came to Columbus and met me. We had an interview with Capt. Mills, the commander of the post, at Columbus, Ga., and recommended him to make several arrests, which he declined to do without an order from Gen. Meade. Whitley got an order from Gen. Meade, that Capt. Mills should arrest five or six parties, to be pointed out by myself and Whitley, and they were to be sent to Fort Pulaski. We, before the arrests were made, went to Atlanta, and got an order from Gen. Meade to the Commander of the post at Savannah to give us, myself and Whitley, full control of the prisoners after they arrived at Fort Pulaski. While we were on our way to the fort the following arrests were made in Columbus, Ga.: Stephens and Barber, two white men, and John Stapler and John Wells, two negroes, and sent to Fort Pulaski. Whitley and myself met them, the prisoners, at Savannah, and proceeded to the fort with them. At the fort one of the negroes, John Wells, was taken out of his cell and put into a chair in one of the casements with a cannon pointed at his head, and a soldier hold of the string ready to snap the cap, apparently to shoot the gun; a barber lashed his head full of lather and pretended to be ready to shave his head. This was done to have him give evidence in regard to killing Ashburn. The negro all the time contending he knew nothing about the murder. This farce was kept up about ten minutes; finally they put him back in his cell, with the understanding that if he did not tell something it would be worse for him. They took the other negro, John Stapler, and put him before the gun with no better success. He was afterward put in the sweat-box and kept there in great punishment for at least thirty hours, until his legs swelled, and I took him out of the box, being convinced he knew nothing about the case. At Whitley's and my request the following other arrests were made: Daniel Betz, Amanda Patterson, who were sent to Fort Pulaski. Stevens and Barber were put in one cell. Whitley and myself secreted ourselves in the adjoining cell, but we could hear no conversation between them implicating any of the prisoners. Amanda Patterson was considered an important witness and was put in officers' quarters. Whitley and myself talked with her frequently in regard to the murder, but she earnestly declared she knew none of the parties, as they were masked and painted. She acknowledged being in the house at the time of the shooting. Whitley persevered in questioning said Amanda, and said to me that he would in time get enough evidence out of her to implicate some of the prisoners and other parties, so as to give Whitley an opportunity to make more arrests. Whitley then went to Columbus and arrested other parties. A man was arrested named Bennett, and sent to me at Fort Pulaski to see if I could not draw some evidence from him in regard to the murder. In my frequent conversations with this man Bennett, his prevarications convinced me if any one was guilty of the killing of Ashburn this man Bennett was guilty. After this Bennett was put in the cell with Betz to see if he could not draw some evidence from him. Afterward, he, Bennett, was put in a room with Betz and Stevens, with the view of still obtaining evidence from both of them together. He, Bennett, admitted to me that he was in the crowd that done the shooting at Ashburn, and persuaded Betz and Stevens to acknowledge the complicity of the prisoners arrested with the murder. Whitley and myself placed Bennett with Betz and Stevens for the purpose of working Betz and Stevens up to testify against the prisoners. We, Whitley and myself, promised Bennett, Betz and Stevens, if they would come out and expose the whole story, if they were guilty themselves, they should be protected from punishment by the Government. Amanda Patterson, Bennett, Betz, Marshall and Stevens were all of the prisoners that pretend to know anything about the murder. These parties gave no evidence until they were imprisoned, tired out, and the evidence wrung from them by Whitley and Major Smythe by promises of reward and security from punishment. They, Whitley and Smythe, had frequent conversations with Amanda Patterson, educating her in the evidence she was to give; also Betz and Stevens, making each one repeat the evidence over and over again to have them perfect, so when they were called upon to give their evidence they would not contradict themselves, each one to tell the same story. Whitley remarked to me frequently that this whole case was a political move, and the conviction of the prisoners would be a big thing.

The prisoners that were intended as witnesses were told that the Government had offered a large reward, and if the parties under arrest were convicted, they, the witnesses, would get their share of the reward offered. During the time I was engaged in making up this case in Georgia, I drew money from the Paymaster by Gen. Meade's order.

[Signed,]   WM. H. REED.

Subscribed and sworn to before me, a Justice of the Peace, in and for Washington county, D. C., the 3d day of July, 1868.

[Signed,]   WM. MARTIN, J. P.

From the Columbus (Ga.) Sun.

CARD FROM THE COLUMBUS PRISONERS.

Account of their Arrest, Imprisonment, Treatment, &c.

JULY 25, 1868.

Upon resuming our personal liberty, we, the undersigned, known as the Columbus prisoners, deem it proper to publish the following brief account of our arrest and confinement by the military authorities. During the night of the 30th of March, Geo. W. Ashburn was assassinated in a low negro brothel in Columbus, Ga. On the 6th day of April thirteen citizens were arrested by Capt. Mills, of the U. S. army. On the 10th they were released under bond. Four of this number have never been re-arrested. The man Mills stated that he did not know the charge against the party arrested, but no one believed him, and the fact is only mentioned to show the character of the proceedings. On the 14th day of May four arrests were made, on the 24th four, on the 2d of June four more, on the 16th seven, followed the next day by two others. On the 24th another and the last arrest occurred. These arrests were made by the order of Gen. Meade. Several of the undersigned have in their possession written orders which show this fact. The arrests were made without warrant, affidavit, or charge. No preliminary examination was held. We were kept in total ignorance of the ex parte evidence against us, and the names of our accusers were concealed from us. No one who has followed the trial will be surprised at this apparent neglect.

While we were clamoring for the charges against us. Joe Brown, Whitley, Maj. Smythe and others were suborning Betz, Marshall, Bennett, and Amanda Patterson. The evidence for the prosecution acknowledges that disclosures were made under threats of imprisonment. This is bad enough, but a worse feature is that the date of these disclosures is placed by the witnesses themselves *subsequent* to the arrest of a majority of the prisoners. The question naturally arises, upon what foundation were the arrests based? Of the twenty-two persons arrested on and since the 14th of May, four were *suborned by torture, bribery, and threats.* Nine, after confinement in *felons' cells* and much suffering, were released without any explanation whatever. The remaining nine are the signers of this card. The prisoners arrested in May were at Fort Pulaski before they were removed to Atlanta. Their cells were as dark as dungeons, without ventilation, and but four feet by seven. No bed or blankets were furnished. The rations consisted of a *slice* of *fat* pork three times each week, and beef, too *unsound* to eat, the remaining days. A piece of bread for each meal, soup for dinner and coffee for breakfast, finished the bill of fare. An old *oyster can* was given each prisoner, and in this vessel both coffee and soup were served. It may be said that the soldiers received nothing better, but these citizens were not soldiers, and their friends were able, willing, and anxious to give them every comfort. They were denied the privilege. Refused all communication with their friends, relatives, or counsel, they were forced to live in these horrid cells night and day, prostrated by heat and maddened by myriads of musquitoes. The calls of nature were attended to in a bucket, which was removed but once in twenty-four hours.

At McPherson Barracks we were placed in cells five feet eleven inches wide by ten feet long. These cells were afterward divided, reducing their width to *two feet ten inches.* This is terrible, but true. Upon the arrival of the officer sent from Washington to investigate the arrests, the partitions were removed. Neither bed or bedding was furnished for from two to five days. We were not permitted to see our friends, family, or counsel until after memorials to Congress had aroused the whole country to the enormity of the outrage. Even after this, our LETTERS, breathing the affection and sympathy of a wife or mother, were subjected to inspection. The prison sink was immediately at our cell doors and emitted a stench that was horrible.

At times, when some humane soldier was willing to transcend his orders and give us a breath of fresh air to soothe our distended, bursting veins, we would ask him to *close* the door, preferring to risk suffocation rather than endure the intolerable smell.

During all this time we were ignorant of the charges against us. Of course we accepted the common rumor that our arrest grew out of the murder of Ashburn, but after our counsel was permitted to visit us no definite line of defense could be planned in the absence of all specifications. We were furnished with a copy of the charges against us on the 27th day of June, our trial having been set for the 29th. The intervening day was Sunday and we were 140 miles from the scene of the murder and the residence of our witnesses.

Several of the undersigned never saw the detective, Whitley, until weeks after their arrest. When they did meet him he never *presumed* to treat them with *disrespect.*

Recent developments, new to us, have shown him to be *infamous,* and his treatment of suborned witnesses will be proven by those who know the facts. Our friends and the *press* have not *exaggerated* the barbarity with which we were treated, but they should not *throw the responsibility upon a contemptible detective*, who would only glory in the notoriety his infamy would give him. We fly for higher game. Gen. Meade told Gen. R. H. Chilton (during the war Gen. Lee's Adjutant), upon the eve of his departure from Atlanta, that he had left full instructions with Gen. Sibley concerning the disposition of the Columbus prisoners. These *instructions controlled* our treatment, and leave no issue as to the question of RESPONSIBILITY. At the proper time, and in a manner that will not intrude upon your valuable space, we will make good our position, and will show conclusively that this unparalleled persecution was attempted solely and entirely for *political* purposes.

The officers and soldiers of the garrison were as kind as their orders would permit, and respectful, with but few exceptions. Gen. Dunn's courtesy during the trial, especially after Duke's *alibi*, was in strong contrast with the *vindictive, ungenerous, and unmanly* conduct of Joe Brown.

Of the able and untiring efforts of our counsel, we can not speak in too *high praise*. To the people of Georgia, and especially to our good friends in Atlanta, we return our sincere thanks for their sympathy and assistance.

W. D. CHIPLEY,
C. C. BEDELL,
R. A. WOOD,
E. J. KIRKSEY, M. D.
R. HUDSON,
J. L. WIGGINS,
ALVA C. ROPER,
W. A. DUKE,
JAMES W. BARBER.

PROCEEDINGS OF THE MILITARY COMMISSION.

COUNSEL FOR THE DEFENSE.

ALEXANDER H. STEPHENS,   MARTIN J. CRAWFORD,   JAMES M. SMITH,
JAMES M. RAMSEY,   R. J. MOSES, SR.,   WM. U. GARRARD,
HENRY L. BENNING,   MARSHALL J. WELLBORN,   LUCIUS J. GARTRELL.

The Military Commission convened at McPherson Barracks, Atlanta, Georgia, June 29th, 1868, by virtue of the following orders:

HEADQUARTERS THIRD MILITARY DISTRICT,
Department of Georgia, Florida, and Alabama.
Atlanta, Georgia, June 23, 1868.

[EXTRACT.]

SPECIAL ORDERS, No. 136.

* * * * *

II. A Military Commission is hereby appointed to assemble at McPherson Barracks, Atlanta, Georgia, at 10 o'clock A. M., on Monday, the 29th day of June, 1868, or as soon thereafter as practicable, for the trial of such prisoners as may be brought before it by orders from these headquarters. The Commission will sit without regard to hours.

DETAIL FOR THE COMMISSION.

1. Brevet Brigadier General Caleb C. Sibley, Colonel 16th Infantry.
2. Brevet Brigadier General Rufus Saxton, Major and Quartermaster U. S. Army.
3. Brevet Brigadier General John J. Milhau, Surgeon U. S. Army.
4. Brevet Colonel John R. Lewis, Major 44th Infantry.
5. Brevet Lieutenant Colonel Robert E. A. Crofton, Captain 16th Infantry.
6. Brevet Major Samuel E. St. Onge, Captain 16th Infantry.
7. Brevet Major George M. Brayton, Captain 33d Infantry.

Brevet Brigadier General William McKee Dunn, Assistant Judge Advocate General of the army, is appointed Judge Advocate of the Commission.

* * * * *

By order of Major General Meade.
R. C. DRUM,
Assistant Adjutant General.
Official: W. W. SANDERS, A. A. I. G.

HEADQUARTERS THIRD MILITARY DISTRICT,
Department of Georgia, Florida, and Alabama.
Atlanta, Georgia, June 26, 1868.

[EXTRACT.]

SPECIAL ORDERS, No. 139.

1. Brevet Brigadier General Elisha G. Marshall, Colonel U. S. Army, is hereby detailed a member of the Military Commission instituted in Special Orders No. 136, current series, from these headquarters, in place of Brevet Brigadier General Rufus Saxton, Major and Quartermaster U.·S. Army, hereby relieved from that detail.

* * * * *

By order of Major General Meade.
R. C. DRUM,
Assistant Adjutant General.

Official:
W. W. SANDERS, A. A. I. G.

McPHERSON BARRACKS, ATLANTA, GA.,
June 29, 1868, 10 o'clock A. M.

The Commission met pursuant to the foregoing orders:

PRESENT.

1. Brevet Brigadier General Caleb C. Sibley, Colonel 16th Infantry.
2. Brevet Brigadier General Elisha G. Marshall, Colonel U. S. Army.
3. Brevet Brigadier General John J. Milhau, Surgeon U. S. Army.
4. Brevet Colonel John R. Lewis, Major 44th Infantry.
5. Brevet Lieutenant Colonel Robert E. A. Crofton, Captain 16th Infantry.
6. Brevet Major Samuel E. St. Onge, Captain 16th Infantry.
7. Brevet Major George M. Brayton, Captain 33d Infantry.

Brevet Brigadier General William McKee Dunn, Assistant Judge Advocate General of the Army, Judge Advocate.

The Commission then proceeded to the trial of Elisha J. Kirksey, Columbus C. Bedell, James W. Barber, William A. Duke, Robert Hudson, William D. Chipley, Alva C. Roper, James L. Wiggins, and Robert A. Wood, who being called into court, and having heard the foregoing orders read, and also the following charge and specification against them, and the indorsement thereon:—

CHARGE.—Murder.
SPECIFICATION.—In this, that the said Elisha J. Kirksey, Columbus C. Bedell, Jas. W. Barber, William A. Duke, Robert Hudson, William D. Chipley, Alva C. Roper, Jas. L. Wiggins, Robert A. Wood, Henry Hennis, Herbert W. Blair, and Milton Malone, on the 31st day of March, 1868, in the city of Columbus, in the county of Muscogee, State of Georgia, in and upon one George W. Ashburn, then and there being in the peace of the said State, feloniously and willfully did make an assault; and did then and there feloniously, unlawfully, willfully, and with malice aforethought, discharge pistols loaded with powder and leaden balls at the said George W. Ashburn; and with the said balls discharged as aforesaid, did wound the said George W. Ashburn in the left leg, above and near the ankle joint; and with the said balls discharged as aforesaid, did wound the said George W. Ashburn in the lower part of the nates; and with the said balls, discharged as aforesaid, did wound the said George W. Ashburn in the forehead, which said wound, inflicted in the forehead as aforesaid, was mortal, and of which said mortal wound, inflicted in the manner and form aforesaid, the said George W. Ashburn, then and there died; and the said Elisha J. Kirksey, Columbus C. Bedell, James W. Barber, William A. Duke, Robert Hudson, William D. Chipley, Alva C. Roper, James L. Wiggins, Robert A. Wood, Henry Hennis, Herbert W. Blair, and Milton Malone, the said George W. Ashburn, in the manner and form aforesaid feloniously, unlawfully, willfully and of their malice aforethought, did then and there kill and murder, contrary to the laws of said State, the good order, peace, and dignity thereof.
[Signed.] WM. H. SMYTHE,
Captain 16th Infantry, and Brevet Major U. S. A., Acting Judge Advocate.

INDORSEMENT.—Respectfully referred to Brevet Brigadier General Dunn, Judge Advocate of the Commission for trial.
By order of Major General Meade.
[Signed.] R. C. DUNN, A. A. G.
Third Military District, June 27, 1868.

—Were severally asked if they had any objection to be tried by any member present named in the orders; to which they severally replied in the negative, but stated that in making no such objection, they did not waive any right to object to the jurisdiction of the Commission.

The members of the Commission were then severally duly sworn by the Judge Advocate, and the Judge Advocate was duly sworn by the President of the Commission, all of which oaths were administered in the presence of the accused.

Eugene Davis was duly sworn by the Judge Advocate as phonographic reporter for the Commission, which oath was administered in the presence of the accused.

The accused then applied for permission to introduce as counsel, Messrs. A. H. Stephens, M. J. Crawford, J. M. Smith, H. L. Benning, R. J. Moses, J. N. Ramsey, and L. J. Gartrell.

Permission having been granted, Messrs. A. H. Stephens, M. J. Crawford, J. M. Smith, J. N. Ramsey, and L. J. Gartrell, were introduced and took their seats as counsel for the accused; Messrs. H. L. Benning and R. J. Moses being absent.

The Judge Advocate requested permission to introduce Joseph E. Brown, and Brevet Major W. H. Smythe, Captain 16th Infantry, as assistants to the Judge Advocate.

The accused were then arraigned on the following charge and specification, which charge and specification, and the indorsement thereon, were read aloud by the Judge Advocate in the presence of the accused.

CHARGE.—Murder.
SPECIFICATION.—In this: that the said Elisha J. Kirksey, Columbus C. Bedell, Jas. W. Barber, William A. Duke, Robert Hudson, William D. Chipley, Alva C. Roper, James L. Wiggins, Robert A. Wood, Henry Hennis, Herbert W. Blair, and Milton Malone, on the 31st day of March, 1868, in the city of Columbus, in the county of Muscogee, State of Georgia, in and upon one George W. Ashburn, then and there being in the peace of the said State, feloniously and willfully did make an assault; and did then and there feloniously, unlawfully, willfully, and with malice aforethought, discharge pistols loaded with powder and leaden balls at the said George W. Ashburn; and with the said balls discharged as aforesaid, did wound the said George W. Ashburn in the left leg, above and near the ankle joint; and with the said balls discharged as aforesaid, did wound the said George W. Ashburn in the lower part of the nates; and with the said balls, discharged as aforesaid, did wound the said George W. Ashburn in the forehead, which said wound, inflicted in the forehead as aforesaid, was

MILITARY OUTRAGE IN GEORGIA.

mortal, and of which said mortal wound, inflicted in the manner and form aforesaid, the said George W. Ashburn, then and there died; and the said Elisha J. Kirksey, Columbus C. Bedell, James W. Barber, William A. Duke, Robert Hudson, William D. Chipley, Alva C. Roper, James L. Wiggins, Robert A. Wood, Henry Hennis, Herbert W. Blair, and Milton Malone, the said George W. Ashburn, in the manner and form aforesaid feloniously, unlawfully, willfully and of their malice aforethought, did then and there kill and murder, contrary to the laws of said State, the good order, peace, and dignity thereof.
[Signed.] WM. H. SMYTHE,
Captain 16th Infantry, and Brevet Major U. S. A., Acting Judge Advocate.

INDORSEMENT.—Respectfully referred to Brevet Brigadier General Dunn, Judge Advocate of the Commission for trial.
By order of Major General Meade.
[Signed.] R. C. DRUM, A. A. G.
Third Military District, June 27, 1868.

The counsel for the accused here asked that they may be allowed until to-morrow to file their answer or plea to the charge, for the following reasons, viz: that Alex. H. Stephens, who had been assigned to the position of leading counsel for the accused, had had no personal acquaintance with any of the prisoners until he met them in the court-room, and had never seen the charges until a short time ago—this morning.

The Commission was then cleared, and after deliberation the doors were again opened, and the Judge Advocate announced to the accused in open court, that the request of counsel was granted.

The Commission then adjourned until to-morrow (Tuesday, the 30th inst.) at 10 o'clock A. M.

McPHERSON BARRACKS, ATLANTA, GA., }
10 o'clock A. M., June 30, 1868. }

Commission met pursuant to adjournment.

Present, same members as yesterday, the Judge Advocate, the prisoners on trial, and their counsel.

The record of yesterday's proceedings was read and approved.

The Judge Advocate then asked permission to introduce John D. Pope, of the firm of Brown & Pope, as assistant to the Judge Advocate. Permission having been granted, he was accordingly introduced and took his seat as assistant to the Judge Advocate.

The accused asked permission to introduce Marshall J. Wellborn as additional counsel for the defense.

Permission having been granted, he was accordingly introduced and took his seat as additional counsel for the defense.

The counsel for the accused then entered the following plea to the charge and specification, which is appended and marked document "A."

The Judge Advocate stated that it would be necessary for each of the accused to plead separately to the charge and specification. The accused were then severally asked by the Judge Advocate how they pleaded to the charge and specification which was read to them yesterday. The accused then severally pleaded as follows:
To the specification, "Not guilty."
To the charge, "Not guilty."

Examined by the Judge Advocate.

Charles Marshall, a witness for the prosecution, was then called, and having been duly sworn, testifies as follows:

Q. What is your name, your age, and your occupation? *A.* Charles Marshall; age, twenty-seven;. occupation, soldier.

Q. In what service are you a soldier, how long have you been in that service, and to what company do you belong? *A.* The United States service; in that service since 1861; belong to company G of the 16th infantry.

Q. Where have you been on duty during the last year? *A.* In Columbus, Ga.

Q. Were you acquainted with George W. Ashburn, late of Columbus, Ga.? *A.* Yes, sir.

Q. Were you present at his death? *A.* Yes, sir.

Q. Did he die a natural death or a death by violence? *A.* By violence, sir.

Q. State how you came to be present at his death. *A.* I was induced to go there, sir.

Q. Who induced you to go there? State all the circumstances attending the death of Ashburn, so far as you know them. *A.* The first person that spoke to me about it was Doctor Kirksey, about three weeks before the affair took place; I had another interview with him about three days before it took place. The night that the affair took place I went down there, about between the hours of half past eleven and half past twelve, as near as I can judge; I met a party in a vacant lot near the house—the party that committed the deed; we then crossed the street; one of the party asked for admission into the house—knocked at the door; the answer came from the inside, "Who is there?" The answer was then made by the party outside, "Mary Tillinghurst," or some such name as that; I can't exactly remember the name; the party inside asked, "What do you want?" the answer was then made, "I want to see Hannah Flourney." She says, "I can't let you in; it's too late," or "at this time of night," I am not positive which, but it was one of those two. The party outside made answer and said: "If you don't let me in I'll break the door down." The panel of the door was then broken and the door opened. There were three rooms in the house. As soon as the door was broken open the party made through the house to where Mr. Ashburn's room was; it was the third room, in the rear of the house; he asked, "Who comes there?" and then opened the door and stepped back. There was a round table in the middle of the floor and he lit a candle; the candle was sitting on the table. As soon as the door was open one of the party made the remark, "There's the d—d s—t." Ashburn was behind the table that time, when the firing commenced. As soon as the firing commenced he fell; after he was down one of the party stooped down to the side of the door and fired. There were from ten to fourteen shots fired altogether, as near as I can recollect. After that was over I went out of the house immediately; went across toward the Perry House and up Jackson street to my quarters—the court-house. In the first part of my statement I forgot to say that there was a coat handed to me nearly opposite the house as I went down.

Q. You say that the first person who spoke to you of this matter was Doctor Kirksey? *A.* Yes, sir.

Q. If he is present, point him out. *A.* There he is, sir (pointing to one of the accused).

Q. How long was that, did you say, before the death? *A.* About three weeks.

Q. Where did the interview first spoken of, between you and Dr. Kirksey, take place? *A.* On Broad street, Columbus, Ga.

Q. What did Dr. Kirksey say to you in that interview? *A.* Well, sir, he spoke of getting Ashburn "out of the way."

Q. What did he say about getting Ashburn "out of the way?" *A.* He spoke of a party being gotten up for that purpose, sir.

Q. What did he say about the party? *A.* He didn't mention no names to me, sir.

Q. Do you know whether Dr. Kirksey asked any person to join the party? *A.* He asked me.

Q. What did he say to you about joining the party? *A.* He told me it would be all right if I did.

Q. Anything else? *A.* Yes, sir; that I hadn't long to serve in the army, and could come back to Columbus to live.

Q. Did he state any reason why Ashburn should be put out of the way? *A.* No, sir; not directly there.

Q. Did he say anything about the number who would probably be of the party to dispose of Ashburn? *A.* He said there would be a crowd, sir; that was all.

Q. Did he name any person who would be of the crowd? *A.* No, sir.

Q. Was there anything said in that conversation by Dr. Kirksey in regard to any reward or profit that you or any one else might get by joining in the party against Ashburn? *A.* Nothing more than that I would be all right, sir; have anything I wanted.

Q. When did the second interview with Dr. Kirksey, of which you have spoken, take place? *A.* A few days before the affair took place, sir.

Q. Where? *A.* On Broad street.

Q. State what passed between you in that interview? *A.* He told me that the party was made up and the affair would soon take place, and that when it did I should know of it.

Q. Did you afterward get notice when the "affair," as you call it, was to take place? *A.* Yes, sir.

Q. How, when, and where did you get that notice? *A.* At my quarters, about a little before three o'clock on the afternoon of the 30th, the day it took place; it was brought to me by a negro boy.

Q. Brought, how? *A.* It was wrapped up in a piece of brown paper; there was a mask with writing on a piece of paper on the inside of it; the writing stated, "meet to-night at twelve o'clock."

Q. What has become of that writing? *A.* I tore it up, sir, as soon as I read it.

Q. State, if you remember, what that writing contained? *A.* Meet to-night at twelve o'clock, sir.

Q. Did you know the negro boy who left the bundle, as you have said? *A.* I did not, sir; had never seen him before as I know of.

Q. What kind of a mask was it? *A.* An ordinary false-face, sir, made out of pasteboard.

Q. Was there any signature to the notice you say you received? *A.* No, sir.

Q. Did you know the handwriting? *A.* No, sir.

Q. Did you act upon the notice you have mentioned, and if so when did you go and whom did you meet? *A.* I left my quarters that night between half past eleven and twelve o'clock; went over toward the Perry House, which is across from the place where this occurrence took place; I met this party in a vacant lot opposite from the house on the other side of the street. Before I met the party I was handed a coat.

Q. Who was the person who handed you a coat? *A.* Henry Hennis.

Q. How did he come to hand you a coat? *A.* I met him just below the Perry House and he handed me the coat and said, "put this on."

Q. Had you any previous arrangement with him about a coat for that occasion? *A.* Not with him I hadn't, sir.

Q. Had you with any person, and if so, with whom? *A.* Yes, sir; I told Dr. Kirksey I wanted a rig, and he told me it would be there for me.

Q. Why did you want a "rig?" *A.* Because I didn't want to wear my uniform, sir.

Q. When did Dr. Kirksey inform you that there would be a rig there for you? *A.* At the second interview I had with him.

Q. What do you mean by a "rig?" *A.* I mean a suit, sir.

Q. What kind of a coat was the one given to you, as you have said? *A.* It was a grayish coat, sir; an English walking coat.

Q. What kind of buttons did it have on? *A.* The buttons were of bone; what their color was I don't know.

Q. Large or small buttons? *A.* Rather large, sir. I would not be positive about the exact size.

Q. What kind of pantaloons and covering for the head did you have on at that time? *A.* I had on a black slouched hat and a pair of dark pantaloons—not uniform.

Q. Whom else did you meet there about the time Hennis gave you the coat? *A.* About a few minutes afterward—a very short time afterward—I met the other party. I met Hudson, Duke, Barber, Bedell, Dr. Kirksey, and Milton Malone. [Here the witness, at the request of the Judge Advocate, identified each of the parties just named as being among the accused.]

Q. Where did you meet those persons whom you have named and pointed out? *A.* I met them in a vacant lot across from the house.

Q. What house? *A.* The house where Ashburn was killed.

Q. How far from that house? *A.* I should judge two hundred yards, one hundred and fifty, somewhere along there.

Q. Where did you proceed from there? *A.* To the house, sir.

Q. What house? *A.* Where Ashburn was killed.

Q. Where is that house situated? *A.* On Oglethorpe street, in the city of Columbus; I forget the name of the streets it is between.

Q. Describe the house as to how it stands with reference to the points of the compass, the number of rooms, and particularly as to the room in which Ashburn was killed. *A.* The house stands on the west side of the street; it is a one-story frame house, three rooms; the front door is in the center; I am not positive whether there were two windows in the front or not; there is a side door in the third room leading into an alleyway; as regards the back of the house I know nothing; the door of the second room faces the front door as it opens; the front door opens to the right, and the door of the second room opens to the left; the door of Mr. Ashburn's room opened to the left; the door of his room is toward the left side of the house as you go in, it doesn't face the door of the second room; there is a fire-place in the center of the back room in which Mr. Ashburn was killed; those are about all the points I know of.

Q. Does the house stand lengthways with the street or endways to the street? *A.* Endways to the street.

Q. Did you go into the house you have described the night Ashburn was killed? If so, state when you entered, and what

other persons, if any, went in with you.
A. I did, sir, somewhere in the neighborhood of midnight; the parties that went in with me are those that I have mentioned; there were others there, but those I could not recognize, and don't know who they are; there were from twenty to thirty in the party.

Q. Did you see anything of George Betz that night? and if so, where did you see him? A. I saw him there in the party, sir.

Q. Was he in the house with you? A. Yes, sir.

Q. Were there any others in the house besides those you have named? A. Yes, sir.

Q. Name them. A. I could not name them, sir; I am not positive who they were.

Q. Why don't you know who they were? A. It was impossible for me to know all of them, sir.

Q. Why was it impossible? A. There was too large a party, and I was not in the party only a short time before the affair commenced.

Q. How large was the party? A. From twenty to thirty, sir.

Q. Were any of them disguised? A. Yes, sir, all that I saw and talked with were disguised in a manner.

Q. How were they disguised? A. By masks, the majority of them.

Q. Were there any persons in the house besides Ashburn when you entered it? A. Yes, sir.

Q. State who? A. There was a colored woman and a white woman.

Q. Do you know their names? A. I have heard their names, sir; the white woman's name was Amanda Patterson, the colored woman's name Hannah Flournoy.

Q. Did you see any man in the house besides the party you were with and Ashburn? A. I did not, sir.

Q. What did your party do after they entered the house? A. Proceeded to the back room where Mr. Ashburn was.

Q. Tell what took place there? A. The firing commenced there, and he was killed there, sir.

Q. Who fired upon him? A. A party in the door.

Q. In what door? A. The door of his room, sir.

Q. Who constituted that party? A. Myself, Duke, Barber, Hudson, and another man, I am not positive who it was. I rather think it was Betz, but I am not positive about it.

Q. Did all those persons fire on Ashburn? A. Yes, sir.

Q. State what conversation, if any, took place between Ashburn and your party previous to his death? A. The remark he made was, "Who comes there?" then he opened the door and stepped back and one of the party then made the remark, "There's the d—d s—t," and then the firing commenced.

Q. Who was the person who made the vulgar remark you have just mentioned? A. Hudson, sir.

Q. How were your party armed? A. With revolvers.

Q. Did you see Ashburn that night after he was dead? A. I saw him fall, sir.

Q. Did you see any other persons go into the room after Ashburn fell; and if so, who were they? A. I seen two look into the room; there was not any person went into the room as I know of; I would not be positive whether any went in or not.

Q. Who were the two persons who you say looked into the room after he fell? A. Kirksey and Bedell.

Q. Did either of them do or say anything? A. No, sir; somebody made the remark then, "Come on, boys," and the party went out.

Q. Was it immediately after Ashburn fell that Kirksey and Bedell looked into the room where he was? A. Yes, sir.

Q. Was there a light in Ashburn's room at the time the assault was made upon him, and if so, what kind of a light was it? A. Yes, sir; a candle.

Q. How long did your party remain in the house after Ashburn was killed? A. Hardly any time at all, sir.

Q. Where did they go to from there? A. They dispersed, sir.

Q. Where did you go? A. I went home, sir, to my quarters.

Q. You say, I believe, in your previous evidence, that one of your party stooped down and fired at Ashburn; who was that? A. It was Hudson, sir.

Q. Where was Ashburn at the time Hudson so fired? A. He was behind the table, sir, lying on the floor.

Q. Did Hudson make any remark at the time he fired? A. No, sir.

Q. Could he have shot Ashburn without stooping down, after Ashburn fell? A. The table was in the way, sir.

Q. Did you see the remains of Ashburn after that night? A. No, sir.

Q. Did you have any conversation with any of the other parties connected with the assassination of Ashburn previous to the meeting for that purpose? A. No, sir.

Q. Had you heard the matter of disposing of Ashburn discussed previous to that night? A. No, sir; not particularly.

Q. What induced you to take part in the killing of Ashburn? A. Well, sir, there was a great many inducements.

Q. State them. A. The various associations I had, sir; I always had it instilled into my mind that he was better out of the community than in it.

Q. To what associations do you refer? A. People in town, sir.

Q. Was there any sort of organization that you know of where the propriety of getting clear of Ashburn was discussed or considered? A. Not as I know of, sir.

Q. How did it get instilled into your mind that Ashburn should be disposed of? A. Well, sir, by conversation I had with different people; all my companions were outside of my company; I attended very little to my duty as I should have done, and I was warned by my commanding officer to stop my associations, but I failed to do that, and kept headlong in my course, which brought me where I am; had I taken his advice I should have done right instead of wrong.

Q. Were any of these men on trial your associates in Columbus? A. I used to speak to them; would meet them very frequently, nearly all of them.

Q. Have you had much acquaintance with the defendant Chipley? A. No, sir. I have not; I never spoke to him in my life until after the occurrence.

Q. What conversation did you have with him after the occurrence? A. I merely spoke to him up in the court-house when he was under arrest; merely passed the time of day with him, sir.

Q. Have you had no other conversation with him? A. No, sir.

Q. Since this occurrence have you received any valuable presents from any person in Columbus; if so, state what? A. I received a watch since that occurrence, sir.

Q. What kind of a watch? A. A gold hunting-case watch.

Q. Worth about how much? A. Three or four hundred dollars, sir.

Q. Who gave it to you? A. It was handed to me by a clerk in a jeweler's store.

Q. State his name, when and where he handed the watch to you? A. Ingmire is his name; he handed me the watch on the night of the 24th of April, in front of the Presbyterian Church.

Q. Do you know who provided that watch for a present to you? A. I do not, sir.

Q. Did any person tell you before you received it that it was to be presented to you? A. Yes, sir; several spoke to me about it.

Q. Name them. A. Barber and a young gentleman named Gunby spoke to me about it; said that I would receive it; a man by the name of Williams spoke to me about it also.

Q. Was there anything besides the watch given to you at that time? A. A chain, sir, with the watch.

Q. Was Mr. Ingmire a particular friend of yours? A. No, sir; I was not much acquainted with him.

Q. Did you receive any other present of value, at the death of Ashburn, from any of the citizens of Columbus? A. No, sir; I received no present.

Q. Did you not receive money? A. Yes, sir; I received that in form of a loan.

Q. How much, and from whom? A. I received one hundred dollars from Mr. Wilkins, formerly Mayor of the town.

Q. How did you, a private soldier, come to have such good credit with Mr. Wilkins? A. I don't know, sir; I asked him for the loan of it, and he told me I could have it.

Q. Did he let you have it immediately upon your asking for it? A. No, sir; about a week afterward.

Q. What conversation passed between you at the time you asked for this loan? A. I asked him for the loan of it, saying that I wanted to go home on furlough. He says, "I will let you have it before you go."

Q. Had you and the Mayor been on intimate terms previously? A. Yes, sir.

Q. Did anybody else suggest to you to apply to him for a loan? A. No, sir.

Q. Did you go home on furlough, and if so, when? A. Left on the 25th of April and returned about the 24th of May.

Q. How did it happen that you and the

Mayor were on such good terms? A. Nothing as I know of, sir.

Q. Have you ever returned the money so borrowed, or have you ever been asked to return it? A. No, sir.

Q. Did you give any note or surety for the loan? A. No, sir.

Q. What did Ingmire say to you when he handed you the watch and chain? A. He told me to take it; that is about all the remark he made: "Take this and take care of it."

Q. Didn't he tell you, or intimate to you, who the present was from? A. He said it was from my friends.

Q. Did he tell you, or did you know, what friends he referred to? A. No, sir; none particular.

Q. When were you to pay the money borrowed from the Mayor? A. There was no time mentioned, sir.

Q. Has he applied to you since you returned for payment? A. No, sir.

Q. Has any person, for him, applied to you for payment? A. No, sir.

Q. Have you seen him since you returned? A. Yes, sir; frequently.

Q. State the day of the month and the day of the week, if you can, when Ashburn was killed? A. It was Monday, the 30th of March, 1868.

Q. Was he killed before or after midnight? A. It was about midnight; Monday was the 30th, and it was the night between Monday and Tuesday that he was killed.

Q. Do you know what county and State Columbus is in? A. State of Georgia; I believe it is in Muscogee county, sir; I am not certain.

Q. Were your interviews with Kirksey in the day time or in the night, and was any person present at either interview? A. In the day time; no person was present at the interviews.

Q. How long had you been acquainted with Kirksey? A. About a year, sir—nearly a year.

Q. How many shots were fired at Ashburn? A. About ten or fifteen.

Q. Do you know how the pistols were loaded that were fired at him? A. No, sir; I couldn't say that.

Q. Can you say as to your own? A. Yes, sir; mine was loaded with powder and ball, an oblong leaden ball.

Q. How many shots did you fire at Ashburn? A. I fired one, sir.

Q. Do you know whether your shot struck him? A. I do not, sir.

Q. Have you had any conversations with any of these prisoners about the killing of Ashburn since the occurrence? A. No, sir.

Q. Did all the persons engaged in this affair enter the house that night? A. No, sir.

Q. Did you see any others about except those in the house with you? A. There were some others at the side.

Q. How do you know that? A. Because the side door was broken in.

Q. What door do say was broken in? A. The side door; the door from the alley into Ashburn's room.

Q. When was that door broken in? A. During the firing, sir.

Q. Was it thrown open? A. I would not swear whether it was or not; I am not positive.

Q. Could you recognize the persons outside, about the door broken in? A. No, sir.

Q. Does the size and form of any one of the prisoners here, whom you have not indentified, correspond with those of any person whom you saw in the house, and whom you then did not recognize? A. Yes, sir; I saw one man that night I thought was Mr. Chipley; I would not be positive, but I thought so from the size of the man.

Q. Was the person whom you thought was Mr. Chipley disguised, and if so, how? A. Yes, sir; disguised with a mask.

Q. Who seemed to be the leader of your party? A. This man I speak of.

Q. Which man? A. The man I supposed to be Chipley.

Q. What did this leader do? A. He appeared to have all the say in the party, sir.

Q. Was there much noise or talk in your operations? A. No, sir; excepting when there was knocking at the door; that was the only noise that was made of any account.

Q. Was there any shouting or noise made by your party after the affair was over? A. No, sir; not as I heard.

Q. Do you know what was the object of this party in killing Ashburn? A. The object was to kill him; that was all, I suppose.

Q. Why were they so anxious to kill Ashburn? A. Well, sir; most everybody held an animosity against him.

Q. What was the cause of this animosity; do you know? *A.* He was politically opposed to the majority of the people, sir.

Q. Was that the reason for this organization to kill him? *A.* That is all the reason, I suppose, sir.

Q. What makes you so suppose? *A.* From hearsay.

Q. Why did you take part in killing him? *A.* I don't know, sir; the influence was so great over me I suppose, I could not resist it; I didn't resist it anyhow.

Q. What influence? *A.* My associations, sir.

Q. Were those influences social or political? *A.* Both, sir.

Q. Were you opposed to Ashburn politically? *A.* I was, sir.

Q. Was that fact well known among your associates in the city? *A.* Yes, sir.

Cross-Examination by A. H. Stephens for the Defense.

Q. Did you not have a personal difficulty with Ashburn? *A.* Yes, sir, I had.

Q. Did you not slap his jaws, or strike him the evening before he was killed? *A.* I can not say whether I struck him or not, sir, when I had the difficulty with him; it was early in the afternoon and I was under the influence of liquor; it was about half past three in the afternoon.

Q. Where did this occur? *A.* In the upper part of the city, in Broad street.

Q. Whose house was it at? *A.* In nobody's house; it was on the street.

Q. Was it not at Jack Clark's grocery? *A.* No, sir.

Q. Were you or not too much intoxicated to recollect distinctly what occurred, or where it occurred? *A.* No, sir, I was not; I recollect where it occurred.

Q. But you do not recollect whether you slapped his jaws or not? *A.* No, sir; I think I didn't.

Q. Do you now recollect whether you struck him at all or not? *A.* I did strike him, sir.

Q. Did you or not say to Wm. H. Williams, captain of the fire company in Columbus, that you intended to kill Ashburn, or words to that effect? *A.* I might have said so that night; I would not swear to it though; I don't remember it.

Q. Did Ashburn shoot or fire his pistol in the crowd that entered his room? *A.* I think not, sir.

Q. Did he have a pistol or did you see a pistol in his hands? *A.* I did not see a pistol in his hands.

Q. Are you certain and positive that you say Kirksey, Duke, Barber, and Hudson, the accused now before you, in the house where Ashburn was killed that night? *A.* I did not see them all in the house; I saw some in the house and some outside.

Q. Which were in and which out? *A.* Duke, Hudson, and Barber, were inside; they were in the door leading out of the second room into the third; I saw them all before I went in; Kirksey and Bedell were in the second room; myself, Barber, Hudson, Duke, and this man, I take for Betz, were standing right in the door where the shooting took place; the other two were in the room, and Malone was in that room too, in the second room.

Q. You are certain and positive then that all those parties were in the house at or about the time of killing? *A.* I am, sir.

Q. Are you just as positive in this statement as in any you have made? *A.* I am, sir.

Q. Had you any intimacy or personal association with Hudson? *A.* Not of any account; I have seen him hundreds of times.

Q. Did you ever spend five minutes of conversation with him in your life? *A.* I don't know as I have, sir.

Q. Who did you say talked with you about the present of the watch you have testified about? *A.* A young man named Gunby, and Barber also told me I would receive it.

Q. You said somebody else on your direct examination whose name I did not hear; who was it? *A.* Mr. Williams, I think, sir.

Q. Which Williams? *A.* One of two brothers, I don't know his first name, but think it is Dan. Williams.

Q. What Gunby do you refer to? *A.* His father keeps a store on St. Clair street; I don't know his first name.

Q. Is it the son of Robert M. Gunby? *A.* I don't know, sir; I don't know his first name.

Q. Where is the storehouse located that his father occupies? *A.* In St. Clair street, below Broad, toward the river.

Q. These are the parties that told you beforehand that the watch would be given to you? *A.* Yes, sir.

Q. When did you say the watch was

given to you? *A.* On the night of the 24th of April.

Q. Was or not this the night of the day on which the election on the adoption of the Constitution, and election of officers of the State under it, closed? *A.* It was the night of the day after, sir; the election closed on Thursday and this was on Friday night.

Q. Had you not been very active before the election, and during its four days' duration, in opposition to the adoption of the Constitution and in co-operation with all those parties? *A.* Yes, sir.

Q. What was your position in your company before the election? *A.* First Sergeant, sir.

Q. Were you arrested during the election, and by whose orders, and for what? *A.* I was arrested by Captain Mills and reduced to First Duty Sergeant by his order, for trying to influence the election—that is what he charged me with.

Q. Was or was not Mayor Wilkins an opponent of the Constitution? and did not the opponents of that measure generally express sympathy with you because of the treatment you received for the course you had taken? *A.* Yes, sir.

Q. After you were reduced to the position of Duty Sergeant, did you not immediately apply for a furlough? and do you not know that the money Mayor Wilkins let you have was raised by contribution among the people? *A.* I applied for a furlough about a week before I was reduced; I do not know that the money Mayor Wilkins let me have was raised by contribution among the people.

Q. When did you get the furlough? *A.* It dated from the 25th of April, sir.

Q. That was how many days after you were reduced? *A.* About three days, sir.

Q. How long after this was it Mayor Wilkins let you have the money, and did you or not tell him you wanted it to bear your expenses home? *A.* He gave it to me on Friday night, the night of the 24th of April; I told him that I wanted it to take me home.

The counsel for the accused asked that the Commission adjourn until to-morrow.

The Commission retired for deliberation, and on returning the Commission adjourned to meet to-morrow morning at 10 o'clock.

McPHERSON BARRACKS, ATLANTA, GA., July 1, 1868, 10 o'clock, A. M.

The Commission met pursuant to adjournment.

Present—The same members as yesterday, the Judge Advocate, the prisoners on trial and their counsel. The record of yesterday's proceedings was read and approved.

Cross-Examination of Charles Marshall resumed by the Defense.

Q. What was the character of the house where Ashburn was killed? *A.* I never was in the house before and know nothing of its character.

Q. What is its character by public reputation? *A.* I heard it spoken of as a bad house.

Q. Is it not notoriously a house of ill-fame? *A.* Not as I know of; I have heard say so.

Q. Who is it reputed to be kept by? *A.* I believe this Hannah Flourney spoken of was the proprietress of the house; I have heard say so; I could not be positive about it.

Q. Is she the white woman or the colored woman? *A.* The colored woman.

Q. Did Mr. Ashburn live in that house? *A.* As far as I know he did, sir; I am not positive.

Q. Did you ever see Mr. Bedell before that night? *A.* Yes, sir.

Q. Did you ever speak to him in your life? *A.* Yes, sir.

Q. Before this occurrence? *A.* I think I have, sir, I won't be positive.

Q. When? *A.* I am not positive, sir, when.

Q. Where? *A.* In Columbus, sir.

Q. Whereabouts in Columbus? *A.* I will not specify any particular part, sir.

Q. Was it on the street or where he was engaged in business? *A.* If I have spoken to him it is on the street; I am not positive whether I spoke to him before that affair.

Q. If you had ever spoken to him do not you think you would recollect it? *A.* I am not positive, sir, I speak to a great many persons.

Q. Do you speak to a great many people that you are not made acquainted with —have no acquaintance with at all? *A.* No, sir.

Q. Would it be likely for you to have spoken to Mr. Bedell, having no acquaintance with him? *A.* Well, sir; I have spoken to a great many persons in Columbus without any introduction.

Q. You are not positive that you ever did speak to him? *A.* Not positive; no, sir; I would not swear to it.

Q. What time in the evening was it when you had the difficulty with Mr. Ashburn? *A.* The forepart of the afternoon.

Q. About what hour? *A.* I should judge, between three and four o'clock; I would not be positive about the hour, sir.

Q. Where did you go after that interview with Mr. Ashburn? *A.* Went round town, sir.

Q. Where to; what place? *A.* Went to several places.

Q. Name any one? *A.* I stopped in a saloon—two saloons.

Q. What saloons? *A.* Stopped in at the "Arbor," sir, on St. Clair street, above Broad.

Q. Did you meet anybody there you knew? *A.* Met the bar-tender there.

Q. Anybody else? *A.* Not as I remember, sir.

Q. What other saloon did you go to? *A.* Cooke's Hotel, sir.

Q. Did you meet anybody there you knew? *A.* The man who kept the place, sir.

Q. Anybody else? *A.* Not as I remember; there was some one in there, sir, but I am not positive who they were.

Q. Where did you go then? *A.* Went down to my quarters.

Q. At what hour did you reach your quarters? *A.* I judge about five o'clock, sir; somewhere about then.

Q. Did you remain there until eleven o'clock, or half past? *A.* No, sir.

Q. Where did you go? *A.* I went down town, sir, to supper.

Q. Where did you take your supper? *A.* Took it in a friend's house, lower part of Jackson street.

Q. What is the name of your friend? *A.* MacSpadden, sir.

Q. At what time did you take supper? *A.* I judge between seven and eight o'clock.

Q. Where did you go then? *A.* Came out to my quarters about half past eight.

Q. Where did you go then? *A.* Remained there until after roll-call.

Q. When you went from your supper at MacSpadden's who went with you? *A.* Mr. Harris, sir.

Q. What was the hour of roll-call? *A.* Nine o'clock, sir.

Q. What became of you then? *A.* I remained in my quarters about half an hour.

Q. Where did you go then? *A.* Went around on Broad street and got a drink, sir.

Q. Where at? *A.* A saloon called the "Ruby."

Q. Where did you go then? *A.* Went back to my quarters.

Q. Did you take another drink at the "Ruby"? *A.* I took one drink there, sir, and then went round to my quarters.

Q. Where did you say you stopped when you came to Broad street? *A.* I stopped at the "Ruby," sir; the saloon called the "Ruby."

Q. After nine o'clock? *A.* Yes.

Q. Where did you go then? *A.* Back to my quarters, sir.

Q. How long did you remain there? *A.* Until about half past eleven o'clock.

Q. Was that the time you left to go to the meeting of the party? *A.* Yes, sir; somewhere between eleven and twelve.

Q. Did you pass the sentry? *A.* I did, sir.

Q. Who was on sentry that night? *A.* I do not remember, sir.

Q. Were the men permitted to pass in and out any time of the night? *A.* No, sir; not generally.

Q. How were you allowed to pass? *A.* There was never any restriction on me passing out.

Q. How did that occur, that there was no restriction on your passing? *A.* I was in charge of the company then, sir.

Q. Where was the coat given you that you have testified about? *A.* Near the Perry House.

Q. You say Mr. Hennis handed that to you? *A.* Yes, sir.

Q. Which side of the Perry House? *A.* Above it, sir.

Q. In Oglethorpe street or Jackson street? *A.* In Oglethorpe street, sir; the Perry House is on Oglethorpe street, not on Jackson street.

Q. Did not you have three citizens' suits? *A.* No, sir.

Q. When you were working for the Democratic Club did not you tell them that you had citizens' suits to put on the soldiers to go out electioneering for them—three citizens' suits? *A.* I never knew I was working for the Democratic Club, sir.

Q. The question is, did not you tell one of the Democratic Club that you had three citizens' suits to put on soldiers? *A.* I didn't tell him I had the suits, sir; I told him I could get the suits.

Q. Did not you tell him that you had sent them out with these suits on? *A.* Not as I remember, sir.

Q. You say you did not know you were working for the Democratic Club; what interference was it that you had in the election that caused your arrest by Capt. Mills? *A.* The Captain accused me of trying to influence men to vote, sir.

Q. You stated yesterday, I believe, that you were co-operating with those parties that spoke to you about the watch in the election; were they or not known to be Democrats? *A.* Yes, sir, they were.

Q. In what way did you co-operate with them in the election? *A.* By endeavoring to influence the freedmen's votes, sir.

Q. How was the election conducted at the polls? *A.* Conducted as nearly all the elections were; there were sentries at the door and judges of election at the door.

Q. Was there a guard of soldiers in a row, through which the voters had to pass? *A.* There were two sentries, sir; there was no "row."

Q. Was it a matter of difficulty or not, to your knowledge, for a colored man who was going to vote the Democratic ticket to get access to the polls? *A.* No, sir.

Q. Was not your main business—being an officer—to conduct that class of voters to the polls? *A.* No, sir.

Q. Did you take any of that class of voters to the polls?

[Objection to the question was made by the Court and it was withdrawn.]

Q. You say these parties were masked? *A.* Yes, sir.

Q. What kind of masks did they have? *A.* Different kinds, sir.

Q. What were the kinds—some of them? *A.* I would not be positive what they were made of, sir.

Q. What sort of mask did you have? *A.* I had an ordinary pasteboard mask, sir.

Q. How many had the same kind? *A.* That I would not be positive of, sir.

Q. What sort of a mask did Bedell have? *A.* I would not be positive as to his mask, sir.

Q. Positive as to *him* and not as to his mask? *A.* Yes, sir.

Q. What sort of mask did Barber have?

A. Barber's mask I should judge to be one he made himself; I am not positive, but it looked to me like a concern he made himself; it was a dark affair.

Q. What sort of a mask did Hudson have? *A.* Hudson had a mask something like Barber's.

Q. What sort of a mask did Duke have? *A.* Duke's mask, sir, was a small mask; came about down just about the chin.

Q. What sort of a mask did Kirksey have? *A.* I would not be positive about his mask, sir.

Q. What sort of a mask did Malone have? *A.* Malone had a mask something like mine, sir.

Q. What sort of mask did Betz have? *A.* I did not see Betz full in the face, sir; could not swear to it.

Q. Who first spoke when the party left the vacant lot? *A.* The first remark that I heard was when we got to the house.

Q. Did nobody speak when you left the vacant lot? *A.* I am not positive of it, sir.

Q. Did anybody speak after you arrived there? *A.* There was something spoken, sir, but I am not positive as to what it was.

Q. Was there anything said by anybody when you left the vacant lot? *A.* Yes, sir, I said there was something said.

Q. Who said it? *A.* That I am not positive of.

Q. What was said? *A.* That I am not positive about.

Q. What became of Hennis after he gave you the coat? *A.* He joined the party, sir.

Q. Did he lead it? *A.* No, sir, I think not.

Q. After you got into the middle room of the house where Ashburn was, who opened the door into his bed-room? *A.* He opened it himself, sir.

Q. Who were with you in there did you say? *A.* I said there was Barber, Duke, Malone, Hudson, and this man I took for Betz.

Q. How was Betz dressed? *A.* The man I take for Betz had on a pair of plaid pantaloons and thin coat.

Q. Which of the parties entered the door of Ashburn's bed-room first? *A.* They entered about simultaneously; I could not swear to any one being in advance or in the rear.

Q. You and all the other parties? *A.*

Yes, sir; not *all* the others; it was impossible for all to get there at the same time.

Q. Which one went first, that is my question, and I repeat it? *A.* The man I took for Barber is the man who went first.

Q. Who next? *A.* That I am not positive about, sir.

Q. Where were you? *A.* Right there at the door, sir.

Q. Did either one get into Ashburn's room? *A.* No, sir, they remained on the threshold of the door.

Q. Did you all shoot standing there in the door? *A.* Yes.

Q. Did you shoot over anybody's shoulders? *A.* No, sir.

Q. Who was to your left? *A.* The man I took for Hudson.

Q. Who was to your right? *A.* The man I took for Barber.

Q. Then where were the others standing? *A.* Right in the rear of us.

Q. Did they shoot over your shoulders? *A.* They did, sir.

Q. But none of you got into the room? *A.* No, sir, no person got inside the room.

Q. Where was Ashburn when you first saw him? *A.* In the third room standing in the rear of the table.

Q. What sort of table was that? *A.* As near as I can remember it was a round table.

Q. What part of the room was it in? *A.* In the center of the room.

Q. What other furniture was there in the room? *A.* There was a bed, sir.

Q. What part of the room was the bed in? *A.* At the right hand as you went in the door.

Q. Any other furniture in it? *A.* I would not be positive, sir?

Q. Where was the candle when the door was opened? *A.* On the table, sir.

Q. Did it remain there all the time? *A.* I think it did, sir.

Q. What did you do with your mask? *A.* I threw it away, sir.

Q. Where did you throw it? *A.* In Jackson street.

Q. Threw it down in the street? *A.* Tore it up, sir, and threw it away.

Q. What did you do with the coat? *A.* I threw it off, sir, as soon as I left the house, sir.

Q. Left it in the street? *A.* I don't know whether it remained on the street or not.

Q. You threw it away in the street? *A.* I did, sir.

Q. In which street? *A.* Oglethorpe street.

Q. What did you strike Mr. Ashburn for, the evening before he was killed? *A.* I had some words with him, sir.

Q. Was it not because you knew that he was going to report you to Capt. Mills next day? *A.* No, sir; I never knew anything of the kind.

Q. Did not you tell Foster Chapman at his drug-store that evening, that that was what you struck him for, that he was going to report you next day to Captain Mills? *A.* No, sir; I did not; I told him I struck him, and that he was going to report me for striking him; and Foster Chapman told me I could get any bond I wanted if he *did* report me.

Q. Didn't you tell Foster Chapman then that you intended to kill Ashburn? *A.* I don't remember having told him anything of the kind, sir.

Q. Do you swear that you didn't tell Foster Chapman that Ashburn was going to report you, and that you would kill him, Ashburn? *A.* I swear that Ashburn said he was going to report me, and I told Mr. Chapman so, sir; but as regards my saying that I would kill him, I will not swear to.

Q. You will not swear that you did not tell him so? *A.* No sir; I will not.

Q. Did you not make a similar statement, or the same statement, to Van Marcus the same evening, and to Julius Clapp? *A.* I did, sir; I made the same statement as regards me having the fuss with Mr. Ashburn, and my striking him, and that he was going to report me for it; this took place in the interview I had with Mr. Clapp in the saloon under Cooke's Hotel, just below the drug-store; he and a party were playing cards in the back part of the saloon, and when I told him, he told me if I wanted bond I could have it.

Q. Was that the time that you passed by Cooke's saloon, as you have testified before? *A.* It was, sir.

Q. Was there a political meeting in Columbus that night? *A.* I heard say there was; I am not positive, sir.

Q. Which party had the meeting?
[Objected to by a member of the Court, and withdrawn.]

Q. Is it within your knowledge that Mr. Ashburn was at a public meeting that night? *A.* It is not, sir.

Q. You stated that he was a very unpopular man in Columbus, and that it was on account of his political principles being against the majority of the people; was not the majority of the same party with himself? *A.* Not the majority of those having influence, sir.

Q. Was, or not, the majority of those who voted at the polls of Mr. Ashburn's party? *A.* As far as I understand, sir, the returns of the election prove that they were.

Q. Is it within your knowledge that there was strong opposition to Mr. Ashburn within his own party? *A.* I never heard of any, sir.

Q. Do you know a Mr. Bennett? *A.* I do, sir.

Q. Did he live in this house with Mr. Ashburn? *A.* I do not know, sir.

Q. Did you see him in that room that night? *A.* No, sir.

Q. If he had been in the room, do you think you would have seen him? *A.* No, sir; there were plenty of opportunities for him to secrete himself, sir.

Q. Did you have any conversation with Bennett, about Ashburn, before? *A.* Never spoke to the man in my life, as I know of, before the affair took place.

Q. Was there anybody in the room that you first entered? Did you see anybody in it? *A.* Not when I first entered, sir.

Q. Did you see anybody in the second room? *A.* I did, sir.

Q. Who did you see there? *A.* I seen a white woman.

Q. Who was she? *A.* I would not swear to the woman, sir; never seen her before in my life, nor since, that I know of.

Q. Did you hear her name called that night? *A.* No, sir.

Q. Have you ever seen her since? *A.* Not to know her, sir; I seen a woman said to be her; but whether it is her or not I do not know.

Q. Would you know her if you were to see her? *A.* I do not think I would, sir.

Q. Did you see any other person; any other woman in the house that night? *A.* No, sir; I would not swear to it.

Q. Where did you first see this white woman? *A.* I seen her in the middle room, sir.

Q. Where did she go? *A.* She remained there, sir.

Q. What part of the room was she in?

A. In the right-hand side of the room, when I seen her.

Q. Did she do anything but stand still? *A.* I would not swear to what she done, sir; I passed her quickly; and then my back was to her, and what she did I am not positive of.

Q. Was she still there as you returned? *A.* She was, sir; there was a candle lit in that room.

Q. Did she say anything? *A.* Not that I heard.

Q. Do you state that you saw another woman, either white or colored, in either of the rooms? *A.* There was a colored woman got out of the side window as we got into the second room; she was not in the room at the time we got in; she got out the side window, on the right-hand side of the room.

Q. You saw a colored woman then get out of the window? *A.* Yes, sir.

Q. Who was it? *A.* I didn't know her then; I suppose it is this Hannah Flourney.

Q. Was she in the room again as you returned back? *A.* I didn't see her, sir.

Q. When did you say you enlisted? *A.* In 1861, sir.

Q. Where? *A.* The first place was in Trenton, New Jersy.

Q. How long a term for? *A.* Three months, sir.

Q. Where and when did you next enlist? *A.* In Philadelphia; about the 1st October, 1861.

Q. How long for? *A.* Three years, sir.

Q. Where did you next enlist, and when? *A.* In December, 1864, at Brandy Station, Virginia; 1863; I should say, sir.

Q. How long for? *A.* Three years, sir.

Q. When and where did you next enlist? *A.* Buffalo, New York, sir; on the 8th day of January, 1866.

Q. For how long? *A.* Three years.

Q. When were you arrested for your connection with this matter? *A.* About three weeks ago, sir; between three and four weeks; I was not aware that it was for connection with this matter that I was arrested.

Q. When did you become aware of it? *A.* When I was brought here, sir.

Q. How did you become aware of it? *A.* I was told of it by Major Whitley.

Q. Did Major Whitley have you arrested? *A.* That I would not swear to, sir; I do not know who had me arrested.

MILITARY OUTRAGE IN GEORGIA.

Q. Have you ever received a letter since your arrest, in relation to the arrest, from anybody? *A.* Never received a letter from any one.

Q. Did you ever receive a written statement from any one? *A.* No, sir.

Q. Did you tell private Price, of company C, 16th infantry, that you had received such a statement from some person? *A.* No, sir; I don't know such a man in company C, 16th infantry.

Q. Any private in company C? *A.* No, sir; I *know* them, but I never told them anything of the kind.

Q. Any such to anybody? *A.* No, sir.

Q. How was the matter disclosed to you by Major Whitley? *A.* Well, he told me what I was arrested for, sir.

Q. What else did he state? *A.* He told me that if I knew anything about it, I had better make a full confession of the affair.

Q. What reason did he give you for that? *A.* He gave me the reason that it was my duty, sir, and proved to me that the evidence against me was sufficient.

Q. Did he hold out any inducements to you? *A.* He did not, sir; nothing whatever.

Q. Did he tell you that if you would testify to certain facts, which he stated to you, there would be no prosecution against you? *A.* He did not mention any "certain facts" at all, sir; he told me to tell what I knew, sir.

Q. How many conferences have you had with Maj. Whitley? *A.* I spoke to Maj. Whitley three or four times before I said anything of the affair to him.

Q. Did he make any statement to you that in case you testified to the implication of these gentlemen you would not be punished? *A.* He made no statement to me as regards my testifying against any particular person, sir; he told me to tell what I knew of the affair, and I did, openly and frankly; he offered me no inducements.

Q. Did he tell you that you would not be punished if you would so testify? *A.* He told me I would not be prosecuted; he did not tell me whether I would be punished or not; after I made the confession to him he told me that.

Q. Did he make that statement to you before you made any confession to him? *A.* Not that I remember, sir; I knew myself I could not be placed on the stand and at the same time be tried; it was not necessary for Major Whitley to tell me that.

Q. You knew, then, that by making the statement you have you would be saved yourself? *A.* I don't know, sir; I didn't know whether my evidence would be sufficient to do, sir; consequently I wished to implicate no one; I did not do it for that purpose, sir.

Q. You stated that you didn't know your evidence would be sufficient to do; what do you mean; "sufficient to do" what? *A.* I didn't know whether my evidence would convict or not, sir.

Q. If it convicted, you knew that you would be discharged—not hurt yourself? *A.* I did not know positively, sir.

Q. Was that the impression under which you made the statement to Maj. Whitley? *A.* The impression I labored under when I made that statement was that it was my *duty* to do so, and I did so, openly and frankly—not looking forward to anything that may come hereafter.

Q. You stated that it did not require Maj. Whitley to tell you that you would not be liable to punishment if you made this statement; now, my question is, whether you were under the impression at the time you made it that by making it you would be free from hurt or harm; was that your impression? *A.* I was not positive as regards that.

Q. Was it your impression; was it what you thought? *A.* I say I am not positive, sir.

Q. Did not Maj. Whitley tell you that he would guarantee you against harm from Government if you would? *A.* No, sir; never talked of the Government harming me, sir.

Q. Did not Maj. Whitley tell you he would guarantee you against all harm on account of this if you would? *A.* He told me he would guarantee me protection, sir.

Q. Did Maj. Whitley have exclusive control of you since your arrest? *A.* No, sir.

Q. Any person permitted to see you without his authority? *A.* There was no one came to see me, sir, to have any interview with me.

Q. Did you have any interview with anybody but Maj. Whitley since your arrest? Yes, sir; I had.

Q. Whom? *A.* Gen. Dunn and Gov. Brown, sir.

Q. At your quarters or at their quarters? *A.* At the Adjutant's office in this garrison.

Q. Who took you there? *A.* The sentry.

Q. Who had the control of your prison door? *A.* The Sergeant of the guard.

Q. Under whose control was the Sergeant of the guard? *A.* I suppose he was under the officer of the day, sir, as far as I know; that is how I understand.

Q. Did Maj. Whitley come to see you when he pleased? *A.* I don't know, sir, whether he come when he pleased or whether he had to get permission; I am not positive about that, sir.

Q. Did anybody else except him come to see you then? *A.* Not in the cell, sir.

Q. How often was he with you there? *A.* I spoke to him once in the cell and once outside, sir; that is all I remember—yes, sir, I spoke to him three times: the first time I was in the third cell, next time I was in the first cell, after the partition was put up, and the next time I was in the hall, last Sunday night a week.

Q. What sort of a cell were you first put in? *A.* In one of those cells over there at the guard-room, sir; the cell before it was altered was, I suppose, five or six feet wide and eight or ten feet long.

Q. How long did it remain in that condition? *A.* I don't know, sir; I was taken out of that cell and put in the end one.

Q. How long was it before you were changed from one cell to the other? *A.* It was about eighteen hours.

Q. Who was there when you was so changed? *A.* The Sergeant of the guard, and I think Maj. Smythe was in the hall, sir.

Q. Maj. Whitley there? *A.* I did not see him, sir.

Q. What is the size of the second room you were put in? *A.* It is one of the large cells split in two by a partition; it is about three feet wide.

Q. Did you have any conference with Maj. Whitley in the first room you were put into? *A.* I spoke to him as regards getting a blanket and one thing or another.

Q. In which room was it that he first told you what you were arrested for? *A.* In that room, sir.

Q. The first one? *A.* Yes, sir.

Q. You had a talk with him in that room then about something beside a blanket? *A.* He just asked me if I knew what I was arrested for, and I told him I did, sir.

Q. You have just stated that you never knew what you were arrested for until he told you; how do you explain that? *A.* I was not positive; I knew what I was arrested for; my own conscience told me that; I might have been brought here on some other charges, just as easily as not, if there had been any evidence against me.

Q. Did not you expressly state that you never knew what you were arrested for until Maj. Whitley told you? *A.* I did, sir; that is, I never was informed by anybody; I knew myself what I was arrested for.

Q. Did Maj. Whitley then tell you what you were arrested for by simply asking you if you knew what you were arrested for and your telling him yes? *A.* That is not the way he told it; no, sir.

Q. How did he tell it? *A.* He told it in a rather indirect way.

Q. Well, how did he tell it? Just answer that question; how did he begin? Narrate it just as it occurred; as near as you can recollect, word for word. *A.* He spoke to me about this affair, sir.

Q. Just state how he began; what he said; his own words, as near as you can recollect. *A.* He told me what I knew to make a statement of, sir.

Q. What is the first word he said? How did the conversation begin; what did he state? *A.* I would not swear to the first word, sir.

Q. Well, just as near as you can; bring to your mind now how it began and what he said. *A.* That is what he said, sir; he told me to make a statement of what I knew about the affair, if I knew anything; he did not demand it of me—nothing of that kind; merely asked me to do it.

Q. When was that? When did that occur? *A.* Just after I had gotten here.

Q. Which room were you in? *A.* I was in the third cell, sir; the same thing took place also in the second cell.

Q. Which first—the second or third? *A.* The first time he spoke to me about it was in the third cell; there was less said there than in the other.

Q. Which one were you in first? *A.* In the third cell.

Q. What do you mean by third cell? *A.* I mean the third door.

Q. Were you ever put in that cell when you first came? *A.* No, sir; I was not put in there when I first came.

Q. Was that the first cell you were put in? *A.* Yes, sir.

Q. He mentioned it then to you the first twenty-four hours after you came? *A.* I think it was, sir; yes, sir.

Q. Then you were taken to the second cell? *A.* I was taken to the end, sir.

Q. The second cell you were in? *A.* Yes, sir.

Q. That is the one you say was about three feet by eight? *A.* Yes, sir.

Q. How long were you in that? *A.* I was in there over twenty-four hours.

Q. How long? *A.* Put there one afternoon and kept there until the second morning after.

Q. Where were you taken then? *A.* To the cell in the lower end, sir.

Q. What is the size of it? *A.* About six by eight, sir; somewhere about there.

Q. Was that the first cell you were put in? *A.* No, sir.

Q. How long did you remain in that place? *A.* Until the next morning.

Q. Where were you taken then? *A.* Into the guard-room with the prisoners.

Q. How long did you remain there? *A.* Until last Monday morning; a week, sir.

Q. Where were you taken then? *A.* Put in the end room, sir.

Q. Did you remain there ever since? *A.* Yes, sir.

Q. Where was it that you first made the confession to Major Whitley? *A.* It was in the Adjutant's office.

Q. Was there any person present with you? *A.* No, sir.

Q. Do you swear that Major Whitley did not have free and full access to you at all times since you have been here? *A.* I could not swear to that sir; I don't know what Major Whitley's orders were, sir, no more than you do.

Q. Did Major Whitley tell you what other parties had confessed about this matter? *A.* No, sir.

Q. Did he ever make any statement to you of what other parties had stated, by way of inducement to you? *A.* He did not; never made any inducements to me of any kind.

Re-direct Examination.

Q. For what did Maj. Whitley tell you he would guarantee you protection; was it that you should tell the whole truth and that you should implicate any particular individuals? *A.* That I should tell the truth.

Q. Did or did not Major Whitley charge you not to implicate any innocent person in any statement that you might make? *A.* He did, sir.

Q. When, in your examination yesterday, you stated that the majority of the people of Columbus were against Ashburn, in regard to which statement you have been examined to-day, were you speaking of the sentiments of the whole people of that locality or a class, and if a class, what class of the people were you speaking of? *A.* I was speaking of the class having the most influence.

Q. Were you speaking of the white population or of the black? *A.* Of the white, sir.

Q. How many drinks did you take that night, the night of Ashburn's assassination? *A.* I took one, sir, at the "Ruby."

Q. Were you more or less intoxicated that night than you were in the afternoon? *A.* More in the afternoon.

Q. You stated in your cross-examination that you were not certain whether you had spoken to Bedell before the night of the killing of Ashburn; had you not often seen him previous to that time, and did you not know him well by sight? *A.* I seen him most every day, sir, and knew him well by sight.

Q. Were you intoxicated at all the time of Ashburn's assassination? *A.* I was not under the influence of liquor, sir.

Questions by the Court.

Q. Did you at the time you received the loan from Mr. Wilkins promise and intend to pay it in the future? *A.* I did not, sir.

Q. Did the person you believed you recognized as Chipley have a revolver and fire it on Ashburn on the night in question? *A.* No, sir.

Q. Had you made application for your furlough before you were relieved as first sergeant? *A.* Yes, sir.

Q. Look at this paper and say if it is a correct diagram of the house in which Ashburn was killed; examine it carefully. [The Judge Advocate here handed a paper to witness.] *A.* I believe it is, sir.

Q. During your conversation with the accused, Chipley, after the murder of Ashburn, was there anything said in reference to the said murder? If so, state all that was said to you. *A.* There was not, sir.

Q. Was there anything said to you after

Ashburn was killed by any of the accused on the subject in question? *A*. No, sir.

[Question by defense, by permission of the Court.]

Q. Did Mr. Chipley say more than "good morning" at the only time you spoke to him after the death of Ashburn? *A*. Not as I remember, sir.

[A. E. Marshall was then duly sworn as an additional short-hand reporter for the Court, by the Judge Advocate, in the presence of the Court and the accused.

Questions by Prosecution.

George F. Betz, witness for the prosecution, was brought into Court and duly sworn.

Q. What is your name? *A*. My name is George F. Betz.

Q. Where do you live? *A*. In Columbus.

Q. Where were you raised? *A*. In Columbus.

Q. Where do your parents live? *A*. In Columbus.

Q. Columbus? In what State and county? *A*. State of Georgia, Muscogee county.

Q. What is your occupation? *A*. I have none particularly, sir.

Q. In what business were you last employed before you were arrested? *A*. I was on the railroad, sir.

Q. How long had you been running on the railroad? *A*. About seven or eight months.

Q. In what capacity? *A*. Fireman, sir.

Q. Were you acquainted with George W. Ashburn? *A*. Not personally.

Q. Did you know him by sight? *A*. I did, sir.

Q. Is he dead or alive? *A*. He is dead, sir.

Q. Were you present at his death? *A*. I was sir.

Q. How did he die? *A*. He was shot.

Q. How many persons were present when he was shot? *A*. Between twenty-five and thirty, I think, sir.

Q. Where was he killed? *A*. In Columbus.

Q. At what locality in Columbus? *A*. On Oglethorpe street, sir.

Q. In the street or in a house? *A*. In a house, sir.

Q. Where was that house located? *A*. Located on Oglethorpe street.

Q. Can you give any description as to its location? *A*. No, sir; none particularly.

Q. Do you know the cross streets near it? *A*. I do not recollect their names.

Q. How far was it from the Perry House? *A*. About two hundred yards, sir.

Q. Was there any vacant lot near it? *A*. There was.

Q. Was the vacant lot on the same side of the street or the opposite side of the street from the house where Ashburn was killed? *A*. It was on the opposite side.

Q. Look upon that diagram (one handed to witness) and say whether, in your opinion, it is a correct diagram of the house in which Ashburn was killed. *A*. Well, I can not tell, for I was not acquainted with the house.

Q. Had you ever been in it before that night? *A*. I had not, sir.

Q. Was the end or the side of the house to the street? *A*. The end of it was to the street.

Q. State whether there was any door in the end of the street. *A*. There was, sir.

Q. Where did the persons meet who killed Ashburn? *A*. In that vacant lot, I suppose.

Q. Where did they go from that lot? *A*. To the house.

Q. What did they do when they got there? *A*. Knocked at the door.

Q. Did any one say anything; and if so, what? *A*. They did.

Q. Well, what? *A*. They asked for admittance; some one inside asked who was there, they said it was Mary Tillinghurst.

Q. What did the person inside reply? *A*. Asked, who do you want to see?

Q. What did the person outside say? *A*. Hannah Flournoy.

Q. What reply was made to that? *A*. Can't let you in; it is too late.

Q. Do you know who outside demanded admittance? *A*. No, sir; I do not.

Q. Did the person seem to speak in his own natural voice or in an effeminate voice not his own? *A*. I can't tell.

Q. Did you hear him speak when he demanded admittance? *A*. I did, sir.

Q. Did you know his voice? *A*. I could not recognize it.

Q. After admittance was denied, what then occurred? *A*. The door was knocked down, or a part of it knocked down.

Q. Did anybody enter? *A*. They did, sir.

Q. How many persons, and who were they, to the best of your knowledge, who entered? *A.* I can't tell how many came into the house.

Q. Did you go in? *A.* I did, sir.

Q. Do you know any persons whom you can identify who went in? *A.* I do.

Q. Who were they? *A.* Mr. Dukes.

Q. If he is here, point him out. *A.* (Witness, pointing to one of the prisoners) There he is, sir.

Q. Who else? *A.* Mr. Hudson.

Q. Can you point him out? *A.* I can.

Q. Do so. *A.* (Witness pointed to one of the prisoners.)

Q. Do you see any one else present who was in there? *A.* I do.

Q. State who, and point him out. *A.* All of them, sir?

Q. Point out one at a time. *A.* (The witness pointed to each prisoner severally, who, at the order of the Court, rose up in full view of the Court as his name was called by witness.) Mr. Robt. A. Woods, Mr. James W. Barber, William Duke, Robert Hudson, Alva C. Roper, Jas. Wiggins, Doctor Kirksey, Columbus Bedell.

Q. Any one else? *A.* I am not certain of Captain Chipley.

Q. Well, if there is any reason that induces you to believe that he is the man, or any description of his person, state them. *A.* The man in command of that squad I take to be Captain Chipley.

Q. Why did you take him to be Chipley? *A.* From his appearance, sir.

Q. What was his appearance? *A.* Just as it is now—a large man.

Q. If he was disguised in any way, state it—how? *A.* He was disguised; had on a dough-face.

Q. What do you mean by a dough-face? *A.* False-face.

Q. What sort of a false-face was it? *A.* It was dark; I believe, to my best knowledge, it was black.

Q. Do you know of what it was made? *A.* No, sir.

Q. What did it look like? *A.* Looked like a false-face, that's all I know.

Q. When you say dough-face, do you mean it was made of dough or some other material? *A.* There wasn't much dough about it.

Q. What did this person do there that night who you took to be Capt. Chipley? *A.* He seemed to have command of a squad.

Q. How many of those persons, if any, whom you have named went with you into the house? *A.* Mr. Duke, Mr. Hudson, Mr. Barber.

Q. Any one else? *A.* No, sir. They came behind me, whoever else came into the house.

Q. Did you see Marshall anywhere that night—a soldier? *A.* I did, sir.

Q. Where was he when you went into the house? *A.* He was with me.

Q. You have stated that Duke, Hudson, Barber, Marshall, and yourself went into the house together; did you see any one else in the house after you came in besides the names you have mentioned? *A.* I did, sir.

Q. Who were there? *A.* Milton Malone, Henry Hennis, Doctor Kirksey, Columbus Bedell, and a fellow by the name of Blair; that is all I know about him.

Q. Did you see Bedell and Kirksey do anything? *A.* I did not, sir.

Q. Were you and the others who first went in with you armed? *A.* They were, sir.

Q. With what? *A.* With pistols.

Q. What sort of pistols? *A.* I did not notice closely; revolvers, I believe.

Q. What was yours? *A.* A revolver, sir.

Q. When the door was broken down, and you went in, what did you do? *A.* Went on through the room.

Q. To what room? *A.* Ashburn's room, I suppose, sir.

Q. What room was that—the first, second, or third room? *A.* The third room, sir.

Q. Did you hear Ashburn say anything, and if so, what? *A.* He asked who came there.

Q. What did he then do? *A.* He didn't do anything particularly, not as I seen.

Q. Who opened the door? *A.* He opened his door.

Q. Was there any burning candle in his room or not? *A.* There was.

Q. Where was it? *A.* It was on the table, sir.

Q. Where was the table? *A.* In the middle of the floor, or about.

Q. What sort of table, if you recollect? *A.* A round table, sir.

Q. Where was Ashburn as you got into the door? *A.* He was in his room.

Q. What part of his room? *A.* He was on the right-hand side.

Q. Was there any bed in the room? *A.* There was.

Q. Where was it located? *A.* In the corner of the room.

Q. As you went in was it on the left-hand or right-hand corner? *A.* Right-hand corner.

Q. When you got to Ashburn's door, if anybody said anything, who was it and what did he say? *A.* Bob. Hudson said, "You are a d—n s—t."

Q. What then occurred? *A.* Firing, sir.

Q. How many shots were fired? *A.* To the best of my belief there were thirteen or fourteen.

Q. Who fired? *A.* I did, sir.

Q. Who else? *A.* Mr. Duke.

Q. Who else? *A.* Mr. Hudson.

Q. Anybody else? *A.* Mr. Barber.

Q. Any one else? *A.* Mr. Marshall.

Q. Was there any one else? *A.* I think not, sir.

Q. Did you see Ashburn fall? *A.* I did, sir.

Q. Did anybody fire after he fell? *A.* I think they did.

A. Who? *A.* Mr. Hudson.

Q. In what position was he when he fired? *A.* He was on his knees, squatting down.

Q. Why did he stoop down to fire? *A.* I do not know,

Q. Was there anything in the way, after Ashburn fell, to render it necessary for him to stoop in order to hit him? *A.* I believe the table was between him and Ashburn.

Q. What did you all do after the firing, and after Ashburn fell? *A.* Went out, sir.

Q. Did anybody go and look upon him after he fell before you went out, and if so, who? *A.* I did not see anybody.

Q. Did anybody's mask fall off as you retired from the room? *A.* There did.

Q. Whose? *A.* I believe it was Sam. Bedell's.

Q. Did you hear him make any remarks to a woman or anybody else? *A.* I think he did.

Q. What was the remark? *A.* The best I can recollect is, he said he would kill her if she told on him.

Q. Did all the party go in the house, or did a part remain outside? *A.* They didn't all go in.

Q. State whether the man you took to be Capt. Chipley went in? *A.* I didn't see him go in.

Q. Did you see any women in the house when you entered? *A.* I did.

Q. Who were they? *A.* A white woman and a negro woman.

Q. Can you give their names? *A.* I can.

Q. Do so? *A.* Amanda Patterson and Hannah Flourney.

Q. Do you know Mr. Bennett? *A.* I do.

Q. Did you see anything of him in the room? *A.* I did not.

Q. Were there any places in the room where he could have concealed himself; if so, what sort of places? *A.* I do not know that.

Q. Could he have been in the room without your seeing him? *A.* I suppose he could, sir.

Q. After you retired from the house what did the party then do? *A.* They went on across the street and went through the lot.

Q. How many do you think were present? *A.* Between twenty and thirty.

Q. When they passed the vacant lot what did they do? *A.* I do not know.

Q. State whether they remained together, or whether they scattered. *A.* I can not tell.

Q. Where did you go? *A.* Went home.

Q. Where were they when you separated from them? *A.* In that lot, sir.

Q. Who did you first meet when you got there that night? *A.* Met Bill Duke.

Q. Who next? *A.* Met the crowd next.

Q. How long after you got there before you advanced to Ashburn's house? *A.* About ten minutes, sir.

Q. Why did you go there that night? *A.* I went there to help kill Ashburn.

Q. Did you expect to meet anybody else there? *A.* I did, sir.

Q. Why? *A.* Because I was told so.

Q. Who told you so? *A.* Dr. Kirksey.

Q. How many conversations had you with Dr. Kirksey on this subject? *A.* One, sir.

Q. Where was it? *A.* In Columbus.

Q. In what part of the city? *A.* In Oglethorpe street.

Q. How did the conversation occur? *A.* He just called me to him.

Q. What did he say? *A.* He told me he wanted me to join that party.

Q. What party? *A.* The party to help kill Ashburn.

Q. Why did they say they wanted to kill Ashburn? *A.* They didn't tell me that.

Q. Why did he say it? *A.* He didn't tell me.

Q. Did he say anything about money, or anything of value, and what? *A.* He did, sir. He said he would give me so much money to go there.

Q. What sum? *A.* Fifty or a hundred dollars.

Q. State whether you agreed to go. *A.* I did.

Q. Was any time fixed? *A.* There was.

Q. When was it? *A.* Monday night.

Q. What month and what day of the month was that Monday night? *A.* It was March, 30th day of the month.

Q. Was anything said about the time of night the meeting was to take place? *A.* There was.

Q. What time? *A.* Between twelve and one o'clock.

Q. At what place? *A.* At that vacant lot.

Q. What vacant lot do you mean? *A.* On Oglethorpe street.

Q. Where were you in the early hours of that night? *A.* I was knocking around town.

Q. Did you go home any time of the night before the killing? *A.* I did, sir.

Q. What time in the night did you go home? *A.* Between ten and eleven o'clock, sir.

Q. What did you do when you got home? *A.* Went to bed.

Q. How long did you remain in bed? *A.* About half an hour or three quarters.

Q. What did you then do? *A.* Got up.

Q. How did you get out the room? *A.* Got out of the window.

Q. Where did you go from your room? *A.* Went up on Broad street.

Q. Then where did go? *A.* Went on up town.

Q. How long after that before you went to the vacant lot? *A.* I went on up there, sir.

Q. After the killing of Ashburn, how long before you returned home? *A.* I suppose it was about an hour.

Q. Where did you go in the meantime? *A.* I went away down town.

Q. When you got home how did you get into the house? *A.* I got in at the window.

Q. What did you then do? *A.* Went to bed.

Q. Where were you next morning? *A.* Was there.

Q. Did you get up as usual? *A.* I did.

Q. State whether the family, or any of them, knew you were absent after you went to bed that night. *A.* I do not think they did, sir.

Q. Did Doctor Kirksey give you any reasons why they intended to kill Ashburn, and if so, what? *A.* No, sir; he did not. I knew them, though.

Q. How did you know them? *A.* They wanted to get him out of the way in election times.

Q. When you went down town after the killing, with whom did you go? *A.* Went by myself.

Cross-examination — Questions for Defense by Mr. Stephens.

Q. Leave all the rest there? *A.* No, sir; I didn't leave them.

Q. Which way did the others go. *A.* Went on through the lot.

Q. Did you go back to the lot? *A.* Not right then.

Q. Did you go back to the lot? that is my question. *A.* I did, sir.

Q. Did anybody leave the lot with you? *A.* No, sir.

Q. Did anybody leave before you? *A.* I went with the crowd; I went one way, they went the other.

Q. You went with the crowd, and you went one way and they went the other? *A.* When I left them.

Q. Did you leave the crowd all at the lot? *A.* I left them going through the lot, sir.

Q. Did anybody go with you when you left? *A.* No, sir.

Q. Did you go into the lot? *A.* I did.

Q. And then did you turn right round and go back? *A.* I didn't.

Q. Which way then did you go? *A.* Went up the street.

Q. Which street? *A.* I believe it is Church street.

Q. Which street is the vacant lot on? *A.* It is on both of them.

Q. Which both? *A.* Oglethorpe and Church.

Q. Did you go then through the lot to Church street? *A.* I did.

Q. Did they all go through with you to Church street? *A.* I left them all about half way, sir.

Q. You left all about half way in the lot? *A.* I did not leave them all.

Q. Where were the balance? *A.* Some went down the other street—down Oglethorpe street.

Q. Did you not state that they all went back with you into the lot? *A.* I believe I did.

Q. Is it true? *A.* Some of them turned off down Oglethorpe street.

Q. Which ones of them? *A.* I do not know.

Q. Which ones of them were with you? *A.* I do not know that.

Q. Do you know a single one that did? *A.* I do.

Q. Which one was it? *A.* Bill Duke.

Q. Which other one went? *A.* Bob Hudson.

Q. Which other one? *A.* Jim Barber.
Q. Which other one? *A.* Dr. Kirksey.
Q. Which other one? *A.* Lum Bedell.
Q. Which other one? *A.* Henry Hennis.

Q. Any other one? *A.* I do not recollect; they are all I know went through the lot with me, I believe.

Q. Are you certain of it or not? *A.* No, sir, I ain't.

Q. Well, then, did you leave them all there? Do I understand your testimony to be that you left them all there? *A.* I went by myself.

Q. Did you leave them there? is my question. *A.* There's where I left them; there is where I turned off from the crowd.

Q. You say you left them there? *A.* I did.

Q. And went alone? *A.* Yes, sir.

Q. Did you say you went down Church street? *A.* No, sir.

Q. What did you say about Church street? *A.* I went up Church street.

Q. And you left Bedell, and Barber, and Duke, and Hudson, and Kirksey in the middle of the vacant lot? *A.* About the middle.

Q. Was there any conversation had between you, or any of you, after the crowd got into the middle of the vacant lot? *A.* Going from the house there was.

Q. What was that conversation? *A.* Milton Malone asked me why I did not shoot all the barrels of my pistol off.

Q. Anything else? *A.* No, sir.

Q. You say that all the crowd you know went into the middle of the vacant lot with you? *A.* I believe so.

Q. Did Hennis go? *A.* I think he did.

Q. Marshall? *A.* I did not see him.

Q. What did you do with your mask? *A.* Tore it up.

Q. Where did you tear it up? *A.* Tore it up in the street.

Q. Which street? *A.* I do not know what street it was—it was in Columbus.

Q. What kind of a mask did you have? *A.* Had a black one, sir.

Q. What kind of a mask did Bedell have? *A.* Had a black one.

Q. Where did you get the mask you had? *A.* I made it.

Q. Did you ever ask Dr. Kirksey for the fifty dollars, or the hundred he promised to pay you? *A.* No, sir; I never asked him for it.

Q. Did he ever say anything to you about paying it? *A.* He said he would send it through the post-office to me.

Q. When did he say that? *A.* He said when I received it I would get it through the post-office.

Q. Did you ever get it through the post-office? *A.* No, sir.

Q. And you never said anything to him about it? *A.* No, sir.

Q. Now, upon your oath, Mr. Betz, will you swear that you ever spoke to Dr. Kirksey or Dr. Kirksey to you in your life, about anything? *A.* I have.

Q. Did anybody ever see you speak to Dr. Kirksey, or see you in company with him; or is there anybody living by whom you can prove that you ever had a conversation with him, or that he ever knew you? *A.* I do not know whether I can or not.

Q. How high is that window of your bedroom? *A.* I do not know exactly how high it is.

Q. How high do you suppose it is? *A.* Higher than my head.

Q. How were you dressed that night? *A.* I had on a black coat.

Q. What sort of pants? *A.* A pair of dark pants.

Q. When were you arrested? *A.* I was arrested on the 21st of May, I believe.

Q. In whose custody have you been since? *A.* Been in the military custody.

Q. Who had charge of you? *A.* Capt. Cook, at this place.

Q. Where were you first taken after your arrest? *A.* To Fort Pulaski.

Q. In whose charge were you put then? *A.* Capt. Cook was in charge of the fort, I believe, I do not know.

Q. Where did you first get acquainted with Mr. Whitley? *A.* I never seen him before till I got to the fort.

Q. Did you have any acquaintance with Capt. Chipley? *A.* Not personally.

Q. Did you ever speak to him, or he to you, in your life until since your arrest? *A.* I do not recollect.

Q. You have no recollection of any words passing between you and him in your life? *A.* No, sir.

Q. Is it not true that a word never did pass between you and him, in your life, until since your arrest? *A.* I do not recollect.

Q. Did you ever speak to Mr. Bedell in your life? *A.* I have.

Q. Did he speak to you? *A.* He did.

Q. Can you state any occasion? *A.* I can.

Q. State it. *A.* Mr. Bedell was shooting in his lot one day; and I was an officer; I went to his lot and told him not to do it; he said is was his lot and he would shoot when he pleased; he was shooting a hog.

Q. Has Mr. Bedell any lot? *A.* I do not know.

Q. You don't know? *A.* It was the lot where he lived; I don't know whether it was his or who it belonged to.

Q. When was that? *A.* Been a good while ago.

Q. How many years? *A.* No years at all.

Q. How long ago, then? *A.* I don't recollect.

Q. Three months? *A.* More.

Q. Six? *A.* More than that.

Q. Twelve? *A.* I don't think it was that long.

Q. How was Mr. Woods dressed that night? *A.* I don't recollect, sir.

Q. How was Mr. Duke dressed that night? *A.* He had on black clothes.

Q. How was Mr. Bedell dressed? *A.* I don't recollect.

Q. Was it a dark night or a moonshine night? *A.* I think the moon had just gone down, sir.

Q. How was Mr. Roper dressed? *A.* I don't recollect that either.

Q. How did you know them? You stated that they were all masked. *A.* I spoke to them, sir.

Q. Which ones did you speak to? *A.* I spoke to all I mentioned.

Q. When did you speak to them— before you got to the house or afterward? *A.* Going to the house.

Q. Did they tell you their names? *A.* No, sir.

Q. Were they all masked when you first saw them? *A.* Will Duke was not.

Q. Did he put on a mask afterward? *A.* I do not know whether he did or not.

Q. Were all the rest masked except Bill Duke? *A.* I think they were, sir.

Q. Well, how did you know them? *A.* By their talk.

Q. How did you know them individually? *A.* Because I had been raised up with them. I knowed them as good as I know myself.

Q. Were you as intimate with Mr. Bedell as with yourself? *A.* No, sir.

Q. Did you ever hear Mr. Bedell talk except when you heard him say he would shoot the hog? *A.* I have.

Q. Ever on any other occasion except that? *A.* No, sir.

Q. He never did on any other occasion except that? *A.* Not as I recollect.

Q. You never heard him utter a word in your life except that he would shoot when he pleased on his lot? *A.* Yes, sir, I have.

Q. If so, state when and where. *A.* On the street, sir.

Q. State on what occasion it was. *A.* I heard him talk; he was not talking to me.

Q. Can you state what you ever heard him talk about, and who were present? *A.* I do not know, sir, what he was talking about. I heard him speak; that was the question you asked me—whether I have ever heard him speak.

Q. Do you say that you have ever heard him speak often enough to be as familiar with his voice as to recognize him under a mask and swear positively to his identity from his voice? *A.* I do not think I would.

Q. Would you say the same of Doctor Kirksey? *A.* No, sir.

Q. Are you more familiar with him than with Bedell—more intimate? *A.* I would know him sooner by his voice.

Q. How long have you known Doctor Kirksey? *A.* I don't exactly recollect.

Q. How long, as near as you can tell? *A.* I don't know; I could not say.

Q. Raised with him? *A.* No, sir.

Q. Did you not say you were raised with all of them? *A.* No, sir.

Q. What did you say about being raised with them? I understood you that way.
A. Raised with the biggest part of them.
Q. Dr. Kirksey was not one of them? *A.* No, sir.
Q. I want you now to state as near as you can when you first knew him. *A.* I knew him some eight or nine months, I reckon.
Q. How long have you known Mr. Woods? *A.* I can not tell that.
Q. Longer than Kirksey or shorter? *A.* Longer.
Q. Can you swear that you could recognize his voice? *A.* Yes, sir, to the best of my knowledge and belief I could.
Q. How was he dressed that night? *A.* I don't recollect, sir.
Q. You say you recognize these gentlemen by their voices, as they were talking, as they went from the vacant lot to the house where Ashburn was killed; can you state anything that any one of them said? *A.* I can.
Q. State it. *A.* Mr. Hudson—Bob Hudson—said we would give him hell.
Q. Anything that any other said? *A.* No, sir; I don't believe I do; I don't recollect particularly what they said.
Q. Do you state upon your oath that the only ground of your recognizing them was their voice? *A.* I knowed them very well.
Q. Have you not just stated that you knowed them by their voices? *A.* Yes, sir, I did.
Q. You said you were first taken to Savannah? *A.* Taken to Fort Pulaski.
Q. Where did you first get acquainted with Mr. Whitley? *A.* At Fort Pulaski.
Q. Did he have charge of you there? *A.* Capt. Cook had charge.
Q. Have any interview with Mr. Whitley there? *A.* I did, sir.
Q. When did you first know what you were arrested for? *A.* I don't recollect that; I don't recollect the time.
Q. Who told you? *A.* I don't recollect.
Q. Who was present the first interview you had with Mr. Whitley? *A.* Nobody, sir.
Q. Where did the interview take place? *A.* At Fort Pulaski.
Q. Did he tell you what you were arrested for? *A.* No, sir; I don't believe he did.
Q. Who did tell you? *A.* I don't recollect.
Q. To whom did you first make the disclosure that you have made here? *A.* To Major Whitley, sir.
Q. Where was it at? *A.* Down here in one of those houses.
Q. Did you make no disclosure to him at Fort Pulaski? *A.* No, sir.
Q. Did he endeavor to get you to make any? *A.* Not particularly, sir.
Q. What did he do? *A.* Didn't do anything.
Q. What did he say on the subject of your making a disclosure? *A.* I don't recollect, sir.
Q. Did he tell you that he had proof of your guilt, and that if you would testify against the other parties, you would be protected? *A.* I know that, sir.
Q. You know what? *A.* I know that I would be protected.
Q. Didn't Mr. Whitley tell you so? *A.* He did, sir; I knew it before ever he told me though, I knew his business very well.
Q. What was his business? *A.* He was a detective.
Q. He is no Major in the army then? *A.* I do not know whether he is or not.
Q. You say you knew his business? *A.* From what I have heard.
Q. His business is a Government detective you say? *A.* Yes, sir, a Government detective, or a Government agent of some kind.
Q. Didn't he tell you that if you didn't make a disclosure that you would be hung? *A.* I don't recollect, sir.
Q. Didn't he tell you in substance that you had better save your neck? *A.* I don't recollect it, sir.
Q. Didn't he tell you that these other gentlemen were men of property, and that they would let you be hung, and that you had better save your neck by coming out with the truth against them? *A.* I don't recollect that either; something of the kind was said.
Q. State as near as you can what was said. *A.* I don't recollect anything particularly; I knew it though before he told me so.
Q. Did he tell you to say that on your oath? *A.* No, he didn't.
Q. Was Mr. Daniel under arrest here? *A.* He was.
Q. Did Mr. Whitley have the exclusive control of you; did anybody see you except by the permission of Mr. Whitley? *A.* Officers came there; soldiers saw us without his permission.

Q. Did they go into the room? *A.* We were not in a room.

Q. Where were you then? *A.* In the cell.

Q. Did the soldiers go into the cells at any time—have free access to you? *A.* They came if they chose.

Q. Did they do it? that is my question. *A.* No, sir; the cook came there to bring rations to us.

Q. Were you permitted to have any intercourse with friends without the permission of Mr. Whitley? *A.* I never had any at all.

Q. Did Mr. Whitley tell you the arrest of the other parties? *A.* I think he did.

Q. Don't you know he did? *A.* I am not certain he did.

Q. Didn't he take you to a place and show Mr. Daniel in another part so that you could see him? *A.* No, sir, he didn't.

Q. Didn't he tell you where he was? *A.* I knew where he was.

Q. Didn't Mr. Whitley tell you so? *A.* I don't recollect, sir.

Q. Didn't he tell you how he got there? *A.* I believe he did.

Q. How did he tell you he got there? *A.* Gave a bond.

Q. What else did he tell you about it? *A.* I don't recollect that.

Q. You don't recollect? *A.* No.

Q. Didn't he tell you distinctly that Kirksey and Chipley had bonded him (Daniel) and was leaving you to be hung because you were poor? Didn't he tell you that Kirksey and Chipley said that their money would save them? *A.* I believe he did.

Q. And also that you would be hung and thereby they would get rid of you? *A.* No, sir, he didn't.

Q. Well, did he say they would get rid of you? *A.* I don't recollect that either.

Q. Didn't he tell you that Kirksey and Chipley said that their money would save them? *A.* I believe he did, sir.

Q. Didn't he give you assurance that if you would come out and make a statement you would not be hurt? *A.* I knew that, sir.

Q. That is not my question: I ask you did he tell you so? *A.* He did, sir.

Q. I'll put this question: Didn't he tell you that Kirksey and Chipley said that their money would save them, and d—n the other fellows; we want to get them out of the way? *A.* No, sir.

Q. Didn't he tell you any words to that effect? *A.* I don't think he did, sir.

Q. Did he not tell you in the presence of your father to remember that the halter was still around your neck? *A.* No, sir.

Q. Did Mr. Whitley allow you to see your father by yourself? *A.* He (Mr. Whitley) was in the same room, sir.

Re-examination by Prosecution.

Q. If the promise of protection made by Maj. Whitley was depending upon your testifying against any particular person or persons, name such persons. *A.* No, sir; it was not.

Q. Upon what was it depending? *A.* Upon telling all that I knew, sir.

Q. If he gave you any warning to criminate no innocent person, state what it was. *A.* I don't recollect particularly, but he told me not to do it.

Q. I will ask you if you have done it in any statement you have made here— whether you have criminated any innocent person? *A.* No, sir.

Q. State whether or not you were well acquainted with Mr. Bedell by sight? *A.* I was, sir.

Q. Do you not know many persons by sight to whom you have never been introduced and with whom you have never spoken? *A.* I do, sir.

Q. You testify that you heard these persons in conversation before you went into the house; I ask you whether there was any light in Ashburn's room after you went in? *A.* There was.

Q. State whether you saw them in the house when the light shone upon them? *A.* I did, sir.

Q. State whether that did or did not aid you in identifying them. *A.* Not particularly; I knowed who they were.

Q. Do you mean to say that you knew before they went in who they were? *A.* Yes, sir.

Q. State whether on seeing them in the light you found yourself mistaken as to any one of them, and if so, who? *A.* I did not.

Q. State whether or not, in the crowd that night, you heard any of those present call others by name, and if so whose names you heard called. *A.* I heard Dr. Kirksey's name called.

Q. Do you know by whom it was called? *A.* No, sir.

Q. State whether you heard any other

name called. *A.* I heard Jim Barber's name called.

Q. Any other? *A.* I heard Henry Hennis' name called.

Q. Any other? *A.* I don't recollect; I don't think there was.

Questions by Court.

Q. State the year of the occurrence. *A.* 1868, sir.

Q. Did any one go as Captain of the party and give you directions; and if so, who was it? *A.* I think there was, sir, a commander. Well, sir, I think he was; I would not swear it, but I think it was Captain Chipley.

Q. Did any person fire from your rear on Ashburn? If so, state about the number of shots, and the names of the persons who fired them, to the best of your knowledge. *A.* There were two shots fired from behind me—Jim Barber; I think it was him, to the best of my knowledge and belief.

Q. You state that Bedell's mask fell off—did you recognize Bedell at that time? *A.* I did, sir.

Q. How long have you lived in the same town with Dr. Kirksey, Wood, and Bedell, and known them? *A.* I could not exactly say; a good while.

Q. What were your reasons for assisting in killing Ashburn? *A.* Because I thought he was a tyrant to the place, and ought to be out of the way.

Prosecution.

Q. State what time of night the killing took place. *A.* Between twelve and one o'clock.

Defense.

Q. Were you or not very much intoxicated the early part of that night? *A.* I was not.

Q. You say that the person you suppose to be Chipley did not go into the house; you then did not see him by the light? *A.* I did not see him go in and did not see him by the light; there was a gaslight in the street close to the house.

Q. How near is the gaslight to that house? *A.* It is right cat-a-cornered across—I suppose a hundred yards.

Q. Berringer's corner? *A.* No, sir.

Q. What place was it? *A.* Right in front of a house, about one third of the block.

Q. Do they have gaslights moonlight nights? *A.* The moon had gone down.

Questions by Court.

A. Did your party pass a gaslight in going from the vacant lot to Ashburn's house? *A.* No, sir.

[At three o'clock the Court adjourned till to-morrow morning, at 10 o'clock, July 2d.]

McPherson Barracks, Atlanta, Ga., }
10 o'clock a. m., July 2, 1868. }

Commission met pursuant to adjournment.

Present, same members as yesterday, the Judge Advocate, the prisoners on trial, and their counsel.

The record of yesterday's proceedings was read and approved.

George F. Betz, whose testimony was taken yesterday as a witness before this Commission, was present, and on hearing his testimony read by the Judge Advocate asked permission of the court to make the following correction, viz: Where, in his answer to a question from the defense, which will be found on the ——— of his testimony, he says, "There was a gaslight in the street close to the house," he desires now to say, "In regard to the gaslight, I will not be so positive whether it was lighted or not." Permission was granted and the correction accordingly embodied in this day's proceedings.

The counsel for the defense aforesaid, asked permission of the Court to further interrogate the witness, which permission having been granted, the witness, George F. Betz, again took the stand and was interrogated as follows :

Questions by Defense.

Q. Have you had conversation with anybody about that portion of your testimony since it was delivered here yesterday? *A.* Have I had any? No, sir, none particular.

Q. Have you had any? is my question. *A.* No, sir, I have not had any.

Q. You conversed with nobody upon this subject since yesterday—upon the subject of this gaslight? Has your testimony about that been mentioned to you since you retired from this Court yesterday? *A.* No, sir.

The counsel for the defense then asked

the further permission of the Court to propound to the witness a few general questions, which in yesterday's examination were omitted. Permission having been granted, the witness was further interrogated as follows:

Questions by Defense.

Q. Do you know Jacob and Isaac Marks, of Columbus, Georgia? A. I do, sir.

Q. Have they lately been under arrest here? A. I think they have.

Q. When were they brought before you, and if so, by whom? A. They were brought before me by Maj. Whitley?

Q. Were you asked if they were present at the killing of Ashburn, or words to that effect? A. Yes, sir.

Q. What was your reply? A. "No," sir.

Q. Did not Whitley then say that you had sworn that they were? A. He did, sir.

Q. Did not you say, "Well, you dictated the names"? A. Yes, sir.

The Judge Advocate then asked permission of the Court to further interrogate the witness on behalf of the prosecution. Permission having been obtained, the Judge Advocate interrogated the witness as follows:

Questions by Prosecution.

Q. What do you mean by "dictated the names?" A. Well, sir, with regard to that last question, I think I gave a wrong answer. I don't think "dictate" was mentioned at all.

Q. Do you know what the word "dictate" means? A. Not exactly, sir.

Q. Did Mr. Whitley ever name any persons to you and tell you that you should make an accusation against them in regard to the murder of Ashburn? A. I don't think he did, sir.

Q. Didn't you make the statements to him voluntarily, implicating the parties in regard to whom you have testified here? A. I did, sir. Only Maj. Whitley talked to me as a friend—advised me what to do; there was no inducement, sir, whatever, made to me; I done this voluntarily.

Q. Did Maj. Whitley ever advise you or suggest to you to bring an accusation against any particular persons? A. No, sir.

Further questions by defense, by permission of the Court:

Questions by Defense.

Q. What did you say when Mr. Whitley told you that you had sworn that the Markses were at the killing? A. I said I would not indentify them, or "could not;" I don't know which; one or the other.

Q. Did you say anything about dictating or giving the name, or words to that effect? A. I do not recollect, sir.

Questions by the Prosecution.

THOMAS S. TUGGLE, a witness for the prosecution, was then called, and having been duly sworn, testified as follows:

Q. State your name, age, residence, and occupation. A. My name is Thomas S. Tuggle; I reside in Columbus, Georgia, and my profession is that of a physician.

Q. Did you see the body of George W. Ashburn after his death? A. Yes, sir.

Q. Where did you see his body, and when? A. The day after he died; I suppose between nine and ten, or probably ten o'clock in the morning; the house was on Oglethorpe street, nearly opposite the Perry House; he was in the third room, I think, from the street, entering at the end of the house; I do not know how many rooms the house had; it was a long row going back, and I was not further back than the room his body was in.

Q. Where was his body in the room? A. Lying in what I would call the northwest corner of that room; his head was towards a window, which was to the right of the chimney. Q. Was his body on a bed? A. No, sir; lying on the floor with nothing under him at all.

Q. How was he dressed? A. With a long shirt—you might term it a gown—and an overcoat, a sort of sack overcoat probably; no other clothing that I remember.

Q. If you made any examinations of the wounds upon his body, state what they were? A. I only looked on while Dr. Kirksey and Dr. Moses, and Dr. De Graffenried and Dr. Terry turned the body; I do not think I put my hand on the body at all; I made no examination with my own hands; I saw Dr. Kirksey probe the wound on his head with a pencil or pen staff.

Q. State where that wound was. A. Well, as well as I could say now, it was right in the center of the forehead, ranging back and little down, as if his head had been leaning forward at the time; I suppose that it was probably one in above the eyes, as well as I recollect now; there were other wounds on his body; he had one on the right side of the nates, that seemed to be a superficial one; he had one on the left leg, if I am not mistaken, that seemed to have passed through the leg; I think there was an abrasion probably on his right foot; it might have been a bullet hole, I am not certain about that; there was blood there, and I thought from the looks of it that it was; there was a crowd in the room, and it was not very light, and I did not put a probe in it; I could not swear positively that there was a wound on the right foot, but I think there was; I know there was blood there at least.

Q. State whether from the probing of the wound in the head, which you saw made as you say by Dr. Kirksey, that wound was a mortal one or not? A. I should consider that it was a mortal wound, from the direction that it went; that is, provided there is such a thing as wounding a man mortally in the brain; it seemed to have entered centrally, going directly toward the center and base of the brain.

Q. Is it your opinion that he did or did not die of that wound? A. Well, sir, if that wound was there before he was dead, I think it produced his death.

Q. Did you observe any bullet holes in his garments? A. Yes, sir; I saw Dr. De Graffenried turn him over like, and saw where a bullet hole or two, or probably more, had gone through the coat that apparently had not struck his body.

Q. Did the body, when you saw it, appear to be in a condition in which it had died? A. Yes, sir; I do not presume from the appearance it presented that it had been moved much from the extravasation of the blood, which appeared to be on the body next to the floor, between the skin and cellular tissue.

Q. What, in your opinion, had inflicted that wound? A. Well, sir, if I should judge from its appearance, it was a bullet.

The defense did not desire to cross-examine this witness.

Questions by the Prosecution.

ALEXANDER G. BENNETT, a witness for the prosecution, having been first duly sworn, testifies as follows:

Q. State your name, age, and occupation? A. Alexander Gordon Bennett; age, forty-eight; machinist.

Q. Where is your residence? A. In Columbus, Georgia, for the past two years.

Q. Were you acquainted with George W. Ashburn in his lifetime? A. Yes, sir.

Q. How long had you known him previous to his death? A. About ten months.

Q. Were you and he living in the same house at the time of his death? A. Yes, sir.

Q. Were you in that house the night of his death? A. Yes, sir.

Q. State to this Court all you know about his death? A. I had been out with Mr. Woodfield, the master machinist of the Muscogee road, until about eleven o'clock; came in some time past eleven, and went to bed; I could not say how long it had been between that time and the time a rap came at the door; some one in the house, I think it was Hannah Flourney, asked who was there; they said it was one Mary Tillinghurst; she said no one could come in at that time of the night, and they said if they would not be let in they would break the door in; I got out of bed, and went into Ashburn's room, and asked him if he had any weapons; he said he had; I asked him to give them to me, as some one was going to break in the door; he said no, he would use them himself; I then tried the back door and side door; there are two doors, one leading into an alleyway, and one into a back porch; some one at the back door said, "Get back, you s—n of a b—h;" I then asked Ashburn again if he would not give me the pistol, instead of using it himself; he said no, and then put on his overcoat, and told me to look out for myself, and that God would take care of him; I then left the room, and told him not to light any light; when I got to the door between the front door and the middle room, the front door was broke in; the rush of men coming in, I got behind the middle door, at the back of the bed; some women's clothes were hanging on the back of the door, on some nails, and they hid me entirely; one article of clothing also hung on the bed-post; Mr. Ashburn opened the door of the room, having a lighted candle, and said, "Who comes there?" the party that was coming in said, "You are a d—d s—t;" three then came into the light of Mr. Ashburn's room; I could see them; they commenced firing; then one of them withdrew back—the one on the left-hand side of the door—the same side on which the door opened; then two others came up and fired in the place of those who were firing first; the last one that fired sat down on his knees, and fired under the table; all I heard Mr. Ashburn say afterward was, "Stop, stop," I think, three times distinctly uttered, after the firing commenced, and about the same time they commenced firing; I think the side door from the alley was broke in, but can't say whether there was any firing from that point or not; after the firing, I heard some one say, "Come on, boys;" with that they started and run out of the door; then I came out after that, and the girl and boy, standing in the front room, said, "Go back, they are coming again;" so I went back to the same place again, but it proved to be the police.

Q. Was that room Mr. Ashburn's home? A. Yes, sir, it was all the home he had while in Columbus this last time.

Q. Do you know whether he owned or rented it? A. Rented it, I think.

Q. Do you know from whom he rented it? A. I think it was the colored woman.

Q. Name her? A. Hannah Flourney.

Q. Where did he take his meals? A. In that room.

Q. Who furnished them? A. I think he was furnishing himself, and the colored woman was cooking for him.

Q. Did you know why he went there to occupy that room? A. I knew, what he told me himself and what I seen in the papers at the time, that he could not get a bed at no hotel.

Q. How was he dressed when you first saw him that night after he came out of his bed? A. He had nothing on but his night-shirt, and then he put on his overcoat when he came out of bed.

Q. Was it by the light from his room that you saw these parties who were firing upon him? A. Yes, sir.

Q. Did you know either of the parties who fired upon him? A. I believe I did.

Q. Name any one whom you knew. A. Hudson, William Duke, and Jim Barber, and one Marshall and George Betz; I did not recognize Hudson nor Marshall so certain as I did the other three.

Q. Did you recognize any other persons in that house that night about the time that Ashburn was killed? A. There was more in the room, but I could not see them; they were in the shade; there was more in the front room; I could hear them talking to the girl in the front room.

Q. How many persons, in your opinion, were in the house that night beside the ordinary occupants? A. I suppose between twenty and—about twenty, I think, by the number apparently walking about.

Q. Do you mean that many in the house or that many in and about the house? A. About that many in the house; I could not say for certain.

Q. Did there appear to be many without and about the house at that time? A. Yes, sir; they seemed to be in an alleyway; I could not say about the door before it was broken in.

Q. Did you see Ashburn's body that night after his death? A. I did before the police had been in the room and the Mayor came in.

Q. Did you see any person go into the room shortly after Ashburn's death, or about the time it occurred? A. The first man that went in was one Lawrence, a policeman.

Q. Where was his body when you first saw it after his death? A. Lying with his head against the wall at the back part of the room, and his feet pointing toward the table at a kind of an angle across the room.

Q. Were you present the next day when Dr. Tuggles was there? A. Yes, sir.

Q. Was the body in the same position when he was there as it was when you first saw it after Ashburn's death? A. With the single exception of being drawn about a foot toward the table; that was done for the purpose of straightening him out, so that he might not stiffen before he was straightened; it was done by the Mayor, or by his order.

Q. How many shots did it appear to you were fired at him? A. I think about fourteen, but won't be certain.

Q. Do you know how many wounds there were on his body? A. I think there was three or four; I won't be certain on that head, as I did not look at any of them except those on the head.

Q. Did you observe whether there were any shot holes through his clothes? A. There were some in the coat, but I didn't examine it closely.

Q. Were there many marks of shots in the walls or in the rooms? A. Yes, a good many.

Q. Did any person occupy that room with Ashburn? A. Nobody excepting me sometimes; there had been a gentleman in the same room, some nights previous to that, named Edwards.

Q. Who occupied the room next to his,

toward the street? *A.* Amanda Patterson and a colored woman.

Q. What is the name of the colored woman? *A.* Hannah Flourney.

Q. Who occupied the front room? *A.* Nobody in general occupied it; it was only rarely occupied by any party; I was late coming that night and I occupied it.

Q. Were there any other occupied rooms in that house? *A.* There was a back kitchen—two rooms—occupied by colored people; I don't know who they were.

Q. Were you examined before a coroner's inquest that was held there? *A.* Yes, sir.

Q. Did you make the same statement there that you have made here to-day? *A.* No, sir.

Q. Were you not under oath? *A.* I was under oath, but did not tell that I knew any of them or suspicioned any.

Q. Why? *A.* Because I should have been cutting my own throat if I had done so.

Q. What do you mean by "cutting your own throat?" *A.* I mean simply this, that I believe the Klu-klux Klan would have put an end to me, as they threatened to do so any way.

Q. Was it then because you were in fear of your life? *A.* Certainly.

Q. Have you at any time since the death of Ashburn, had any conversation with either of these persons on trial? *A.* Yes, sir.

Q. With whom? *A.* I have spoken to them all since I came here, I think.

Q. I mean had you any conversation with any of them in Columbus after the trial? *A.* I had one conversation with Mr. Chipley and Kirksey, I believe, about six or eight weeks after the occurrence; that is the only conversation with any of the prisoners that I have had.

Q. Where did that conversation take place? *A.* At the jail, I believe.

Q. Which side of the jail were you on? Inside or outside? *A.* We were in a room in the second story occupied by the sheriff.

Q. Did they come there to see you? *A.* Yes, sir.

Q. What business did they say they had come for? *A.* The principal of it was about politics—and to know what evidence would be against them—or what evidence I knew would be against them; that was the most of the conversation.

Q. State what they said on the subject of the evidence? *A.* I could not state all that they said; it was principally that they thought there was nothing against them but this colored woman Flourney, or some other colored people; they wanted to know if I knew any of them that had told anything against them.

Q. Was there anything said in that conversation about Amanda Patterson? *A.* No, sir; not that time; nothing with these two men at all.

Q. Did they make any request of you in regard to these colored people? *A.* Nothing, except asking the question what it was they had said against them.

Q. Did they ask you for any assistance or aid of any kind in this trouble? *A.* No, not particular; they never asked me for any assistance; the assistance they asked of me was political, more or less.

Q. You referred awhile ago to a conversation with somebody else about Amanda Patterson? *A.* That was with one Mr. Hughes, a cotton merchant, and the other was Mr. Bowers, the banker.

Q. Will you state what that conversation was? *A.* He asked me, Hughes did, about Robert Daniel, if he was in the custom of coming to see this girl, and I told him that he was; could not say how often, but I had seen him there; and asked me if I thought she could have any evidence against Daniel. and I said I could not say; he asked me if it would not be as well to get her away from the place; I said "I do not know whether it would be suitable or not;" he said if she would go away there would be plenty of money furnished.

Q. Did he or any one else ask you to interest yourself to get Amanda Patterson away from there? *A.* I believe Mr. Bowers was the only one that ever asked me; Mr. Bowers and Hughes the only two.

Q. Did they both ask you or only one in the presence of the other? *A.* One at a time: they were not in the presence of each other; one was in the barber-shop, kept by Sandy Danfall, I think, and the other was in the bar-room behind Speers' jewelry store, in a back room.

Q. Which one had the conversation with you in the barber-shop? *A.* Hughes.

Q. When was that? *A.* It was about two or three days before Amanda Patterson's arrest.

Q. Was it before or after a number of persons had been arrested in Columbus on the charge of having murdered Ashburn?

A. I think it was three of them had been arrested; no, only two—Stevens and Barber—and the two colored people.

Q. Where and when did you have the conversation you mentioned with Bowers? *A.* In a back room of this bar-room kept by one Tom Campbell; I think it was about the same day that Hughes had spoke to me in the barber shop; I think one was in the forenoon and the other in the afternoon.

Q. Did either of these men ask you to try to get Amanda Patterson away? *A.* Not directly; merely hinted if she would go away that money would be had or plenty of money would be got, provided she would consent.

Q. Did they or any other person offer any inducements to you to leave? *A.* No; I was about to leave anyhow; about to come to Atlanta.

Q. Did you make any effort to get Amanda Patterson to leave? *A.* No, sir, but went to her one night when I was the worst for liquor and had a talk with her; I do not know what I said to her.

Q. Do you remember whether, in the conversation you have spoken of at the jail or anywhere else, Mr. Chipley said anything about Amanda Patterson? *A.* I believe there was some questions asked me; if she screamed when the party came in or made any noise; I believe there was some such question as that asked me.

Q. Did Mr. Chipley have any conversation about the "Ku-kluxes" that time or any time in the jail? *A.* Well, something about it; that I need not be afraid of the "Ku-kluxes" if I did —— [witness hesitates].

Q. Did what? *A.* If I helped them politically, or something of that sort, there would be no danger for me from the "Ku-kluxes;" that is how I understood it.

Q. Did Kirksey have anything to say to you in this conversation about that interesting organization? *A.* I disrecollect; I think not; perhaps some little talk about it, but it had become so notorious—the talk of these Ku-kluxes—that I didn't pay any attention much to it.

Q. Did you receive any money from either of these parties on trial? *A.* No, sir; believe they were to pay fifty dollars for me, but I don't know whether they did or not.

Q. Were you in jail when they came to visit you? *A.* Yes, sir.

Q. Who got you out? *A.* I think it was them, but I can't say; the fine was paid; I did not see it paid.

Q. Did they say anything to you about paying your fine when they were there? *A.* I believe they did.

Q. You do not know who paid your fine? *A.* No, I don't know which of the two it was, or if it was any of them; but they said they would get it done.

Q. You were released soon afterward? *A.* Yes, sir.

Q. Do you know a man by the name of Thomas Clark? *A.* I know a man by the name of Joe Clark—a barber; that is all.

Q. Did you receive any money from him? *A.* I received $3.75, I think, if I am not mistaken.

Q. What was that for? *A.* To pay for some affidavits.

Q. What affidavits? *A.* Against one Justice of the Peace, named Bostwick.

Q. What was that for? *A.* That he was not a citizen.

Q. What had that Justice been doing? *A.* Nothing particular at that time.

Q. Hadn't he issued warrants for somebody? *A.* Yes, sir; some time previous to that.

Q. Who had he issued the warrants against and had arrested that you know of? *A.* I believe most of the prisoners here present.

Q. Then you were employed, were you, by him to get up a prosecution against this Justice of the Peace? *A.* No, sir, but for myself; it was he that had commenced the prosecution against me, and it was on my own account that I did that.

Q. I will ask you now to point out or call out the names of those persons among the accused here who you saw in Ashburn's house the night that he was killed. (The witness here named and pointed to James Barber, William Duke, and Robert Hudson, the accused, who, at the request of the Judge Advocate, severally rose to their feet as their names were called. Witness then said, "The other two I don't see here.")

Q. Were these the three that fired? *A.* These three fired, I think.

Q. Are there any others here that fired that night? *A.* No, I don't see any others.

Q. Did you see there that night any others of the prisoners that you see here present to-day? *A.* No, I didn't see any others that I knowed.

Q. If you had been acquainted with all the parties in the house could you have recognized them? *A.* I don't know that I could have recognized more than two others that I had seen, but I didn't know them; I only seen about seven in all.

Q. Were you in a position to see everybody in the house? *A.* No, sir.

Q. Were you particularly anxious to be seen yourself? *A.* No, sir; I was not.

Q. Were you not really hiding from observation? *A.* I was.

Q. Were you not excited and alarmed? *A.* I was.

Cross-Examined— Questions by Defense.

Q. Didn't you say, Mr. Bennett, that you were not certain whether Hudson was there in your direct examination? *A.* I ain't certain positively as to the man; I would not like to swear positively as to the man; the other three I am pretty certain of.

Q. Which three are you certain of? *A.* I believe it is James Barber, Duke, and Betz.

Q. You said you would not be certain positively as to Hudson, because he was masked; how can you be certain as to the other three, as they were masked? *A.* I seen them standing up, he was in a stooping position and his coat was hanging over his face, and I could not see him so well; I saw only one side of his head as he passed by the door.

Q. Who was stooping? *A.* Hudson.

Q. Where was he stooping? *A.* In the edge of the door, rather on the side of the door.

Q. Do you mean the door where the shooting was? *A.* Yes, sir.

Q. How did you know the other three who were masked as well as the other persons? *A.* By their personal appearance, and the light shone better on them.

Q. What do you mean by the personal appearance? *A.* The shape; I mean their bodily appearance; I could know I was well acquainted with his back to me, or if they were at a distance, I could recognize them by their personal appearance.

Q. Is that the only ground on which you made the statement that you knew these three persons? *A.* I can't explain why I know a man when I see him; I can't describe the optical between two men.

Q. You judge then just from the size and conformation of the body? *A.* And their walk and movement.

Q. You were very much excited, were you? *A.* Yes, sir; I was considerably excited.

A. You have already stated on oath that at the coroner's inquest, you stated that you knew none of these parties? *A.* I did not say that I knew anybody.

Q. Were you asked if you knew any of those persons that came into the house? *A.* I think I was, but I ain't certain; I disrecollect what was said.

Q. If you were, what did you say? *A.* I disrecollect; I evaded the question as far as I could.

Q. Have you not stated on your direct examination here to-day, that you did swear that you did not know them on that occasion? *A.* I think I stated that.

Q. You do now swear, that you did then swear at the coroner's inquest that you did not know them? *A.* I think I stated to them that I did not know any person.

Q. Didn't you state on the direct examination, that at the coroner's inquest you testified that you didn't know the parties? *A.* I did testify that way, I think.

Q. You assigned as a reason why you testified that way, personal fear or apprehension? *A.* Yes, sir.

Q. Was not a military garrison in Columbus at the time? *A.* Yes, sir.

Q. Who was in command there? *A.* Captain Mills.

Q. What number of troops were garrisoned there? *A.* I don't know the number.

Q. Were there quite enough to protect every person who would appeal to the commanding officer for protection? *A.* If I went to the barracks and staid there; I believe there was.

Q. When was it you stated you were imprisoned in Columbus? *A.* I believe it was the second Monday in May; I don't know precisely.

Q. How did Mr. Chipley and Dr. Kirksey happen to visit you at the jail? *A.* I don't know, sir.

Q. Were you sick? *A.* No, sir.

Q. Didn't Dr. Kirksey attend you there as a physician? *A.* He did not attend me; he was the county physician.

Q. Is Dr. Kirksey the county physician? *A.* He was the county physician.

Q. Did he visit the sick in jail, those that were confined by the orders of the county court? *A.* I do not know.

Q. What were you in jail for? *A.* I

believe it was a whisky bill, obtained partly by the Union League and partly by myself.
Q. Was it for debt? A. It was for a fine of fifty dollars that they put me in.
Q. What was the fine imposed upon you for? Q. I do not know what it was imposed upon me for, more than that was the main cause of it.
Q. Was it not for getting whisky under false pretenses? A. I do not know; that was said to be the cause, but I do not know that you can drink by the glass and get it on false pretenses, going backwards and forward.
Q. Was not the charge on which you were convicted for getting whisky under false pretenses? A. I do not know what the charge was; I never read it.
Q. Was not the charge brought by a member of the Loyal League? A. I believe it was.
Q. Who was it that prosecuted you? A. I believed it was an old Jew called Coleman.
Q. Did you then appeal to members of the Democratic party for assistance? A. No, sir; I had no means of communicating with them unless they came to the jail to me.
Q. Didn't you send word through George Horton, the Sheriff, to the leading members of the Democratic party? A. I did not; if he sent any word, it was on his own responsibility, not mine.
Q. Did you not send word to them by John Cleghorn, the Jailer? A. I do not know if I knew any of them or had spoken to them.
Q. Have you not sworn that you knew Mr. Barber at night and under a mask? A. I did.
Q. Was he not one of the leading members of the Democratic party? A. I do not know.
Q. Didn't you know that he was a candidate for the clerkship of the county? A. Yes, sir, I knew that he was a candidate, but knew nothing about the Democratic party.
Q. You knew he was running on the party opposed to the one to which you belong? A. I knew he was running on the party opposed to the one to which I belong.
Q. To which party do you belong. A. Republican.
Q. What name does the party opposed to the Republican party in Columbus take? A. Democracy.
Q. Well, then, you now swear that you did know that Mr. Barber was the candidate of the Democratic party for Clerk of the Court? A. I did; he was that.
Q. Didn't you know that Mr. Chipley was Chairman of the Executive Committee of the Democratic party? A. I did not know; I paid no attention to the Democratic party whatever. I had no knowledge of it, no knowledge as to who was chairman, nothing of its organization; might have seen it stated, but didn't pay any attention to it.
Q. Did you not tell Mr. Cleghorn, the Jailer, that you would deliver to Mr. Chipley, Chairman of the Executive Committee of the Democratic Club, certain letters and other political papers if he, Chipley, would get you out of jail? A. I told Mr. Chipley that; he demanded that of me; he demanded no political papers of me for that; I was to send them to him by Cleghorn, as security, if I would work with their political party to a certain extent.
Q. Did you agree with Mr. Chipley to turn over the papers to him and work with the Democratic party if he would get you out of jail? A. No, sir; I did not agree to work with the Democratic party. I was to work with the Republican party, and was to tell him what white members belong to the Union League?
Q. You were to be in the League and communicate to Chipley what white members belong there? A. Yes, the white members belonging to the League.
Q. Was not that the consideration on which you were taken out of jail? A. That was part of it, I think.
Q. Was not the other part that you were to furnish them a list of the Loyal League and a letter from Foster Blodgett? A. I believe he asked something of that kind, that I had a letter of Foster Blodgett; I think that was his demand, but I do not think he ever got it.
Q. Was not that consideration the other part of it? Didn't you tell him you had such a letter from Foster Blodgett, and that you would furnish him that, besides giving him a list of the Loyal League, if he would get you out of jail? A. I think he made that demand, but I didn't comply with it.
Q. You speak of a demand; I speak of

the agreement between you. *A.* I do not think there was any agreement, but it was voluntary upon both parties; there was no specified agreement whatever.

Q. You were in jail under a fine of fifty dollars and the costs, and you proposed that if he would pay this fine and get you out of jail, you would give him a list of the Loyal League and furnish him the names of all the white men in the Loyal League, and also a letter from Foster Blodgett, you said you would do that, and he would do the other—voluntary on both sides? *A.* No, the proposition came from them, not from me—that was the proposition.

Q. Did you agree to that proposition? *A.* In part I did.

Q. In what part did you not agree? *A.* In furnishing the list of the Union League.

Q. You didn't furnish the list of the Union League? *A.* I did not.

Q. Was the other part of the proposition carried out? *A.* So far as the sending over of some four letters in my possession one year.

Q. Were you released from jail, and the fine paid, and you turned over some of the letters. *A.* I did. I gave an order to the jailor to go and find what letters were in the trunk. One of the letters there was Mr. Ashburn's, and one from Costino.

Q. Did you tell Mr. Chipley that the letter from Foster Blodgett was political, and would do the Democratic party good to have it. *A.* I did not. The idea was this, that I was to write to Foster Blodgett, and aid Foster Blodgett in getting a city election, instead of an appointment. That was the object of it.

Q. Didn't you deliver to Mr. Chipley a letter from Foster Blodgett? *A.* I do not know what was in the trunk. All the letters there, I think I gave him, one from Bryant, the foot of it little torn, the signature torn.

Q. Didn't you say that the Foster Blodgett letter was delivered by Mrs. McCarter to Mr. Chipley. *A.* I do not know such a person in Muscogee county.

Q. Who was it you gave the order to to deliver the letter? *A.* It was to one Mrs. McClary.

Q. Didn't Mrs. McClary deliver it? Don't you know that Mrs. McClary delivered it? *A.* I don't know, because I have not seen the woman since.

Q. Have you ever seen the letter since? *A.* No, sir.

Q. Was it in your trunk? *A.* I think so.

Q. Have you examined the trunk since? *A.* No, sir.

Q. Never examined it since? *A.* No, sir.

Q. You gave the order to Mrs. McClary to deliver it. *A.* I gave the order to deliver what letters she could find in the trunk, I think was the wording of it.

Q. Who is Mr. Costino that the other letter was from or to? *A.* Mr. Costino, I believe he is a colored man, a member of the present Legislature of Georgia, and the letter, I believe, I got from Mr. Ashburn the night he was killed.

Q. Mr. Costino, then, was a man of political influence with his party, or supposed to be so? *A.* In Talbotton, I suppose he was. He did not belong to Columbus or Muscogee County.

Q. Didn't you represent to Mr. Chipley that the possession of this and other letters would be valuable to him or the Democratic party, politically. *A.* I did not. He demanded this as security that I would aid him in obtaining a city election. The letter was given as security.

Q. Did you promise them to aid him in the city election? *A.* I believe I promised to aid in obtaining a city election, instead of an appointment. There was talk that there was to be a military appointment, and I was to use my influence in getting an election instead of an appointment.

Q. If that was the object, how did Mr. Chipley know that you had those letters in your possession?

A member of the Court here objected to further examination on this point, as being irrelevant.

The counsel for the defense rose to state the object, to show relevancy of the testimony.

The President of the Court asked that it be put in writing, which was done in the following words:

The object of the testimony is to show that the money that Chipley furnished witness in getting him discharged from jail was in no way connected with the Ashburn assassination, but was in consideration of certain services, that witness was to render the Democratic party. It is to fully and clearly account for this entire transaction, disconnecting it entirely from the object which the prosecution intended to establish by its introduction.

The Commission here retired, and after due deliberation returned; and, after the members were seated, the decision of the Commission was announced by the Judge Advocate, "That the Court sustains the objection in question."

The Court deems it proper to state, that the defendants C. and K. have a right to show, if they can, a different motive for their interference in behalf of the witness when in jail from the one attempted to be established by the prosecution, but in doing so they must confine themselves within proper limits. The Court is of opinion that the cross-examination of the witness on the stand has extended to irrelevant matter.

Q. What business were you engaged in at the time of the decease of Ashburn? *A.* I was keeping a bar-room.

Q. Whose bar-room? *A.* It was partly owned by myself, and partly by a fellow named Turner—a man named Turner.

Q. You said that man Turner, or that fellow Turner—who is Turner? *A.* Matthew Turner.

Q. How far was your place of business from the house where Ashburn was killed? *A.* It was about a mile, nearly.

Q. Did you not go to the house where Ashburn was killed on the night of the killing, in company with Mr. Woodfield, to see Ashburn, to get money that you claimed that Ashburn owed you? *A.* I went in company with Mr. Woodfield, early in the evening, about money that he owed Mr. Woodfield. I was to get mine the next day.

Q. Did Mr. Ashburn owe you, and how much? *A.* He owed me considerable. I could not tell exactly how much he owed me—a little over sixty-seven dollars at one time, and several other bills that I looked over.

Q. Did Mr. Ashburn settle with you that night? *A.* He did not; he was to settle with me the next day.

Q. Did you and he come to an agreement as to how much he owed you, that night? *A.* We did not come to any solution that night. Mr. Woodfield's was talked about, and only his, as he was going out to a meeting that night.

Q. Did you not say the next morning after the killing, on Broad street, in Columbus, to Mr. Horton, that you went down with Woodfield to get your money, and that Ashburn gave you an order on Dr. Tuggle for it? *A.* Who is Mr. Horton? I don't know the man. I don't think I ever spoke to him. I spoke to Mr. Wilkins the next morning. I don't know any man named Horton.

Q. Did you tell anybody in Columbus that if Ashburn had not settled with you that night you would kill him? *A.* I did not.

Q. Were your relations with Ashburn friendly or unfriendly? *A.* They were not unfriendly at that time—they were friendly. We had explained the matter. It was a difference on election matters.

Q. Do you know Mr. John Duncan, of Columbus? *A.* I know him by sight.

Q. Do you know his father? *A.* I had the same acquaintance that I did with John.

Q. Did you ever say anything to either of them, or both of them together, about the killing of Ashburn? *A.* I did.

Q. What did you say? *A.* Do you want me to state the whole conversation that occurred between us?

Q. Didn't you state to him, if that d—d old Ashburn had not been killed when he was, you would have killed him? *A.* No, sir.

Q. You say you did not state to either of them, or both of them, those words? *A.* No, sir.

Q. What time did you reach the house in which Mr. Ashburn lived, and in which he was killed? *A.* I think it was between seven and eight, or six and seven. I don't exactly know what time he came there. I had seen him in the afternoon, previously to that, me and Woodfield both, and then we were to meet him at night. I came there for that purpose.

Q. Was Mr. Ashburn there when you got there? *A.* Yes, sir.

Q. Did Mr. Ashburn remain there? *A.* No, sir; he went to the meeting at the Temperance Hall.

Q. Was that a political meeting? *A.* It was.

Q. What time did he come from that meeting? *A.* I don't know; I was at Mr. Woodfield's house when he came home; he was home before me.

Q. What time did you go back to Hannah Flourney's? *A.* I think it was 11 o'clock, or after 11; it was somewhere after 11.

Q. Did you usually sleep in that house? *A.* I had been in the habit of sleeping there since Mr. Ashburn came back from Atlanta; sometimes I would sleep at the shop, but very little.

Q. Had you slept there the night before? *A.* I disrecollect whether I had or not; rather think I did.

Q. You state that you usually slept there; that is your statement? *A.* Since Mr. Ashburn came back from Atlanta.

Q. Did Mr. Woodfield return to that house that night with you? *A.* He didn't return after he went to his house.

Q. Didn't you state to Mr. Horton next day after this occurred, that Mr. Woodfield returned with you to that house, and that the firing commenced, or the party came, within fifteen minutes after he left? *A.* I did not. I did not speak to Mr. Horton the next day. Mr. Horton was not in the habit of speaking to me under any circumstances.

Q. Did Ashburn fire his pistol that night in the room? *A.* I think not; I wouldn't be certain, but I think not.

Q. Didn't you tell Mr. Murphy and others that Ashburn fired one shot and you thought two; but was positive that he fired one shot that night? *A.* Mr. Murphy was looking at the pistol, and seeing it was not fired, seeing that there was not a chamber empty, there was no necessity for my saying that.

Q. You state that you did not make that statement to Mr. Murphy? *A.* I made no statement to Mr. Murphy at all; it was to Mr. Mayor that I made any statement that was made.

A. What time were you arrested? *A.* The first day of last month, June.

Q. Where were you taken? *A.* To Fort Pulaski.

Q. Where were you put there? *A.* In a cell.

Q. What was you arrested for? *A.* I don't know.

Q. Were you ever told what you were arrested for? *A.* No.

Q. How were you treated there? *A.* Received the same fare as soldiers generally received — soldiers' rations; only closely confined; that was the only trouble that was to it.

Q. Were you confined in a cell? *A.* I was.

Q. What was the size of the cell? *A.* I should suppose it was about seven or eight feet long by four or five feet wide.

Q. Who visited you there? *A.* An officer named Reid, I believe.

Q. Was he a Government detective? *A.* I think he was, but do not know.

Q. Did he ask you to make any disclosures about Ashburn's assassination? *A.* He asked me why I should have gone to this girl while I was full of whisky, and this affair about Mr. Woodfield is the only thing I am aware of.

Q. Had you ever before stated to anybody about your knowledge of these three persons accused? *A.* I had.

Q. Whom had you stated it to? *A.* To Captain Mills, and, I believe, to Major Smythe.

Q. Was that before you were arrested? *A.* I think that was one day after the occurrence that I told Capt. Mills; it was but a short time; it was three or four days after the occurrence that I told Major Smythe; I wouldn't be certain.

Q. Did Mr. Reid ask you about the same? *A.* No, sir; it was about the conversation at the jail, and about going to see Amanda Patterson.

Q. When did you first see Mr. Whitley? *A.* At Capt. Mills' office, the morning I was arrested.

Q. Did he go to Savannah with you? *A.* No, sir.

Q. Did you see him in Savannah while you were under arrest at Fort Pulaski? *A.* I did not see him while I remained a prisoner at Fort Pulaski, but after I came away.

Q. Where did you see him after you came away? *A.* At Atlanta.

Q. You did not see him from the time of your arrest till you came to Atlanta? *A.* I think not.

Q. Where were you put when you were brought here? *A.* I was put in a room where there was some other witnesses.

Q. Where were you placed after that? *A.* In a cell in the guard-house.

Q. Been kept in a cell ever since? *A.* No.

Q. How long were you kept in a cell? *A.* I disrecollect how long.

Q. Were there any statements made to you that by making disclosures you would be removed from the cell? *A.* No, sir; no offers of any kind were ever made to me.

Q. Can you account for your being arrested and put in a cell and kept in a cell for so long a time as you were? Any reason assigned you for it? *A.* I understand it was attempting to leave Columbus, or to go away with this girl; I do not know exactly.

Q. Had Mr. Whitley ever had any conversation with you about your testimony? *A.* I disrecollect; we have spoken many times on various subjects; I do not think there was any specified conversation on that subject.

Q. Were you confined with any of the other prisoners, or were you together at any time? *A.* George Betz was the only one and Marshall and a boy named Stephens.

Q. Were you confined for a part of the time in close confinement with Betz alone? *A.* I was.

Q. What did Mr. Whitley tell you, the third day of your close confinement with Betz, would be the result if you did not disclose? *A.* I believe he said that I should stay there till I rotted, or something to that effect; I believe that was the amount of it.

Q. Did you see the affidavit that Mr. Whitley got Betz to make there? *A.* It was not made in the cell I was in; I merely got a sight of it—did not read it at all.

Q. You do not know the substance of it? *A.* I do not; I know a few of the names; I know nothing of the substance.

Q. Was Betz with you last night? *A.* Yes, sir; he was in the room all night.

Q. Sent to your room? *A.* I think so.

Re-direct Examination by Prosecution.

Q. Do you know why you were confined in the cell with Betz alone? *A.* I do not exactly know why; I have an idea, but do not exactly know the real cause of it; I believe Mr. Whitley asked me if I would go in the cell and I said I would; when I was taken there I believed strongly that he was one of the parties that did the shooting of Ashburn.

Q. Did you go in at the suggestion of Mr. Whitley or by his direction? *A.* I volunteered to go.

Q. For what purpose did you volunteer? *A.* I believe it was to see if I could induce him to go over to the State's evidence.

Questions by the Court.

Q. What did you state to the Duncans? *A.* Well, sir, Mr. John Duncan, some time previous—I think it was three days previous—strongly induced me to turn a Democrat, saying that something was going to happen; he strongly advised me to quit Ashburn and stop with him altogether; I said I'd see about it; at that particular time, and the morning after Mr. Ashburn's death, I went there; thinking he was one of the party, I said, after taking a drink or two, "I wonder why I escaped that night?" and he said "because you had turned a Democrat;" he then said nobody would be hurt for killing old Ashburn in a whorehouse anywhere else except in the United States; I don't recollect what I said in answer to various inquiries made.

Q. What kind of arms were used by the accused ṛamed? *A.* Revolvers.

Q. Were you released from jail and your fine paid in consideration that you would not say what you know about the death of Ashburn? *A.* No, sir, there was no such thing as that.

The Court then adjourned till 10 o'clock to-morrow morning.

McPHERSON BARRACKS, ATLANTA, GA., } July 3, 1868. }

The Commission met pursuant to adjournment.

Present—The same members as yesterday, the Judge Advocate, the prisoners on trial and their counsel.

The record of yesterday's proceedings was read and approved.

Henry L. Benning, Esq., of counsel for accused, appeared and took his seat.

The counsel for accused requested that the court instruct Capt. Mills, who had in charge the testimony taken at the coroner's inquest, to forward the same, for the purpose of being used upon the trial now proceeding.

The Judge Advocate stated that he would have Captain Mills subpœnaed, with instructions to bring with him the document referred to, if in his possession.

Questions by the Judge Advocate.

AMANDA PATTERSON, a witness on behalf of the prosecution was then introduced, and having been duly sworn, testified as follows:

Q. What is your name? *A.* Patterson.

Q. Your full name? *A.* Amanda Patterson.

Q. Your age? *A.* Going on eighteen.

Q. Where do you reside? *A.* Columbus.

Q. What State? *A.* Georgia.

Q. How long have you resided there? *A.* About six years.

Q. Were you acquainted with George W. Ashburn, in his lifetime? *A.* About two weeks was as long as I was acquainted with him.
Q. Were you living in the same house with him at the time of his death? *A.* Yes, sir.
Q. Had you known him previous to going to that house to live? *A.* Yes, sir.
Q. How many rooms are there in that house? *A.* Five, sir.
Q. Did you occupy either of these rooms? *A.* Occupied one of them.
Q. Will you state which one of them; that is, whether first, second, third or fourth from the front? *A.* Second from the front.
Q. Which room did Mr. Ashburn occupy? *A.* Third room.
Q. Were you in your room the night that Ashburn was killed? *A.* Yes, sir.
Q. Now, state to the court, in your own way, what happened that night in relation to his death? *A.* There came a crowd of men to the door, knocked and asked for the door to be opened; Hannah says, I shan't open the door this time o' night for nobody; she asked them who was there; they said "Mary Tillinghurst;" Hannah asked 'em who they wanted to see; they said they wanted to see "Mandy;" she told them they couldn't see "Mandy;" then they asked for her; she wanted to know what they wanted with her; they said for her to come to the door a minute; she told them she shouldn't do it: they told her if she would not open the door they would burst it open; she told them they might burst it if they wanted to; so they burst it open and come in.
Q. Well, what did they do when they came in? *A.* When they asked Hannah who was in there, she said nobody but me and her; then they went to Mr. Ashburn's door and told him to open it; he asked what was wanting, and they told him to open the door; then he opened the door and they commenced firing.
Q. Was there any light in the front room when these persons broke in? *A.* No, sir; there wasn't no light in either one of the rooms.
Q. Was there a light in that room—the front room—at all, that night after they broke in? *A.* No; no light at all, only what they brought in; they lighted a light in the room after they came in.
Q. Did you see the persons who fired on Ashburn? *A.* No, sir; I didn't see them; I went into the front room.
Q. Did you see Bennett there that night? *A.* Yes, sir, I saw Mr. Bennett.
Q. Were any females there that night? If so, state who they were. *A.* None but me and Hannah Flourney.
Q. How many persons seemed to come into the house at that time? *A.* Well, I could not tell how many there was in the front room; there was a good many; there was not so many come into the middle room, though; I don't know exactly how many did come into the middle room.
Q. Which room were you in when these parties broke into the front room? *A.* In the second room.
Q. Was there any person in there with you at the time? *A.* No, sir; no one but Hannah Flourney.
Q. Did you see any persons that night in your room besides the usual occupants of the house? *A.* Yes, sir, I did.
Q. State who you saw. *A.* I saw Chipley, Dr. Kirksey, and Bob Hudson, Columbus Bedell, Jim Barber, and George Betz, and Bill Duke.
Q. Do you see any of the parties you have named now in this room? If so, point them out. *A.* Yes, I do. [Witness here pointed out the three mentioned among the accused.]
Q. Were these parties disguised in any way? *A.* Yes, sir; they had on masked faces.
Q. Did you see any one or more of them that night without masks? *A.* I didn't see but one.
Q. Who was that? *A.* I don't know, sir; a stranger to me.
Q. Did any of these that were masked lose their masks that night? *A.* Yes, sir; Columbus Bedell lost his.
Q. Where did he lose his mask? *A.* It dropped off his face when he went out the front door.
Q. Did any conversation take place between you and him at that time? If so, state what it was. *A.* None at all, only as he went out the door, he told me if I told on him he would kill me.
Q. Did this take place in the daytime or at night? *A.* Night.
Q. Do you know what day of the month or week? *A.* I don't know, sir; it was Monday night.
Q. What time in the night? *A.* It was between twelve and one o'clock.

Q. Had you had any conversation with any of these parties previously in regard to the killing of Ashburn? *A.* I had a conversation with Chipley, Dr. Kirksey, and Jim Barber.

Q. Where did that conversation take place? *A.* Up over Spears'.

Q. State how you came to be there. *A.* I went to see the Doctor.

Q. What Doctor? *A.* Moses.

Q. Were they in the Doctor's office? *A.* No, sir, they wasn't.

Q. Where were they? *A.* They were in another room.

Q. State the conversation you had with them. *A.* Well, I went up there; they were in a room, and when I come out Barber says "Mandy;" and I says, "What do you want?" and he says, "Come here." I just walked to the door—never went inside—and him and Chipley says, "We are going to kill old Ashburn the night of the day he speaks." I told them not to do it while I lived there.

Q. When did this conversation take place? how long before Ashburn's death? *A.* On the Tuesday evening before the Monday night they killed him.

Q. Was that all the conversation that took place between you and them at that time? *A.* No, sir; I told them not to come while I lived there, and I told them that they did not know how to get in; they said they knew as well how the house was fixed as I did; and they said if I told what they said they would kill me.

Q. Did you hear either of these parties, at any other time before Ashburn's death, say anything about killing him. *A.* I heard Columbus Bedell and Jim Barber.

Q. When and where was that? *A.* It was on the street, on the Wednesday, I believe, before the killing, Monday.

Q. On what street was it? *A.* Broad street.

Q. In what place? *A.* Down close to the new bank, Columbus.

Q. What did you hear said by either of these parties at the time? *A.* As I was passing by I heard Jim Barber say to Columbus Bedell, says he, "We're going to kill Ashburn."

Q. Had you any personal acquaintance with Columbus Bedell at that time? *A.* No, sir; I had talked to him some few times; not often.

Q. Have you seen him to talk to him since the killing of Ashburn? *A.* Yes, sir.

Q. When and where? *A.* He came up to my house about a week before I came from home.

Q. What did he say to you then and there? *A.* He said not much of anything, only he said he wanted me to come to his room with him.

Q. Did he ever visit you before? *A.* No, sir; never was in my house before in his life.

Q. How long did he stay that time? *A.* He didn't stay more than half an hour.

Q. Any person present when he was there? *A.* Yes, sir.

Q. Who were they? *A.* Agnes Kyles, Georgie Allston, and Almeda Ridley.

Q. Did you go with him as requested? *A.* No, sir; I did not.

Q. Did he give any reason why he wished you to go with him? *A.* No, sir.

Q. Did you make him any promise? *A.* No, sir, I didn't make him no promise.

Q. Did he tell you where his room was? *A.* Yes, sir; he told me where it was.

Q. Did he tell you to come some other time if you could not go then, or anything of that kind? *A.* Yes, sir; I was sick at that time and he asked me when I got well if I would come.

Q. Have you had any conversation with any person, since the death of Ashburn, about leaving Columbus? *A.* No; none except with Mr. Bennett; Mr. Bennett came to my house and wanted me to go away.

Q. Well, what did he say to you about going away? *A.* He asked me if I didn't want to go away; I told him no; I asked him why he wanted me to go away; he said the Ku-kluxes would kill us; he said if the Yankees carried us off and put us in prison we would die; he said he didn't want to swear anything against the men; I told him I would not go at all; he said Mr. Bowers and Columbus Bedell was to furnish the money to go away if we would go and not swear anything against them.

Q. Why did you not go with Bedell, as he requested? *A.* Because I didn't want to go; I was afraid he wanted to get me down there and kill me.

Q. What would he want to kill you for? *A.* Afraid I would tell anything on him.

Cross-examined by Defense.

Q. Were you examined at the Coroner's inquest? *A.* Yes, sir.

Q. In that examination did you not

testify that you did not know any of these parties? *A.* Yes, sir, I did; I would not tell 'em I knowed 'em.

Q. Do you know Mr. McCanlis, that lives near your house? *A.* Yes, sir, I know him.

Q. Did you see him that night after the death of Ashburn? *A.* Yes, sir, I tced him.

Q. Did he come into your house? *A.* No; I saw him standing out by his gate.

Q. Any conversation between him and you as to the persons in the party immediately after the death of Mr. Ashburn? *A.* No, I had never no conversation with him; I never spoke to him.

Q. Did not you speak to Mr. McCanlis that night after Mr. Ashburn's death? *A.* No, sir; I never spoke to the man.

Q. Did not he ask you if you knew any of them? *A.* No; I never spoke to him.

Q. Didn't you tell him that you did not know any of them? *A.* No; never spoke to him at all that night.

Q. Did you see the son of Mr. Ashburn there that night after his father was killed? *A.* Yes, sir.

Q. Did he ask you if you knew any of the parties that killed him? *A.* No; his son never asked me if I knew any of them at all.

Q. Were you in the room with his son where the body was lying? *A.* Yes, sir; I was in there.

Q. Didn't he ask you if you knew any of them there in the room? *A.* He never asked me if I knowed 'em.

Q. Who were present at the time you say Dr. Kirksey, Chipley and Barber told you that they were going to kill Ashburn? *A.* I don't know; there was some more men in the room I didn't know; there was no one with me at all.

Q. What time was it that you had this conversation with Mr. Chipley and Barber and Kirksey? *A.* It was in the evening on Tuesday before they killed him, Monday night.

Q. Was that the time you say you went to Dr. Moses' office? *A.* Yes, sir.

Q. Was it at Dr. Moses' office? *A.* No, sir; it was not.

Q. Where was it then? *A.* It was in another room, in the same building.

Q. Where was that building? *A.* Where was the building? Up over Spears'.

Q. Do you mean Spears' jewelers' store? *A.* Yes; I mean Spears' jewelers' store.

Q. When were you first arrested? *A.* I don't know what day it was, now.

Q. As much as three weeks ago? *A.* Three weeks? It will be six weeks or seven weeks to-morrow since I left home.

Q. Who arrested you? *A.* Captain Mills sent up and had me arrested; I never asked him anything about it, or who had it done.

Q. Where were you first taken to? *A.* Me? I was taken down to Fort Pulaski.

Q. How were you treated there? *A.* Oh, I was treated mighty well.

Q. Where were you put? *A.* I was put in a room.

Q. By yourself? *A.* Yes; by myself.

Q. What was the size of the room? *A.* A tolerable large room.

Q. Any person visit you there? *A.* Yes, Captain Cook visited me there.

Q. Did he converse with you about this affair of Ashburn's assassination? *A.* No, I never said anything to him about it.

Q. Who first mentioned the subject to you, of the assassination of Ashburn, after your arrest? *A.* Mr. Whitley.

Q. Did he tell you that that was what you were arrested for; to give evidence on that subject? *A.* Yes, sir.

Q. What did he state to you about your evidence? *A.* He asked me what I knew about it.

Q. Did he tell you that you would be confined until you made a disclosure? *A.* No.

Q. Did he tell you that you would be confined—not released—until you made a disclosure? *A.* Yes, he told me I would be imprisoned until I told about it.

Q. Did he tell you what could be proven by other parties? *A.* No.

Q. Did he tell you that he knew that Kirksey and Bedell and Chipley and Duke were there? *A.* No, he never said anything about it; he never told me that he knew they were there.

Q. Did he ever mention the names of those gentlemen to you? *A.* He never mentioned their names until I told him they were there.

Q. How long was it before you told him they were there? how long after your arrest? *A.* Not long.

Q. Did you ever see Mr. Whitley until you came to Atlanta? *A.* Yes, sir.

Q. Where did you first see him? *A.* I saw him down at Fort Pulaski.

Q. How long have you been in Atlanta—how long since you came up? *A.* Been here four weeks.

Q. How much a day did he tell you he would give you? *A.* Never told me he would give me anything.

Q. Did you not tell the guard that Mr. Whitley told you he would give you a certain amount of money, and if so what amount? *A.* No, I did not.

Q. What time of day was it when you heard Bedell and Barber speak of killing Ashburn? *A.* In the evening, between two and three o'clock.

Q. Who were present when Bedell and Barber spoke to you on the street. *A.* There wasn't no one at all. They didn't speak to me; I just heard them speaking, when I was passing by.

Q. Were any persons present with them? *A.* No, they were by themselves.

Q. What part of the street was it, and what street was it? *A.* Broad Street.

Q. What part? *A.* Not very far from the new bank.

Q. Where is the new bank? *A.* On Broad Street.

Q. What part of the city is it in? *A.* About middle-way in the city.

Q. How far from the Perry House is it? *A.* It is nowhere's near the Perry House.

Q. How far from the Post-office is it? *A.* Post-office! It is nowhere's near it.

Q. How far from the City Hall is it? *A.* I don't know where the City Hall is.

Q. How far from Spears' jewelers' store? *A.* A good piece below.

Q. Which side of the street was it on? *A.* On the left-hand side as you go down.

Re-examined— Questions by Judge Advocate.

Q. In your cross-examination, you stated that you would not tell the Coroner's Jury what you knew about the persons who killed Ashburn, or words to that effect; now tell me why you would not tell before the Coroner's Jury all that you know about that matter? *A.* Because I was afraid of my life. That's the reason I didn't tell it.

Q. Why were you afraid of your life? *A.* Because I was. I was afraid they would kill me.

Q. Why were you afraid they would kill you? *A.* Because I knew they would have killed me if I had told anything on them.

Q. State whether or not you had been warned by any one not to tell? *A.* I was warned by Chipley and Barber before it occurred, that if I told anything on them they would kill me.

Q. But I mean by any officer? *A.* No, by no officer.

Q. Did anybody else warn you, before the Coroner's inquest met, not to tell what you knew about it? *A.* Yes, Mr. Bennett told me not to tell anything there about it.

Q. What did Mr. Bennett say to you? *A.* He told me not to tell anything there that I knew about it. He said he was not going to tell anything he knew, and if we did tell, they would kill us all.

Q. Did the conversation you had with Chipley, and Barber, and Kirksey, over Spears' store, take place in the room, or in the hall, or where? *A.* They were in the room.

Q. Where were you? *A.* Standing in the hall, right by the side of the door.

Q. Whereabouts were they standing? *A.* In the door.

Q. Were the other persons whom you there saw in the room, near to those with whom you were conversing, or not? *A.* No, they were standing about middle-ways in the room.

Q. Did they speak in a loud voice? *A.* Not very loud.

Q. Did they speak to you loud enough to be heard by the other persons in the room? *A.* Yes, sir, they did.

Re-cross-examined— Questions by Defense.

Q. Had you left Dr. Moses' office before this thing took place? *A.* Yes, sir, he was not there.

Q. How far was his office door from the door where these gentlemen were? *A.* not far.

Q. On the same floor? *A.* Yes, sir.

Q. How far from the door—six feet, or ten, or what? *A.* The Doctor's office was on one side of the hall, and they were on the other.

Q. Is his office door right opposite? *A.* No, not opposite.

Q. What distance do you think it is from one door to the other? *A.* I don't know; I never took no notice.

Q. Is it eight or ten feet? *A.* I don't know how far it was.

Q. Which is nearest to the entrance of the hall—the door of Dr. Moses' office or the one these gentlemen were standing in? *A.* The door these here men was in.

Q. Was Dr. Moses' office door open? *A.* No, sir.

Q. Any other office door open? *A.* No; no doors were open at all, only the door them men were in.

The Court then took a recess of ten minutes at the request of one of the accused, after which the Commission was again called to order by the President.

Questions by Judge Advocate.

WADE H. STEPHENS, a witness on behalf of the prosecution, was then called, and having been duly sworn, testified as follows:

Q. State your name, age, and occupation. *A.* Wade H. Stephens; 21 years of age; occupation, harness-maker.

Q. Where do you reside? *A.* Columbus, sir.

Q. There are about forty Columbuses in the United States; in which do you reside? *A.* Columbus, Georgia, sir; Muscogee county.

Q. How long have you resided there? *A.* About eight years.

Q. Are you acquainted with Dr. Kirksey? *A.* Yes, sir.

Q. How long have you known him? *A.* Seven or eight months; probably more.

Q. Is he here? *A.* Yes, sir.

Q. Which is he? *A.* There he is over there, sir; next to Mr. Roper (pointing to one of the accused).

Q. State whether you had any conversation with him in regard to the killing of George W. Ashburn. *A.* I had a conversation with him before the killing of Mr. Ashburn; about three weeks.

Q. State that conversation, if it related to the killing of Ashburn. *A.* I met him on the street, sir, a few blocks below the court-house; he stopped me and called me to his buggy; he was in his buggy at the time; he asked could I keep a secret; I told him of course I could; he told me there was a party got up in that place to go to a certain place at a certain time and there put an end to old Ashburn, and if I would join the party he would give me fifty dollars; I refused his money and went away; he called me back to him and said if I would not go with the party not to expose what he said to me; nothing further occurred at that time; I spoke a few words afterward to him when we were prisoners in the court-house.

Q. What was your conversation in the court-house, if it related to the killing of Ashburn? *A.* Well, sir, the party refused to give bond for me; Capt. Mills, I believe, told me he was required to take bond from each one of them to the amount of twenty-five hundred dollars, and they refused to give bond for me; I think Mr. Moses was the man who refused; he said the reason was he didn't know me; I made myself known to him, and he knew me very well after I told who I was; I stepped to the window and told a negro boy to go to my mother and aunt and to bring them and the titles of the property; shortly after they came up; I gave them seats and walked up to my mother and looked at some papers, and handed them back to her, and stepped off some three or four paces; Kirksey walked up to me and said, "That's all right now; we didn't know you; we didn't know but what you was guilty, and if you was you would have got money to go away upon."

Q. Didn't he know you at that time? *A.* He did very well, sir; he was the first man that spoke to me when I got into the court-house; I was arrested, I believe, on Tuesday, though all the rest were arrested on Monday; no one was arrested that day but myself; when I stepped into the court room he called me by name; I supposed he knew me by his calling me; he was the first man that spoke to me; I knew him; he spoke to me a great many times before that.

Q. Do you remember the month and the day of the month that you went to prison? *A.* Not exactly.

Q. About what time was it? *A.* I do not remember, sir, what time it was, because I knew I was innocent and didn't care about it; I was not dreaming of being arrested and brought to this place or any other on the Ashburn affair.

Q. Do you remember how long it was after Ashburn was killed, before you were arrested and taken to the court-house? *A.* I can not say the length of time, but it was a few weeks before the election; that's all I could say about that, sir.

Cross-Examined—Questions by Defense.

Q. When were you first arrested? *A.* When? It must have been a good while ago, sir; I don't remember what time it was. As I said before, I didn't pay any attention to anything concerning the arrest during the time I was confined in the court-house; what I heard there I of course, knew very well; recollected it, and do until to-day, but the day of my arrest I could not remember, sir; I remember when I was arrested and carried to Fort Pulaski.

Q. Were you discharged on your arrest? *A.* On my bond, sir, I was released.

Q. Did you state that that was shortly previous to the election? *A.* Some time before the election, sir, and after the death of Mr. Ashburn, that I was in the court-house.

Q. How long before the election? *A.* I don't remember, sir; as I have explained before, I do not remember the time; I think it was a few weeks, probably more; I don't remember the date or anything about it.

Q. When were you arrested a second time? *A.* The 14th of May, sir, I believe, when I was carried to Fort Pulaski.

Q. Who were arrested with you at that time? *A.* Mr. Barber, sir; I found him in the court-house when I went there, or rather he was in a room off separate from the cells; I do not know whether it was in the guard-room or not; was called about twelve o'clock to go to the depot and get on the train; he came out also, and two negroes.

Q. What were the names of the colored people? *A.* John Wells and John Stapler, sir; they pass by these names; I could not swear to their names.

Q. Where were you put in Fort Pulaski? *A.* In a cell, sir.

Q. What was the size of the cell? *A.* About four by six and about fifteen feet deep.

Q. In close confinement? *A.* Yes, sir.

Q. Who visited you there? *A.* Captain Reid, Major Whitley, and Captain Cook, sir.

Q. When were you informed of what you were arrested for? *A.* I was not told, sir; I was asked if I knew anything about the Ashburn affair.

Q. When were you asked that? *A.* Shortly after I got to Fort Pulaski.

Q. What did you say in reply to that question? *A.* Told 'em I knowed nothing, sir.

Q. Did anybody adopt any course of punishment to compel you to answer? *A.* No, sir.

Q. What did they do? What treatment did they subject you to? *A.* I was confined in a cell, received Government rations, and found as well as a prisoner could fare; as well as they generally do fare.

Q. Were you told that you would be kept in close confinement until you did? *A.* No, sir.

Q. How long did you remain there before making any disclosure? *A.* Never made any at all, sir, there.

Q. Where did you make a disclosure? *A.* At McPherson Barracks, sir.

Q. You made no disclosures at Fort Pulaski, of what you have here to-day? *A.* No, sir, none at all; I may have spoken some few words to some of them about it; I won't be certain that I never mentioned anything at all about it while there; but I made no confession there.

Q. Were you removed from the first cell you were put in? *A.* Yes, sir.

Q. Where were you put then? *A.* Into another cell opposite; it was the left cell I was in—on the opposite side—the side facing the side I was first in.

Q. What was the object? *A.* I don't know, sir.

Q. Was there any change in your personal condition? *A.* No, sir.

Q. Cell of same character and size? *A.* Yes, sir; I think the reason I was changed was they wanted to put one of those freedmen in the cell that I was in; but I won't be positive.

Q. Were you put at any time in a close box? *A.* No, sir.

Q. No restraint at all put over your person—your limbs? *A.* No, sir.

Q. Did you receive any letter from any person? *A.* Yes, sir; I received two; my mother's name was signed to them; I don't know whether she sent them or not.

Q. Who delivered them to you? *A.* I won't be positive, sir; it was either Major Whitley or Captain Reid.

Q. Did you get a letter from any one telling you that Kirksey, Bedell, and the others had confessed? *A.* No, sir.

Q. Or that they intended to convict you? *A.* No, sir.

Q. Did you not get a letter from anybody telling you that their money would save them and you had better save yourself? *A.* No, sir; I have received no letters from any one except my mother since I left Columbus, with the exception that the officers were taking my letters and brought them to me; of course, I could not get out to get them myself; they had to handle them.

Q. Did you make any affidavit before any person in Savannah—Fort Pulaski? *A.* No, sir.

Q. Make any here? *A.* Yes, sir.

Q. Before whom did you make it? *A.* Major Whitley; I made it before him and another gentleman; I forgot his name; it was here in the barracks.

Q. What was the substance of that affidavit, as far as you know or recollect? *A.* What I spoke here concerning Dr. Kirksey.

Q. Did you consider that affidavit binding or not? *A.* I did, sir.

Q. Did you ask anybody afterward if an affidavit made before a Quartermaster was binding? *A.* No, sir; I did not.

Q. And you did not reply that you were "all right," then? *A.* I spoke those words, sir, there in the cell, I believe, with Mr. Roper, and spoke to Mr. Barber after I had been speaking to Mr. Roper some time; I didn't speak to him except merely to pass away the time—lonesome hours; I says to Jim Barber, says I, "Do you know anything about law," and he said, "No;" I didn't tell him that I had made an affidavit before anybody; I merely asked him if a man was to make an affidavit without going before a court of justice, or something of that kind; I don't remember now the exact words; I asked him if it was binding; I believe "no" was his answer; I didn't have any more to say, and didn't pay any attention scarcely to to it, because what I say is not what I swear to.

Q. Did you not distinctly say to Mr. Barber, " Then I am all right"? *A.* No, sir; I told him no such words.

Q. Nor nothing to that effect? *A.* No, sir.

Q. Did anybody that you know of, or can name, ever see you in conversation to Dr. Kirksey, or hear you speak to him, or he to you, in your life, before your first arrest? *A.* No, sir; Dr. Kirksey is a rich man, sir, and I am a poor man; you don't suppose he will speak to such "small potatoes" unless he intends to get 'em into trouble, or something of that kind? that is about the amount of it.

Re-examined—Questions by Judge Advocate.

Q. When you were asked at Fort Pulaski to tell what you knew about this affair, why did you not tell what you have testified here in regard to Dr. Kirksey? *A.* The reason I didn't tell? I started to come out and tell what I knew, and some conversation raised Whitley, Captain Reid, and others, and they stopped me, and I then turned off and went back to my cell, and didn't finish the conversation; I started at it and they stopped me; after that I didn't care to make a statement while I was in such a place as that.

Q. When in Columbus, before your arrest, when you knew that efforts were being made to ferret out the murderers of Ashburn, why did you not tell what Dr. Kirksey had said to you? *A.* I thought in all probability, sir, I would be murdered in the same way that Ashburn was if I told anything.

Q. Did you hear any conversation yesterday, in the prison here, between any of these prisoners and Betz? *A.* No, sir, I didn't. Couldn't distinguish a word their voice is all I could hear.

Q. About the time of Ashburn's murder, was there much excitement about an organization commonly called the "Kuklux Klan," in and about Columbus? *A.* Well, sir, there was a good deal of marks on my fence, and—

Q. (Interrupting). I don't want particulars—I only want to know generally, whether there was much excitement and alarm about it? *A.* I suppose there was, sir.

Q. Did the fear of that organization, if any such existed, operate upon you at all? *A.* No, sir. I supposed those "K's" and "D's" they put on my fence, some one put there to plague me. But I heard some others speak, and it seems there was a good deal of excitement.

Q. Do you know whether there was alarm among those who were known not to be connected with the Democratic party, for fear of this organization? *A.* You mean the Radical party?

Q. Yes. *A.* Yes, sir.

Q. Do you know whether about that time there were apprehensions of assassination among men of the Radical party? *A.* I didn't hear any such thing as that, sir.

Re-cross-Examined—Questions by Defense.

Q. You say "K. K." was marked on your fence? What do you mean by that? Have you got a fence? *A.* I have, sir; I have a piece of ground, with a plank nailed on it, and a shanty or two.

Q. Do you live on that? *A.* I live in the house, sir, on that piece of ground.

The lot my mother bought from Major Moses, I believe, in 1859.

Q. Does your mother live there? *A.* Yes, sir; did when I left.

Q. Is it your lot or your mother's? *A.* I should consider it mine, sir—or part of it—some of the improvements are mine. It is hers though, as it stands, 'cause I don't want any of it.

Q. Does your mother's husband live there? *A.* No, sir, he's dead.

Q. Who keeps house with her? *A.* A colored girl, a cook, keeps the back room.

Q. Does John Wells, a colored man, live with your mother? *A.* No sir. He did, until I was ready to shoot his brains out, then he left. I don't think, sir, that any such conversation should be used here, and I ain't agoin' to answer any more questions like that.

Q. Was John Wells arrested with you? *A.* No, sir—he was put in the same room that I was. He was arrested first. He lives down two or three blocks from where I do. I don't know what time of the day he was arrested.

Q. Was he taken to Savannah with you? *A.* Yes, sir, in the same car.

Q. Was he not known to be a Democratic colored man? *A.* I heard him say he was a Democrat, and others called him a Democrat.

Q. Are you a Democrat, yourself? *A.* No, sir. I voted a Democratic ticket, but was a fool for it.

Q. Were you not known to be a Democrat at that time in Columbus? *A.* No, sir, I wasn't.

Questions by the Prosecution.

SALLY BEDELL, a witness for the prosecution, was next called, who, having been duly sworn, was interrogated as follows:

Q. What is your name? *A.* Sally.

Q. Sally what? *A.* Sally Bedell.

Q. Where do you live? *A.* In Columbus.

Q. In what State is Columbus? *A.* In Georgia.

Q. Where were you on the night of the 30th of March—the night that Mr. Ashburn was killed? *A.* At Norah Winters.

Q. Whom did you see there that night? *A.* I saw Mr. Wiggins and Mr. Wood.

Q. Is Mr. Wiggins, the gentleman whom you saw there that night, here present? *A.* Yes, sir.

Q. Point him out? *A.* There he sits over there (pointing to Mr. Wiggins, one of the accused, who, at the request of the Judge Advocate, rises to his feet).

Q. Is that the man? *A.* Yes, sir.

Q. Do you see Mr. Wood present? *A.* Yes, sir.

Q. Point him out? *A.* There he sits over there (witness points to Mr. Wood, one of the accused, who, at the request of the Judge Advocate, rises to his feet).

Q. Is that Mr. Wood? *A.* Yes, sir.

Q. What time of the night did you see them at Norah Winters'? *A.* The clock was not running when I saw them.

Q. Was it before or after supper? *A.* It was after supper.

Q. About how long do you think it was after supper? *A.* I don't know exactly how long it was; we didn't have any time in the house.

Q. Did anybody there have any masks, or masquerade suits that night? *A.* Mr. Wiggins had some masquerade suit.

Q. How many suits? *A.* There was only one suit.

Q. Where did he say he got it? *A.* The suit was got from Mollie Jones'.

Q. What did he say he was going to do with it? *A.* He didn't say what he was going to do with it; he brought them there.

Q. If he said anything about a party going out masked that night, state what he said? *A.* He said there was thirty of them going out disguised.

Q. Whom did he say it to? *A.* To Aunt Norah.

Q. Norah who? *A.* Aunt Norah Winters.

Q. How long did Mr. Wood and Mr. Wiggins stay there? *A.* There was no time-piece in the house.

Q. Where did they say they were going when they left? *A.* When they first left the house they were going down to Temperance Hall, where the speaking was, out there that night.

Q. Did they come back after they went to the speaking? *A.* Yes, sir.

Q. Both of them? *A.* Mr. Wiggins came back, Mr. Wood didn't.

Q. What did Mr. Wiggins do after he came back? *A.* Went to bed.

Q. About what time did he go to bed, do you think? *A.* It was after the speaking was out in the hall; I don't know what time it was.

Q. Where was the mask suit when he

went to bed? *A.* It was laying in the chest in the room.

Q. In what room? *A.* In Aunt Norah's room.

Q. In what room did he go to bed? *A.* Went to bed in Aunt Norah's room.

Q. Did you see him any more that night? *A.* After he went to bed?

Q. Yes. *A.* Yes; I saw him after he went to bed.

Q. About what time in the night? *A.* I don't know, sir, what time it was.

Q. Where was he, and what was he doing? *A.* He wasn't doing anything till he went to bed.

Q. Was he in the room or out doors when you saw him? *A.* He was in the room when I saw him.

Q. Was he in bed or out of it? *A.* In bed.

Q. Where did you next see him—outdoors or coming in from outdoors? *A.* I saw him coming in from outdoors.

Q. When was that? *A.* That was the night Mr. Ashburn was killed.

Q. What time in the night? *A.* I don't know, the clock wasn't running that night; I don't know what time it was.

Q. Was it after he had gone to bed? *A.* Yes, sir.

Q. Which way did he seem to be coming from? *A.* I could not tell which way he come; he had to come up stairs.

Q. Was Norah's room up stairs. *A.* Yes, sir.

Q. Was he below stairs or above stairs when you saw him come in? *A.* He was up stairs.

Q. How far was he from Norah's room? *A.* Just come right up the steps and walked across the passage into Aunt Norah's room.

Q. If you heard anything said by him to Norah about her swearing that he was there in bed that night after Ashburn was killed, state it. *A.* No, sir; Aunt Norah didn't say it to Mr. Wiggins; she said it to me and little Norah.

Q. What did she say? *A.* She said if they would take him up she would say that he was in the bed with her, and make me and little Norah say the same.

Q. You say that the masquerade suit lay on the chest in Norah's room when you went to bed; where was it the next morning when you got up? *A.* It was on the bed—the clothes was; the mask was lying on the floor.

Q. What was the condition of the mask when it lay on the floor? *A.* It was broke up.

Q. What sort of mask was it? *A.* The upper part was pasteboard and the rest was black silk.

Q. Anything like fringe about it? *A.* No, sir; it was plain black silk.

Q. You say it was broke up; what did you do with it? *A.* I threw it in the fire, sir.

Q. Where did you sleep that night? *A.* I slept in Aunt Norah's room, on the couch.

Q. Where were you when you saw Mr. Wiggins come in, after he had been out? I mean the time you saw him coming up the stairs. *A.* I was in the room, sitting down on the foot of the couch.

Q. What time of night was that? *A.* I don't know what time it was; it was after that meeting was out at the hall; we didn't have any time-piece.

Q. I refer to the time when he came back after he had gone to bed; what time was that? *A.* It was about day; I don't know exactly—about four o'clock when he came in.

Q. Do you know how long after he first went to bed before he got up and went out? *A.* No, sir; I don't know how long it was, but he didn't stay in bed very long.

Q. State whether he went to bed again after he came in at four o'clock. *A.* Yes, sir, he went to bed again.

Q. When Norah Winters said she would make you and little Norah swear that he was there that night in bed with her, what did you say? *A.* I told her I could swear that he was there for such a time, but no longer.

Q. When Norah spoke about having you to swear, did she say anything about his being killed, and what did she say? *A.* That was the time she said that before she would see him killed she would make me and little Norah swear that he was in bed with her.

Q. Whom do you mean by him when you say "him killed?" *A.* Mr. Wiggins she meant.

Q. What is your age? *A.* I don't know how old I am.

Q. You are a grown woman, are you? *A.* Yes, sir, I am.

Cross-examined by Defense.

Q. Were these questions ever put to you before? *A.* Not in Court they have not been.

Q. Have they ever been put to you out of Court? *A.* Yes, sir.
Q. How often? *A.* Four—five times.
Q. By whom? *A.* Mr. Bostock and that gentleman sitting over there.
Q. What is his name? *A.* I don't know what his name is. (Witness points to Major Whitley.)
Q. Do you mean the magistrate in Columbus, Mr. Bostock? *A.* Yes, sir.
Q. Did Norah Winters keep a boarding-house? *A.* Yes, sir.
Q. What sort of a masquerade suit do you speak of; can you describe it? *A.* They were calico pants and worsted coat.
Q. Were not several of them there? *A.* There were two or three suits in the house, but there was not but one of them taken out of the house that night after I went to bed.
Q. Do you know that there was any one of them taken out that night? *A.* There was one of them taken; it was taken out of the room; whether it was carried out of the house I don't know.
Q. You state that Mr. Wiggins brought one of these suits in? *A.* Yes, sir.
Q. That was before he went to bed? *A.* Yes, sir.
Q. What did he say when he threw it on the bed? *A.* He didn't say anything when he threw his suit on the bed.
Q. Did he then, or any time when you were there, tell Norah that there was the suit that Emma Hines sent back that she had borrowed? *A.* Yes, sir.
Q. Is that suit there yet? *A.* I don't know whether it is there or not.
Q. Was it there as long as your stay? *A.* Yes, sir.
Q. Was Mr. Wiggins a police officer? *A.* Yes, sir, he was a police officer.
Q. What time did you go to bed? *A.* I went to bed before the speaking was out at the hall, but did not go to sleep.
Q. How did Mr. Wood happen to go up into the room with Mr. Wiggins? *A.* Aunt Norah asked him up stairs to take a drink.
Q. That was about what time? *A.* That was before the speaking was out at the hall; it was the soon part of the night.
Q. Was there anybody else present? *A.* Caslin.
Q. Was not little Norah? *A.* Little Norah was down at the door too.

Questions by Court.
Q. Did Mr. Wiggins have a masquerade suit on when he went or returned? *A.* No, sir; he didn't have it on when he went out or returned.
Q. Did he take it with him? *A.* He took it out of the room with him; I don't know whether he carried it down stairs or not.

Questions by Prosecution.

ABRAHAM JOHNSON, a witness for the prosecution, was then called, and having been duly sworn, was interrogated as follows:
Q. What is your name? *A.* Abraham Johnson.
Q. Where do you live? *A.* In Columbus.
Q. State whether you were at Mr. Chafin's store, in Columbus, Ga., on the Thursday after Mr. Ashburn was killed. *A.* Yes, sir.
Q. Look at those gentlemen and state whether you saw any of them there, and if so, state whom. *A.* I saw one of them.
Q. Point him out and name him. *A.* (Witness pointing to Dr. Kirksey, one of the accused.) Dr. Kirksey. (Witness also pointing to Mr. Bedell, one of the accused.) Mr. Biddell.
Q. Bedell, as they usually call him? *A.* Yes, sir, Mr. Bedell.
Q. Look along the whole line and see if you see any other one there. *A.* I see Mr. Chipley.
Q. Any other? *A.* No, sir.
Q. If you heard them say anything about Mr. Bennett, state what they said. *A.* I was staying at the widow McClary's boarding-house, and I was going down the street and stopped at Mr. Chafin's store, and Mr. Hamp Stewart asked me in and I went in; and Mr. Hamp Stewart asked me where I staid, and I told him at Mrs. Clary's boarding-house, and Dr. Kirksey asked me was that where Mr. Bostock boards; I told him yes, sir, that was where Mr. Bostock boarded; and Mr. Bedell asked me if I heard Mr. Bostock say he was going to arrest anybody about Mr. Ashburn again ; I told him no, sir, I didn't know whether he was or no.
Q. Go on and state what else was said. *A.* Dr. Kirksey told me to find out whether he was going to arrest any one or no, and I told him yes, sir, I would; then he said

find out whether he was going to arrest any one or no and let him know, and I told him yes, sir, I would; and Dr. Kirksey asked me where was Mr. Bennett the night Mr. Ashburn was killed; I told him Mr. Bennett said he was behind the middle door, and he said if he had known that Mr. Bennett would have been behind the door, first he said the Ku-kluxes and then he said the Ku-kluxes would have fixed him like we fixed Mr. Ashburn.

Q. Did he say anything more? *A.* He told me to see if Gen. Meade was coming down in Mr. Ashburn's place or no, and said if he do to find out and let him know; first he said the Ku-kluxes, and then he said the Ku-kluxes would fix him like we fixed Mr. Ashburn.

Q. Did anybody try to stop him? *A.* Dr. Kirksey touched him and tried to stop him from talking, when he said that, and he said never mind Abram; he was in the war with me.

Q. Who was it touched Mr. Bedell and said that? *A.* Dr. Kirksey.

Q. Who was it replied, never mind Abram, he has been in the war with me? *A.* Hamp Stewart.

Q. Repeat Mr. Hamp Stewart's language as near as you can? *A.* Mr. Hamp Stewart didn't have anything to say, only asked me where I staid.

Q. That sentence about the war? *A.* He said, never mind Abram, he is a good boy, he was in the war with me; I took care of him.

Q. Who was it first made the remark about the Ku-kluxes? *A.* Dr. Kirksey.

Q. Who touched one of the crowd to stop him while they were talking? *A.* Dr. Kirksey.

Q. Whom did he touch? *A.* Mr. Bedell.

Q. When Dr. Kirksey touched Mr. Bedell what was Mr. Bedell saying? *A.* He was saying, find out whether Gen. Meade was going down or no, and let him know.

Q. Who has said anything to you about coming here to testify? *A.* Mrs. Williams.

Q. What did she say? *A.* Mr. Bostock called me to go down there one night to his office, and I went; I was staying at Mrs. Williams' then; I told her, Mr. Bostock wanted to find out whether I knew anything about the Ku-klux or no, and I told her I didn't know anything about them at all; and she said if you do, and find it out, these men will blow your head off and shoot you, just so.

Q. I didn't ask you that, I asked you if anybody had said anything to you about being a witness in this case? *A.* No, sir; nobody has said anything to me about it but Mr. Bostock.

Q. Has anybody threatened you if you swore in the case? *A.* Yes, sir.

Q. Who? *A.* Mr. Moses—young lawyer Moses.

Q. What did Mr. Moses say? *A.* Damn Bostock, if he wants you to go up yonder as witness, don't you witness to nothing; he said if you do, these men will shoot you when you come back, and if they don't do it I will do it myself.

Q. What Mr. Moses is that? *A.* Young lawyer Moses; I don't know what his name is.

Q. Do you know who his father is? *A.* Yes, sir, I know his father.

Q. State whether his father is a lawyer? *A.* Yes, sir, his father is a lawyer.

Q. Do you know whether he and his father are partners in the same law office? *A.* Yes, sir.

Q. Do you know what his father's given name is? *A.* No, sir.

Q. Are there any lawyers in Columbus named Moses, but these two that you know? *A.* None that I know of.

Cross-examined—Questions by Defense.

Q. Whose store do you say this conversation between Kirksey, Bedell, and Hamp Stewart was at? *A.* Mr. Chafin's.

Q. Whereabouts is that store? *A.* It is on Broad street.

Q. What time of the day did this conversation occur? *A.* It was an hour by sun, I think.

Q. What part of the street is that store on? *A.* It is on the right-hand side going down.

Q. Who stays in that store? *A.* Mr. Chafin and Mr. Redd.

Q. Does Mr. Taliaferr stay in that store? *A.* I do not know, sir, whether Mr. Taliaferr stays there.

Q. Mr. Redd stay in that store? *A.* I don't know, but I have seen him there; I don't know whether he clerks for Mr. Chafin or no.

Q. Who were present when this conversation took place? *A.* There were there but Dr. Kirksey, Mr. Chipley, Bedell, Chafin, and Mr. Hamp. Stewart; I don't know whether they heard me talking to him or no, but they were in the store.

Q. Was Mr. Redd there? *A.* Yes, sir; he was in the back part of the store writing.

Q. Have you ever been sworn in this case before? *A.* Yes, sir.

Q. Did you swear to this statement that Bostock said to you, that they would give you one hundred dollars if you would swear what Barber and George Betz said to Henry Kimbro? *A.* Yes, sir.

Q. Did you take the money? *A.* No, sir.

Q. What reply did you swear you made to Mr. Bostock when he made that offer to you? what did you tell Bostock? *A.* [Witness hesitates.]

Q. Did you tell him this: that George Ashburn, the young man, son of Ashburn, would give you one hundred and fifty dollars if you would swear to having heard what Barber and George Betz said to Henry Kimbro. *A.* No, sir.

Q. You didn't make that reply to Mr. Bostock, then? *A.* No, sir.

Q. What did you say to him? *A.* I disremember what I said to him then.

Q. Did he offer the one hundred and fifty dollars? *A.* No, sir; he told me he would give one hundred.

Q. Did you expect to get it? *A.* I told him I didn't care anything about any money; I just believed in the right thing; I told him that if he was a mind to give it to me he could do it.

Q. Rather expect he will give it to you, don't you? rather looking that way? *A.* No, sir.

Q. How long have you been here? *A.* Been up here since Tuesday evening.

Q. Who sent you here? *A.* Captain Mills.

Q. Who sent you to Captain Mills? *A.* As I was passing by he called me and told me not to get out of the way; he wanted me to go to Atlanta; that was Monday evening.

Q. Who was it told Captain Mills about your testimony? Mr. Bostock? *A.* Yes, sir.

Q. Was Mr. Bostock the Justice of the Peace, the magistrate that had these gentleman arrested first? *A.* Mr. Bostock first told Captain Mills, and had me to go down and repeat the same words to Capt. Mills and to Major Smythe.

Q. Was this Mr. Bostock the man that issued the warrant against these parties at the first arrest? *A.* Yes, sir; they say he was.

Q. Were these questions asked to-day ever read over to you before? *A.* Yes, sir; once.

Q. By whom? who read them to you? *A.* Mr. Bostock.

Q. Mr. Bostock read them to you? *A.* Yes, sir.

Q. Did young Mr. Ashburn offer you the one hundred and fifty dollars if you would swear against Barber and Betz? *A.* No, sir.

Q. Didn't you tell Mrs. Williams that young Mr. Ashburn had offered you one hundred and fifty dollars? *A.* No, sir.

Q. Didn't you tell Mrs. Williams that young Mr. Ashburn had offered you one hundred and fifty dollars if you would swear against Barber and Betz? *A.* No, sir.

Q. Or any of the others? *A.* No, sir; she didn't ask me if I would swear to it.

Q. I ask you if you didn't tell Mrs. Marie Anne Williams that young George Ashburn had offered you one hundred and fifty dollars if you would swear against any of these parties? *A.* He didn't offer it to me; he told me that I would get that much, and I told him I didn't care anything about the money; I believed in the right thing, and he said, That's all right.

Q. Did you tell Mrs. Williams that? *A.* I told her so, but I didn't swear it.

Q. Did young George Ashburn say that you would get one hundred and fifty dollars if you would swear against any of these parties? *A.* He didn't ask me if I would swear to it, but stated to me that I would get it.

Q. He told you that you would get one hundred and fifty dollars if you would swear that way? *A.* Yes, sir.

Re-direct Examination.

Q. Do you intend to say that the same questions I have asked you here to-day were asked you by Mr. Bostock in Columbus? *A.* Yes, sir; I can say they are.

Q. Have I not asked you some questions that he didn't ask you? *A.* No, sir.

Q. Have I not asked some questions here that Mr. Bostock didn't ask you. *A.* Yes, sir.

Q. Did Mr. Moses get you to swear anything before him? *A.* No, sir, he didn't get me to swear anything before him.

Q. Didn't he draw up a paper and get you to swear to it before him? *A.* No, sir, he just drawed up a paper of what I told you.

Q. Did he read it to you?   A. Yes, sir.

Q. Can you read?   A. No, sir.

Q. Do you know whether he read it right when he read it to you?   A. No, sir, I don't, whether he did or not.

Q. Did you understand that you was swearing to that paper before him?   A. No, sir.

Q. Did he offer you anything if you would make the statement before him?   A. Yes, sir.

Q. What did he offer you?   A. His father gave me two dollars, a two dollar bill.

Q. What did he give it to you for?   A. For telling him what he sat down on that paper; Mrs. Williams sent me to him.

Q. Did he tell you you was swearing to it at the time?   A. No, sir.

Questions by Prosecution.

BURRILL DAVIS, witness for the prosecution, was next called into court, and having taken the stand, was duly sworn, and interrogated as follows:

Q. What is your name?   A. Burrill Davis.

Q. Where do you live?   A. In Columbus, Ga.

Q. What is your age?   A. About 68 years, sir; not quite.

Q. How long have you resided in Columbus?   A. About twenty-four years.

Q. Where were you on the thirtieth of March last, on the day before Mr. Ashburn was killed?   A. In the city of Columbus, sir.

Q. Did you have any talk that day with Mr. James W. Barber?   A. No, sir.

Q. Did you see him that day?   A. Yes, sir.

Q. Did you drive anybody in a buggy that day?   A. In a express wagon, I did, sir.

Q. Whom?   A. Mr. James Barber.

Q. Anybody in with him?   A. No, sir.

Q. Did you hear him talk any.   A. Yes, sir.

Q. State what he said.   A. I was standing in the livery stable down on Broad street, with my wagon wheels just off the pavement; Mr. James Barber came up; had a new pair of shoes in his hand; threw them in, and jumps upon the wagon; about half drunk, I suppose; he said to me was I a Democrat; I said, yes, sir; he said you are posted on the dots; I said no, sir, and he asked me if I had been to the club; I said no, sir; he says why don't you go; because I don't feel like it, says I; why don't you to-night; I says I don't much care about it; says he, when you go up to town to Captain Ramsey, he will post you on the dots; I then put whip to my horse to get shed of him; got tired of the conversation; he said, just then, we Ku-kluxes, what they say they will do, in spite of men and hell; and then he said we hung seventy-five the other day in Tennessee; says I, is it possible; about this time we were near home, and says he, be certain to go up to Captain Ramsey; and I whips up the horse and lets him out; he says again, go up yonder; and I says, yes, sir. Well, that is all.

Q. If anything was said about what the Ku-kluxes were going up there for, state it.   A. Yes, that.I forgot; says he, Mr. Ashburn will be a dead man shorter than any of you have knowledge of; and I said is it possible; that was before some words I said.

Q. State all he said in connection with the Ku-kluxes and Mr. Ashburn.   A. Well, he said in the latter clause of his conversation, after he said they had hung seventy-five men in Tennessee, he said Ashburn will be dead shorter than any of you have any knowledge of; he talked about some trifling thing; being a drunken man, I did not pay any attention to it.

Q. What time of the day was this?   A. It was in the neighborhood of sunset.

Q. What day?   A. Monday.

Q. How long afterward before you heard Mr. Ashburn had been killed?   A. Next morning, between daybreak and sun-up.

Cross-examined.

Q. I understand you to say that you told Mr. Barber that you were a Democrat?   A. Yes, sir; I told him so.

Q. Did you tell him the truth?   A. No, sir.

Q. Did Mr. Barber know you very well when he was sober?   A. Knowed him very well ever since he was a child.

Q. Didn't he know perfectly well that you were not a Democrat, but a Republican?   A. No, sir; I don't know as he did.

Q. Was not your position in politics very well known throughout the town?   A. I don't know as it was at that time.

Q. Was Mr. Barber a very active politician? *A.* No, sir, I think not.

Q. Were you not very active in party politics? *A.* No, sir, but most determined in principle.

Q. Was not Mr. Barber very drunk that evening? *A.* Well, sir, as well as you can judge a drunken man, I supposed him to be about half drunk.

Q. When do you consider a man half drunk—what is your idea? *A.* When a man is half drunk?—when a man is full drunk, he forgets everything he does or says.

Q. When a man is half drunk does he not forget half of everything he says and does? *A.* No, sir, I never said that.

Re-examined—Questions by Prosecution.

Q. State whether Mr. Barber was or was not in a condition at that time to know what he was doing? *A.* To my judgment I think he knowed what he was doing.

Q. Did you take him to his house? *A.* Yes, sir.

Q. What time did you say you got to his house? *A.* In the neighborhood of sunset, sir.

Q. Did you have to help him out of the wagon? *A.* No, sir.

Q. Did anybody? *A.* No, sir.

The court then adjourned, in consideration of to-morrow being the 4th of July, until Monday, the 6th instant, at 10 o'clock.

McPHERSON BARRACKS, ATLANTA, GA., }
10 o'clock A. M., July 6, 1868. }

The Commission met pursuant to adjournment.

Present, same members as yesterday, the Judge Advocate, the prisoners on trial, and their counsel.

Abraham Johnson, a witness on behalf of the prosecution, whose testimony was taken yesterday, on having it read to him by the Judge Advocate, in the presence of the Court and of the accused, requested permission to make the following correction:

"The man spoken of as Henry Kimbro, we call him Gainwell."

Permission was granted.

R. J. Moses, Esq., of counsel for defense, was introduced and took his seat.

The accused requested permission to introduce Wm. W. Garrard, Esq., as additional counsel for defense. Permission having been granted, he was accordingly introduced and took his seat.

The Judge Advocate then stated that the prosecution was here closed.

Counsel for defense asked permission of the Court to retire for a few moments for the purpose of consulting their witnesses. Permission was granted, and the Court then took a recess of ten minutes, at the expiration of which time the Court was again called to order.

Questions by Defense.

MARTIN M. BECK, a witness on behalf of the defense, having been duly sworn, testified as follows:

Q. What is your name and age? *A.* My age is forty-five; Martin M. Beck is my name.

Q. What is your occupation? *A.* Merchandise.

Q. Where do you reside? *A.* In Columbus, Georgia.

Q. Are you acquainted with Mr. Duke, who is under arraignment here? *A.* Yes, sir.

Q. This is the gentleman here, is it? *A.* Yes, sir. (Witness points to one of the accused.)

Q. Did he board with you at any time this year? *A.* Yes, sir; he boarded with me in March and April, up to the 26th or 27th of April; I disremember what day it was.

Q. Did he leave your house at any time during March? *A.* Yes, sir.

Q. What time? *A.* It was the 26th or 27th. I believe.

Q. Who left with him? *A.* Joe Ab. Abner.

Q. How did they leave? *A.* They left in a buggy.

Q. Where for? *A.* To go to Merriwether county, where he lives; that was his home.

Q. When did you see him again? *A.* He came back to my house on the first day of May—the first time I saw him after that.

Q. Did you see him from the 26th or 27th of March until the 1st day of May? *A.* I didn't see him.

Q. Did he not settle up his board when he left in March? *A.* Yes, sir.

The Judge Advocate did not desire to cross-examine this witness.

The witness' testimony having been read to him in the presence of the Court and of the accused, he asked permission, which was granted, to make the following correction, viz:

Where, on lines nine and ten of the third page of this day's record, the words March and April occur, he wishes to insert instead "February and March," so that his answer may read:

"Yes, sir; he boarded with me in February and March, up to the 26th or 27th of March; I disremember which day it was."

Questions by Defense by permission of the Court.

Q. Is Joe Abner a white man? A. Yes, sir.

Q. Where is this Mr. Abner now? A. I suppose in Columbus at this time; he was off in the country when I left; he lives in the suburbs of Columbus, not in the city.

Questions by the Court.

Q. How do you remember that it was on the 27th March Duke left your house? A. It was by some business that was transacted them days; that is my recollection of it.

Q. You are sure that it was not later than the 27th March, 1868, that Duke left your house? A. Yes, sir.

Questions by Defense by permission of the Court.

Q. Do you know what day of the week it was when he left there? A. I think it was on Friday; that is my recollection—Thursday or Friday.

Q. Are you certain that it was the Thursday or Friday before the death of Ashburn? A. I am.

Questions by the Court.

Q. Are you certain that he left town when he left your house, and did not return at any time, night or day, until May 1st. A. Well, sir, I could not say positively about that, for I don't know what a man does after he gets out of my sight; I never seen him, and I received a note from him that he was in Merriwether a few days after he got there; and Mr. Abner, when he returned, told me he left him there.

The Judge Advocate moved to strike from the record that portion of the last answer which referred to Mr. Abner's statement to the witness, said statement not being evidence.

The counsel for defense objected.

The Commission was then retired, and after due deliberation returned to Court, and the Judge Advocate announced that the Court sustained the objection of the Judge Advocate, and the matter referred to would therefore be stricken from the evidence.

Questions by Defense.

HENRY WELSH, a witness for the defense, being duly sworn, testified as follows:
Q. What's your full name? A. Henry Welsh.
Q. What is your age? A. Twenty-eight years old.
Q. What's your occupation? A. Carpenter by trade, before I lost my arm.
Q. Where do you live? A. Muscogee county, Georgia.
Q. Are you acquainted with William Duke, who is arraigned on this trial? A. I am, sir.
Q. Do you see him here? A. Yes, sir.
Q. Can you point him out? A. Yes, sir.
Q. Which is he? A. That gentleman, sir (pointing to one of the accused).
Q. Do you reside in the county or in the town of Columbus? A. I reside in the town.
Q. Did you see Mr. Duke at any time during the latter part of March, this year? A. I did, sir.
Q. State when, where, and who was with him. A. I saw Mr. William Duke about the 26th or 27th March; he was accompanied by Joseph Abner; he was about one mile from the Court-house, on the Harris county road.
Q. How were they traveling? A. In a buggy.
Q. Did you have any conversation with them? A. I only remarked to the gentlemen where they were going.
Q. What was the reply? A. Mr. Duke answered he was going home.
Q. You say 26th or 27th; what day of the week was it? A. I think on Thursday or Friday.
Q. Are you certain it was before the death of Mr. Ashburn? A. I am certain.

Cross-Examined by Judge Advocate.

Q. Are you acquainted with Mr. M. M. Beck? A. I am, sir.
Q. Have you had any conversation with him in regard to the matter about which you have been testifying? A. Yes, sir; we talked it over a few days before we left town.
Q. Have you not talked it over together

this morning? *A.* No, sir; not—— that; I think, however, to the best of my we was only speaking about coming up knowledge, it was on 26th.
here this morning; we didn't talk anything *Q.* Well, then, what makes you talk in regard to the evidence of the case. about 27th? *A.* Well, sir, I would not
Q. Did not you and he, this morning, be positive that it was on the 26th; I talk it over, and one or the other say that know it was some trades I had in Colum-it was the 26th or 27th March that Duke bus on the 26th and 27th; I was up right left town, or something to that effect? *A.* by the place where I saw Mr. Duke both Not as I recollect of. mornings—26th and 27th; I don't recollect
Q. Were not these words—the 26th or for certain which morning it was I met him.
27th March—mentioned by one of you to *Q.* Do you remember what day of the the other this very morning? *A.* These week it was? *A.* No, sir; either Thursday words has been mentioned; I don't recollect or Friday.
whether me or Mr. Beck mentioned them. *Q.* Wasn't mentioned with same con-
Q. Mentioned this morning were they versation this morning the words "Thurs-not? *A.* Yes, sir, but I don't think by day or Friday?" *A.* No, sir; I don't either one of us. think it was; if it was I don't recollect it.
Q. Who were they mentioned by? *A.* *Q.* Have you been acquainted with Duke I do not recollect now, sir; there was a long while? *A.* Acquainted with Mr. several talking. Duke some three years.
Q. Those several persons talking; were *Q.* Did you have any conversation with they not talking about these dates? *A.* him that morning? *A.* Nothing; only Yes, sir. I suppose they were: I was sitting just asked him which way he was going.
by them and never paid no attention how *Q.* When did you first remember, after the conversation came up. you heard of Ashburn's death, that it was
Q. State who these several persons the 26th or 27th of March that you had were. *A.* I believe they was Mr. Wood- seen Duke traveling away from Columbus?
ward, Mr. Norman, Mr. Duke—the two *A.* I remembered it when I heard that Mr. Dukes—and another gentleman, I Duke was arrested and brought to prison.
don't recollect his name, sir; (witness *Q.* Did you remember it or was your pauses) it was Mr. Reese, sir. attention called to it by some one? *A.*
Q. Where did this conversation take No, sir; my attention was not called to it.
place? *A.* Right out here, sir, on the *Q.* How long was it after you saw Duke piazza of this building. on the road until he was arrested? *A.*
Q. What was said? *A.* I don't recol- Two or three months; three months, I be-lect of anything being said, any more than lieve, very nearly.
some one mentioned about the date; he *Q.* What time in the morning was it came home on the 26th or 27th. when you met him? *A.* I think about six
Q. Was Mr. Beck present at that con- or seven o'clock in the morning.
versation? *A.* I am not certain whether
he was or not.

Re-examined by Defense.

Q. Would you have remembered that it was the 26th or 27th March if you had not *Q.* Does the Harris county road lead to heard it? *A.* Yes, sir, I believe I should. Merriwether county? *A.* Yes, sir; Harris
Q. Do you know anything else that county lies between.
happened on the 26th March? *A.* Yes, *Q.* Columbus and Merriwether county?
sir. *A.* Yes, sir.
Q. Is there anything that happened on *Q.* If he had started to Merriwether the 26th March that makes you remember county he would have taken the road you what time it was when you met this man? seen him going out by, would he not? *A.*
A. Yes, sir. Yes, sir; there's no other road leading out
Q. What? *A.* Some private business to Merriwether county that I know of.
with some gentlemen in Columbus.
Q. It was on account of this private *Questions by Defense.*
business, then, that you remember it? *A.*
Yes, sir. EMILY DUKE, a witness for defense, hav-
Q. It was 26th March, was it? *A.* ing been duly sworn, testified as follows:
Yes, sir; 26th or 27th, I am satisfied of *Q.* What is your Christian name, Mrs. Duke? *A.* Emily.

Q. Where do you reside? *A.* Merriwether county.

Q. How long have you been living there? *A.* About last Christmas was a year ago—a little before Christmas.

Q. Where did you live before? *A.* Lived in Jerrard.

Q. Where is Jerrard? *A.* In Alabama; right across the river from Columbus.

Q. Is William Duke, the person arraigned, your son? *A.* Yes, sir.

Q. Where did he reside the early part of this year? *A.* He resided with me, where I live in Merriwether county, most of the time.

Q. Was he sometimes in Columbus and sometimes at home? *A.* Well, he went with me to Columbus and we was gone there about a couple of weeks, a little more, I believe, but he came back with me when I was coming home.

Q. Was he in Columbus in any part of March of this year? *A.* Yes, sir, he came home about the 26th of March.

Q. Who came with him? *A.* Mr. Abner.

Q. How did they travel? *A.* In a buggy.

Q. Do you recollect the day of the week? *A.* I think it was Thursday, I won't be positive; some says Thursday and some Friday, but I think it was Thursday; though it might have been Friday; I won't be sure, but it was one or the other.

Q. What day did Mr. Abner return with the buggy—how long did he stay there? *A.* Well, he only stayed all night with us; he went to his brothers next day, about Greenville; I think he went home Sunday; that is what we heard anyway.

Q. State how long he was there after coming home? *A.* Well, he was there until the last of April; me and him went back to town, and got there the first day of May.

Q. Where did he sleep when he was at home? *A.* Slept in the same room where I did.

Q. Do you know that he was there Monday and Monday night, after he came home? *A.* Yes, sir, he was there.

Q. The time you state that you and he went to Columbus together, when was that? *A.* When was it?

Q. Yes. You stated that he went to Columbus with you, and you stayed two weeks? *A.* That was the first of May; I went on business to Crawford court and he went with me—the Friday before Crawford court—got there 1st day of May.

Q. The time that he went with you and came back with you? *A.* Yes, sir.

Q. How far do you live in Merriwether county from Columbus? *A.* Forty miles.

Cross-examination—Questions by Judge Advocate.

Q. When did you first hear of the murder of G. W. Ashburn? *A.* Heard it on Wednesday, I think, after it was done Monday.

Q. How long after that was it before you heard the name of your son mentioned in connection with that murder? *A.* I don't recollect; I didn't hear it at all, but just a little while before they came after him; a little before that—I don't recollect exactly; not mighty long though; it was two weeks last Wednesday when he was taken.

Q. Was he arrested at your house? *A.* Yes; he was at the shop at work, but it was close to the house; I saw him when he came.

Q. When he was arrested did you remember, as you state it now, where he was the week before Ashburn's murder? *A.* Yes, sir, I knowed mighty well he was at home.

Q. How did you come to remember so well the date of his arrival home? *A.* Well, I reckon what made me was, I knowed the date Mr. Ashburn was killed, and I knowed that he had come before that—knowed how long he had been home before.

Q. Who went away with Mr. Abner next morning? *A.* Nobody at all.

Q. Where did your son sleep the night he arrived home? *A.* Well, he slept in the same room where he did all the time—where I do; him and Mr. Abner slept together.

Q. Is your room his usual place of sleeping? *A.* Well, it is all in one room.

Q. Is there but one room to your house? *A.* It is just one large room; we did have a partition in it, but had it taken down.

Q. Did any other persons sleep in that room? *A.* Yes, sir, the balance of the family.

Q. Who constituted the balance of the family? *A.* Well, a couple of daughters, a son and his wife, and son-in-law.

Q. Were all these persons in the habit of sleeping in the same room? *A.* Yes,

MILITARY OUTRAGE IN GEORGIA.

sir; they didn't have anywhere else to sleep; all homefolks; it didn't matter.

Q. Was Mr. Abner "homefolks?" A. Well, he was not particular homefolks; he was an old acquaintance—a neighbor—an old gentleman.

Q. Who slept in the room the Monday of which you have spoken? A. The Monday night of Mr. Ashburn's death?

Q. Yes. A. My brother slept in there—slept with William.

Q. Well, who else? A. I slept in there, and them that I told you awhile ago.

Q. You slept there and your two daughters—your married daughter and her husband? A. Yes, sir.

Q. What is your brother's name? A. Arington.

Q. What was he doing there that night? A. Well, he had come down the Sunday before to see us; he lives in Carroll county, and he just happened to be there.

Q. When did your brother leave? A. Left on the Thursday after he come, Sunday.

Q. How did he travel? A. He was walking.

Q. Didn't your son leave home from the time that he arrived before Ashburn's murder until you and he went up to Crawford court? A. No, sir.

Q. Neither day nor night? A. Not to be gone all night nor all day; he went round there; close about; he had not been ne'er a day nor o'er a night.

Q. Do you know Mr. Welsh? A. Yes, sir.

Q. Mr. Beck? A. Yes, sir.

Q. Have any conversation with either of them this morning? A. No, sir.

Q. Were you present where they or others were conversing? A. No, sir; I ain't been with them, only coming out here; I was not with Mr. Beck then; Mr. Welsh come in the carriage that I did.

Q. Haven't you heard some persons this morning talking about the 26th or 27th of March? A. No, sir.

Q. Did you hear Mr. Welsh say anything about the 26th or 27th of March? A. No, sir, nothing about it.

Q. Nor Mr. Beck? A. I have not spoken to Mr. Beck to-day.

Q. Have you not had conversation with some of the witnesses in this case? A. No, sir.

Q. This morning or any time? A. Have had nothing to say about it.

Q. No conversation with any one about the time your son arrived home? A. The witnesses?

Q. Yes; the members of your own family that are here now. A. No, sir; not as I recollect.

Q. Have you not talked it over by yourselves as to the time he got home from Columbus? A. Not to-day.

Q. Haven't you before? A. Well, may be I have some time before—I expect may be I did.

Q. Did you remember these dates until they were told you by somebody else? A. Yes, sir.

Q. How came you to remember so particularly the two dates? A. Well, I knowed it was the last of the month, and I always knew the day of the month.

Q. Can you, two months after a thing has happened, always remember when it occurred—the day it occurred? A. Well, I reckon I recollect it because he come home that day.

Q. Where was your son in February, 1868? A. He was at home, I reckon.

Q. What was he doing at home? A. He was working in the shop; a blacksmith shop and a wagon shop.

Q. Was he at home every day and every night in February? A. There is nowhere for them to go at night where we live; it ain't like living in town—nowhere to go out.

Q. He was at home every day and every night of February, 1868? A. Yes, sir.

Q. Where was he in the early days of March, 1868? A. He was at home.

Q. Was he at home in the middle of March? (Witness hesitates.)

Judge Advocate.—Answer the question, madam, if you please.

Witness.—You have got me bothered so that I don't know.

Q. You recollect where he was on the 26th and 27th of March—can't you recollect where he was in the middle of March? A. Yes, he was at home.

Q. When he returned with this Mr. Abner, how long had he been absent? A. Not mighty long; I don't recollect how long.

Q. Had he been gone a week? A. Yes, sir; I reckon, he had.

Q. Can you say that he had been gone a week, certain? A. Well, I wouldn't be positive; I think so.

Q. Can you read? A. No, sir.

Q. Have you any almanac at your house? *A.* No, sir.

Q. I think you said you had heard of your sons name in connection with the murder of Ashburn before he was arrested? *A.* Well, sir, we heard it.

Q. Did you hear it from your son, or from whom did you hear it? *A.* No, sir, I didn't hear it from my son; this gentleman that brought him up was there a peddling, and he told us about it; he said that was the chap he had heard down there.

Q. How long after your son had got home before he brought that chap to the house? *A.* Whom, Mr. Abner?

Q. Yes. *A.* Oh, that was a week or two, before they come after him.

Q. What kind of a buggy was that in which your son came home? *A.* A one-horse buggy.

Q. Describe the horse? *A.* A dark bay horse, to the best of my recollection.

Q. Had the buggy a top? *A.* No, sir, no top at all.

Q. Do you know to whom the buggy belonged? *A.* Well, I don't know whether it belonged to old man Abner or not.

Q. What time did they arrive at your house? *A.* I reckon the sun was about an hour high, or hardly so much? It was raining when they came.

Q. Was it a rainy day? *A.* It hadn't been raining all day. It rained in the evening a little, not much.

Re-examined—Questions by Defense.

Q. What is your age? *A.* I don't know exactly, about fifty-six, though, I reckon.

Q. During the months of February and March did your son pass up and down from Columbus home? *A.* Well, he did once, I think.

Q. What is his trade or occupation? *A.* Working in the shop.

Q. What kind of shop? *A.* Blacksmith shop and wood shop.

Questions by the Defense.

. JORDAN REESE, a witness in behalf of the defense, having been duly sworn, testified as follows:

Q. State your name in full? *A.* Jordan Reese is my name, sir.

Q. What is your age, and where do you reside, and what is your occupation? *A.* I shall soon be seventy years old, sir; I am a farmer; I reside in Merriwether County, near Sulphur Springs.

Q. Do you know Wm. Duke, who is under arraignment here? *A.* Yes, sir, well acquainted with him; that is, I have been acquainted with him about sixteen or eighteen months, since he moved from Columbus up to my neighborhood. He lives about between four and five hundred yards from where I live.

Q. Did you say he moved, or his father? *A.* Well, the whole family moved together; all have been there ever since—all the family. Occasionally some would be off, backwards and forwards to Columbus, and about, but that is their residence—their home.

Q. What is William Duke's business or occupation? *A.* Well, sir, he is a blacksmith, and works in a work-shop on buggies, etc.; most anything—wood work; sometimes in the blacksmith shop and sometimes in the wood shop.

Q. Do you know where he was the last week in March of this year? *A.* Well, sir, I was with him on the 30th day of March, at the shop. His shop is a kind of resort for the neighborhood. He was there between sunset and dark. I left him there, with several others.

Q. What day of the week was that? *A.* Monday evening, the 30th, there were some seven or eight there.

Q. Were you at the same place next morning? *A.* Yes, sir. I went up there on Monday evening, to have some work done. The old man Duke was at work on my plows, and he didn't get them quite finished, so I started very early Tuesday morning, and went up after my plows. I was also there Wednesday morning.

Q. Was William there Tuesday morning, when you went for your plows? *A.* Yes, sir.

Q. Was he there Wednesday also? *A.* Yes, sir, he was there on Wednesday.

Q. When did you first hear of the murder of Mr. Ashburn? *A.* Well, sir, as well as I recollect, it was about Thursday or Friday afterwards. I think one of my neighbors, Jimmy Tucker, perhaps, if I am not mistaken, went up to Lagrange, and heard it there—I think about Thursday—I won't say—Wednesday or Thursday.

Q. How far is it from your house and Mr. Duke's father's to Columbus? *A.* It is fully forty miles. We always call it that—that is what we generally call it. It is a very long day's drive, sir.

Cross-examined—Questions by the Judge Advocate.

Q. When did you first hear the name of William Duke connected with the murder of Ashburn? A. Well, sir, the first I heard of it was at the time they arrested him—the day after they had arrested him I think. I did not charge my memory exactly to a day, but about Thursday, I think, they arrested him. I heard of it about Friday evening or Saturday morning, I won't be certain which, and I was very much astonished.

Q. When was he arrested? A. Well, I never charged my memory, sir, in regard to it. I think it was about Thursday, but I don't know the day of the month.

Q. Was it last Thursday? A. Not last Thursday—last Thursday week, if I am not mistaken.

Q. Do you remember what day of the month he was arrested on? A. No, sir. I go there almost every day, to the shop, walking about, and think it was Friday I went up to the shop, and some of the family told me William was arrested and carried off.

Q. Do you know when Mr. Ashburn was murdered—the date of the murder? A. Only from hearsay. I heard it was on Monday night, the 30th.

Q. You don't remember when William was arrested—the day of the month—although it was a week ago last Thursday? A. No, sir. I did not charge my memory with it.

Q. But, do you remember the day that he mended your plow? A. Yes, sir. I carried the plows on Monday, the 30th, and I went after them on Tuesday.

Q. How are you able to remember so distinctly the day you took the plows there to be mended? A. How?

Q. Yes, how are you able to remember so distinctly? A. What makes me certain that that is the day, sir, it was either Friday or Saturday that a gentleman brought William Duke up from Columbus, and I think it was Saturday morning that I saw him, and asked him about matters and things in Columbus—what was the news, and so on—that's the reason why I know. William had been for some time from home, and I saw him Saturday morning, I think—either Friday or Saturday.

Q. Well, how did you remember afterwards what day of the month it was on which you first saw William, on his return from Columbus? Did it make so much impression on your mind as that? A. Well, sir, I think it was on the day, the 26th—no, the 27th or 28th, on refreshing my memory about it—what I recollected was that William was there from, I would say, the Saturday morning before until some seven or eight days after—well, may be a week or more after Ashburn was killed. That is why I recollect that William was there, because I seen him there every day.

Q. When were you first inquired of as to the time when William returned from Columbus to his home? A. Why, I saw him myself. I was with him two days.

Q. Since his arrest, has not some person come to you to inquire of you as to the time when William returned from Columbus? A. No, sir, not a soul.

Q. Did no one speak to you as to the time when William returned home? A. When he returned home from Columbus?

Q. Has no one since his arrest talked to you as to the time when William returned from Columbus? A. Several have talked about the time that Ashburn was killed—on Monday. Being at the shop there (there were several of us there, some seven or eight men, that Monday evening), there was a general talk among the neighbors about William being arrested. They were rather suprised at it—everybody in the whole neighborhood—seven or eight men—in the shop at the time I was there.

Q. Who first spoke to you about coming here as a witness? A. Well, I didn't know that I was coming here until they sent for me.

Q. Since you arrived here, have you not had conversation with some one as to the date of Ashburn's murder? A. No, sir, I recollect that very well.

Q. Well, you say you remember now the date of Mr. Ashburn's murder? A. Well, I did not say positive. The murder took place, as I understood it, on the 30th of March, Monday night. That's what we heard some three or four days afterward. This man, from our neighborhood, Mr. Tucker, went up to Lagrange, and brought the news down. That's all I know about it.

Q. Explain, if you please, how it happens that you remember now the date of Ashburn's murder, and you can not remember the day of the arrest of your neighbor, as one of the parties connected with that murder, although that arrest took place not more than ten days ago? A. Well, I stated that I thought it was either Thursday—last Thursday was a week, that's what I—(witness hesitates)—I think it was on Thursday.

Q. Do you remember the day of the month that your neighbor Duke was arrested on? A. No, sir, I did not charge my memory with it.

Q. Did you charge your memory with the date of Ashburn's murder? A. Yes, sir.

Q. Were you in the habit of going frequently to the shop in which William worked? A. Yes, sir, sometimes twice a day I would go up there, and stay there with the neighbors, and we would talk.

Q. Did you go there frequently in the month of February? A. Well, sir, sometimes it is every day, and sometimes three or four days before I go there. I would be off from home.

Q. Was William at home in the month of February? A. Yes, sir.

Q. Was he at home in the month of March? A. Well, he was not at home the first part of March much; he went down to Columbus, and, as I said, he came up the last of March.

Q. Do you know when he left home to go to Columbus? A. No, sir, they pass back and forwards frequently, the family does, and I don't charge my memory with such things.

Q. Do you know how long he was absent at any one time in March? A. No, sir, I don't recollect.

Q. Did you frequently have work done at that shop? A. Yes, sir, had all my work done there sir.

Q. Was he at home all the month of February? A. Well, I don't know, sir. It seems to me that he was most of February, because he had chills and fever. I think he was sick most of February if I am not mistaken.

Q. Do you know whom William came home with the last time he came, before Ashburn's murder? A. The last time?;

Q. Yes. A. No, sir, I did'nt see the man who brought him up. I heard a man brought him up, but that was all.

Re-examined—Questions by Defense.

Q. Did you have any notice at all of your testimony being needed here until you got a subpœna? A. No, sir, I have not had a subpœna yet, sir.

Q. And no notice? A. I had a notice, sir. There was a man came for us. A gentleman was sent from here who told us we were required, so he said; I don't know. He said he was sent from this body down there to bring us up.

Q. Had you spoken very publicly and freely about your knowledge of where William was, and expressed your surprise at his arrest? Had you spoken thus freely and publicly everywhere? A. Well, the neighbors talked about it in the neighborhood, after he was arrested. We were all very much surprised at his arrest.

Q. Have you been to Lagrange? A. I had to go up to Lagrange to get on the cars.

Q. Were you there last week, or the week before? A. Yes, sir, last week I was up there—Tuesday.

Q. Did you speak up there to anybody, or publicly, as to your knowledge of this transaction? A. Well, sir, Mr. Abrams and Dr. Wymbush was there—the way they come to ask me about it, both of these gentlemen knew that I lived in sight of him, and asked me something about it.

Q. That's the explanation of the first notification you got of it, is it? A. Yes, sir.

Questions by the Defense.

J. T. WOODWARD, a witness for the defense, having been duly sworn, testified as follows:

Q. Give your name in full, Mr. Woodward. A. J. T. Woodward.

Q. What is your age? A. Twenty-three years old—twenty-four my next birthday.

Q. What is your occupation? A. Farmer, sir.

Q. Where do you live? A. Merriwether County.

Q. Do you know William Duke who is now on arraignment here? A. Yes, sir.

Q. Which is he? A. There is Mr. Duke, (witness points to Duke, one of the accused.)

Q. How far do you live from his father's house? A. About a mile and a half, sir.

Q. Did you see William Duke at any time during the latter part of March, this year? A. Yes, sir, I saw him on the 27th,

28th, 30th, and 31st, and 1st of April. All through April I was with him.

Q. Where was he on the 27th of March? A. ..... at his father's house, sir.

Q. W... hour of the day did you see or A. I saw him directly after ... ck, soon in the evening.

... re was he on the 28th? A. He was shop at his father's.

... t days of the week—do you ... . Friday and Saturday.

Q. ...re did you see him Monday, the 30th? A. Saw him at his father's.

Q. What time of the day did you see him there? A. I saw him in the evening about dusk.

Q. Where was he then? A. He was at his father's, at the house.

Q. You said you saw him the 31st; when did you see him then, and at what time of the day? A. I saw him very early in the morning at his father's.

Q. How far does Mr. Duke's father, where you saw him, live from Columbus? A. Forty miles, sir, it is called.

Q. When did you first hear of the murder of Ashburn? A. The second day of April; I was at the shop when I heard it.

Q. Do you recollect the day of the week that was? A. It was Monday, sir.

A. Do you know how the news got there—how did you hear it? A. Well, sir, there was an old gentleman come up from below there, two or three miles, he told me about it; and then there was a young man in the settlement, was in Lagrange on Tuesday; we met there that evening, and he told me about it.

Cross-examined—Questions by the Judge Advocate.

Q. When did you first hear that William was charged with taking part in the murder of Ashburn? A. William Duke?

Q. Yes. A. Well, sir, I never heard of it till he was arrested.

Q. When was he arrested? A. Well, sir, I don't recollect; I was not at home at the time.

Q. Can't you recollect now the day that he was arrested? A. No, sir, I can't, because I was not in the settlement at all.

Q. Can't you recollect the day that you heard he was arrested? A. I think he was arrested on Thursday; I won't be certain of it; Thursday or Friday—Thursday, I think.

Q. When did you first hear of it? A. I think I heard of it the day he was arrested.

Q. What day of the month was that? A. Well, sir, I can not tell you.

Q. I wish you would try to tell me. A. I can't tell that, sir; 1 ——. (Witness hesitates).

Q. It interested you, did it not, to know that your neighbor was charged with so serious a crime? A. It did, sir.

Q. Very much? A. Yes, sir.

Q. But you can't remember the day of the month? A. No, sir, I was out on other business; I was not at home myself; my father told me about it; he had been down to my place.

Q. You think it was Thursday? A. Yes, sir, I think it was Thursday.

Q. You do remember though, very distinctly, the days that you saw him in the shop, some three months before that? A. Yes, sir, I do.

Q. You say you were with him all the month of April? A. The most of April I was—I will not say all April; I had my work done at the shop, and was there every day mighty near; his father keeps a blacksmith and wood shop too.

Q. When you heard of his arrest, did you then remember these dates, as you have given them on your examination in chief? A. Yes, sir.

Q. You remember then that it was Friday, the 27th, that you first saw him? A. Yes, sir; I commenced thinking about the death of Ashburn, and I knew Mr. Duke was at home when I heard that he was arrested.

Q. Did you know the date of Ashburn's death when you first heard of his arrest? A. Yes, sir.

Q. Had you charged your mind with that when you heard of it? A. Yes, sir.

Q. The date of his death? A. Yes, sir.

Q. Why did you charge your mind with that date? A. Because I knew that Mr. Duke was at home at that time after I heard that he was arrested.

Q. Did you, at the time you heard of Ashburn's death, charge your mind with the date of his death? A. Yes, sir.

Q. Why did you do that? A. Well, because I just happened to know that it was that date; I was reading of it in the papers.

Q. Recollect that, but you can't now remember the date when you heard of the arrest of your neighbor on a charge murder? A. I don't recollect the date, sir—the time he was arrested.

Q. Had anything occurred since Ashburn's death and before Duke's arrest to cause you to reflect on the days you had seen William Duke at the shop, and if so, what was it? A. Nothing, sir.

Q. Has your attention been called to these dates by conversation with other persons? A. We have been talking about them, sir.

Q. Have you not been talking about them to-day? A. No, sir, I have not been talking about them to-day.

Q. Yesterday? A. I don't recollect talking about them yesterday, sir.

Q. The day before? A. It may have been, I don't know for certain—I would not say for certain.

Q. Whom did you talk about them with? A. Well, I had talked about them before I came to Atlanta with my brother and brother-in-law, my father—no, not my father—and Mr. Florence. These were the first I had talked to about it.

Q. Had you talked with any of the witnesses here? A. Yes, sir, I think I have. I have talked to one of them about it.

Q. What witness here have you talked with? A. Talked with young Mr. Duke—Wayne Duke is his name—about it.

Q. Who else? A. Well, sir, I talked with his brother, John Duke I think is his name. "Dug" Duke I thing they call him.

Q. When did you talk with them? A. I talked with them the day we came up here, sir—last Friday I believe—Friday evening.

Q. Do you remember the day William Duke went to Columbus, the last time he left home to go to Columbus, before the murder of Ashburn? A. No, sir, I do not.

Q. Do you remember the day he left home to go to Columbus with his mother, after the death of Ashburn? A. No, sir, I do not. I think, though, it was some time in April—'long towards the last of April, I won't be certain of it.

Q. Can't you remember any other days since Christmas, except those you have named, that you can swear that you saw Duke at the shop, at work—particular days. A. "Particular days," sir? I don't know as I can, but I am pretty certain he was there directly after Christmas.

Q. Do you know where he was in the month of February? A. No, sir, I don't. I had not made arrangements with him to do any work at all, at that time. 'Long towards the first of March I made arrangements with him to do my work. I had my work done in another place—didn't go to the shop so often.

Q. Where was he in the month of March before the days you have mentioned? A. I think he came from Columbus on the 26th.

Q. Where was he before that? A. I think he was in Columbus.

Q. Was he at home no part of March, except those days? A. I don't recollect, sir, whether he was or not.

Q. What kind of day was it on which Duke came home? do you remember? was it cold, wet or dry, or what? A. I don't recollect, I was at the shop on Friday, I think—I am pretty certain it was Friday, and I saw him; I had not seen him before in some time, I think; I don't recollect anything about the day or what day it was.

Q. When was it you made arrangements with him to do your work for you? A. I didn't make arrangements with him, I made arrangements with his father about the first of March.

Q. From what fact was it that the date, the 30th of March, was impressed upon your memory more than any date? A. I don't understand the question exactly.

Re-examined—Questions by Defense.

Q. Did the news of the death of Mr. Ashburn produce a great sensation in your neighborhood or not? A. Yes, sir, it did.

Q. Was it a sensation as was calculated to make a deep impression upon all who heard of it? A. Yes, the people seemed to be very much surprised to hear of it. I was in Mr. Duke's there when I heard of it.

Q. You say it was published in the papers. A. Yes, sir, I saw it in the papers after these gentlemen told me?

Q. Was it or not from these facts you have just stated, of your being there at the time, that the date was more impressed upon your mind than other dates? A. Yes, sir.

Cross-examination—Questions by Judge Advocate.

Q. Did you not go with William Duke to Montgomery, Alabama, a day or two before or a day or two after the murder of Ashburn? *A.* No, sir, I never was in Montgomery in my life.

Q. Didn't you go in that direction? *A.* No, sir, I was never in Columbus but once in my life and that was when I was very small; my father carried me there.

The Court then adjourned until to-morrow morning at 10 o'clock.

McPHERSON BARRACKS, ATLANTA, GA., July 7, 1868.

The Commission met pursuant to adjournment.

Present—The same members as yesterday, the Judge Advocate and assistants, the prisoners on trial, and their counsel.

The record of yesterday's proceedings was read and approved.

Emily Duke, a witness for the defense, examined before the Commission yesterday, on hearing her testimony read by the Judge Advocate in open court, asked permission of the court to correct some points in her testimony. Permission having been granted, the witness made the following statement:

"I made a mistake in the description of my house—there is one bed-room, a large one—but there is a dining-room, and a cook-room besides. My son and his wife did not stay there all night—they live close by us. My son William was not at home all the time through February and March —but I don't know exactly how long he was there. I know he passed up and down the road a time or two, but what time I don't know. I think it was last Wednesday was a week he was taken. I think it was the 24th. My son-in-law did not sleep in the house, he has a little house just adjoining mine."

The witness, Jordan Reese, also examined before the Commission yesterday, on hearing his testimony read in open Court by the Judge Advocate, asked and obtained permission of the Court to make the following correction:

"When I come to think about it, I think that William Duke was arrested on Wednesday instead of Thursday."

The witness, J. T. Woodward, also examined yesterday before this Commission, on hearing his testimony read by the Judge Advocate, asked and obtained permission of the Court to make the following correction:

"It was Wednesday, the first day of April, that I first heard of the murder of Ashburn. I talked about that before I came to Atlanta with my brother-in-law, and so forth, not my brother, as recorded in my testimony of yesterday. With regard to William Duke, I was with him part of April, not all the time."

The counsel for the accused then submitted a paper, of which the following is a copy:

"The counsel for the prisoners ask that the court order a copy of the testimony of record be made for the use of the defense; the counsel for the prisoners ask that subpœnas be issued for Mr. W. H. Reed, now in Washington City, and for H. C. Whitley, now in Atlanta, and that the witness Whitley be ordered by the court not to leave Atlanta without the permission of court."

The Commission decided to leave the matter in the hands of the Judge Advocate. The Judge Advocate stated that he would furnish a true copy of the testimony of record to the defense. Also that he would subpœna Mr. Whitley, and, when so subpœned, Mr. Whitley could not leave Atlanta without permission of the court; and that with regard to the other party, Mr. W. H. Reed, who is said to be in Washington City, he would also have him subpœnaed, as desired, that the defense in this case may have the utmost latitude for the obtaining of testimony necessary to their case. The defense stated that with the permission of the court they would for the present suspend the taking of testimony in the case of the accused, William Duke, although several other witnesses in his behalf were waiting. This was desirable, they said, for the accommodation of some ladies who were present as witnesses in behalf of another of the accused, one of which ladies was ill and anxious to return to her home. The court granted the desired permission.

Questions by Defense.

MRS. EDWARD SHEPPARD, a witness on behalf of the defense, being duly sworn, testified as follows:

Q. What is your name? *A.* Mrs. Edward Sheppard.

Q. Where do you live? *A.* In Wintou, near Columbus.

Q. Do you know Dr. Kirksey? *A.* Yes, sir.

Q. Can you point him out in the court? *A.* Yes, sir.

Q. Do so. (Witness points out Dr. Kirksey, the accused).

Q. Are you related to Dr. Kirksey? *A.* Yes, sir.

Q. What relationship? *A.* My son-in-law, sir.

Q. Where does Dr. Kirksey live? *A.* Lives in Winton.

Q. With whom? *A.* With me.

Q. Please describe the house—the internal arrangement and situation of the house as to the rooms. *A.* The house is one story high; the front part of the house is a long hall, running through, with three rooms on each side, each door opening into the hall; there are two large outside doors that are fastened; one of the inside doors is a large folding door.

Q. Is the room that Dr. Kirksey sleeps in on either side of the passage, and which side? *A.* It is one of the front rooms on the right-hand side.

Q. Where is your sleeping-room situated? *A.* My sleeping-room is two rooms below, on the left-hand side.

Q. Whose sleeping-rooms are opposite to Dr. Kirksey's? *A.* My son's.

Q. What is his name—which of them? *A.* Andrew Sheppard.

Q. Whose sleeping-room is next to Dr. Kirksey's? *A.* My daughter, Mrs. Moore, and Miss Woodville Sheppard and Miss Winne.

Q. Do you recollect upon what day of the month Mr. Ashburn was killed? *A.* No, sir, I don't.

Q. Do you recollect the month? *A.* No, sir.

Q. Do you recollect the day of the week? *A.* No, sir.

Q. When did you first hear of the killing of Mr. Ashburn? *A.* Next morning.

Q. Do you know where Dr. Kirksey was the night before? *A.* The night before he was killed?

Q. No, the night before you heard of it. *A.* No.

Q. You say you heard the next morning that Ashburn was killed? *A.* The Doctor was at home.

Q. The night that he was killed? *A.* The Doctor was at home.

Q. What time did he come home that night? *A.* Came home to tea, after dark—some time after dark.

Q. Did he go out after dark? *A.* No, sir.

Q. Were you in his bed-room after he retired? *A.* Yes, sir.

Q. How came you to be there? *A.* He had a sick baby.

Q. About what time of the night were you in his room? *A.* I don't know exactly the hour, but it was very late in the night; we had no time in the house; it was late in the night.

Q. Who was in the room when you went into the room? *A.* His wife and baby and servant girl.

Q. No one else? *A.* Not that I recollect, sir.

Q. The Doctor himself was not there? *A.* The Doctor was in bed.

Q. In what room was the bed? *A.* In the front room.

Q. I mean was that the room that his wife and child were in? *A.* Yes, all were in one room together.

Q. Was the Doctor awake? *A.* Yes, sir.

Q. Can you recollect how late at night it was? *A.* No, sir, I can not tell how late it was, but we were up unusually late that night anyway; we had some three or four sick ones in the house.

Q. Did you remain long in the room? *A.* Yes, sir, remained some time in the room.

Q. When you left the room did you go to bed? *A.* No, sir.

Q. Why? *A.* I had a little boy with a toothache that I had to attend to.

Q. Were you kept up much of the night? *A.* Yes, I was up and down nearly all night, trying everything that I could to ease his tooth.

Q. Did you send this child—this little boy of yours—anywhere for medicine that night for his tooth? *A.* Yes, sir, I sent him to the Doctor's room for morphine.

Q. Did you get it? *A.* Yes, sir, he got it.

Q. What Doctor do you refer to? *A.* Dr. Kirksey.

Q. This the same gentleman who is now a prisoner? *A.* Yes, sir.

Q. Mrs. Sheppard, from the manner in which those rooms are situated to each other, could Dr. Kirksey have left the house that night without your knowledge? *A.* No, sir.

Q. Are you very clear upon that point? *A.* Yes, sir, because I am very easily awaked, and the least noise wakes me, and he could not have got out without raising the win-

MILITARY OUTRAGE IN GEORGIA.

dows or opening the doors, and I should certainly have heard it, because I was up anyway.

Q. Have you severe dogs? *A.* Yes, sir, two.

Q. Could Dr. Kirksey pass those dogs without their barking at him severely? If so, why? *A.* No, sir, because he is always teasing of them and whipping at them with his whip, and he is always teasing them and they always bark at him.

Q. Could Mr. Sheppard himself pass those dogs at night without their barking at him? *A.* I don't know, he hardly ever goes out of the house of a night—very seldom.

Q. How are the doors of the house fastened? *A.* The inside doors are fastened by locks, the outside doors are fastened with bars—iron pieces to hold the bars.

Q. Is the house barred at night? *A.* Yes, sir, always.

Q. Have you a daughter by the name of Mrs. Moore? *A.* Yes, sir.

Q. Is Mrs. Moore a very nervous woman or not? *A.* Yes, sir, she is very nervous indeed. She has been sick a great while and she is very nervous.

Q. Is she not very timid about anything occurring at night and always very watchful? *A.* Yes, sir.

Q. How far is your house from Columbus? *A.* A mile and a quarter.

Q. Do you remember where Dr. Kirksey was on Monday night, a week before Ashburn was killed? *A.* I think he must have been at home, but I do not remember particularly. He has not for a month or so hardly ever been out at night.

Q. Why is it that you remember with so much particularity about his being home that night—the night that Ashburn was killed? *A.* Well, after they commenced arresting some of our men, everybody got to thinking about it, and thinking what had happened that night, and it made us call to mind everything of the kind, and thinking of four own. Of course we were trying to think where they were. It made us particular about that night. I had a feeling recollection of it otherways, being up all night and sick ones in the house.

Q. Who was the first person you heard had been arrested? *A.* Mr. Bedell, I believe, was the first I heard.

Q. How long was that after you heard of Ashburn's murder? *A.* I think it was the same evening. A young lady came up from Columbus, and told me they were arresting them.

Q. You say you commenced immediately locating your own family, after you heard of the arrest of Bedell; now state whether you are certain or not of where Dr. Kirksey was that night? *A.* Yes, sir, he was at home and in bed that night.

Cross-examination—Questions by the Judge Advocate..

Q. How long since Dr. Kirksey married your daughter? *A.* He was married in October after the surrender.

Q. How many children has his wife? *A.* One, sir.

Q. What is its age? *A.* Two years the 17th of this month.

Q. What was the matter with the child that night? *A.* She was threatened with croup, I think.

Q. How did you learn that there was anything the matter with the child? *A.* My daughter's calling me. She always calls me whenever the baby is the least sick.

Q. About how far is it from the door of her room to the door of your room? *A.* My room is one room below hers.

Q. Did you not say it was across the hall on the opposite side? *A.* Yes, sir.

Q. About how many feet would you say? *A.* Well, I have no idea how many feet it is. It may be ten feet—I have no idea.

Q. Will you please point out some object in this room about the distance that it is from the door of her room to yours? *A.* Yes, sir, about as far as from here to that window. (Witness points to window behind the President, about ten or twelve feet from herself.)

Q. How large are those rooms? *A.* I really don't know how large they are; they are common-sized rooms.

Q. What sized carpet does it take to cover the floor? *A.* I don't know, sir; I never measured it.

Q. Did Mrs. Kirksey come to your room when she informed you the child was sick? *A.* No, sir, she called me there.

Q. Where was she when she called you? *A.* At her room door.

Q. Was the door open? *A.* Well, I suppose if she was in the door it would be open.

Q. Well, ma'am, do you state on your oath that it was? *A.* I don't recollect about that, sir; I went into the room; she may have shut the door when she got back, after she called me; I did not go right away.

Q. Was your door open at the time she called you? *A.* Yes, sir, my door is always left open at night when any of my children are sick; I always leave my door open, so that if any of them are sick I can hear them when they call.

Q. Did you hear her shut it? *A.* No, sir.

Q. Could she have opened it without your hearing it? *A.* I don't know whether she could or not; I was not paying attention; I might not have heard.

Q. Have you not stated, madam, that Dr. Kirksey could not have gone out of the window that night without your hearing it? *A.* Yes, sir, the doors as I said—the windows are hooked down and the blinds drawn; he could not have gone out without somebody hearing him, because his wife is very easily frightened, and she always has the windows fastened down and hooked in; she never goes to sleep without having it done.

Q. Does she sleep with her door open or closed? *A.* Sometimes open and sometimes shut—the inside door of the room.

Q. How was it that night? *A.* I don't recollect, sir.

Q. Is there an outside door to her room? *A.* No, sir.

Q. Do you know that the windows in Dr. Kirksey's room were fastened down that night? *A.* No, sir, I don't know that night, but they are every night, and I should not see why they should not be that night if they are every night; I did not notice particularly that night.

Q. Is that her habit in summer as well as in winter? *A.* Yes, sir; the windows pull down double from above, and then the green blinds are hooked in; the blinds turn.

Q. You don't undertake to swear that they were fastened that night of your own knowledge? *A.* No, sir, no more than any other night.

Q. Did you notice every door that was open that night? *A.* No, sir.

Q. Can you say whether the windows were shoved up or down in any of the rooms of the house that night? *A.* Don't know, sir; the rooms are all fixed that way at night, because the last thing I do in my children's room—my youngest children—is to do that, on account of robbers and such.

Q. Do you intend to be understood that you fastened down the windows in all the rooms of the house before you went to bed that night? *A.* Yes, sir; if I don't do it myself my little daughter does; that's the last thing done at night—going around to fasten down the windows and doors.

Q. Did you or your little daughter fasten them down in Mrs. Kirksey's room that night? *A.* No, sir, the Doctor always does that himself when he is at home, for his wife will make him do it always before she goes to sleep.

Q. Then you did not intend to say that you or your little daughter fastened down the windows in all the rooms? *A.* She goes round to see all the rooms, and so do I; it is the last thing at night that we go around to see that everything is fastened.

Q. Do you go round on the outside or inside of the house? *A.* Inside; they can all be fastened on the inside, sir; all have hooks.

Q. Do you intend to include Mrs. Kirksey's room in that statement? *A.* Of course; her room is always fastened.

Q. You say you or your little daughter do this each night; which one of you did it that night? *A.* I don't recollect.

Q. Would you swear, madam, that either of you did it that night? *A.* No, sir.

Q. Is Mrs. Moore your daughter? *A.* Yes, sir.

Q. Where is her room located? *A.* Next to Dr. Kirksey's room.

Q. Do you undertake to state that no one of the windows in either of the rooms was opened that night? *A.* No, sir, I think if they had been I should have known it.

Q. How would you have known it? *A.* By the noise they would make, of course.

Q. Would that have made more noise than the opening of Mrs. Kirksey's room door when she called you? *A.* Yes, sir; the windows make a great deal more noise when they are opened; the doors don't make much noise, but the windows make a great deal.

Q. How are the windows hung? *A.* They are hung with weights, sir.

Q. Weights and cord? *A.* Yes, sir.

Q. Is it not very easy then to elevate the lower sash? *A.* I never noticed particularly about that; I never noticed any difference of a lower sash any more than in the other.

Q. Did you sleep any that night? *A.*

Yes, sir, I expect I did; I don't recollect how much though; of course I had to lie down and get up; I don't recollect how much I slept.

Q. Do you recollect how often you were down and up? *A.* No, sir, I don't.

Q. Were you not very much fatigued, waiting upon the child? *A.* Yes, sir, my health is bad anyway.

Q. When you lay down fatigued, having been interrupted in your rest, may you not have slept a little more soundly than usual? *A.* No, sir, I don't in general sleep very sound.

Q. When you have lost sleep, are you not apt to sleep more soundly when you lie down? *A.* Not the same night; I always sleep the next day when I am excited that way—I hardly ever sleep when the children are sick.

Q. Will you swear, ma'am, that the sash could not have been elevated in any one of the rooms of the house that night, when you were asleep, without your having heard it. *A.* No, sir.

Q. Will you swear that it was not elevated in Dr. Kirksey's room? *A.* No, sir.

Q. You stated that Dr. Kirksey was in bed when you went into his room? *A.* Yes, sir.

Q. Why was he not up tending to his sick child? *A.* The child was right by him on the bed; he had been up.

Q. I understand you, that you could not state the time of the night—how late do you believe it was? *A.* It must have been, as well as I recollect, about twelve o'clock at night.

Q. Well, now, madam, what induced you to locate it about twelve o'clock? *A.* Because we were up unusually late that night, and I suppose it to be about that time, sir; we had four sick ones in the house, sir, and I thought so from the chickens crowing shortly after.

Q. What time do your chickens crow at night? *A.* Generally crow about midnight and daylight—same as all other chickens.

Q. Is it a habit with all other chickens to crow at midnight? *A.* I was always taught so from my childhood up, sir.

Q. What is your usual hour of retiring at night? *A.* About ten o'clock, sir.

Q. What time did you retire that night? *A.* I don't recollect in particular; I told you it was unusually late that night; of course it was later than ten, as I repeatedly told you.

Q. Will you pretend to state how long you had slept before you were called by your daughter, after you lay down? *A.* No, sir.

Q. May it not have been as late as two o'clock when you went into the room? *A.* No, sir, I know it was not that late.

Q. May it not have been half after one? *A.* I don't recollect; I can not tell.

Q. Then you will not be positive that it was before half after one? *A.* I ain't positive to the time; I know it was late in the night; it is all that I know about it, as I told you before.

Q. Is Dr. Kirksey a practicing physician? *A.* Yes, sir.

Q. Does he ever attend his patients at night? *A.* Yes, sir.

Q. Is he not county or city physician? *A.* He was.

Q. Was he at that time? *A.* I don't recollect whether he was at that time or not.

Q. Does he not have frequent calls at night from patients? *A.* He has not lately, but he had a great many last year; but not so many this year, because we have not had so much sickness.

Q. Are not calls frequent this year at night? *A.* No, sir, they have not been; I don't know of a single night call the Doctor has had.

Q. This year, do you mean? *A.* This year; yes, sir.

Q. Has his practice greatly fallen off this year? *A.* I don't know; it has been unusually healthy this year.

Q. How long have you had the two severe dogs you testified about? *A.* Well, I don't know; one of them we have had a year or two; we raised them; one is quite young—about a year old, the other about —nearly two years old, as far as I can recollect.

Q. You say they are very severe? *A.* One of them is a very severe dog, sir.

Q. What sort of dog? *A.* Common cur dogs, I guess—large.

Q. Are the people in the neighborhood afraid of them? *A.* Yes, sir; they never come in the yard without a guard, or go out without one.

Q. Were they not in the way of the Doctor's practice? *A.* Well, they generally halloo when they get to the gate, when they come at night, without coming in; the dogs are always in the inside lots; the people always halloo; then we send some one out to them.

Q. Is the inside lots, as you call it, back of the house from the street or road? *A.* There's three inside lots to the house; the house is a very large house and there's three inside lots to it—two front yards, and then there is a back yard, where they keep the dogs; and then at night these gates are all open for the dogs to pass round the house.

Q. Does not the window of Dr. Kirksey's room open into the front yard? *A.* Into one of them, it does; one of the front yards.

Q. Do you pretend to say, if the dogs are in the back yard he could not have got out of the window and left the premises without their barking at him. *A.* He could not have got out without the dogs knowing of it; there could not be a window raised that the dogs did not bark at it, whenever there was a window raised; they always hear the least noise. I notice whenever I raise a window they always generally bark; I suppose when the others do it is the same thing; we keep the dogs right round us, and they are fed from the table, right at the doors, and of course they know everything that is going on.

Q. Do you intend to state that there never is a window raised at night there without their barking at it? *A.* No, sir, I don't pretend to say that; but whenever I raise one they bark, and I suppose it is the same with everybody else.

Q. Might not Dr. Kirksey have raised the window and gone out that night without their barking at him? *A.* I don't think Dr. Kirksey could have got out without the dogs knowing of it; I don't think he could have got the windows up.

Q. Was it not possible that he might? *A.* I don't think so.

Q. Might not the dogs have barked at him if he went out and you not have paid any attention to it? *A.* I can't say.

Q. As they bark so frequently, do you pay special attention every time they do bark? *A.* At night I do, sir, because I am always thinking of some one breaking into the house; I had got up time and again to see what the dogs were barking at.

Q. Do you pretend to say that they never barked at night without your hearing them? *A.* They may bark sometimes that I don't hear them; when I am asleep, may be.

Q. Might not that have been true on that night when you were asleep? *A.* I told you I didn't sleep very much that night.

Q. Did you not tell me you slept some that night? *A.* I say I may have—not sleeping soundly—I may have slept some.

Q. Do you always get up to see what the dogs bark at when they do so? *A.* If I don't get up myself I call some one to see.

Q. Is that rule without exception? *A.* When I hear them barking, and like there was any one about, I most always have some one to see what the dogs are barking at, if I don't get up myself; I think that is sufficient about the dogs.

Q. Will you swear they did not bark at Dr. Kirksey that night? *A.* No, sir.

Q. Are you certain about the time the first arrests were made after Ashburn was killed? *A.* I think it was the evening he was killed that some arrests were made—Mr. Bedell and several others; I don't recollect who now; I recollect Mr. Bedell's name.

Q. May it not have been the second day after he was killed? *A.* I am not certain.

Q. On hearing of Bedell's arrest, why was it you began to think where Dr. Kirksey was that night? Did you suspect him of being implicated? *A.* No, sir, I had not the most distant idea of such a thing.

Q. Then what caused you to reflect about where he was the night of the murder? *A.* Because they were arresting any one and every one.

Q. What do you mean by any one and every one? *A.* Well—just arresting persons—I don't know.

Q. Do you know how many were arrested? *A.* No, sir, I do not.

Q. Do you know of anybody but Bedell? *A.* I know there were others, but I don't recollect their names.

Q. Did you hear how many? *A.* No, I didn't hear how many; I just heard that they were arresting some young men.

Q. Were not the persons arrested in the city? *A.* Yes, sir.

Q. Were they or not the companions of Dr. Kirksey? *A.* I don't know, sir.

Q. How far is your house from the city? *A.* I told you before—a mile and a quarter.

Q. What reason had you to suspect that persons living out a mile and a quarter would be arrested on account of Ashburn's death? *A.* I never thought anything about it.

Q. When was the matter first talked of

in your family as to where the Doctor was on the night of the killing of Ashburn? *A.* After they commenced arresting.

Q. Who first mentioned it? *A.* I don't recollect.

Q. Did Dr. Kirksey say anything about it? *A.* Not that I recollect of.

Q. Was he present when it was talked about? *A.* No, sir, he was not there.

Q. When did he first talk with you and his family on that subject? *A.* I don't recollect, sir, anything about it.

Q. Was it ever spoken of in the family? *A.* About his being arrested?

Q. No, no; about where he was that night? *A.* Only what I said myself when some one was talking about where he was that night; I said for myself I could swear for the Doctor, for he was at home and in bed.

Q. Who were you then conversing with? *A.* With my children.

Q. When was that? *A.* I don't recollect what time it was.

Q. What caused you to think of the necessity of swearing for the Doctor? *A.* Because they were arresting persons.

Q. Did you expect everybody in or about Columbus to be arrested? *A.* Yes, sir, from what I saw, I expected it—women, children and all.

Q. Do you know, madam, that any women and children were arrested? *A.* No, sir; I have heard of such things though.

Q. Did you hear of it in this case? *A.* I think I heard of one woman being arrested.

Q. Who was she? *A.* I don't know, sir; I just heard there was one white woman arrested and sent off.

Q. Did you not hear that she was a woman who was present that night when Ashburn was killed? *A.* No, sir, I didn't know it at the time; I just heard that she was arrested and sent off.

Q. Did you think anything about proving where you was that night? *A.* No, sir, I never thought about it.

Q. Did you expect to be arrested? *A.* I don't know. I laughed about it many a time.

Q. Did you consider it a light matter? *A.* I thought it would be, to arrest women and children.

Q. Was it before or after the arrest of this woman that the conversation occurred in your family, about where the Doctor was that night? *A.* I don't recollect.

Q. Well, give us your best opinion, madam, on that subject. We are entitled to that, I believe. *A.* That is all I recollect—laughing at the idea of arresting women. That is all I know about it.

Q. I regret to press the question, but I must do so—I want your opinion as to whether this conversation took place before or after the arrest of this lady. *A.* I don't recollect anything more than just what I told you. It was just merely a passing thought. I didn't pay no attention at all to it.

Q. Well, but we want your opinion as to whether it was before or after the arrest of the woman. *A.* I don't know, nor don't recollect nothing at all about it.

Q. You will not give an opinion then as to whether it was before or after the arrest of the woman? *A.* I don't recollect anything more about it.

Q. How long after Ashburn's death was the first conversation you had with anybody about where Dr. Kirksey was that night? *A.* I do not recollect, sir.

Q. Was it within a week or after? *A.* I do not know.

Q. Was it a month after? *A.* I cannot tell you anything more than what I have told you. I never remember days, dates, nor months. Whenever I want to know anything of that kind, I always ask somebody about the house.

Q. Then, how can you recollect that the Doctor's child was sick, and that you entered his room on the same night on which Ashburn was killed? *A.* Because, I was up that night, having so many sick ones in the house, and being so anxious, we all sat up. We had four sick ones in the house. I had a little boy with a toothache, which kept me up. My daughter, Mrs. Moore, was very sick, and my niece was very sick, and the baby was very sick. Of course, we all felt sick—the night might have been remembered.

Q. What is there to connect that night of affliction in your family with the death of Ashburn? *A.* Just what I have told you.

Q. How do you know that that night is the same on which Ashburn was killed? *A.* Because I do know it is the same night. I was sitting next morning at breakfast, when the servant came in and told me he was killed. I recollect it all just as well: I do know it was the night.

Q. Did you say anything about the sickness in the family the night before, when the servant told you he was killed? A. No, I didn't say anything at all. The girl was just passing the door, and put her head in, and asked me if I had heard it.

Q. Can you mention any other night when your family was sick? A. Yes, they are very often sick of nights, some one of them. I have a very large family, twelve or fifteen, and there is hardly a week passes that some of them are not sick in some way.

Q. Then, may you not be mistaken, and may it not have been some other member of the family that interrupted your rest on the night Ashburn was killed? A. No, sir, I am not mistaken.

Q. Will you name the next night when any of your family was sick? A. No, sir, they have been sick very often since. I could not name any night in particular.

Q. Will you name any night since that when your family was sick? A. No, sir, I never paid any particular attention to it; they are sick so often.

Q. Can you connect the sickness of your family on any other night, with any other incident that occurred in the city of Columbus? A. No, sir.

Q. Then how can you connect the sickness that night with this particular incident? A. Well, I have already related that to you.

Q. Did you ever think of this until Dr. Kirksey was arrested? A. Well—what I told you about—what I said when they were arresting these persons; of course I told you that.

Q. When was he arrested? A. I don't recollect the day; I know he was arrested twice; he was arrested and put in the court-house; he was put out, and then he was arrested again and brought here; I do not recollect the time.

Q. How long after Ashburn's death before he was arrested and put in the court-house? A. I do not know, sir.

Q. Did you think of the sickness of his family the night of Ashburn's death—when he was first arrested? A. Nothing but what I have already said.

Q. Give me your best opinion as to the length of time after Ashburn's death, before Dr. Kirksey was first arrested? A. I have no idea, sir, of the time; I never paid no particular attention to it at all.

Q. Was it as much as a month? A. I do not know.

Q. Have you no opinion as to the length of time since Dr. Kirksey was last arrested and brought up here? A. Oh, yes, because I knew he was here, and I kept a thinking about him; I think he has been here about five weeks now; I was more interested then and paid more attention to it.

Q. Was he arrested in the day or in the night? A. In the day I think.

Q. Where was he arrested? A. In Columbus.

Q. Do you recollect what occurred in your family the night after his arrest? A. Yes, sir; I recollect having been up most all the night, having something to cook for him, to bring with him, and fixing his clothes, and putting them in his valise, and helping his wife to fix his things.

Q. Was there sickness in the family that night? A. I do not recollect, sir; I do not think there was; his baby has been sick a long time—never has been right well; his wife has been sick; she was sick then and is sick now, and has been sick ever since he has been arrested.

Q. Is she a sickly lady? A. No, sir; she never was sickly until after he was arrested and put in the court-house; she got sick then, going to see him, and has been sick since; she always was healthy, remarkably healthy.

Q. What was he arrested for when he was put in the court-house? A. That is more than he or I knew, I reckon; I don't and he don't himself, I reckon—hardly.

Q. Did you have any idea at the time what he was arrested for? A. No, sir.

Q. Did you think at that time anything about where he was the night Ashburn was killed? A. I do not recollect what I thought then.

Q. Did you have any idea, the last time, what he was arrested for? A. No, sir, I didn't know; there never had been any charges brought against him.

Q. Did you hear from any source the reason of his arrest? A. Persons thought, some perhaps one thing and others another; nobody knew what he was arrested for.

Q. Did you ever hear anybody assign any other reason for his arrest than his connection with the killing of Ashburn? A. I do not know.

Q. Could you name any person who assigned any other reason? A. No, sir, because they didn't know.

Q. Have you ever heard anybody in Columbus say that he was arrested on account of his connection with Ashburn's death, or his *supposed* connection, rather, with Ashburn's death? *A.* I suppose I have heard persons talking, but I do not recollect of their ever saying, but that they didn't know what he was arrested for.

Q. Was the cause of his arrest known in Columbus when you left home? *A.* Of course, because there had been charges preferred against him there.

Q. When was it first known to you and the people of Columbus? *A.* After he was put up here in these cells.

Q. How did it happen that you thought so carefully about where he was the night Ashburn was killed? *A.* Well, I have answered that question.

Q. And, in that connection you say you didn't know what he was arrested for, do you? *A.* No, sir, we didn't know what charges were preferred against him until after they were brought up here.

Re-examined—Questions by Defense.

Q. Mrs. Sheppard, you say you didn't know what Dr. Kirksey was arrested for. Did you not ask his counsel what he was arrested for, and they told you that the Government refused to give any charges against him until recently? *A.* Yes, sir.

Q. Have you known, until these charges were preferred, whether Dr. Kirksey was imprisoned as a witness or a criminal. *A.* No, sir.

Q. Have you not known in your own family—among the family servants—of persons being arrested as witnesses? *A.* Yes.

Q. What became of some of these parties after they were arrested? *A.* They run away.

Q. For what reason? *A.* Because they had been frightened.

Q. Has there been any other incidents occurring in Columbus since the first of January last that created as much excitement as the killing of Ashburn; if so, state it? *A.* No, sir.

Q. You stated, in your direct examination, that having heard of Ashburn's death the morning after the sickness of your family, impressed the occurrences of that night upon your mind; do you still say so? *A.* Yes, sir.

Q. You have been asked to state several other nights—particular nights in which members of your family was sick, or the occurrences of particular nights, and have failed to state but one night, and that was the night of the arrest of your son-in-law; why do you remember particularly the occurrences of the night that the Doctor was arrested? *A.* I have stated that before.

Q. State whether Dr. Kirksey lived at your house from the 1st of January to the 1st of March, and, if not, where did he live? *A.* He stayed the first two months, I think, at the "Cook House," from the 1st of January.

Q. Where is the "Cook House?" *A.* In Columbus.

Q. Then where did you live during that time? *A.* I lived in Winton, near Columbus.

Q. Would you have been apt to have known from Winton whether Dr. Kirksey was called up at nights when he was living at the Cook Hotel. *A.* No, sir.

Q. During the month of March do you recollect any one night in which he was called up? *A.* No, sir.

Q. Is you husband very deaf? *A.* Yes, sir, very deaf.

Q. Did you have your house particularly fastened from apprehension of robbers or any other cause? *A.* From robbers breaking into the house.

Q. Had it ever been broken into; were there many robbers in your neighborhood? *A.* Yes, sir, it has been broken in all around the neighborhood, except on our lot, on account of our severe dogs; the neighbor's places have been broken into.

Q. You say that your husband is very deaf; did that or not cause you to be more watchful at nights? *A.* Yes, sir.

Q. How long has he been so deaf? *A.* He has been so all his life, but it is a great deal worse now. He has been very deaf the last two or three years.

Re-cross-examined—Questions by the Judge Advocate.

Q. Who are your immediate neighbors? *A.* Mr. Bowers, Mr. Biggers, Mr. Thweet, Mr. Dancer, Mr. Markham, and Mr. Brown, these are the nearest neighbors we have.

Q. Have the houses of all these persons been broken into by robbers? *A.* Yes, sir, every one of those houses but one that I can recollect of in that neighborhood, have been broken into.

Q. Which one forms the exception. *A.* Mr. Markham's.

Q. Within what time have they all been

broken into. *A.* Well, they have been broken into several times; I think it is nearly two months since they were all robbed.

Q. Was it all on one night? *A.* The last robbery was all on one night.

Q. Was not that robbery a noted thing there? *A.* Yes, sir, there was a great many talking about it next morning.

Q. Did you hear of it the next morning? *A.* I heard the servants talking about it.

Q. Do you recollect what occurred in your family that night? *A.* No, sir.

Q. Recollect whether anybody was sick that night? *A.* No, sir.

Q. You stated, in answer to a question propounded by Col. Moses, that some servants about your premises, who had been arrested as witnesses, had run away; who were they? *A.* At least they didn't run away; they were frightened off the lot; they were frightened by the Yankees, sir; they came up there and arrested all of them the day the Doctor left, and then some four or five of them left because they told them what they were going to do with them.

Q. Was that the same day the Doctor was arrested? *A.* The day they started up here with the Doctor.

Q. Have you seen any of those servants since? *A.* Yes, sir, I have seen one of them since; the rest didn't come back.

Q. Do you know where they went to? *A.* No, sir; I know where a family went; they went to the foot of the hill and settled there; I found that out afterwards; I didn't know it at the time.

Q. Do you know whether Dr. Kirksey had any conversation with them about leaving before he left? *A.* No, sir.

Q. When Dr. Kirksey was last arrested did you not suspect that it was on account of some alleged connection with the Ashburn murder? *A.* I could not tell what he was arrested for.

Q. Did you not suspect it? *A.* I thought perhaps it might; I don't know what I thought about it at all at the time; I hardly knew what I thought about it.

Q. Please answer the direct question; did you not suspect it? *A.* I told you I didn't know at the time; I don't know what I thought about it; I don't recollect.

Questions by the Court.

Q. How many windows were there in Dr. Kirksey's room? *A.* Four windows.

Q. Does either of these windows open on the piazza? *A.* Two of them do.

Q. How high are they from the ground or from the floor of the piazza? *A.* They are right down on the floor; the two side windows open right down on the floor.

Q. How high are the others from the ground? *A.* I don't know; about like those out there, I reckon (pointing to one of the windows in the Court room); I can't tell exactly; I suppose not more than five feet from the ground.

Q. Do the neighbors you have mentioned own and keep dogs? *A.* One of them does—I think they all do; I think they have all got dogs—little dogs, these little poodle dogs; one of them has five of them.

Q. Do they usually bark at the approach of persons at night? *A.* What dogs?

Q. The neighbors' dogs. *A.* I have heard them a barking over the way.

Q. Did you hear the dogs bark at all the night of the killing of Ashburn? *A.* I don't recollect at all about that.

Q. Had you been into Dr. Kirksey's room that night before his wife called you to see the child? *A.* I don't recollect; I don't think I was; I don't think I had been in the room until I went there to see the child at her call.

Q. What time was it when you saw him last, before you saw him in bed with the sick child? *A.* Well, he was at supper the last I recollect of seeing him. I next saw him in bed; I am generally passing about and attending to my business from supper time until bed time.

Q. How far is your house from the Perry House, Columbus? *A.* Well, I don't know; it is a mile and a quarter to the Court-house and I don't know what is the difference between that and the Perry House.

Q. Has Mrs. Kirksey ever, before the night in question, called you to her room at night? *A.* Yes, sir; many and many a time?

Q. Did you see Dr. Kirksey at any time between supper time and the time you saw him in bed with the sick child? *A.* He was in Mrs. Moore's room at the time between supper time and bed time; I didn't see him, but he was in there.

Q. The question is, did you see Dr. Kirksey at any time between supper time and the time you saw him in bed with the sick child? *A.* I didn't see him, but he was in there; he was in the room there reading; he nurses Mrs. Moore and gives her all her medicine; every time he comes into the house he goes to see her.

Q. Was he dressed in night clothes, when you saw him in bed? *A.* Yes, sir.

Questions by the Judge Advocate by permission of the Court.

Q. How do you know that he was in Mrs. Moore's room at the time spoken of? *A.* Well, I know that he was in there.

Q. Well, but I ask you, how you know it? *A.* Well, just hearing them talking in there, I know by that that he was in there. I knew his voice.

Q. Did you hear the chickens crowing at the time you were in the room where the sick child was? *A.* It was when I was with the little boy.

Questions by the Court.

Q. Do you positively know that Dr. Kirksey was there all the time? *A.* Yes, sir.

Q. Do you know what time Dr. Kirksey went to bed? *A.* I don't know exactly when he went to bed; I was not in his room, and of course I don't know when he went to bed.

Q. Do you know when Dr. Kirksey left Mrs. Moore's room that night, and retired to his own room? *A.* No, sir, I knew he was in the house.

Questions by the Judge Advocate by permission of the Court.

Q. I understand you to state, in answer to the first cross-examination, that your chickens usually crowed at midnight, and that you heard them crow when you went into Dr. Kirksey's room. Did I understand you correctly? *A.* Well, no, I don't think that was it. I said when I went into Dr. Kirksey's room, I heard the chickens crow afterward.

Q. Did you not state that your chickens usually crowed at midnight? *A.* I stated I had been taught from my childhood, that they crowed at midnight and daylight.

Q. Then, was not that before midnight, if they crowed afterwards? *A.* I said I was in his room late at night, and saw him in bed. I didn't say what time. I judged it was about that time, from hearing the chickens crow—about midnight.

Q. How long after you came out of his room before you heard the chickens crow? *A.* Well, I don't recollect what time.

The Commission then adjourned until to-morrow morning at ten o'clock.

McPherson Barracks, Atlanta, Ga., }
10 o'clock a. m., July 8, 1868. }

The Commission met pursuant to adjournment.

Present, same members as yesterday, the Judge Advocate and his assistants, the prisoners on trial, and their counsel.

The record of yesterday's proceedings was read and approved.

The witness, Mrs. Edward Sheppard, who was examined before this Commission yesterday on behalf of the defense, on hearing her testimony read over by the Judge Advocate in open Court, desired to make the following correction with regard to the question given on the 20th line of the 49th page of this day's record, which was, "Do you positively know that Dr. Kirksey was there all the time?" to which the witness yesterday gave for answer, "Yes, sir." She now desires to correct as follows: "It is my firm belief that he was in the house all that night."

Mr. Marshall, one of the reporters to the Commission, having resigned, Charles K. Maddox was then duly sworn by the Judge Advocate as additional phonographic reporter to the Commission.

Questions by the Defense.

Miss Woodville Sheppard, a witness for the defense, having been duly sworn, testified as follows:

Q. What is your name? *A.* Woodie Sheppard.

Q. What is your age. *A.* Seventeen.

Q. How long have you known Dr. Kirksey, and what relation is he to you? *A.* I have known Dr. Kirksey four or five years—I don't exactly know; he is my brother-in-law.

Q. Do you see Dr. Kirksey in the court-house now? If so, point him out. *A.* I see Dr. Kirksey. (Witness points to Dr. Kirksey, one of the accused.)

Q. Do you live with your mother in Winton? *A.* I live with my mother in Winton.

Q. What distance is the house you live in from Columbus? *A.* It is considered a mile and a half from town.

Q. Do you recollect the day of the month, or day of the week, that Ashburn was killed upon—*night* of the day of the month or day of the week? *A.* I do not recollect that.

Q. Do you know where Dr. Kirksey was—the accused—on the night of the murder of Ashburn? *A.* I know where Dr. Kirksey was.

Q. Where was he? *A.* He was at my mother's home, in Winton.

Q. How long after Ashburn was murdered did you hear of it? *A.* We heard it the next day.

Q. Did you hear it in the morning, or in the afternoon? *A.* I heard it in the afternoon.

Q. When you heard it, what did you say in connection with it? *A.* I heard that they had—the Yankees had—arrested Mr. Bedell, supposing him to be connected with it.

Q. Did you hear whether or not they were expecting to make other arrests? *A.* They were making promiscuous arrests, and I did not know whom they might arrest next.

Q. Do you remember whether, at that time, you made any remark in reference to Dr. Kirksey? *A.* Yes, sir. We were trying to locate the different members of our family, to see where they were on that night, as they were arresting everybody.

Q. Do you mean to say that they were arresting everybody, or that there was an apprehension that they were going to arrest everybody? *A.* I mean that the apprehension was very great of their arresting everybody.

Q. Was that apprehension that they would arrest everybody, whatever might be their politics, or was it confined to a particular party? *A.* It was confined to a particular party, because they supposed them to be Democrats—leaders of the Democratic party.

Q. You don't mean to say, or do you mean to say, that that was the reason, or that was what the people thought? *A.* That was what the people thought to be the reason.

Q. When you tried to locate the members of your family the night before, were you able to locate Dr. Kirksey? *A.* I was able to locate Dr. Kirksey.

Q. Be particular in stating from what circumstances you were and are now able to locate Dr. Kirksey. *A.* Dr. Kirksey came home that evening after dark—a little after dark; we eat supper between eight and nine o'clock—our usual hour; Dr. Kirksey stayed in my room—my sister's room, Mrs. Moore's room—perhaps more than an hour after eating supper; he then went to his room; I went up into Dr. Kirksey's room afterwards—a little while afterwards—and stayed up there nearly two hours, talking to him; I then came down into my room and retired; and some time after midnight I was sent to his room to get some medicine for my sister, Mrs. Moore, who was sick; I knocked at Dr. Kirksey's door; he asked me what I wanted; I told him I wanted medicine for my sister; he got up, struck a match and got the medicine, brought it to the door and put it into my hand.

Q. Please state what you did with that medicine and whom it was for. *A.* I carried the medicine back and gave it to my sister, Mrs. Moore; it was for her.

Q. Where is your room situated as to Dr. Kirksey's room—how far from it? *A.* My room is the third room from his.

Q. Whose room adjoins his? *A.* My sister's, Mrs. Moore's.

Q. Was that the room you went into with the morphine? *A.* It was Mrs. Moore's room.

Q. Did you remain in that room any time, or did you go to bed immediately as you carried the medicine? *A.* I remained in the room; did not go to bed immediately.

Q. Can you form an idea of how long you remained in the room with your sister? *A.* It was more than an hour.

Q. When you were in Dr. Kirksey's room, in the early part of the night, did your mother come into the room or not during the time that you were there? *A.* I don't remember.

Q. Was Dr. Kirksey up at that time, when you were in his room—sitting up? *A.* He was lying on his bed.

Q. Had he retired or was he lying on top of the bed? *A.* He had retired.

Q. What induced you particularly that night to go to his room after he had retired? *A.* It is a usual thing for me to go to his room every night after he retires.

Q. For what purpose? *A.* Just merely to be with him and get the news of the day he generally brings at night; he brings them out.

Q. Where was Mrs. Kirksey when you were in the room with the Doctor that night? *A.* She was in her room—Dr. Kirksey's room.

Q. Have they any children? *A.* She has one child.

Q. Was the child at home that night? *A.* The child was at home.

Q. Where was it? *A.* In its mother's room.

Q. Do you recollect whether Mrs. Kirksey and the child, or either of them, were asleep when you were in the room talking to Dr. Kirksey? *A.* I don't recollect.

Q. Do you remember whether Mrs. Kirksey had gone to bed? *A.* I don't remember.

Q. Is your house or not fastened up at night? *A.* Our house is fastened up at night.

Q. Who attends to the fastenings of the house? *A.* I attend to the fastening of the house.

Q. How are the windows and doors fastened? *A.* The doors are fastened with bars; the windows are fastened with catches.

Q. Do you look into that thing—the fastening of the house—invariably, or only occasionally? *A.* I look into it every night.

Q. How are the windows fastened? *A.* They are fastened with catches.

Q. Do either of the windows in Dr. Kirksey's room open on a piazza? *A.* He has two windows that open on a piazza.

Q. How high is the bottom of the window from the piazza floor? *A.* I suppose it is two or three inches.

Q. Do they open down to the floor? *A.* Nearly to the floor.

Q. If those window blinds were not fastened on the inside would there be any difficulty in a person entering that room from the outside? *A.* No, there would be no difficulty in entering it.

Q. Would you consider your house safe from robbers if those window blinds were left open at night? *A.* We have some very bad dogs, and of course noise would be made if any one would attempt to come in.

Q. Why do you fasten the house up? *A.* We think it more secure to fasten the house.

Q. How long have you been in the habit of keeping the house fastened in that way? *A.* I can not remember the number of years.

Q. Is it a number of years? *A.* Yes, sir.

Q. Does any one sleep in the room with you—as a general habit, I mean? *A.* Yes, sir.

Q. Who does? *A.* At the time my cousin was sleeping with me.

Q. Does any one sleep in the room with Mrs. Moore? *A.* Yes, sir.

Q. Who does? *A.* Miss Wynne.

Q. Do your rooms open into each other? *A.* They do.

Q. Would you or not, be afraid to sleep by yourself at night? *A.* I would be afraid.

Q. Have all your sisters been in the habit of having some one sleep in the room with them? *A.* My sisters have all been in the habit of having some one sleep in the room with them.

Q. Does any one sleep with Mrs. Kirksey when the Doctor's out at night? *A.* I sleep with Mrs. Kirksey when the Doctor is out at night.

Q. Have you ever known Dr. Kirksey to sleep out at night and no one to be in the room with Mrs. Kirksey? *A.* No; she always calls me to her room when the Doctor's out at night.

Q. Why is this? *A.* Because she is naturally timid—afraid—does not like to be alone.

Q. From your knowledge of your sister's character and habits, do you believe it possible that Dr. Kirksey could have gone out that night, and that she would not have called somebody to the room? *A.* From my knowledge of her character, I believe that she would have called some one to the room.

Q. Could Dr. Kirksey have got up out of his bed and left that room, in which his wife was that night, without her knowledge? *A.* He could not have done it.

Q. Why do you say that he could not have done it? *A.* Because he generally awakes his wife when he leaves, and would have made a noise at leaving.

Q. In making that noise at leaving, would it have caused the dogs to have done anything? *A.* It would have caused the dogs to bark.

Q. Does not Dr. Kirksey know these dogs well enough to have quieted them immediately? *A.* Dr. Kirksey knows the dogs, but could not have quieted them.

Q. Are they so very severe? *A.* They are very severe.

Q. How do people manage to come there and call him up at night, when they want medical attendance? *A.* They call at the gate.

Q. How far's the gate from the house? *A.* I suppose it is about fifty yards.

Q. Then they must have called very loud, do they not? *A.* They have to call very loud.

Q. Does that cause much barking of the dogs? *A.* Yes; the dogs bark at them.

Q. Does it make noise enough to disturb the different members of the family, at night, when these calls are made? *A.* It does make noise enough.

Q. Have you ever known these dogs to run off persons who were coming there to visit at night, even before bed time? *A.* I have known them to run them off.

Q. When you speak of these dogs being severe dogs, do you mean that they are ordinarily severe, or remarkably severe? *A.* I mean that they are considered very severe.

Q. From your knowledge of the dogs, and the situation of Dr. Kirksey's room, would it have been possible for him to have gone out that night without awakening his wife? *A.* It would not have been possible for him to have gone out that night without awakening his wife.

Q. Do you say it was the invariable habit of Mrs. Kirksey to call you or some other member of the family to sleep with her when he went out? *A.* I say she always did it.

Q. You say that Mrs. Moore was sick that night—were any other members of the family sick that night? If so, state who. *A.* There were three other members of the family sick that night—my brother, Edward Sheppard, Dr. Kirksey's baby, and Miss Wynne.

Q. Were you or not attending upon these persons? *A.* I was attending upon Mrs. Moore.

Q. Were you up most of the night, or in bed most of the night? *A.* I was up most of the night.

Q. Do you think it possible that any one could have left the house that night without your knowledge? *A.* I am certain that no one could have left the house without my knowledge.

Q. Are you very much impressed with the solemnity of an oath? *A.* I consider an oath very binding—very solemn.

Q. Under the solemnity of your oath, are you willing to swear that Dr. Kirksey was in his house that night? *A.* Under the solemnity of my oath, I am willing to swear that Dr. Kirksey was in my mother's house that night.

Q. Have you read your mother's testimony, given on yesterday? *A.* I read the first part. The cross-examination did not come out in the evening. Major Moses came to see me last night, after tea, and advised me not to read the latter part of it.

Q. Did not Major Moses advise you not to read any part of it, and did not you reply that you had already read a part of it? *A.* Major Moses advised me not to read any of it. I told him I had already read a portion of it. Then he advised me not to read the rest of it—the cross-examination.

Q. Did Major Moses converse with you upon the subject of testimony last night, and ask you what you could prove? *A.* Major Moses did converse with me, and ask me what I could prove.

Q. Did you or not state to him what you knew of the case? *A.* I told him what I knew of it.

Q. Did he ask you or not, not to converse with the rest of the family, in regard to what you could prove? *A.* I think he told me not—I don't remember.

Q. Do you remember your younger brother coming up while he was conversing with you, and my sending him away? *A.* Yes, sir, I remember that.

Q. Do you recollect how long after the murder of Ashburn it was that Dr. Kirksey was arrested the first time—when he was carried to the Court-house? *A.* I think it was a few days afterwards, I don't recollect exactly.

Q. You remember who was arrested at the same time? *A.* I remember some of the parties—Mr. Chipley, Mr. William Bedell, and I think Mr. Barber.

Q. Any others you remember? *A.* I don't remember any others.

Q. Do you recollect whether Mr. Tom. Grimes was among the parties arrested at that time? *A.* I think he was.

Q. Do you recollect whether Mr. Columbus Bedell was also arrested at that time? *A.* I don't remember.

Q. Do you remember whether Tom. Grimes was running for any office at that time—candidate for anything—or before that time? *A.* I think he was running for some office.

Q. Do you recollect what it was? *A.* No, I don't recollect.

Q. Do you remember what party he was running a candidate of—whether it was the Radical or Democratic? *A.* The Democratic, of course.

Q. Do you recollect whether Mr. Chipley was a leader of either party in Columbus? *A.* I recollect that he was.

Q. Which party? *A.* A leader of the Democratic party.

Q. You remember whether Mr. Barber was a Democratic candidate for anything? *A.* Yes, sir. I think he was.

Q. Do you remember what it was? *A.* I don't remember.

Q. Do you recollect now, when Dr. Kirksey was arrested at the Court-house, what you thought he was arrested for, or did you have any idea what he was arrested for? *A.* Yes, sir; I had an idea, and I remember what I thought he was arrested for.

Q. What was it? *A.* I thought it was because he was such a strong Democrat.

Q. When did you first learn that he was arrested in consequence of some connection with the Ashburn murder? *A.* It was not long before this trial that I learned that—heard that.

Q. When you first learned that he was arrested for connection with the Ashburn murder, did you or not feel perfectly satisfied that you could establish his innocence?

The above question was then objected to by the Judge Advocate and withdrawn by the defense. In the mean time the witness answered: "Yes; I felt perfectly easy that I could establish his innocence."

Cross-examined—Questions by the Judge Advocate.

Q. I understood you to say that you regard an oath as a very solemn thing, and very binding; does not that depend somewhat upon the authority by which it is administered? *A.* I consider an oath under all circumstances binding.

Q. Do you consider an oath binding upon your conscience if administered by a person who has no legal right to administer an oath? *A.* Yes; if I have taken an oath, of course I consider it binding.

Q. Do you consider that you have taken an oath unless administered by some one having a legal right to administer it? *A.* I consider that I have taken an oath to-day.

Q. Answer my question, please. *A.* That is the answer I wish to give.

Q. I will repeat the question to you. Do you consider that you are taking an oath unless it be administered by some one who has a legal right to administer it?

The counsel for defense objected. The Judge Advocate asked permission to withdraw the question. A member of the Court objected to the withdrawal. The Court then retired, and after due deliberation returned to the Court room and the Judge Advocate announced the decision of the Court, which was that the Judge Advocate had leave to withdraw the question. The Judge Advocate then withdrew the question.

Q. I understood you to say, in your direct examination, that the Yankees were making arrests the next day after Ashburn was killed; are you certain it was that day? *A.* I am certain that it was the next day.

Q. Are you certain that the Yankees made any arrests before the Monday following the night he was killed? *A.* I think they made other arrests.

Q. I asked you whether you are certain that the Yankees made any arrests before the Monday following the night on which Ashburn was killed; you probably didn't understand my question. *A.* I understand your question: I said I think they made other arrests.

Q. What do you mean by "other" arrests, when I ask you about "any" arrests? *A.* I mean because they had arrested one the day afterward; but there were other gentlemen whom they arrested after that; I was thinking of them.

Q. May you not be mistaken about the Yankees having arrested any one the day after he was killed? *A.* I don't think I am mistaken.

Q. Were not the arrests, made the day after he was killed, made by the civil authorities, and not by the "Yankees?" *A.* I think the Yankees made the arrests.

Q. Why do you think so? *A.* Because these gentlemen that they arrested were Democrats, and the Yankees were very much opposed to them, and I supposed it was they that made the arrests.

Q. Have you no other reasons for saying the Yankees made the arrests except that the parties arrested were Democrats? *A.* The parties arrested were belonging to the Democratic Club, and I supposed that they were arrested on that account.

Q. Did you understand that the arrests were made because they belonged to the

Democratic Club or because they were charged with the murder of Ashburn? *A.* Because they were strong leaders of the Democratic Club.

Q. Is it the habit to arrest persons in Columbus simply because they are Democrats, or belong to the Democratic Club? *A.* The Democrats were strong and were very popular, and these men wished to put them down.

Q. Who do you mean by "these men?" *A.* I mean the Radicals—the Yankees.

Q. As the Democrats are very popular there, it is not regarded as a crime for which they arrest persons, is it, that they belong to the Democratic party? *A.* We have thought these arrests were made because they were strong Democrats.

Q. Did you not understand at the same time that they were arrested because they were charged with the murder of Ashburn? *A.* I understood no such thing.

Q. Then you believe they were arrested simply because they were Democrats, did you? *A.* I believe they were arrested because they belonged to the Democratic Club—leaders of the Democratic Club, all of them.

Q. Does Dr. Kirksey belong to the Democratic Club? *A.* Dr. Kirksey belongs to the Democratic Club.

Q. Do you know whether the club is in the habit of holding its meetings at night, and whether he attended. *A.* The club was not in the habit of holding its meetings at night. Dr. Kirksey never attended any Democratic meetings at night.

Q. Do you know when it did hold its meetings, and how often? *A.* I don't know.

Q. Then how do you know that they did not hold them at night? *A.* I know that Dr. Kirksey did not attend them at night.

Q. I understood you to state in a former answer, that they did not hold their meetings at night; do you intend to be so understood? *A.* I intend to say that Dr. Kirksey did not attend them at night.

Q. Did he attend the meetings of the Democratic Club in the day time? *A.* He did attend them in the day time.

Q. At what time in the day were they held? *A.* I don't know.

Q. Where were they held? *A.* I don't know.

Q. Then how do you know that he attended them? *A.* I have heard him say that he attended Democratic meetings in the day time.

Q. Then when you swore that he did attend them, you did not swear it of your own knowledge, did you? *A.* Yes, I swore of my own knowledge.

Q. Do you now swear that you know of your own knowledge that he did attend them? *A.* I swear of my own knowledge that I know he did attend them.

Q. Did you ever see him at one? *A.* I never saw him at one.

Q. Then how can you swear of your own knowledge that he was there? *A.* Because I have heard others say that he was there attending a Democratic meeting.

Q. When you hear other people make statements, can you swear to the truth of those statements from your own knowledge? *A.* If I know the people well, and know what they say to be true, I can swear to what they say to be true.

Q. Is not that swearing from the confidence you have in others and not from your own knowledge? *A.* It is swearing from my own knowledge of the character of others.

Q. But can you swear to the facts of your own knowledge simply from your knowledge of the character of other persons. *A.* If I know a person to be truthful I can swear to what they say to be true.

Q. And swear it of your own knowledge? *A.* I can swear it to be true.

Q. Answer my question, please. (Question repeated.) *A.* I can swear to it from my knowledge of the truthfulness of others.

Q. Do you now swear of your own knowledge that Dr. Kirksey did attend these Democratic meetings? *A.* I know the Democrats held their meetings in the day, and I know Dr. Kirksey was a strong leader of the Democratic Club, and I know then that he attended them.

Counsel for the defense here submitted a document, of which the following is a copy:

"The counsel for the defense ask the court to explain to the witness the difference between swearing to a fact as from her own knowledge and of swearing to a fact on the knowledge of others, because she has confidence in the truth of their statements.

"We desire her to know that nothing is of her own knowledge which she learns from others, never mind how truthful those statements may be; it is then *belief*, not knowledge.

"With this explanation the witness can answer truthfully and understandingly."

The court retired, and, after due deliberation, again entered the court-room, when the witness was requested to withdraw for a few moments, which having been complied with by the witness, the Judge Advocate read the document aloud, and stated that he was directed by the Commission to instruct the witness according to the request of the counsel for the defense.

The witness was then placed again on the stand, and the Judge Advocate explained to her the substance of the request made by the counsel for defense.

The examination was then resumed:

Q. After the instructions which you have received from the court, do you now swear of your own knowledge that Dr. Kirksey did attend those Democratic meetings. *A.* Dr. Kirksey was a strong leader of the Democratic Club, and of course he attended their meetings.

The Judge Advocate again explained to the witness the difference between swearing to a fact of her own knowledge and of swearing to a fact on knowledge derived from others. The question was then repeated as follows:

Q. After the instructions which you have just received from the court, do you now swear of your own knowledge that Dr. Kirksey did attend those Democratic meetings? *A.* No, I do not swear to it of my own knowledge, but I know him to be a strong Democrat, and therefore he attended their meetings.

Q. Do you intend to state that you never suspected when the first arrests were made that they were in any way connected with the death of Ashburn? *A.* I intend to state that I thought the arrests were made because they were strong Democrats; I thought there was no other reason for the arrest.

Q. Were any arrests made of persons prior to the death of Ashburn because they were Democrats? *A.* I do not remember.

Q. Had you heard of any? *A.* I think I had heard of some one.

Q. How long before Ashburn's death? *A.* I do not remember.

Q. Who were they? *A.* I do not remember.

Q. Who told you of their arrest? *A.* I heard of them; I do not know who told me.

Q. Do you know where you were when you heard of it? *A.* I do not remember.

Q. Do you know that it was on account of their being Democrats? *A.* I think it was on account of their being Democrats.

Q. How many persons had you heard were arrested on account of their being Democrats before the death of Ashburn? *A.* I do not remember.

Q. Are you at all confident that you had heard that any persons had been arrested on that account before his death? *A.* Yes; I think I had heard of it.

Q. But you can not state the place, nor time, nor the names of the persons who were arrested, nor of those who arrested them? *A.* I can not state.

Q. Soon after Ashburn's death did you hear of anybody but Democrats being arrested? *A.* I never heard of anybody but Democrats being arrested.

Q. Then what do you mean in your answer to the direct question when you spoke of promiscuous arrests? *A.* Other Democrats—all of them; the town is filled with Democrats; arresting them all; ladies and children—they thought even ladies and children were not safe; no one knew.

Q. Were all the Democrats in town arrested? *A.* The leaders of the Democrats were.

Q. By promiscuous arrests, then, you mean simply the leaders of a particular party? *A.* When they made these arrests of course we did not know for what reason they were arrested, and did not know who else they might arrest.

Q. But you spoke of promiscuous arrests having been made; by that do you mean simply the leaders of a particular party? *A.* I mean that they might arrest any of the Democrats.

Q. But you spoke of what *had been* done? *A.* Because they arrested some, and we did not know for what reason, except that they were Democrats, and as they arrested *them* we did not know but that others of the Democrats might be arrested; we didn't know that even ladies and children were safe.

Q. Is that what you mean by "promiscuous arrests"? *A.* Yes; I mean arrests of ladies and children—any of them.

Q. When you say they had made promiscuous arrests, do you mean that ladies and children had been arrested? *A.* I think we had heard of some lady being arrested and sent off.

Q. Was that immediately after Ashburn's death? A. I do not remember when it was; I think it was afterwards.

Q. Who was the lady? A. I don't know her at all.

Q. Was not that arrest a month or two after Ashburn's death? A. I do not think it was.

Q. Where did you hear she was sent to? A. I did not hear the name of the place.

? Was she sent out of Columbus? A. Q. I think she was.

Q. Was that as much as a week after the death of Ashburn? A. I said it was some time afterwards.

Q. I want your opinion as to definite time. A. I can give no definite reply as to time.

Q. When did you first suspect that Dr. Kirksey had been arrested on account of alleged connection with the death of Ashburn? A. I did not hear that Dr. Kirksey was arrested for the murder of Ashburn until this trial; I never suspected that he was arrested for the murder of Ashburn—never once.

Q. Until when? A. I heard of this trial, here at this trial.

Q. Did you never hear before the trial commenced that that was the cause of the arrest of the Doctor? A. I never heard the cause of his arrest—knew no reason.

Q. Did you not suspect the reason when he was arrested the second time? A. No; I never suspected such a thing.

Q. I mean, did you not suspect when he was arrested the second time that he was arrested on account of alleged connection with the Ashburn murder? A. No; I never suspected such a thing.

Q. What did you suspect was the reason for the second arrest? A. I could assign no reason for it.

Q. Did you suppose that it was on account of his connection with the Democratic party? A. No reason was assigned for his first arrest, therefore I could assign none for his second; I supposed it was from that cause.

Q. Then you never suspected that he was arrested, or likely to be arrested, on account of alleged connection with the Ashburn murder, until about the time this trial commenced, did you? A. I never suspected of his being arrested on account of the murder of Ashburn; not once—I heard of it at the time of this trial.

Q. Were you not apprehensive prior to that time, that he might be arrested on account of his alleged connection with that murder? A. No; I apprehended no such thing.

Q. Were you not apprehensive that he might be accused of connection with it? A. I was apprehensive of no such accusation.

Q. Then how was it that you charged your mind so carefully with the facts that show that he was at home on the night of the murder? A. Because they commenced the arrests, and we did not know who might be arrested—not that we thought the accusation would fall upon him, but we just went locating and finding where he was that night.

Q. When did you first undertake to locate him? A. After the first arrest was made, and before this arrest was made, we discussed the matter.

Q. Well, if you believed he was arrested the first time on account of being a Democrat, and not for any alleged connection with the Ashburn murder, why did you undertake to locate him on the night of the murder? A. Because they had arrested one without any reason, and we didn't know but that they might make other arrests.

Q. Did you not state that that first one was arrested on account of his connection with the Democratic party, and not on account of his connection with the murder of Ashburn? A. Yes, sir, on account of his connection with the Democratic Club.

Q. And without any reference to the murder of Ashburn? A. Without any reference to the murder of Ashburn.

Q. Then why locate the place of Dr. Kirksey on the night Ashburn was killed? A. Because they had made arrests of this one Democrat, and we didn't know but what they might arrest others.

Q. For what? A. We didn't assign any reason for the arrest. They had made one arrest without any reason, and we thought it proper to discuss the matter.

Q. Then why did you connect the discussion with the night of Ashburn's death? A. Because they had made these arrests after the death of Ashburn—they had arrested one Democrat, and we didn't know but what they might arrest others following this murder, and of course we discussed the matter.

Q. Why did you connect the arrest of that Democrat with Ashburn's death? *A.* I did not connect it with Ashburn's death. I said that they arrested him after Ashburn's death, and we could assign no reason whatever for it.

Q. Did you not understand that he was arrested on account of Ashburn's death? *A.* I did not.

Q. You say you did not understand that, but still you connect the discussion as to the whereabouts of Dr. Kirksey with the night of Ashburn's murder—why? *A.* Because they made this one arrest without any reason, and we didn't know but that they might make others.

Q. How do you know that they arrested that one without any reason? *A.* Because I heard they could assign no reason for the arrest.

Q. Then it was not a matter of personal knowledge on your part, was it? *A.* The matter was inquired into to find why the arrest was made, and no reason could be assigned.

Q. Do you refer now to the first or last of these? *A.* I refer to all the arrests.

Q. And you never suspected that any of the arrests were made on account of Ashburn's murder, till about the time this trial commenced? *A.* I never suspected at all that it was on account of the murder of Ashburn; I heard the time of the trial that it was on this account. I never suspected once that it was on account of the murder of Ashburn.

Q. Without any suspicion of that, then, you had already located Dr. Kirksey at home on the night of the killing of Ashburn? *A.* I located him because they had made arrests, and didn't know but what they might make others; without any reason for making one, they might make others.

Q. How many younger sisters have you than yourself? *A.* I am the youngest.

Q. What members of the family were in your mother's house the night that Ashburn was killed? *A.* All the family, and two cousins I had staying with me at the time.

Q. Will you name each person who was in the house that night? *A.* My father, mother, Mrs. Moore, Mrs. Kirksey, Mrs. Kirksey's child, my three brothers, myself, and two cousins.

Q. Was there not a servant girl sleeping in the house that night? *A.* There was a servant girl sleeping in Dr. Kirksey's room.

Q. How old is she? *A.* I suppose about fourteen.

Q. What time of the night did you retire to bed—I mean when you first went to bed? *A.* I suppose it was somewhere near twelve o'clock when I left Dr. Kirksey's room—about there.

Q. What is the usual time for the family to retire? *A.* I don't know the time for the family to retire. I retire later than the rest of them. I am the last member of the family to retire.

Q. Which retired first that night—you or your mother? *A.* I think my mother retired first.

Q. How long before you did? *A.* I don't know.

Q. I understood you to state in your direct examination that you always fastened the doors and windows at night; do you do that every night? *A.* I do it every night.

Q. Does not some other person in the family sometimes attend to it? *A.* My sister, fearing that I may neglect some of it, she goes round; my sister, Mrs. Moore.

Q. Is that so every night? *A.* Yes, that is generally the case.

Q. Then you go round first and close the doors and windows and your sister follows round to see that you have done it well? *A.* Yes.

Q. Does not some other member of the family sometimes close the doors and windows at nights? *A.* It has always been a habit with me to close the doors and windows at night; I do it.

Q. Does not some other member of your family do it some nights? *A.* They may look over it to see that it is well done; I do it.

Q. Do you intend to state then that no one else in the family closes them some nights? *A.* I intend to state that I never neglect it; I go round every night.

Q. Do you sometimes find that other members of the family have closed them before you get there? *A.* I always close them myself.

Q. Do you not sometimes find them closed when you get to them? *A.* No; I always close them myself.

Q. Doesn't your mother close them part of the time? *A.* I attend to the closing of the house myself.

Q. Do you swear that your mother does not divide that duty with you—she sometimes closing them and you sometimes? *A.* I swear that I punctually attend to the closing of the house.

Q. And that your mother never does it? *A.* Mother never does it; I attend to it myself.

Q. If I did not misunderstand you, you stated that you went into Dr. Kirksey's room every night to get the news of the day from him? *A.* It has been a custom with me ever since Dr. Kirksey has been in our family to go and talk with him at night.

Q. How long does it usually take him to detail the news of the day to you? *A.* He does not confine himself to news of the day; he talks to me perhaps two or three hours.

Q. You stated that you were the last member of the family in the habit of retiring; do you spend the last hours before your retirement each night in Dr. Kirksey's room? *A.* I sit in Dr. Kirksey's room every night before retiring.

Q. What time do you usually leave his room at night? *A.* Generally after eleven o'clock.

Q. What time does your mother generally retire? *A.* I don't know.

Q. Have you not a time-piece in the house. *A.* No; the clock is out of order.

Q. Then all you have stated about the time of night is mere guess, is it not? *A.* Well, I guess from what I know to be our usual hours when we had the clock running.

Q. What time did you eat supper that night. *A.* We generally eat supper between eight and nine o'clock.

Q. What time did you eat supper that night? *A.* We generally eat supper between eight and nine o'clock.

Q. What time did you eat supper that night? *A.* There would be no difference between that night and others; we eat supper between eight and nine o'clock.

Q. Do you think it was nearer to eight than nine o'clock. *A.* I can not say.

Q. Are you certain it was between these hours? *A.* I think it was between these hours.

Q. How long after supper was it before Dr. Kirksey went into Mrs. Moore's room? *A.* Directly after eating his supper he went into Mrs. Moore's room.

Q. Did you go in with him? *A.* I went with him.

Q. Did you stay all the time that he stayed there? *A.* I stayed in there all the time that he was in there.

Q. What time of the night did he leave that room? *A.* He stayed in the room perhaps more than an hour.

Q. Give your opinion as to the time of night when he left the room. *A.* I can not state definitely as to the time of night, as we had no time, but I said it was more than an hour.

Q. I asked for your opinion as to the time of night he left the room. *A.* I can not give any opinion as to the time of night, because we had no time; but I said more than an hour.

Q. How long after he left that room before you went into his room? *A.* I went in a little while afterward.

Q. The length of time, as near as you can recollect? *A.* I went in directly afterward.

Q. As much as ten minutes afterward? *A.* Ten or fifteen minutes—about ten minutes afterward.

Q. What time was it, in your opinion, when you left his room? *A.* It was near 12 o'clock when I left his room, or about 12.

Q. As you had no time-piece, how are you able to give an opinion in that case, when you could give none as to the time he left Mrs. Moore's room? *A.* I stayed in his room about two hours; it was about midnight when I left his room; it was late in the night, and I supposed it was 12 o'clock.

Q. You stated that you could give no opinion as to the time he left Mrs. Moore's room because you had no time-piece; how, then, did you arrive at the conclusion, when you had stayed two hours, that it was 12 o'clock when you left Dr. Kirksey's room? *A.* I was not definite as to the time; I said I supposed it was 12 o'clock.

Q. Where did you go from Dr. Kirksey's room? *A.* I went into Mrs. Moore's room.

Q. Where did you next go? *A.* I left Dr. Kirksey's room and then went to Mrs. Moore's room; then went to my own room and retired.

Q. How long did you stay in Mrs. Moore's room, after you left Dr. Kirksey's room, before you retired? *A.* A very little while.

Q. When you reached your own room, how long before you went to sleep? *A.* I don't know.

Q. Your best recollection is all I ask

for. *A.* I don't know how long it was before I went to sleep.

Q. I didn't ask you for your knowledge; I asked you for your opinion. *A.* I don't suppose I went to sleep directly after retiring.

Q. Would you say as much as a quarter of an hour? *A.* I can't say as to what time I went to sleep.

Q. Could it have been as much as half an hour? *A.* I can't say.

Q. Was it as much as an hour? *A.* I don't suppose it was an hour.

Q. After you went to sleep were you up any more that night? *A.* I was up again that night.

Q. How long do you think you slept before you got up? *A.* I had retired perhaps more than two hours when I was woke again and sent to Dr. Kirksey's room.

Q. Who woke you? *A.* Mrs. Moore, my sister.

Q. How long did you stay in Dr. Kirksey's room that time? *A.* I went to his door and knocked, asking for some medicine; he answered me, got up and got the medicine, and put it into my hand.

Q. Where did you then go? *A.* I went back into Mrs. Moore's room.

Q. How long did you stay there? *A.* I stayed there a good while; Mrs. Moore was sick and I was waiting on her.

Q. As much as an hour, do you suppose? *A.* I suppose it was more than an hour.

Q. Where did you then go? *A.* I went back to my own room.

Q. Did you retire to bed again? *A.* I retired, but didn't go to sleep.

Q. Do you sleep soundly, or are you easily awaked? *A.* I am easily awaked.

Q. Are you not much more easily waked of a night when you have been disturbed of your rest than of an ordinary night? *A.* I am easily waked; I am always easily waked.

Q. Do you not believe you would be more easily waked of a night that you have been disturbed of your rest than when there is no disturbance? *A.* I believe I could be woke up any time, for the least noise will wake me any night.

Q. Did Mrs. Moore call you when she wished to get the medicine? *A.* Yes, she called me.

Q. Did you hear any other call that night? *A.* I don't remember.

Q. Did you hear any person in the house call for any other person that night? *A.* I don't remember that I heard any other.

Q. As you are very wakeful, could there have been a call from a person in one room to a person in another, across the passage, without you having heard it? *A.* No, there could not have been. I don't think there could; there could not have been any call without my having heard it.

Q. Are you prepared then to state that there was no such call? *A.* I said I didn't remember anything about any call.

Q. As you remember everything else that took place so distinctly, is it not probable that you would remember that if it had occurred? *A.* I remember everything with regard to myself that was connected with the affair.

Q. Is it not most probable, that you would have heard a call of that sort, if it had been made? *A.* Probably I would have heard it.

Q. Then is it not your opinion that none such was made? *A.* I don't remember anything about it.

Q. Did you hear any one of the doors open that night? *A.* I don't remember that I did.

Q. Did you hear Dr. Kirksey's door open after you retired that night? *A.* Yes, I heard Dr. Kirksey's door open after I had got back into Mrs. Moore's room, a second time, by my brother, who went up after me.

Q. What is your brother's name. *A.* Edward Sheppard.

Q. Am I to understand you that he went up after you when you went there? *A.* After I had made my second visit up there, he went afterwards.

Q. He went after that time? *A.* After that time. I was in Mrs. Moore's after he came back.

Q. Did you see him? *A.* I saw him; Mrs. Moore's door was open.

Q. Didn't you hear Dr. Kirksey's door or window open at any other time during the night? *A.* No, I don't remember hearing Dr. Kirksey's door or window open at any other time during the night.

Q. May not his door or window have been opened at any other time during that night, and you not have noticed it? *A.* His windows could not have been opened without my noticing it. The door, too, makes a noise, and, of course, we would have noticed that.

Q. Do you intend to state then, that Dr. Kirksey's door or window was not opened that night, except the time when your brother went in? *A.* I say, that if Dr. Kirksey's door had been opened, they would have made noise, and of course we would have known it.

Q. May it not have been opened without you hearing it? *A.* The windows?

Q. Or door? *A.* No, the door would make a noise, and would have attracted attention, and the windows could not have been opened without attracting attention.

Q. Might he not have opened the door of his room, and come out, without attracting your attention? *A.* He could not have opened his door and come out, without attracting some attention. I could have heard his door opened.

Q. Can't a person walk through the hall then at night, without waking you? *A.* A person can't walk through the hall without waking me. The slightest noise wakes me.

Q. Are you prepared to state then, positively, that neither Dr. Kirksey, nor anybody else, opened his window or door that night, except the times when you and your brother went to the room? *A.* I am prepared to state, that if anybody had attempted to open the doors or windows, it would have attracted the attention of the family and my attention.

Q. Didn't somebody else open it within your knowledge that night? *A.* Do you mean after I left?

Q. Yes. *A.* My brother opened it after I had left the room—my brother Edward. I said he went there after some medicine.

Q. By somebody else, I mean somebody other than yourself, or your brother? *A.* I don't remember anything about that.

Q. Did you hear Mrs. Kirksey call anybody that night? *A.* Mrs. Kirksey called my mother.

Q. Didn't she open the door when she called? *A.* Yes, I suppose she did. I don't remember.

Q. If she opened the door, did you not hear it? *A.* Yes, I could have heard the door, if she opened it. I don't remember about it.

Q. Will you state positively, that Dr. Kirksey did not open his door or window and come out of his room that night while you were asleep? *A.* I can state that positively.

Q. What time of the night did your mother come into Mrs. Kirksey's room. *A.* I don't remember.

Q. Was it before or after you retired to bed? *A.* She went in before my second visit.

Q. Was your second visit before or after you retired to bed? *A.* My second visit was after I retired to bed.

Q. Did you not leave your room door open when you went to bed? *A.* My room door was open, it opened into Mrs. Moore's room.

Q. Did you not leave the door that opened from your room into the passage open when you went to bed? *A.* I don't remember whether that was closed or not, but we always leave the door between our two rooms open.

Q. Did you see your mother when she went into Mrs. Kirksey's room? *A.* I saw my mother before I went up into Dr. Kirksey's room the second time; I went into her room to get advice about going after the medicine.

Q. I repeat my question, did you see your mother when she went into Dr. Kirksey's room? *A.* No, I don't remember whether I saw her. I don't think I saw her.

Q. How do you know she went there? *A.* I saw her after she came down from Dr. Kirksey's room; she was in her room.

Q. You didn't see her in Dr. Kirksey's room; then how do know she was there? *A.* She had not retired, she had just come down from Dr. Kirksey's room.

Q. You state that you saw her in her own room; how do know she had come from Dr. Kirksey's room? *A.* Because she said she had been up there.

Q. Then what you swear about it is hearsay, and not knowledge, is it not? *A.* I know my mother had been up into Dr. Kirksey's room; what I swear to is what I know.

Q. Can you swear that you know she had been there when you did not see her there? *A.* If she was up at that time, I supposed she had been into Dr. Kirksey's room, and she told me so. She had not retired.

Q. As you had retired, how can you state that she had not retired? *A.* She had not retired when I went into her room to get advice about the medicine.

Q. I believe you said in substance that that was about 2 o'clock in the morning; do you now state that she had not retired until about 2 o'clock in the morning? *A.* I said it was some time after midnight that I went up to the door of Dr. Kirksey's room the second time; I did not state any definite time.

Q. Do you know what time your mother did retire that night? *A.* I don't know.

Q. Then how do you know that she had not retired before she went into Dr. Kirksey's room? *A.* I say that she had been up, I mean that she had not retired—had not got to 'sleep at that time—I didn't mean that she had not gone to bed, but she was up.

Q. Were you in your mother's room that night after you first went into Dr. Kirksey's room? *A.* I said that I went into Mrs. Moore's room after leaving Dr. Kirksey's room.

Q. I will thank you to answer my question. Were you in your mother's room that night after you first went to Dr. Kirksey's room? *A.* After my first visit to Dr. Kirksey's room, I came back to Mrs. Moore's room, from that to my room, and then retired.

Q. Were you in your mother's room at any time that night after you first went into Dr. Kirksey's room? *A.* I could not have been in mother's room, if I went directly to Mrs. Moore's and from there into my own room.

Q. If you were not in your mother's room, how do you know what time she did retire? *A.* I said I didn't know what time mother retired.

Q. Then how do you know she hadn't retired before she went into Dr. Kirksey's room? *A.* I said I didn't know whether she had retired or not, but at that time she had not retired.

Q. Was it not after you first went into Dr. Kirksey's room that you went into your mother's room to get advice about the medicine? *A.* I went into my sister's room after leaving Dr. Kirksey's the first time.

Q. After the first time that you went to Dr. Kirksey's room, did you not go into your mother's room that night to get advice about medicine for your sister? *A.* I went into my sister's room and then to my own room and then retired; then I was waked up by my sister to get medicine, and then I went to my mother's room to get advice.

Q. Did you not state awhile ago that, after coming out of Dr. Kirksey's room, you went into your own and then retired, and then you were not in your mother's room any more that night? *A.* I stated that I went from Dr. Kirksey's room to Mrs. Moore's, from Mrs. Moore's to my own room, and that I was afterwards waked and went to my mother to get advice about the medicine.

Q. What time of night was it that you went to your mother's room to get advice about the medicine? *A.* I said I could give no definite time; I suppose it was sometime after midnight; I can't state.

Q. How long did your mother stay in Dr. Kirksey's room? *A.* I don't know.

Q. What is your opinion? *A.* I can give no opinion in regard to it; I was not up there with her.

Q. Did you hear her when she came back from there? *A.* I don't remember whether I heard her or not.

Q. Did you hear her when she went in? *A.* I don't remember.

Q. If you can't remember that, how can you remember so distinctly that Dr. Kirksey did not go out that night? *A.* I said, that no noise could have been made without attracting attention; I may have heard my mother and did not remember it.

Q. If your mother might have made a noise, and you not remember hearing it, might not Dr. Kirksey have made a noise and you not have heard it? *A.* If Dr. Kirksey had attempted to go out of the windows it would have attracted the attention of the dogs.

Q. I asked you if your mother might have made a noise and you not remember hearing it, might not Dr. Kirksey have made a noise and you not have heard it. *A.* I could have heard any noise; I said mother may have made a noise, but I don't remember now about it; if Dr. Kirksey made a noise I would have heard it.

Q. As your mother may have made a noise and you not remember it, may not Dr. Kirksey also have made a noise and you not remember it? *A.* He might have made a noise and I not remember it, but I would have heard it.

Q. Was there anything to attract your attention more particularly to a noise made by Dr. Kirksey that night, than to a noise made by any other member of the family? *A.* No; I say I could have heard a noise made by any of them.

Q. In what lot do your dogs stay? *A.* No particular lot; they are around the house at all times of the night.

Q. Where are they in the day time? *A.* They stay in the yard in the day time.

Q. Which yard? *A.* We don't confine them to any yard.

Q. Do you not confine them in the day time to the back lot? *A.* We don't confine them; we don't tie the dogs.

Q. Do you not confine them to the back lot in the day time, by keeping the gates closed? *A.* The gates are closed, but the dogs could jump the fence.

Q. Are the gates open at night? *A.* I don't remember that they are open any more at night than they are in the day; they may be left ajar; I don't know.

Q. Do you allow these severe dogs to remain in the front yard while your visitors approach in the day time? *A.* We allow them to stay about in the day time.

Q. Have they ever injured any visitor? *A.* Yes, they have gotten after persons and run them from the house.

Q. Will you name such persons? *A.* Well, there were two persons visiting at the house, that came to see me, Mr. Bond and Mr. Cooper.

Q. When was that? *A.* I don't remember when it was; it was one night they came to see me.

Q. About how long ago? *A.* I can't remember the time.

Q. Was it this year? *A.* Yes, it was this year.

Q. Was it before or after Ashburn was killed? *A.* I think it was afterwards, but don't remember.

Q. Did the dogs injure either of them? *A.* No, but took after them.

Q. Did he ever run after anybody else? *A.* Yes, he runs after the negroes, or anybody else who comes to the house; the dog takes after them when he is about.

Q. Does not Dr. Kirksey tease the dogs sometimes? *A.* Yes.

Q. Do they ever try to bite him? *A.* They jump at him when he kicks his feet and cuts at them.

Q. Did they ever try to bite him? *A.* I don't remember.

Q. How long has Dr. Kirksey been living in your mother's house? *A.* Since his marriage. He boarded at the hotel awhile, and came back to our house to live with us—he has lived there mostly all the time; he was in business in Pensacola awhile.

Q. How long did he live at the hotel? *A.* I don't remember; I suppose two or three months.

Q. When was that? *A.* If I remember right, it was last fall—not last fall—along in November or December, I think—no, I remember it was after Christmas that Dr. Kirksey—I can't remember exactly in regard to it. I don't remember when he was there.

Q. Was it last year or this year? *A.* I think he moved there in December, and stayed there, probably two months; I don't exactly know about that.

Q. Does not Dr. Kirksey practice medicine? *A.* Dr. Kirksey practices medicine.

Q. And is he not county or city physician? *A.* He was at one time county physician.

Q. Does he have a great many calls? *A.* Yes.

Q. Does he practice at night when called? *A.* Yes.

Q. Are not these dogs in the way of persons coming after him, when he is wanted by patients? *A.* They are in the way; they call at the gate for Dr. Kirksey—those who come for him do—they can not come into the yard.

Q. Was not his night practice better last fall than it has been this spring? *A.* I don't remember that it was.

Q. Has he had many calls at night this spring? *A.* I don't remember that he has.

Q. Can you remember any calls that he had at night this spring? *A.* I can.

Q. Can you remember more than three? *A.* I can't remember the number, but I can remember calls that he has had.

Q. Can you recollect as many as three? *A.* I don't know how many he has had; I don't recollect.

Q. Are you sure he has had any night calls since he moved back from the hotel to your mother's house? *A.* Yes, he has night calls.

Q. Can you recollect more than three calls that he has had at night since he left the hotel, and came to your mother's house? *A.* I can't recollect how many he has had.

Q. Can you recollect a single one? *A.* Yes, I can. I have been up in his room when he was called.

Q. How often? *A.* I don't remember.

Q. Who came to his room after him when you were there? *A.* We would hear some one call at the gate for him, and some one would go out to see who it was; some member of the family, perhaps.

Q. Did that occur more than once? *A.* Yes, it occurred more than once.

Q. Did it occur more than twice? *A.* I can't say how many times it occurred.

Q. Did the Doctor go when he was called? *A.* He went when he was called.

Q. Did you hear the dogs bark the night that Ashburn was killed? *A.* I don't remember hearing the dogs bark that particular night; they generally bark at night.

Q. Were they not back in the servant's lot that night? *A.* I don't remember where they were that night; as I said before, they go all round the house at night.

Q. Might they not have barked and you not notice it? *A.* They attract the attention of us all when they bark; when one barks, all of them bark.

Q. Did they attract the attention of all that night? *A.* I don't remember that they did.

Q. Do not the dogs bark at many little things about the house at night, such as raising the window, or anything of that sort? *A.* The raising of the window would attract the attention of the dogs.

Q. Does not the opening of a door attract their attention? *A.* The opening of the outside door would have attracted their attention—yes.

Q. Do not the dogs invariably bark at night when a window is raised? *A.* They do.

Q. Was any window raised in any part of the house that night? *A.* I don't remember that there was.

Q. May it not have been so and you not remember it? *A.* If a window had been raised—a window was never raised in that house without attracting my attention, because they make noise when they are raised.

Q. May it not have attracted your attention and you not now remember it? *A.* If a window were raised it would have attracted the attention of the dogs. I don't remember that any window was raised that night; I don't remember hearing the dogs bark any more that night than they generally do.

Q. May not this have occurred and you not now remember it? *A.* I think I could remember the raising of a window more distinctly than I could the opening of a door, because the window would make more noise than the door; I think I could remember it better than I could the opening of a door.

Q. May you not have heard it at the time, and it attracted your attention, and not now recollect it? *Q.* I don't remember that any windows were raised that night.

Q. Please answer my question; may you not have heard it at the time and it attract your attention and not now recollect it? *A.* I don't recollect it; I said the dogs would have made considerable noise, and of course that would have made me recollect it if a window had been raised, more than the opening of a door.

Q. May not a door or window have been opened and the dogs barked that night and you now not recollect it? *A.* I think I would have recollected it if any window had been raised that night.

Q. Why do you think you would have recollected it that night any sooner than any other night? *A.* Well, any other night I think I would have recollected a window being raised, because the dogs make considerable noise when it is done.

Q. Will you please tell me what nights in the month of March windows were raised in your house? *A.* I don't remember; we frequently raised them and pulled them down again.

Q. I understand you to say if one had been raised that night you would have recollected it; why could you not have recollected if one had been raised any other night? *A.* I say when windows are raised I can hear it distinctly, because they make more noise than the door.

Q. But do you recollect any other night in the month of March when windows were raised? *A.* Yes, I recollect nights.

Q. Do you recollect whether there was a window raised on the night of the 20th of March in your house? *A.* No, I don't recollect.

Q. Do you recollect whether there was any raised on the night of the 25th of March? *A.* I said I didn't know; I don't recollect that there was any raised that particular night.

Q. Do you recollect whether there was any on the night of the 26th? *A.* No, I don't.

Q. Any on the night of the 27th? *A.* No, I don't recollect; I can't recollect exactly the time, but I know whenever the windows are raised we know it, for we speak of it next day.

Q. Any windows raised on the night of

the 28th of March and spoken of next day? *A.* I don't remember.

Q. Any on the 29th of March and spoken of next day? *A.* I don't remember.

Q. Any on the night of the 31st of March and spoken of next day? *A.* I don't remember.

Q. Was there any raised on the night of the 30th of March and spoken of next day? *A.* I don't remember that there was any raised on the night of the 30th of March.

Questions by Brown.

Q. Can you mention any night in March when the dogs did not bark—from recollection? *A.* No; the dogs generally bark at night; it is a usual thing for them to bark at night.

Q. Do they bark every night? *A.* Yes, sir; as a general thing they bark at night.

Q. Did they bark on the night Ashburn was killed? *A.* I don't remember that they barked any more that night than they generally do.

Q. Do you remember that they barked at all that night? *A.* No, I don't remember that they did.

Q. You would not state they did not bark, would you? *A.* No, but I would state that they did not bark any more than they generally do, because if they had done so, it would have attracted attention.

Q. Did they bark as much as they generally do? *A.* Yes, I suppose they barked just as much as they generally do.

Q. Do you state from your recollection that they barked at all? *A.* I recollect that the dogs bark nearly every night.

Q. Do you recollect whether they barked that night? *A.* I hear them barking nearly every night, and I supposed they barked that night; I don't recollect.

Q. When the Doctor's patients called at the gate, who usually quieted the dogs? *A.* I don't know who quieted the dogs; I didn't go out into the yard to see who quieted the dogs.

Q. Anybody there who could quiet them? *A.* Yes, some of the family could quiet them.

Q. Can any member of the family do it? *A.* Yes, some member of the family can quiet them.

Q. Can't each member of the family do it? *A.* I don't know; I never saw them try.

Q. Can Dr. Kirksey do it? *A.* They generally bark a great deal when Dr. Kirksey comes near, because he has always been in the habit of teasing them; I never saw him quiet them; I never heard of him quieting them down, because they always bark when he is near, because he has always been in the habit of teasing them.

Q. Have you conversed with your mother about her testimony here, since she was sworn yesterday? *A.* I have not conversed with my mother.

Q. Have you heard her converse with others about this thing? *A.* I have not heard her converse with others.

Q. Do you stay at the same place where she stays? *A.* Yes, I stay with her.

Q. Have you been with her much since yesterday? *A.* No, I have not been with her much; I have been out most of the time; I was out all yesterday evening, and with my mother and a gentleman out last night; I was not alone with my mother—have not been with her alone.

Q. Did you say you have not heard her speak of her testimony? *A.* I have not heard her speak of it; she would not speak of it.

Q. Has anybody else spoken to you about her testimony? *A.* No one has spoken to me about her testimony.

Q. Did you not state that a Col. Moses spoke to you about it? *A.* I said Colonel Moses advised me not to read the examination; when he came he asked me if I had read it; I told him I had read the first part of it; he advised me not to read the latter part of it—the cross-examination; I did not read it; it didn't come out.

Q. Did Col. Moses tell you anything that your mother had sworn? *A.* No, he did not tell me anything my mother had sworn.

Q. Did anybody else tell you anything she had sworn? *A.* No, I have not heard anything that my mother swore.

Q. Did you hear her evidence read over this morning here? *A.* I did not hear her evidence read over here.

Q. When did you and your mother first converse about testimony you would give in this case? *A.* I don't remember; I conversed with Mr. Moses about the proof I could give; I don't remember any conversation with my mother about it.

Q. When was that? *A.* It was a few days ago that I had a conversation with Col. Moses.

Q. Did you never converse with any

one else about it? A. Yes, I had stated to them that I could prove Dr. Kirksey's innocence.

Q. To whom did you state that? A. I don't know; I don't remember to whom I had stated it; I may have said so to my mother or some of them; I don't remember.

Q. Can you name no person? A. No; I may have said to my mother that I could have proved it.

Q. How long after Ashburn's death before you and your mother first talked about it? A. This subject was discussed; we did not know, after they had made the first arrest, who would be arrested, and we commenced the discussion of the subject in order to locate the different members of our family on the night of Ashburn's death.

Q. Did you then say you could prove his innocence? A. I say we were trying to locate where the different members of our family were that night; we did not know what the reason of the arrest was, and we merely discussed among ourselves as to where they were located; we knew nothing about—had no suspicion—of their being arrested for the murder of Ashburn, but merely for the purpose of locating the different members of our family, as they were making arrests at the time.

Q. When did you first say you could prove his innocence? A. I said I could prove his innocence when I heard of the trial here and that he had been arrested for the murder of Ashburn.

Q. Did you never say so before that time? A. I knew nothing before that time as to what he was arrested for.

Q. Had you ever thought about the necessity of proving his innocence? A. I never had thought of the necessity of proving his innocence before—never suspected his being arrested for the murder of Ashburn.

Q. You have stated that you understood the first arrests were made on account of the persons arrested being Democrats. Is that the reason you thought it necessary to recollect the facts and prove his innocence? A. We did not know why any of the arrests were made; we merely discussed the matter; we wanted to know where the different members of our family were located that night; we did not know why the arrests were made.

Q. If you believe that the arrests were made because the persons were Democrats, why did you locate Dr. Kirksey that night rather than on the night before? A. Because they had commenced making arrests and we did not know who might be arrested; any of the family might be arrested.

Q. Were they arresting them for being Democrats on any particular night? A. We supposed that they were arrested for being Democrats; we could assign no other reason for their arrest.

Q. Was it for being Democrats on the night of the 30th of March, rather than the 29th of March? A. The arrests were made after the 30th of March, and of course we thought of that night.

Q. Had the Democrats done anything that night that was peculiar that they hadn't done on any other night? A. No; the Democrats had done nothing; we knew not why the arrests were made, and merely located the different members of our family in regard to that night after the arrests were being made the next day.

Q. Did you think the arrests were made on account of their being Democrats on that particular night? A. I didn't know why the arrests were made.

Q. Did you apprehend that Dr. Kirksey would be accused of getting up and going out after he had gone to bed on that particular night? A. I did not know what they might accuse him of, and we merely wanted to locate him.

Q. Why did you want to locate him on that particular night, rather than any other night? A. Because they had commenced making arrests the next day after that night.

Q. Did you suppose then that the arrests made next day were for something that occurred that night? A. I did not know why the arrests were made—could assign no reason; we merely wished to locate the different members of our family; we didn't know what accusation was against them.

Q. Did you suppose that the arrests were made that day on account of some occurrence that had taken place the night before? A. We did not know from what occurrence it sprung.

Q. Did you suppose it was spoken of in the family that the arrests made that day were on account of occurrences that had taken place the previous night? A. The arrests were made on the next day after that night, and of course we were discussing what had happened that night in our family.

Q. Did you suppose the arrests made were made on account of anything that did happen that night? *A.* I did not know what it happened from.

Q. Did you suppose or believe it was so? *A.* I have answered that question.

Q. No, you have not; I beg your pardon; did you suppose or believe the arrests made that day were made on account of anything that happened the night before? *A.* I said we did not know why.

Q. I don't ask for your knowledge at all, but for your belief or supposition. *A.* I did not think of their being arrested from anything that happened that night.

Q. Were you at home on the day after Ashburn's death? *A.* Yes, sir, I was at home.

Q. Were you there all day? *A.* Yes, I think I was there all day.

Q. What time did you say you first heard of the death of Ashburn? *A.* I said I heard it in the evening.

Q. Were you with your mother that day? *A.* I don't remember whether I was with my mother any more that day than I generally am.

Q. Whom did you first hear speak of it? *A.* I don't remember; I heard some one; it was after dinner, I think, that the murder of Ashburn—some member of the family, I believe, I heard speak of it.

Q. Where was Dr. Kirksey that day? *A.* I suppose he was attending to his business.

Q. Do you know where he was? *A.* I don't; I can't say positively; he was practicing medicine, and I suppose he was attending to it.

Q. Did you see him that day; *A.* I saw him next morning at his breakfast; I don't remember whether he came next day to his dinner or not; I saw him next night at his supper.

Q. Did you see your mother at breakfast that morning? *A.* My mother generally attends at table when we are all at breakfast.

Q. Did you see her at breakfast that morning? *A.* Yes, sir; I think she—yes, my mother was at breakfast.

Q. Did you hear her or her servant say anything that morning, about breakfast time, about Ashburn being killed? *A.* No, I heard nothing about Ashburn's death that morning.

Q. When did you first hear Dr. Kirksey speak of it? *A.* I heard Dr. Kirksey speak of it—I think it was after supper the next night.

Q. Where was Dr. Kirksey the next night—that is, the night after Ashburn was killed? *A.* He was in my sister's room, Mrs. Moore's room.

Q. All night? *A.* All night? I reckon he retired to his room.

Q. Do you know that he retired to his room that night? *A.* He went from her room—yes; I know that he retired to his room, for I am in the habit of going to Dr. Kirksey's room before retiring.

Q. Were you at his room that night? *A.* I stated that it was a habit for me to go to Dr. Kirksey's room after supper—after we stopped talking in her room to go to his room and talk with him.

Q. Please answer the question; were you there that night? *A.* As I was there other nights, I was there that night; I go to Dr. Kirksey's room every night.

Q. How late did you stay there that night? *A.* I generally sit with him a long while.

Q. I don't ask generally, I say how long that night? *A.* I can give no definite reply as to the time I stayed there; I generally stay there a long while.

Q. Do you recollect what room you went from that night when you went into Dr. Kirksey's room. *A.* I think I went from my sister's room into Dr. Kirksey's room; he generally talks in my sister's room; I think I went from there into his room.

Q. Where did you go from his room that night? *A.* I generally go through her room to go to my room. It is the nearest way into my room.

Q. You say you generally go that way—did you go that way that night? *A.* It is the nearest into my room, and I suppose I went that way that night. The door was open.

Q. Have you no distinct recollection about it? *A.* I have a distinct recollection about going up into his room and talking with him, and going back again.

Q. Have you a distinct recollection that you went back from your sister's room? *A.* No, I have no distinct recollection with regard to my going from my sister's room; but I suppose I went that way. It is the nearest way. I am generally in the habit of going through her room to go into my room.

Q. What time did you retire that night? *A.* I say I am the last member of the family to bed. I usually retire late; always late.

Q. I asked you what time you retired that night? *A.* It may have been after eleven o'clock that I retired, I don't know. I can not give any definite time. I know it was late.

Q. Was there any sickness in the family that night? *A.* I don't remember that there was any sickness in the family that night.

Q. Had the four persons who were sick the night before all recovered that night? *A.* My sister may have been sick; she was sick the next morning. I don't remember her complaining that night. We were not up as much next night as we were that night—not so many sick. I don't suppose there were many sick.

Q. Was Dr. Kirksey's child well that night? *A.* I don't remember whether it was well the next night or not. I only know it was sick the night before. I don't remember whether it was well the next night or not.

Q. Were the other two members of the family who were sick the night before, well that night? *A.* My little brother's face was swollen; he had the toothache—sick with the toothache, and he had taken something to ease his tooth. His face was slightly swollen.

Q. Was any member of the family sick the night before Ashburn was killed? *A.* I don't remember that there were any sick the night before he was killed.

Q. Can you mention any other particular night when they were sick? *A.* My sister, Mrs. Moore, is in bad health, and she is frequently sick at night. There were more sick that night, that's the reason I remember it more distinctly.

Q. I must repeat my question. Can you remember any other particular night, when any particular member of the family was sick? *A.* No, I can not remember any particular night.

Re-examined by Moses for Defense.

Q. Can you state what was the matter with Mrs. Moore that night particularly, that required her to have medicine? *A.* No, I can not state. She was nervous. She had a sick headache, or something of that kind, and she wanted some morphine. I went to the Doctor's room to get it.

Q. What was the matter with your brother that night? *A.* Edward?

Q. Yes, Edward. *A.* Had the toothache.

Q. Recollect what was the matter with Dr. Kirksey's baby that night—what particular disease it was? *A.* No, sir, I don't recollect what was the matter.

Q. Do you remember what was the matter with your cousin? *A.* No, I don't remember with her. I suppose she had a headache, or something of tha tkind.

Q. It was nothing permanent, was it— any permanent sickness? *A.* No, sir.

Q. Does Dr. Kirksey have his office, that he does his business in in the day time, in Columbus, or at his house? *A.* Dr. Kirksey's office is in Columbus.

Q. You have spoken of some calls that Dr. Kirksey had at night, in the spring of this year; do you remember whether they were before or after Ashburn's murder? *A.* He may have had some before and some afterwards; I don't recollect these calls at night.

Q. Do you recollect the names of any of the parties that he was calledto see at night? *A.* No; frequently he is called out to a plantation to see some of the negroes; I don't know whom he was called to see.

Q. Is Dr. Kirksey at home much in the day time? *A.* He takes breakfast there, and sometimes comes home to his dinner—sometimes he doesn't; he comes home to his supper.

Q. Does Dr. Kirksey see much of the dogs in the day time? *A.* Dr. Kirksey generally teases the dogs when he comes home in the day time.

Q. You stated in the cross-examination, that you did not remember the dogs barking more the night of Ashburn's death-than any other night—if any one had attempted to go out of the house that night, or any other night, would they not have barked more than usual? *A.* They would bark a great deal if anybody attempted to go out—make considerable noise—but no more that night than they were accustomed to do.

Q. If any one passes in or out of your house after bed time, do the dogs make such an unusual barking as would attract the attention of the family? *A.* The dogs make an unusual noise; it would attract the attention of the family if anybody passed out.

Q. You have stated repeatedly that you never knew that the reason of your brother-in-law's arrest was because of Ashburn's murder, but that you believed it was because he was a Democrat? *A.* That was my belief—that it was because he was a Democrat.

Q. Do you mean to say that that was the real reason—his being a Democrat—in your opinion? *A.* We thought that was the reason.

Q. Did you not suppose that the Ashburn murder was an excuse for arresting the Democrats? *A.* We did not suppose that they could have accused gentlemen of such an act.

Q. Does any one go round with you at night to carry a light when you go to close down the windows and doors? *A.* Sometimes, when it is late, some one goes round with me, when I am late closing.

Q. Who goes with you? *A.* There is no particular one—sometimes one goes with me; no particular one goes with me.

Q. Do you usually go to breakfast as early as the rest of the family? *A.* I do not go to breakfast as early as the rest of the family; I go there when they are at the table; I don't go as soon as they do.

Q. Your father ever complain of your going to bed too early or too late? *A.* Father complains of my going to bed too late.

Q. You say that the last time you went into your mother's room she had not retired, do you mean that she had not been to bed before, or that she was then up? *A.* I mean that she was up at that time; I did not say that she had not been to bed before.

Re-cross-examined—Questions by Brown.

Q. I believe you stated that the dogs usually bark at a person going out at night? *A.* Yes, I said the dogs make a noise—they bark—the dogs bark.

Q. Is it always regarded so remarkable as to be remembered when they bark at a person going out at night? *A.* Yes, sir, when a noise is made it is always spoken of next day—when the dogs make an unusual noise; they make a noise when any one goes c

Q. How long is it usually remembered in the fam. when the dogs bark at a person going out—would you say as much as a month? *A.* We speak of it the next day; we wish to know if the other members of the family heard it; I don't know how long it is remembered.

Q. Is it regarded so unusual an occurrence that all the members of the family recollect it months afterwards? *A.* When any one goes out the dogs make an unusual noise, and attract the attention of the family, of course we all speak of it afterwards.

Q. Is it remembered by each member of the family months afterward? *A.* I don't remember that we speak of it months afterward.

Q. Can you recollect any other particular night when the dogs barked at persons going out that is remembered and spoken of by the members of the family now? *A.* I can not remember any particular night.

Q. Can you recollect any time that there was an unusual barking of the dogs at night that the family, in discussing the matter next day, could not account for the way the barking occurred? *A.* I can not any particular time, but I know times that they have done it.

Q. Can you recollect any time that there was an unusual barking of the dogs at night that the family could not account for? *A.* Yes, frequently the dogs barked at night and we could not account for it.

Questions by the Court.

Q. Has it been your custom, when arrests previous to the death of Ashburn have been made, to talk it over with the family and become cognizant of the presence or absence of Dr. Kirksey? *A.* I state as before, after the first arrest was made we had discussed to find out among ourselves and locate Dr. Kirksey that night.

Q. Has it been your custom, when arrests previous to the death of Ashburn have been made, to talk it over with the family and become cognizant of the absence or presence of Dr. Kirksey? *A.* Before the murder of Ashburn, has it been our custom to talk over these arrests? They didn't commence arresting—they didn't make any arrests. They made one or two arrests and we had talked over those; before the murder of Ashburn they arrested a woman and we had spoken of that, but I don't suppose we located him on those arrests.

Q. Does it often occur that so many persons in your family are sick the same night? *A.* Yes, sir; it frequently occurs.

Q. When you heard of the death of Ashburn did the incident create much excitement or talk in your family? A. No; it didn't excite any; there was no great excitement; I don't remember any unusual excitement.

The Commission then adjourned until to-morrow morning at ten o'clock.

McPHERSON BARRACKS, ATLANTA, GA., } 10 o'clock A. M., July 9, 1868.

The Commission met pursuant to adjournment.

Present, same members as yesterday, the Judge Advocate and his assistants, the prisoners on trial, and their counsel.

The record of yesterday's proceedings, and the testimony of Miss Woodville Sheppard, up to and including question 248, were read and approved.

Miss Woodville Sheppard, on hearing her testimony read by the Judge Advocate in open Court, desired to make the following corrections: Answer No. 12, add—"I don't mean the Yankees, because some of them are Democrats, but I mean the Radicals." On the 12th line of answer to question No. 19, after the word "retired," add, "I went through Mrs. Moore's room to go into my own room."

Answer to question No. 21, correctly saying—"There are three rooms on the side of the hall, mine is the third room but the second from his." Answer to question 114, add—"By the Yankees I mean the Radicals." Answer to question 197, add, "And Dr. Kirksey." Answer to question No. 205, add—"My mother sometimes goes round to look over it, for fear I may have left something wrong." Answer to question No. 215, add—"Mother goes around sometimes with me, and afterwards, perhaps, to see that it is well done."

A motion was made that the balance of this witness' testimony be read over from the reporter's notes to witness, and that the record be read to the Court when made. The Judge Advocate asked that the Court might retire.

The Commission then retired, and after deliberation, returned to the Court-room, and the Judge Advocate announced that the motion was withdrawn.

The Judge Advocate stated to the Commission that an omission had thus far been made in the record of each day's proceedings, in this, that it did not show the fact that the prisoners on trial and their counsel are present each day. The Judge Advocate asked that the Commission empower

him to insert that fact on each day's record, dating from the convening of the Commission. The permission was granted.

The counsel for defense requested that the record be made up so as to show the names of those counsel who conduct the examination of each witness.

The Commission gave instructions to the Judge Advocate to this effect.

Mr. Davis, one of the phonographers to the Commission, stated that he would be unable before to-morrow morning to have his notes of yesterday's testimony transcribed in full, and stated further, that the taking of further testimony at present, would, therefore, only retard the proceedings of the Commission.

The Commission then adjourned until to-morrow at 10 o'clock A. M.

McPHERSON BARRACKS, ATLANTA, GA. } 10 o'clock A. M. July 10, 1868.

The Commission met pursuant to adjournment.

Present, the same members as yesterday, the Judge Advocate and his assistants, the prisoners on trial and their counsel.

The record of yesterday's proceedings was read and approved.

That portion of the testimony of Miss Woodville Sheppard, comprising questions No. 249 to 503, both inclusive, which the reporters had been unable to transcribe until this morning, was then read aloud by the Judge Advocate in the presence of the witness, who on hearing the same read, desired to make the following corrections: Answer to question No. 344, the witness wishes to correct by saying, "it was either in December or January, I don't recollect exactly." Answer to question No. 418, the witness wishes to add, "I mean the subject of their arrest; I don't mean the subject with regard of proving their innocence, because we didn't know what they were arrested for until this trial."

The Court then put the following questions to the witness:

Questions by the Court.

Q. Has any one suggested to you to make any corrections in any part of your testimony since you were examined? A. No one has suggested to me to make any corrections.

Q. As the corrections made by you refer in several instances to points where your testimony does not fully agree with that of your mother, have not you and your mother conversed about the evidence you gave since you were examined? *A.* My mother has not conversed with me.

Q. Have you conversed with any one about your testimony since it was given? *A.* I have conversed with no one since it was given about it.

Questions for Defense by Major Moses.

Mrs. J. B. MOORE, witness for the defense, having been duly sworn, testified as follows:

Q. What is your name? *A.* Mrs. Moore.

Q. Where do you reside? *A.* Columbus, Georgia.

Q. Do you live in the city of Columbus? *A.* I live in the suburbs—in Winton.

Q. Who lives in the same house with you? *A.* My father, mother, brother-in-law, Dr. Kirksey, my sisters and brothers, and two cousins who are staying with us for a few months.

Q. Do you remember the night on which Ashburn was killed? *A.* I do.

Q. What was the day of the month? *A.* I don't know.

Q. What circumstances do you remember it by? *A.* By several of the family being sick.

Q. Please state the particular occurrences that night that impressed it upon your memory. *A.* That night I was very sick with headache, and the next morning the servant came in and told me that Ashburn was killed.

Q. Was that the only occurrence of that night that tended to impress it upon your memory? *A.* No, there were several others of the family sick beside myself; I was sick and I recollect the servant telling me about it next morning.

Q. What others of the family were sick? *A.* My sister's baby and my cousin and my little brother were sick, and myself.

Q. What was the matter with your little brother? *A.* He had the toothache.

Q. What was the matter with Dr. Kirksey's child? *A.* It was threatened with croup.

Q. Did you send for any medicine that night? *A.* I sent for a dose of morphine.

Q. To whom and by whom? *A.* I sent to Dr. Kirksey by my sister, Woodie Sheppard.

Q. Did you take the medicine? *A.* I did.

Q. Did you sleep any after that time. *A.* I did not.

Q. Did you have any conversation with Dr. Kirksey the next morning as to the medicine he had sent you? *A.* I did not.

Q. Was it morphine? *A.* I thought it was morphine, but heard afterwards it was quinine.

Q. How far is your room from Dr. Kirksey's. *A.* I don't know what distance.

Q. I mean is it the next room or the third room? *A.* It is the next room.

Q. Could you hear noise from one room to the other? *A.* I could, but could not hear what was said.

Q. Did the female members of your family ever sleep alone? *A.* They never did.

Q. If Dr. Kirksey went out at night, did Mrs. Kirksey remain alone? *A.* She never did.

Q. Was it her habit to send for a member of the family, or did she go to their rooms? *A.* It was her habit to send for some member of the family.

Q. Was this occasional or invariable? *A.* It was occasional.

Q. You say that Mrs. Kirksey sent occasionally for some member of the family to sleep with her when Dr. Kirksey was away; then do you mean to say that she sometimes slept by herself when he was away? *A.* I don't mean to say that she slept by herself. I mean that whenever he was absent, she sent for some member of the family to stay with her.

Q. You say you were awake all of that night after taking this medicine; had you been asleep long before you sent for it? *A.* I had not.

Q. What was the matter with you? *A.* A severe headache.

Q. Could any one have gone out of that house that night without your knowledge? *A.* They could not.

Q. Why? *A.* Because I could have heard the noise.

Q. Are you satisfied whether Dr. Kirksey went out of the house that night or not? *A.* I am.

Q. Did he go out? *A.* He did not.

Q. Did he spend any part of the evening in your room? *A.* He did.

Cross-examination—Conducted on behalf of the Prosecution, by Governor Brown.

Q. What time of night did you eat supper that night? A. I don't know what time, sir; we had no time-piece.

Q. What was your usual time to eat supper? A. Between seven and eight o'clock.

Q. Do you recollect whether you took supper that night about the usual time? A. I do not.

Q. Were you at the supper table with the family? A. I was.

Q. Was Dr. Kirksey there? A. He was.

Q. Where did you go from the supper table? A. I went to my room.

Q. Where did Dr. Kirksey go? A. He also went to my room.

Q. How long after supper did he go to your room? A. A few moments after supper.

Q. How long did he remain there? A. I don't know how long.

Q. Please give us your best opinion. A. About an hour or more.

Q. What time of night was it, in your opinion, when he left your room? A. About ten o'clock.

Q. Where did he go from your room? A. He went to his room.

Q. Did you see him any more that night? A. I did not.

Q. How long after he left your room before you went to sleep? A. About a half an hour.

Q. Have you any means of knowing how long you slept? A. I have not.

Q. Where was your sister that night who has been examined here. A. In the room with me.

Q. How long after supper did she go to your room? A. A few moments after supper.

Q. How long did she stay there before she left your room? A. About an hour or more.

Q. Where did she go from your room? A. To Dr. Kirksey's room.

Q. Do you know how long she stayed in Dr. Kirksey's room? A. I do not.

Q. Where did you next see her after she left your room for Dr. Kirksey's room? A. In my own room.

Q. Was that after you had been asleep? A. It was.

Q. Did you call her to the room or did she come without being called? A. I called her.

Q. Where was she when she answered your call? A. She was in the adjoining room.

Q. Doesn't your room join hers and Dr. Kirksey's—one on each side? A. It does.

Q. Which one of the adjoining rooms was she in? A. In the lower room.

Q. Was that her own room or Dr. Kirksey's? A. That was her room.

Q. Do you know when she went from Dr. Kirksey's room to her own room? A. I do not.

Q. Do you know whether she went through your room or not? A. I do not.

Q. Is there a door opening from your room into your sister's room. A. There is.

Q. Is there a door from each of your rooms into the hall or passage. A. There is.

Q. Was your door left open or was it closed that night? A. It was partially open.

Q. Was that its condition when you went to sleep? A. It was.

Q. Do you mean the door into your sister's room or the door into the hall. A. I mean the door into the hall.

Q. Was the door between yours and your sister's room closed when you called your sister? A. It was not.

Q. After your sister went to Dr. Kirksey's room and brought you the medicine, how long did she remain in your room? A. A few minutes, perhaps a half hour.

Q. Where did she then go? A. She went to her room.

Q. Did you see her any more that night? A. I did not.

Q. Where was your mother that night? A. She was in Dr. Kirksey's room the early part of the evening, afterwards she went to her own room.

Q. Do you know what time she left Dr. Kirksey's room and went to her own room? A. I do not.

Q. Do you know whether she was in Dr. Kirksey's room any more that night? A. I do not.

Q. Are you very easy to wake? A. I am.

Q. Could a person walk across the hall in the night without waking you? A. They could not unless they should tread very easily; they could wake me with shoes on.

Q. Could they not have walked across the hall with shoes on without waking you? A. They could not.

Q. Could a person have opened a door or a window in that house that night without waking you? *A.* They could not.

Q. Did you hear any door or window opened in that house that night after you first retired? *A.* I did not.

Q. Do you intend to include an inner door as well as an outer door? *A.* I do.

Q. Could anybody have called another in that house without waking you? *A.* They could not.

Q. Did you hear any such call? *A.* I did not.

Q. Do you know what time of night Dr. Kirksey's child was taken sick? *A.* I do not.

Q. Do you know what time your mother retired to bed that night? *A.* I do not.

Q. Did you hear anything more of your mother that night after you first retired and went to sleep? *A.* I did not.

Q. I believe you stated it was always a habit of your family for some one to sleep with the females of the family; who usually slept with your younger sister—the one who has been examined here? *A.* My cousin was sleeping with her for the last six months.

Q. You also stated, that when Dr. Kirksey was absent at night, some member of the family slept with Mrs. Kirksey. Who usually slept with her in the absence of the Doctor? *A.* My sister, Woodie Sheppard.

Q. Did any other member of the family ever sleep with her in the absence of the Doctor? *A.* I don't recollect.

Q. You stated that Dr. Kirksey couldn't have left the house that night without your knowledge; was it not possible that a window might have been raised and he gone out, while you were asleep, without your knowing it? *A.* It was not.

Q. Will you state the reason why you are able to be so positive, that the Doctor was there on that particular night? *A.* Because, after hearing of the military arrests in Columbus, we were all trying to locate the male members of the family.

Q. Why did you wish to locate them? Did you suspect that any member of your family was to be arrested? *A.* I did not.

Q. Is it a habit in your family always to locate the members of the family the previous night whenever you hear of an arrest the next day? *A.* It is not, because we had never heard of an arrest of this kind being made.

Q. What do you mean by an arrest of "this kind being made"? *A.* I mean arresting the gentlemen of the place.

Q. Did you never before hear of a gentleman being arrested in Columbus? *A.* I don't recollect.

Q. You stated that you did not suspect that any member of your family would be arrested; did you suspect, when Dr. Kirksey was first arrested, what he was arrested for? *A.* I did not; I merely supposed that he was arrested as being a prominent Democrat, and that they wanted to try and implicate him in the murder of Ashburn.

Q. When did you first hear he was accused of any connection with the murder of Ashburn? *A.* I didn't hear of his being accused of any connection with the murder of Ashburn.

Q. Have you never heard that he was accused of any connection with it? *A.* I never did.

Q. Do you not understand that he is now on trial under that accusation? *A.* I do now.

Q. Is to-day the first time you ever so understood it? *A.* No; I supposed after their bringing them up here that the military suspected that he was implicated in the murder—I mean, I supposed that he was suspected by the military of being implicated in the murder.

Q. When did you first suppose he was suspected by the military of being implicated in the murder? *A.* When they brought him here.

Q. Did you never hear that that was the reason of his arrest? *A.* I never did.

Q. What did you hear was the cause of the first arrest? *A.* We heard they didn't know what he was arrested for.

Q. Did you hear of any other arrests about that time? *A.* I did.

Q. Who? *A.* Mr. Bedell, Mr. Chipley, and several others—Mr. Roper, Mr. Grimes—I don't know the names of the others.

Q. What did you understand they were arrested for? *A.* I don't know; I only supposed that, on account of their being Democrats, they were arrested as being implicated in the murder of Ashburn.

Q. When did you first talk the matter over in the family as to the necessity of locating Dr. Kirksey on the night Ashburn was killed? *A.* On the evening of the Doctor's arrest.

Q. Was that the first or the second arrest? *A.* The first arrest.

Q. How long was that after Ashburn was killed? *A.* I don't know.

Q. What was said in the family about it at the time? *A.* My mother said that she could testify that Dr. Kirksey was at home on the night of Ashburn's murder.

Q. Why did she say she would give that testimony? *A.* Because she was in his room off and on during the night.

Q. I believe you stated awhile ago that you didn't hear her in his room after you first went to sleep; am I correct? *A.* I didn't hear her in the room; I could hear the voices, but could not distinguish who they were that were in the room.

Q. I understood you to say that you didn't hear any one call after you went to sleep and that you didn't know where your mother was after that time? *A.* I didn't hear any one call; I heard my mother say that she was in the room and I heard a number of voices, but I could not distinguish who they were.

Q. Did any other member of the family say anything about locating him that night? *A.* My sister Woodie did; we all spoke of it; all the family spoke of locating Doctor—sister Woodie in particular, and mother.

Q. What did your sister Woodie say about it? *A.* She said she was in the room at the time that they supposed Ashburn was killed.

Q. What time was that? *A.* Some time between 12 and 1, I suppose; we had no time-piece.

Q. If you had no time-piece, how did she know that she was in the room between 12 and 1?

Objected to by Major Moses, on behalf of the defense.

Gov. Brown—I will withdraw that and put this question:

Q. Did your sister state how she knew the time of night, when she was in the room? *A.* She said she had heard the chickens crowing, and she supposed it was after midnight.

Q. What did you say about the time? *A.* I supposed it was that time.

Q. What caused you to suppose that your sister was that time of night, as you were asleep? *A.* I was not asleep at that hour of the night. I called her, and sent her for morphine.

Q. What time did you send her for the morphine *A.* I suppose it was between the hours of twelve and one.

Q. Why do you suppose it was between these hours? *A.* Because the chickens were crowing for midnight until some time after that, perhaps half an hour.

Q. As you did not suspect that Dr. Kirksey would be arrested for the murder of Ashburn, why did you all think it necessary to locate him that night? *A.* We did not try to locate him until after his arrest.

Q. Was there nothing said in the family the next day after Ashburn's death about locating him? *A.* There was not.

Q. There was nothing said then about locating him, until after his first arrest, was there? *A.* There was not.

Q. Do you feel very confident that you are not mistaken in that statement? *A.* I do.

Q. Did you attempt to locate any other member of the family that night? *A.* We did.

Q. Who? *A.* My brother, and all the male members of the family.

Q. Why locate only the male members of the family? *A.* Because they were arresting gentlemen, not arresting ladies.

Q. Did you not suspect that ladies and children would be arrested? *A.* I did not know.

Q. Was there any talk in the family about the probability of arresting ladies and children? *A.* There was not.

Q. What are the names of your brothers whom you located that night? *A.* Andrew and Albert.

Q. Where was Andrew that night. *A.* He was in his room.

Q. How were you all able to locate him, and know that he was there? *A.* Because his room was opening into the hall, and it was open, and we knew that he was in his room, as he was not in the habit of going out after night—never goes out after night, very seldom, unless some of the school-boys come for him.

Q. How old is Andrew? *A.* Fifteen or sixteen—I have forgotten which.

Q. Did you suppose there was any danger of his arrest on account of Ashburn's murder? *A.* I did not. I only thought; didn't know who they might take up, and try to implicate in this murder.

Q. Is Albert older or younger than Andrew? *A.* Younger.

Q. What is his age? *A.* Fourteen, I think.

Q. Did you have any fear of hir arrest? *A.* I didn't know but what they might arrest him.

Q. Where was he that night? *A.* In his room.

Q. Were either of these brothers leading Democrats? *A.* They are not. They didn't belong to any party. They are too young.

Q. Did you suspect that any one but leading Democrats would be arrested? *A.* I didn't know. I thought all who were in favor of the Democrats might be arrested.

Q. Did you locate your father that night? *A.* I did not, for my father never goes out after night at all.

Q. Was not most of the talk about locating Dr. Kirksey? *A.* It was, because he was arrested. He was the only one of the family that had been arrested, and we didn't attempt to locate him until after his arrest.

Q. How long after his arrest before you did attempt to locate him? *A.* The evening of his arrest.

Q. At what time of the day was he arrested? *A.* I don't know.

Q. Was it in the forenoon or in the afternoon? *A.* I don't know what time he was arrested, I only heard it late in the evening, between five and six o'clock, that he was arrested. I didn't know at what hour he was arrested.

Q. Did you hear what he was arrested for? *A.* I did not.

Q. Did you at that time suspect what he was arrested for? *A.* I did not; I supposed afterwards that he might be arrested as being a prominent Democrat, and they wanted to implicate him in the death of Ashburn.

Q. Was that your supposition the evening of his arrest? *A.* It was not.

Q. When was that first your supposition? *A.* The next day we commenced speaking of it; we had not spoken of it much the evening before; we only tried to locate the Doctor, and the next morning we got together and talked about it to know what they could have arrested them for, knowing them to be innocent men.

Q. Who was present during that conversation? *A.* My mother, myself, my sister, Mrs. Kirksey, my two cousins, the Misses Wynne; I don't recollect any other members of the family being present.

Q. Was your sister Woodie present? *A.* I don't recollect.

Q. Did you have any more than one conversation? *A.* Yes, we have been speaking of it ever since their arrest.

Q. Do you remember the first time it was spoken of when your sister Woodie was present? *A.* I do not.

Q. Do you remember whether she was ever present when it was spoken of? *A.* I do not.

Q. Are you sure that your mother was present when it was spoken of? *A.* Yes, because she was speaking of it herself.

Q. Who first mentioned the death of Ashburn during that conversation? *A.* I don't know; we were all speaking at once; I can't tell who first mentioned it.

Q. Are you sure your mother was there then? *A.* I am.

Q. What time did you first hear of the death of Ashburn? *A.* The morning after his death one of the servants came in and told me.

Q. Who was present? *A.* She told me of it and I went and told the other members of the family; I was the first one to hear it.

Q. What time of the morning was it? *A.* Directly after breakfast; about eight o'clock, I suppose.

Q. Where was your mother then? *A.* In my room; I was in the hall.

Q. Did you tell your mother of it? *A.* I did.

Q. Where was your sister Woodie then? *A.* I don't know.

Q. How long before you saw her? *A.* I don't know.

Q. Did you see her any more that morning? *A.* I don't recollect.

Q. Was not she at home? *A.* Yes, but she generally spends her mornings in study, and I hardly ever see her during the day, unless at meals.

Q. Where were your brothers? *A.* They were at school.

Q. When you state you first heard of Ashburn's death and told it to the other members of the family, who do you mean by the other members of the family? *A.* I mean my mother, cousins and sister, Mrs. Kirksey.

Q. Did it create any excitement in the family? *A.* It did not; we all said we was glad he was dead.

Q. Did Mrs. Kirksey and your brothers join in that expression? *A.* We all did; I don't recollect about my brothers joining in, but I recollect the female members of the family delighting in his death—being glad to hear of it.

Q. Where was Dr. Kirksey at that time?

A. Dr. K. had left for town or some place, I don't know where.

Q. When did you next see him? *A.* I saw him that afternoon; that evening he came home to tea.

Q. Did he say anything about Ashburn being killed? *A.* He did, and he said he regretted to know that he was killed; that it was so near the time of the election that his death would cause a great deal of excitement among the negroes.

Q. Why were the female members of the family glad he was dead? *A.* Because he was a Radical.

Q. How long did Dr. K. converse with the family on the subject of his death? *A.* I don't recollect; he was talking to my father about it.

Q. Did the female members of your family desire the death of all the Radicals? The defense, through Major Moses, objected to this question, but before the objection could be laid before the Commission the witness answered "We do."

A member of the Commission desired to be informed whether the objection was withdrawn or insisted upon.

Major Moses, for the defense, then rose and said:

"I will state to the court that I have understood from the little reading I have had, that I could only make objections to this court, through the Judge Advocate, and I did so as soon as I could possibly get to him. I don't withdraw the objection."

The question was answered before the court had decided upon it.

A member of the Commission—What do you propose to do with it?

Major Moses—I don't propose to touch it, sir.

Re-examined by Major Moses.

Q. Mrs. Moore, you have said that the ladies of your family were glad to hear of the death of A., and that they desired the death of all the Radicals; you don't mean by a Radical, a person merely differing in political opinion with a Democrat? *A.* No, I mean a scalawag.

Q. Do you understand a scalawag to be a representative of a party who is endeavoring to excite—

Judge Advocate (to Counsel)—Don't be quite so leading.

Major Moses—I want to get at what she means.

Witness—I mean by scalawags those who are trying to excite the negroes against us.

Q. Are you not apprehensive that the influence of the class of people whom you call scalawags, may produce an insurrection, in which women and children may be killed; and it is not alone to that class of persons you refer when you say you wish they were all dead?

Judge Advocate—I object to that question as being irrelevant.

Major Moses—I want to show how this animosity arises.

Judge Advocate—I object.

Major Moses—I will not press the question, sir, but I can not withdraw it.

The Commission then retired for deliberation, and on returning to the court-room the Judge Advocate announced the decision of the Commission, which was, that the objection was overruled.

The question was therefore repeated to the witness as follows:

Q. Are you not apprehensive that the influence of the class of people who you call scalawags may produce an insurrection in which the women and children may be killed; and is it not alone to this class of persons you refer, when you said you wished they were all dead? *A.* It is.

A member of the Commission presented the following, which was read in open court by the Judge Advocate:

"A member of the court asks that the record be corrected. As it now stands, it appears that time was not given by the Judge Advocate for the objection to the question. It also would appear that the court has not decided upon that objection, and therefore, as the record now stands, it appears that no attention has been given him. It should appear upon the record, if the counsel still objects or withdraws his objection, or allows the record to stand, question and answers, as it now is."

Counsel for Defense—Major Moses—In reply, presented the following:

"The witness having answered before the Judge Advocate could possibly present the objection to the court, defense withdraws its objection to the following question: 'Did the female members of your family desire the death of all the Radicals?' The defense still having upon the record the answer of witness to the subsequent question propounded by the defense."

The Commission then retired, and after deliberation returned to the Court-room,

Questions by Moses for Defense.

EDWARD SHEPPARD, a witness for defense, having been duly sworn, testified as follows:

Q. What is your name and age? A. Edward; thirteen.

Q. Where were you the night of the Ashburn murder? A. At home.

Q. How do you know that you were at home? A. Having the toothache I went into the Doctor's room to get something to put into it.

Q. How do you know that that was the night Ashburn was murdered? A. Because next morning, when I went to school, we went down to see his body, and my face was swollen up.

Q. Whom did you get the medicine from when you went to Dr. K.'s room? A. The Doctor himself came to the door and gave it to me.

Q. Did you take the medicine immediately or did you go anywhere before taking it? A. I went through mother's room and asked her whether it was too much or not.

Q. Did you get to sleep after that from the effects of the medicine? A. I went to sleep a little before morning; not right afterward.

Q. Had you been asleep before you took the medicine? A. No, sir.

Q. What time did you go to bed? A. After ten o'clock, or some time after ten o'clock.

Q. Did you lie in bed long before you went to Dr. K.'s room? A. About two hours and a half.

Q. Were you in much pain while you were lying down? A. Yes, sir.

Q. Don't that make time seem very long? A. I don't know, sir, about that.

Cross-examined—Questions by Brown.

Q. Has Dr. K. a horse and buggy? A. Yes, sir.

Q. Describe the horse. A. He is a white horse.

Q. Entirely white? A. Yes, sir; he's entirely white.

Q. Is he a large horse or a small horse? A. Middle-sized horse.

Q. Do you know about his age? A. No.

Q. Is the Doctor practicing medicine? A. He is.

Q. Is this the horse he drives regularly in his practice? A. It is.

Q. Describe his buggy. A. Common buggy.

Q. Has it any top? A. It has.

Q. Can you give no other description of it? A. I can not.

Q. Is it old or new? A. It is a tolerably new buggy.

Q. Does the Doctor usually travel in it when he goes to town and back? A. He does.

Q. Does he usually go to town and back every day? A. Yes, sir.

Q. What time of the night do you usually eat supper at your house? A. About 7 or 8 o'clock.

Q. May it not be as late as 8 or 9 o'clock? A. It is not often at 9.

Q. Is it not frequently as late as 8 o'clock? A. It is.

Q. Do you recollect what time you ate supper that night? A. I do not.

Q. Do you recollect whether Dr. K. was at supper? A. He was.

Q. Who else was there? A. No one else but the family.

Q. Where did the Doctor go after supper? A. Nowhere, as I know of.

Q. Do you know what time he went to bed? A. I do not.

Q. Where was your mother? A. She was in her room.

Q. Do you know what time she retired? A. I do not.

Q. Do you know whether she was up during the night after she retired? A. She was.

Q. How often? A. I don't know.

Q. Then how do you know she was up at all? A. She was up when I came through her room to show her the medicine.

Q. What time of night was that. A. I don't know.

Q. Had you been asleep before that? A. I had not.

Q. Who put the medicine in your tooth? A. She did.

Q. Do you know what it was? A. Morphine.

Q. Did you hear anything of your mother that night after you went to your room? A. I did not.

Q. How long did you say it was before you went to bed after you got to your room? *A.* I don't know; I stayed in the room by the fire awhile.

Q. Do you know whether Dr. Kirksey stayed there all that night or not? *A.* I don't know.

Q. Where did you first see him next morning? *A.* At breakfast.

Q. Where was the Doctor's room? *A.* On the right-hand side of the hall.

Q. How far from the entrance door? *A.* I don't know.

Q. Was it the first, second or third room? *A.* The first one.

Q. Any windows in it? *A.* There is.

Q. How many? *A.* Four.

Q. Any of them open on to a piazza? *A.* Two of them.

Q. Might not the Doctor have got up that night and gone out of a window without your hearing? *A.* I don't know.

Q. When did you first hear that Mr. Ashburn had been killed? *A.* The next morning.

Q. What time of the morning? *A.* When I got to school, about ten o'clock.

Q. Did you eat breakfast at home before you went to school? *A.* I did.

Q. Did you not hear your mother or Mrs. Moore speak of his death before you went to school? *A.* I did not.

Q. I understood you that you went to see his body; why did you go? *A.* It was twelve o'clock and all the boys were going down in town, and I went with them.

Q. When did you first hear the subject of his death discussed in the family at home? *A.* It was that night.

Q. What was said about it there? [This question was objected to by Major Moses in behalf of the defense, and withdrawn by Gov. Brown.]

Q. Was Dr. Kirksey at home that night? *A.* He was.

Q. Was he present when you heard it discussed in the family? *A.* I don't know.

Q. I refer to the night after Ashburn's death; is that the night you refer to? *A.* Yes, sir.

Q. At what time during that night was it discussed in the family? *A.* I don't know.

Q. Give your best recollection. *A.* At the table at supper.

Q. Did Dr. Kirksey take supper that night with the family? *A.* He did.

Q. Did they all eat supper at once? *A.* Yes.

Q. Now, what was said in the family about Ashburn's death at that time, at the table, when Dr. Kirksey was present, and in his hearing? [This question was objected to by Major Moses for the defense, and withdrawn by Gov. Brown, by consent of counsel.]

Q. What was said there in the family that night about the necessity of locating where Dr. Kirksey was the night before? *A.* They were talking about the arrest of Mr. Bedell, and they said they could prove that the Doctor was at home that night.

Q. Who said that? *A.* They all were talking about it.

Q. Whom do mean by "they all?" *A.* The family.

Q. Can you mention any one who spoke of it? *A.* I did myself.

Q. What did you say about it? *A.* I told them that I could prove that the Doctor was there.

Q. Did you mean that you could prove he was there all night? *A.* That he was there the night Ashburn was murdered.

Q. But did you mean you could prove he was there all night? *A.* He may not have been there the first part of the night. He was at supper.

Q. What part of the night do you mean he may not have been there? *A.* The forepart, after supper.

Q. Where was he then? *A.* He may have gone to see some of his patients. I don't know.

Q. Do you recollect whether he went in his buggy? *A.* I do not.

Q. Do you recollect how long after supper he started? *A.* I do not.

Q. Do you recollect what time he got back? *A.* I do not. He was in his room when I went after the medicine. He came to the door.

Q. Then do you know whether he did go? *A.* I don't know whether he did or not; but he did sometimes go after supper to see some patients.

Q. Does he have many calls at night to see patients? *A.* He does.

Q. Did he have many about that time? *A.* I don't know exactly.

Q. How often upon an average do you think he was called out at night to see patients—as much as once a week or oftener? *A.* Oftener.

Q. Has that been the case all this year? *A.* It has while he was at home.

Q. Did not he and his wife board at the hotel awhile in town? *A.* They did the first part of the year.

Q. Did he have as many calls at night before the time they went to the hotel as he has had since? *A.* I don't recollect.

Q. Do you recollect that he has had frequent calls at night since they returned from the hotel? *A.* He has.

Q. Have you some severe dogs there? *A.* We have.

Q. Do they bark at persons who come for him to go to patients? *A.* They do. Nobody can come into the yard at night after supper.

Q. Is that one of the reasons why you know persons called for him frequently to see patients? *A.* It is.

Q. May you not have been mistaken about his having had many calls to go to see patients at night, since he and his wife returned from the hotel? *A.* I am not.

Q. Where was Dr. Kirksey the night before Mr. Ashburn was killed? *A.* I don't know. He was at home at supper.

Q. Was it not his habit to go down in town occasionally to attend political meetings? *A.* I don't know unless it was for Masonic meetings. He went to them sometimes.

Q. Was he frequently gone at night when you did not know where he was gone? *A.* He was.

Q. What time of night did he usually return when he went out? *A.* I don't know exactly, as he was called any time of night.

Q. Is it easy to wake you when you are asleep? *A.* It is.

Q. Did you hear the dogs bark that night that Ashburn was killed? *A.* Not as I recollect.

Q. Do they not bark very often at night? *A.* Not unless some one is about.

Q. Don't they bark at the slightest noise, as the raising of a window or anything of that sort? *A.* They do.

Q. Do they always bark when a window is raised? *A.* Not always. Not unless it is late at night.

Q. Are you generally awake late of a night? *A.* I am not.

Q. Then how can you say that they bark at a window raised late of a night? *A.* They stay at my window, and wake me up sometimes barking, when mother's up in her room.

Q. Is it the raising of the window or the barking of the dogs that wakes you? *A.* The barking of the dogs.

Q. Then how do you know they bark at the raising of a window? *A.* Because I hear mother raise a window, and they still bark at it when she is up.

Q. Who usually fastens down the windows, and closes the doors of a night, when the family retire? *A.* My sister Woodie.

Q. Does not your mother attend to that sometimes? *A.* She goes with her sometimes, to hold the candle.

Q. Does your mother never go and attend to it herself? *A.* She does sometimes, when my sister is sick.

Q. Is your sister Woodie often sick? *A.* Not very often.

Q. Do you know who closed the windows the night Ashburn was killed? *A.* She closed them.

Q. Did you see her? *A.* She went from my room to do it in the other part of the house.

Q. Who closed them in Dr. Kirksey's room that night? *A.* She goes all over the house, and closes them herself. I don't know whether she done it that night or not.

Q. Do you mean that she goes into the rooms of the other members of the family, and closes the windows there? *A.* She does.

Q. Why did you all consider it necessary to locate Dr. Kirksey on that night? *A.* Because they were taking up the Democrats, and he was a prominent Democrat among the rest.

Q. Whom had they taken up? *A.* Mr. Bedell, I heard first, was taken up.

Q. What were they taking Democrats up for? *A.* I don't know, unless they supposed them to be connected with the murder of Ashburn.

Q. Do you know when Dr. Kirksey was first arrested? *A.* I don't recollect.

Q. About how long after Ashburn's death was it? *A.* I don't know.

Q. Do you think it was as much as a week? *A.* I don't know.

Q. Have you any opinion? *A.* No, sir.

Q. Was anything said in the family about locating Dr. Kirksey on the night of Ashburn's death, prior to his first arrest? *A.* There was. They were all talking about it.

Q. Why did they say it was necessary to locate him? *A.* Because they were taking up the other Democrats. Everybody thought they would take up their children, their sons, and their fathers.

Q. Was any thing said about locating

any other member of the family, except Dr. Kirksey? A. There was not. He was the only gentleman, except father, in the house.

Q. Have not you a brother? A. I have. He is young.

Q. Younger than yourself? A. No, sir.

Q. How much older? A. Two or three years. I don't know exactly.

Q. Was nothing said in the family about locating him or you? A. No, sir.

Q. Why did they think then that it was necessary to locate Dr. Kirksey? A. Because they were taking up other Democrats, and they thought they would take up any one.

Q. Did you expect all the Democrats would be arrested? A. I did not know.

Q. Did you hear anything said in the family about arresting women and children? A. I did not.

Q. Would you have heard it if anything had been said about it? A. I don't know that I would.

Q. Did you ever have the toothache before that night? A. I had it sometimes before.

Q. Was your face swollen before that night—if so, how long? A. It was not; that night was the worst I had of it.

Q. How many days was your face swollen after you had the toothache that night? A. About a day and a half.

Q. Give the substance of all the conversation of yourself and family referred to by you, about the time of the arrest—stating all that referred to the killing of Ashburn, arrest of parties, absence or presence of Dr. Kirksey on the night of the murder? A. They were talking about the taking of Mr. Bedell, and they thought they would see whether they could remember when he was at home; I don't remember what was said about the killing of Ashburn; they were talking about the arrest of Democrats, and thought they would take up any of them that they supposed were connected with the murder of Ashburn; they were all talking about how they could see when he was at home and off, and that he was there that night; I don't remember all the conversation.

Q. Was it a front tooth or a back tooth, or a jaw tooth that ached that night—have you had it pulled out? A. It was a front tooth; I have not had it pulled out.

Q. Can you show the court the unsound tooth, and the cavity in it that ached? (Witness shows his tooth to the whole court.)

The court then remanded the prisoners into custody, and adjourned until to-morrow morning at 10 o'clock.

McPHERSON BARRACKS, ATLANTA, GA.,
10 A. M., July 11, 1868.

The Commission met pursuant to adjournment.

Present, the same members as yesterday, the Judge Advocate and his assistants, the prisoners on trial, and their counsel.

The record of yesterday's proceedings was read and approved.

The testimony of the witness, Mrs. Moore, taken before the Commission yesterday, having been read to her, she desired to make the following corrections:

"Instead of saying that my sister occasionally sent for some member of the family to stay with her, I wish to say she invariably does so when the Doctor is away. In saying that the ladies of our family desired the death of all the Radicals, I meant only to say such Radicals as Ashburn, who were trying to excite the negroes against their former masters."

Questions by Major Moses for Defense.

MISS CLIFFORD WYNNE, witness for defense, having been duly sworn, testified as follows:

Q. What is your name and where do you reside? A. Clifford Wynne; I live in Banks county, Georgia.

Q. Where were you staying on the night of Ashburn's murder? A. At Col. Sheppard's.

Q. Who else was staying in the house with you? A. Col. Sheppard's family.

Q. Any one else? A. No one else.

Q. Where was your sister at that time? A. She was there.

Q. Do you know whether Dr. Kirksey was at home that night or not? A. Yes, sir.

Q. Were you well that night? A. I had sick headache that night.

Q. Did you sleep much that night? A. No, sir; I was awake nearly all night.

Q. Did you hear any one come in or go out of the house that night. A. I did not.

Q. Were there any other members of the family sick that night? A. There were three others sick.

Q. Who were they and what was the matter with them? *A.* Mrs. Moore, Dr. Kirksey's baby, and Eddy Sheppard.

Q. Do you know what was the matter with them? *A.* Eddie had the toothache, Dr. K.'s baby had the croup, and Mrs. Moore had nervous headache.

Q. Whom did you occupy the room with? *A.* Mrs. Moore.

Cross-examined by Brown.

Q. What time of the night did the family eat supper on that night? *A.* After dark—some time after dark.

Q. What time of the year was it? *A.* In March.

Q. What time of March? *A.* The latter part.

Q. Do you recollect what day of the month? *A.* I do not.

Q. What time does dark come in the latter part of March? *A.* I don't know.

Q. Does it come earlier or later than it does in July? *A.* It comes earlier.

Q. When you say the family had supper after dark, what time of the night do you mean it was? *A.* I don't know what time of the night it was.

Q. Does not dark come about 7½ o'clock in the latter part of March? *A.* I don't know what time it comes.

Q. How long after dark did they eat supper that night? *A.* I don't know; we didn't have any time-piece.

Q. Who were present at the supper table? *A.* Col. Sheppard and his family, Dr. Kirksey, myself, and my sister Matty.

Q. Was Edward Sheppard there? *A.* Yes.

Q. Was Mrs. Moore there? *A.* Yes.

Q. The sick ones of the family all eat supper there, did they? *A.* Mrs. Moore took some coffee.

Q. What did you take? *A.* I drank some coffee.

Q. Anything else? *A.* No.

Q. What did Edward take? *A.* I don't remember his being at the table; they were all there but him.

Q. What did Dr. Kirksey take for supper? *A.* I don't know what he ate for his supper.

Q. Do you recollect what any other member of the family took for supper? *A.* No, I don't remember now.

Q. Where did you go after supper? *A.* I went into Mrs. Moore's room.

Q. How long did you stay in Mrs. Moore's room? *A.* I slept with Mrs. Moore.

Q. How long before you went to bed? *A.* I retired very late that night; had sick headache.

Q. Do you usually sit up when you have the sick headache? *A.* I very often do.

Q. If you are very sick do you not lie down on the bed? *A.* Sometimes I do.

Q. What time, in your opinion, did you lie down that night? *A.* About eleven o'clock.

Q. How long before you went to sleep? *A.* I did not go to sleep till nearly day.

Q. Did you and Mrs. Moore sleep on the same bed? *A.* Yes, sir.

Q. Do you know what time she went to sleep? *A.* It was nearly day when she went to sleep.

Q. Had she been to sleep at all before you went to sleep? *A.* Yes.

Q. How long before you went to sleep had she been asleep? *A.* Not very long.

Q. Are you sure she did not go to sleep before midnight? *A.* I don't know whether it was before midnight or not.

Q. Have you not just stated that it was nearly day? *A.* She had been asleep once and waked up again; it was nearly day before she went to sleep again.

Q. Well, now tell us what time it was when she went to sleep the first time. *A.* I can not tell; not having any time-piece, I can not tell exactly when she went to sleep first.

Q. How long was it after you went to sleep? *A.* It was some time after I went to bed.

Q. As much as two hours? *A.* About two hours and a half, I think.

Q. How long did she sleep? *A.* She didn't sleep very long.

Q. What did she do when she woke? *A.* She called to Woodie to go to Dr. Kirksey's room for medicine for her.

Q. Where was Woodie when she called her? *A.* In the next room adjoining ours.

Q. After Woodie came back with the medicine how long did she stay in Mrs. Moore's room? *A.* She sat on the bed some time.

Q. As much as an hour? *A.* I suppose it was.

Q. May it have been two hours? *A.* I don't think it was two hours.

Q. Think it was an hour and a half? *A.* About an hour, I reckon.

Q. Where did Woodie go then? *A.* She went to her room then.
Q. Did you see her any more that night? *A.* No.
Q. How long had you been at Col. Sheppard's before Ashburn's death? *A.* Three months.
Q. Was Dr. Kirksey out at night frequently during that three months? *A.* No.
Q. Do you recollect any instance in which he was out at night during that three months. *A.* No, I don't.
Q. Did he not have calls from patients at night occasionally? *A.* Yes, he had calls.
Q. Well, did he not go? *A.* Yes, he went very often.
Q. Was he not then out at night? *A.* Yes, he was out at night.
Q. Were you not incorrect in the answer you made a few minutes ago, that he was never out at night during the three months? *A.* Yes, I was incorrect.
Q. Were his calls to patients frequent at night, during that time? *A.* I don't remember whether they were frequent or not.
Q. Do you remember any call he had? *A.* I don't remember any in particular.
Q. May you not be incorrect then when you stated he had any calls at night? *A.* No, I don't think I am.
Q. Was Mrs. Sheppard usually at home? *A.* Yes.
Q. If the Doctor had been called to patients at night would she have known it? *A.* Yes.
Q. Was Edward usually there at night? *A.* Yes, sir.
Q. If the Doctor had been called to patients at night, would Edward have known it? *A.* Yes.
Q. Was Mrs. Moore usually there at night? *A.* Yes, sir.
Q. If the Doctor had been called to patients at night, would Mrs. Moore have known it? *A.* Yes.
Q. Did he not go at night sometimes to attend meetings of the Masonic Fraternity? *A.* I believe he did.
Q. Did he not go sometimes at night to attend the meetings of the Democratic Club? *A.* I don't remember his going.
Q. When he went out at night, did he usually travel in his buggy? *A.* Yes.
Q. When did you first hear of the death of Ashburn? *A.* Next morning.
Q. Where were you? *A.* I was at Col. Sheppard's.

Q. In what room of the house? *A.* Second room on the right hand of the hall.
Q. Was that Mrs. Moore's room? *A.* It is.
Q. Who told you of Ashburn's death? *A.* I don't remember who told me.
Q. Didn't a servant come in and tell Mrs. Moore? *A.* I think she did.
Q. Where was Miss Woodie at that time? *A.* She was off studying; I don't know where she was.
Q. Was it before or after breakfast? *A.* I don't remember now.
Q. Have you talked with Mrs. Moore within the last twenty-four hours about where Miss Woodie was at that time? *A.* I have not.
Q. Have you read any of Mrs. Moore's testimony in the newspapers? *A.* I have not.
Q. Have you heard any of it read. *A.* No.
Q. Have you heard anybody speak of it? *A.* No, I have not.
Q. Are you and Mrs. Moore and Mrs. Sheppard and Miss Woodie staying at the same house? *A.* We are.
Q. Have you heard any conversation since the court adjourned yesterday, about what Mrs. Moore stated in her testimony? *Q.* No, I have not.
Q. Any about what Miss Woodie stated? *A.* No.
Q. Any about what she did here in the court-room? *A.* I have heard a good deal of talk about how she acted.
Q. Did you hear nothing about what she said or about what Mrs. Moore said in their testimony? *A.* No, I have not.
Q. Where was Edward Sheppard when you first heard of Ashburn's death? *A.* At school, I believe.
Q. What time did the family take dinner that day? *A.* I don't remember what time they took dinner that day.
Q. What time do they usually take dinner? *A.* About one o'clock.
Q. Was Miss Woodie at dinner that day? *A.* I don't remember whether she was or not.
Q. When did you first see Miss Woodie after Ashburn's death? *A.* Some time next day. The day we heard of it.
Q. What did she say about it? *A.* I don't know.
Q. When did you first hear the question discussed in the family as to where

Dr. Kirksey was on the night of Ashburn's death? A. When they commenced making the arrests of the young men belonging to the Democratic Club.

Q. When was that? A. When they arrested them and put them in the Courthouse.

Q. Was that the day after Ashburn's death? A. It was when they arrested Dr. Kirksey, and put him in the Court-house. Then we located where he was that night; found he was at home.

Q. Do you remember when the Doctor was arrested? A. I do not.

Q. When you say the young men of the Democratic Club, whom do you mean. A. All those that were arrested, and belonged to the Club.

Q. Will you please name them? A. I am not acquainted with any of them except Dr. Kirksey.

Q. Then, how do you know that anybody was arrested who belonged to the Democratic Club, except Dr. Kirksey? A. I heard it.

Re-examined by Mr. Moses.

Q. Was Dr. Kirksey living at Col. Sheppard's in the early part of the year, or was he living elsewhere? A. He was living at Col. Sheppard's.

Q. Are you certain that Dr. Kirksey was living at Col. Sheppard's from the first of January until the death of Ashburn, first of March—just think it over? A. He did not live there all the time.

Q. Where did he live when he was not there? A. Cook's Hotel.

Hereupon, the counsel for the defense submitted the following paper to the Court, which was read by General Dunn, Judge Advocate:

"In the case of this witness, counsel for defense would state to the Court that they consent that the evidence be read over to her from the reporter's notes, and she be permitted to make any corrections in it that she may desire, and that the record may be made up by the reporters from the notes thus corrected, if the Judge Advocate will give his consent; and if such consent shall be granted, they ask the Court to allow this course to be taken in this case, as the witness lives in Banks county, and wishes to leave for her home."

General Dunn, Judge Advocate—I certainly have no objection to that course.

Whereupon the Court allowed this course to be taken in this case, and the evidence was read to the witness from the reporter's notes.

The witness desired to make the following correction:

To question No. 61, which was, "Well, did he not go?" to which witness answered "Yes, he went very often," witness wishes to answer, "Yes, when he was called out to his patients, he went."

Questions by Moses for Defense.

ANDREW SHEPPARD, a witness for defense, was duly sworn, and testified as follows:

Q. What is your name, and where do you live? A. Andrew Sheppard is my name. I live in Winton, near Columbus.

Q. Where were you on the night of Ashburn's murder? A. At home.

Q. Do you know where Dr. Kirksey was that night? A. He was at home between ten and eleven o'clock, as far as I know.

Q. How do you know he was at home at that time? A. Because I saw him go in his room.

Q. Do you know where he was the rest of the night? A. I do not.

Cross-examined by Brown.

Q. What month and what time of the month was Ashburn killed? A. I think it was on the 30th March.

Q. What time does the sun set on the 30th March? A. I don't know.

Q. Is not it a few minutes after 6 o'clock? A. I don't know.

Q. Are not the nights longer then than they are in July? A. They are.

Q. What time does Mr. Sheppard's family usually take supper? A. About 8 o'clock.

Q. Does that rule apply as well in the winter as in the summer? A. Yes.

Q. In midwinter is not that about two hours after dark? A. Yes, I think it is.

Q. Does not 8 o'clock come now just at dark? A. Yes.

Q. In the winter do the family take supper two hours after close dark? A. Yes, about that time.

Q. Do they now take supper just at dusk? A. A little after dusk.

Q. Is it not frequently after 8 o'clock when the family eat supper? A. I don't know; they take supper about 8 o'clock generally.

Q. Who were at supper that night? *A.* The family.

Q. Who were the family? *A.* My mother and father, Dr. Kirksey and his wife, and my two cousins were there—Mrs. Moore and my sisters and brothers.

Q. What time did you go to bed? *A.* I think I went to bed between 10 and 11 o'clock.

Q. Was it before you went to bed that you saw Dr. Kirksey go into his room? *A.* A little before I went to bed.

Q. Were you up any more that night? *A.* No, I was not.

Q. Did you sleep with Edward? *A.* No, I slept by myself.

Q. Was it in the same room with Edward? *A.* No, the room opposite Dr. Kirksey's.

Q. With whom did Edward sleep? *A.* With my brother Albert.

Q. Who slept in the middle room opposite Mrs. Moore's room? *A.* My mother.

Q. Who slept in the third room on the side where your mother slept? *A.* My brothers.

Q. Where's the parlor? *A.* The parlor is in a different part of the house altogether.

Re-examined by Moses.

Q. What were you doing between supper and the time you retired? *A.* I was studying.

Q. Where were you studying? *A.* In the hall; the table at which I was studying is about twenty feet from Dr. Kirksey's room.

Q. Did you read there until you retired? *A.* Yes, I studied there.

C. T. ARRINGTON, a witness for the defense, was then introduced and duly sworn.

The Judge Advocate ordered all the witnesses whose testimony would refer to Mr. Duke, the accused, to withdraw from the room, so as not to hear any of the testimony of Mr. Arrington. Mr. Arrington testified as follows:

Questions by Stephens in behalf of the defense.

Q. What is your name in full? *A.* C. T. Arrington.

Q. Where do you reside? *A.* Carroll county.

Q. Where were you when you heard of the assassination of Mr. Ashburn? *A.* I was down at Mr. Duke's.

Q. Where were you there when you first heard of it? *A.* Down at the blacksmiths shop.

Q. Recollect the day of the week? *A.* No, sir, I don't; it was Tuesday or Wednesday, I disrecollect.

Q. Was Mr. Duke present at the shop when you first heard the news? *A.* Yes, sir.

Q. When did you go to Mr. Duke's—the father? *A.* Went the Sunday before.

A. How long did you stay there on that visit? *A.* Four days.

Q. Was Mr. Duke, the accused, at his father's when you reached there on Sunday? *A.* Yes, sir.

Q. Do you know where he was the Sunday night after you got there? *A.* Yes, sir.

Q. Where was he? *A.* He was in the house with the balance of the family.

Q. Do you know where he slept? *A.* Yes, sir.

Q. Do you know who slept with him? *A.* Yes, sir.

Q. Who? *A.* I slept with him.

Q. Do you know where he was Monday night? *A.* Yes, sir.

Q. Where? *A.* He was there.

Q. Do you know where he slept that night? *A.* Yes, sir.

Q. Where? *A.* Slept with me.

Q. Where did you and he sleep? *A.* We slept in the house there.

Q. Who else slept in the same room with you? *A.* His mother and father and some of his sisters slept in there.

Q. Do you know where he was on Tuesday night? *A.* Yes, sir.

Q. Where? *A.* He was still there.

Q. Did you and he sleep together every night while you were there during that visit? *A.* Yes, sir.

Q. What day of the week did you return home? *A.* Thursday.

Q. How far is it from there to Columbus? *A.* Well, I don't know sir; I think they call it forty miles. I don't know myself.

Q. What kin are you to the family? If any, state what it is? *A.* Mr. Duke's mother is my sister.

Cross-examined by Judge Advocate.

Q. Are you a man of family, sir? *A.* Yes, sir.

Q. Where do you reside? *A.* In Carroll County.

Q. How far from the residencee of your brother-in-law, Duke? *A.* About forty-three miles.

Q. How did you travel from your residence to your brother-in-law's? *A.* I walked.

Q. Had you any business to take you there? *A.* No, sir; none only just to go on a visit.

Q. How many days did it take you to go from your residence to Duke's? *A.* A day and a piece.

Q. What kind of weather did you have during the journey? *A.* I don't recollect exactly what sort.

Q. Did you leave home Friday or Saturday? *A.* On Saturday.

Q. Do you remember whether or not it rained on Saturday? *A.* No, sir, I do not.

Q. Do you remember whether or not it rained on Sunday while you were pursuing your journey? *A.* No, sir; I don't recollect whether it did or not.

Q. What time of day did you reach Duke's? *A.* I got there about two hours by sun, I reckon, or more; a little more than that.

Q. Was any person with you on your journey? *A.* No, sir.

Q. Whom did you find at home at Duke's on your arrival there? *A.* Just the family.

Q. Was William Duke at home when you arrived there? *A.* Yes, sir.

Q. Where was he? *A.* He was sitting by the fire when I went in.

Q. Was the weather cold? *A.* It was not cold, but he was sitting by the fire.

Q. Where did you spend Monday; the Monday following your arrival at Duke's? *A.* I was there at the blacksmith shop nearly all day.

Q. Who worked in the blacksmith shop? *A.* There was a negro man and one of Mr. Duke's brothers there.

Q. Where was Duke's father? *A.* Well, he had been down below Columbus, and got home on the day I got there—on Sunday.

Q. Well, where was he on Monday? *A.* He was there too.

Q. In the blacksmith shop? *A.* Yes.

Q. Were you at the blacksmith shop all day? *A.* I was not there all day; I was at the house part of the day.

Q. What time did you retire to bed that night? *A.* I don't know, sir, exactly what time; they did not have any time-piece, I don't think; it was somewheres between nine and ten o'clock, I judge.

Q. How many beds were in the room where you slept? *A.* I think there was three.

Q. In what part of the room was the bed located in which you slept? *A.* In the back part of the room.

Q. What size room was this in which you slept? *A.* I don't know, sir; it was a good large room.

Q. How many doors did it have? *A.* Three doors, I think, to it.

Q. What direction did the front door face? *A.* The big road.

Q. What course? *A.* South, I think it is.

Q. South? *A.* Yes, sir, I think so.

Q. What direction was the bed in which you slept in reference to that front door? *A.* Right back to the right.

Q. Do you mean on the east side of the room, entering from the south, or west? *A.* It is on the south side.

Q. You enter the front room from the south—that is, you enter it going north—was the bed in which you slept on your right or on your left hand when so entering? *A.* It was to the right.

Q. Was it against either wall of the house; if so, which wall? *A.* I don't know, sir, whether it was against a wall or not; I didn't notice.

Q. You don't know whether it was against a wall or not, you say? *A.* No, sir; I never noticed.

Q. Was it at the end of the house or the side of the house you entered? *A.* At the end of the house.

Q. Was it about the center of the end of the house, or was it in either corner? *A.* It was in the right-hand corner there.

Q. Where were their beds in that room? *A.* In the other end of the room, to the left.

Q. Will you name over all the persons that slept in that room on the Monday night that you were there? *A.* Mr. Duke, his father and mother, and his two sisters slept there, and I slept there.

Q. Has not Duke a married sister? *A.* Yes, sir; he has two or three of them.

Q. Didn't one of his married sisters and her husband sleep in that same room that night? *A.* He slept in the room adjoining the one I was in.

Q. Has he not a married brother? *A.* Yes, he has two.

Q. Didn't one of those married brothers and his wife sleep in that same room that night? *A.* No, sir, not as I know of.

Q. Where did you spend the Tuesday following this Monday of which you have spoken? *A.* I stayed there at the shop and at the house, backwards and forwards.

Q. Where were you on the Wednesday following? *A.* I was there also; there was several other men there; I don't recollect their names now—neighbors.

Q. What is your business? *A.* I am a farmer.

Q. When did you say you first heard of the murder of Ashburn? *A.* It was on Tuesday or Wednesday, I don't recollect which.

Q. What time of the day was it when you heard the news? *A.* I don't recollect; it seems like it was in the evening like, but I ain't certain.

Q. Can you recollect which of these days it was you heard the news? *A.* I think it was Tuesday, but I ain't certain; Tuesday or Wednesday.

Q. Who brought the news? *A.* I don't know, sir. It was some man in the settlement who came to the shop that was telling it there; I don't know who.

Q. Were the nights about that time moonlight or dark nights? *A.* Light nights, I think.

Q. Now recollect at what time of day it was you heard the news? *A.* I don't know, sir; it was in the evening, I think. I am not positive, but I think it was the evening.

Q. Why do you think it was Tuesday instead of Wednesday? *A.* I don't know, sir, for certain, whether it was Tuesday or Wednesday; but it was one or the other of those days.

Q. Why do you say it was one or the other of those days? *A.* I don't know, sir, for certain, whether it was Tuesday or Wednesday. I don't know which of them it was. There were several at the shop at the time.

Q. How do you know it was either of these days—Tuesday or Wednesday? *A.* I know by the time they said he was killed; it was on the 30th March, and it was a day or two afterward when we heard it.

Q. Do you know what day of the week the 30th of March came on? *A.* It was on Monday, I think.

Q. Do you know? *A.* I got there on the 29th; Monday was the 30th.

Q. How far did you travel from home the first day you left? *A.* I went about thirty miles, I believe.

Q. Where did you stay that night? *A.* I stayed close to Dr. Pierce's.

Q. At whose house? *A.* I don't know, sir, what the man's name is where I stayed.

Q. Did the man keep a tavern? *A.* No, sir.

Q. How far from Pierce's? *A.* It was not very far; I don't know exactly how far.

Q. Give your opinion. *A.* About three quarters of a mile, I think.

Q. Where does Pierce live? *A.* Lives in Merriwether.

Q. On what road? *A.* On the Columbus road, I think.

Q. Did you stop before or after you reached Pierce's? *A.* Before.

Q. Please describe the place you stopped at, so that a person could find it if it were necessary to go there? *A.* It was on the top of the hill, a little house on the left-hand side of the road; the house is built as a sort of double cabin.

Q. What time was it when you stopped there? *A.* After night awhile.

Q. How far is the house where you stayed from the road? *A.* Right close to the road; just a few steps.

Q. Is the front to the road, or the end? *A.* The front, I think.

Q. Can you see Pierce's house from that house? *A.* Yes, sir; I think I can.

Q. Is there any stream of water between that house and Pierce's? *A.* Small branch, I think.

Q. Is there any dwelling-house between these two houses? *A.* Yes, sir; there is one on the right-hand side of the road.

Q. Was the moon shining when you stopped that night? *A.* I think it was a little cloudy; I ain't certain. I think it was.

Q. Do you know whether the moon was shining or not? *A.* No, sir; I don't think it was when I stopped there. It was a little cloudy.

Q. Do you remember the next night, whether the moon was shining or not? *A.* No, sir, I don't.

Q. You don't remember, then, whether Sunday night was moonlight or not? *A.* I don't recollect whether it was moonlight or not.

Q. How was it the Monday night following; was it a moonlight night or not? *A.* I don't recollect.

Q. How was it Tuesday night; was that a moonlight night or not. A. I don't recollect.

Q. How was it Wednesday night? A. I don't recollect, sir.

Q. Don't you remember whether these were dark nights or light nights? A. I think that the moon was shining at that time, when it was not cloudy.

Q. What time did you leave Duke's to go home? A. I left there on Thursday?

Q. What time of the day? A. Soon in the morning.

Q. How far did you travel the first day? A. I don't know exactly. I come eight miles this side of Lagrange.

Q. Where did you stay that night? A. I stayed with my father-in-law.

Q. What is his name and where does he live? A. His name is Ronalds; he lives in Troup county.

Q. How many miles did you travel that day? A. I don't know, sir, what distance.

Q. What time was it when you arrived at your father-in-law's house? A. It was in the evening, just before night.

Q. Do you remember whether that was a moonlight night? A. No, sir; I think it rained that evening, and I think a little that night; I ain't positive.

Q. How long did you remain at your father-in-law's? A. I stayed there until Friday.

Q. Where did you go to from there? A. I went home then.

Q. What is the distance from your father-in-law's to your own house? A. It is about—I don't know exactly how far it is.

Q. You must know something about it; tell me your opinion. A. Between 35 and 40 miles, I think.

Q. What time of the day did you leave your father-in-law's house? A. Soon in the morning.

Q. Did you reach home the same day? A. No, sir.

Q. Where did you stay that night? A. Stayed with my brother-in-law, in the room with him.

Q. What is your brother-in-law's name, and where did he live? A. His name is Handy; he lives in Carroll.

Q. Describe where he lives, so that a person would be able to find it. A. He lives near the Chattahoochie river, with a man by the name of Akres.

Q. That would be a very poor description of a place if a stranger wanted to find it; can't you tell what road he lives on? A. He lives on what is called the Five-notch road, that runs up and down by the Chattahoochie river.

Q. When did you arrive at home? A. On Saturday, I think.

Q. How long were you absent from home? A. I think it was six days.

Q. Can you describe the man that kept the house where you stayed the first night after you left home? A. He is a low, chunky man.

Q. What was his age? Give his age and the color of his hair, so that we would know him if we saw him. A. He was a black man.

Q. Then you can easily tell what the color of his hair was. A. Yes; his hair was black; I don't know what his age is; I reckon forty or forty-five.

Q. Has he a wife? A. Yes, I guess so; there was a woman there.

Q. Describe the size and appearance of the woman. A. She was a good large size; looked like she weighed two hundred.

Q. What appeared to be the age of the oldest child? A. I don't know, sir; I didn't see all the children—didn't go into but one end of the house.

Q. When did you first hear that Duke was accused of being connected with the murder of Ashburn? A. Last night was a week ago.

Q. Where were you when you heard it? A. At home.

Q. Who communicated the information to you? A. Mr. Duke's brother.

Q. Which brother? A. Wayne.

Q. How does it happen that after so long a time you are able to remember so particular by a circumstance that occurred about the 30th of March? A. Well, I recollect about being there and hearing them men speak about that man being killed, about the 30th; I knew he was there that time.

Questions by the Court.

Q. When you visited Duke's house what time of the moon was it—farmers watch the moon generally? A. It was in the morning when I got there.

Q. When you visited Duke's house what time of the moon was it? A. I reckon the moon was full or about full; may be it was done full; I don't recollect exactly.

Examination conducted by Mr. Stephens for Defense.

ROBERT T. C. TUCKER, witness for defense, having been duly sworn, testified as follows:

Q. What is your name? A. Robert T. C. Tucker.

Q. Where do you live? A. In Meriwether county.

Q. Do you know Mr. William Duke, the accused? A. Yes, sir.

Q. Will you point him out to the court? A. There he is, (witness points out the accused, Duke.)

Q. Do you know when you heard of the death of Ashburn? A. I think the first I heard of it was at Duke's shop.

Q. Do you recollect the day of the week? A. I think it was on Wednesday.

Q. Will you state to the court whether or not Mr. Duke, the prisoner here, was there at that time? A. Yes, sir, he was there Wednesday evening; that was the time I went up to his shop.

Q. Had you seen him there any time previous to that? A. Yes, sir, I had seen him there twice previous—once at the shop and once in the field; on Saturday evening before I saw him out in the straw field, near the house, though I did not speak to him; I was not near enough to him; I was some fifty or sixty yards from him.

Q. Did you see him between Saturday and Wednesday? A. Yes, sir.

Q. When and where? A. I saw him at the shop Monday evening, after the sun went down.

Q. Did you see any other person there? A. Yes sir.

Q. Name them. A. Mr. Reese, Mr. Parham, Mr. Woodward and a young man that belonged there at the shop.

Q. Was there any strange person there? A. Well, late in the evening, sir, there was a strange gentleman came down in front of the shop; I was in the back; I understood he was a brother of Mrs. Duke's, though I was not acquainted with him.

The last witness, C. T. Arrington, was here brought into the court-room and placed in the presence of witness.

Q. Will you look at that gentleman and say if he is the one? A. Yes, sir, that is the one, I think, from his face and color of his hair.

Q. You saw him there Monday evening? A. Yes, sir.

Q. Did you or not see the same gentleman the evening you heard of the death of Ashburn? A. I have no recollection, sir.

Q. You saw him there Monday though? A. Yes, sir.

Q. How far is it from your shop to Columbus? A. We call it forty miles, sir, from our neighborhood to Columbus; the road direct has been posted a little east of where I live; I live about a mile west of the Columbus road.

Cross-examined by Brown for Prosecution.

Q. How far do you live from Duke's blacksmith shop? A. From three to four hundred yards.

Q. How long have you lived there? A. From 1852; sixteen years.

Q. Has Duke lived there all that time? A. No, sir.

Q. How long has he lived there? A. He moved up there last winter was a year ago.

Q. Are you very frequently at his house? A. In his shop I am, sir. I have all my work done there.

Q. How often would you say you were there each week? A. Well, sir, sometimes I am there every day for a week, and sometimes not there for perhaps two or three weeks, it depends on my health and business. If I am able to attend to business I don't go so often. I merely go to meet my friends there and have some neighborhood conversation with them. Sometimes, though, my business calls me there, perhaps nearly every day—have something to do there in either wood or iron, and I take it there myself when I have anything to do in that way.

Q. Is not this regarded a very public place in the neighborhood? A. Yes, sir, it is all the place of rendezvous in the neighborhood—the wood and iron shop.

Q. Do you recollect the next time you were there? A. Well, sir I was there that time almost every day of the week. I was preparing my implements for planting my cotton. That took me up to the shop nearly every day in the week.

Q. Who was present the next time you were at the shop after the time about which you testified? A. I really can't call to mind when it was, I don't recollect any day after Wednesday of that week, though I am very certain I was there some day of that week after Wednesday.

Q. Who was present when you were there that time? *A.* On Wednesday?
Q. No, no, this time you speak of after Wednesday? *A.* I can not call to mind who was present, but I recollect that the first information we had of this gentleman being killed in Columbus was on Wednesday. Some person at the shop named that this gentleman in Columbus was shot on the Monday night. I know it was on Wednesday. If you are disposed to have the reason why I know it I will give it to you.
Q. Well, give the reason. *A.* I made arrangements on Tuesday to send my son-in-law to take a load of cotton for a friend to Lagrange with my wagon. He started Wednesday morning to Lagrange; and after he had started to Lagrange, I walked up to the shop and there heard that this gentleman—I can't think of his name, only once in a while—(witness pauses)—Ashburn, was killed in Columbus. Then when my son and son-in-law returned from Lagrange they confirmed the report. They returned on Thursday night.
Q. How long ago has that been? *A.* The last of March or first of April. The first of April was the day they started to Lagrange. Though I started my wagon on Tuesday evening down to get the cotton; next morning they started to Lagrange. I had to send below where I lived to get the cotton, and they went down there over night, and next morning loaded up the cotton and went on to Lagrange.
Q. Has it not been nearly three and a half months since the 30th of March? *A.* Yes, sir.
Q. What circumstance enables you to recollect so distinctly the day of the week on which you started your wagon from home, three months and a half ago. *A.* Well, sir, I had finished planting my corn and preparing my cotton land for planting, when this friend requested that I would take a load of cotton to Lagrange for him, and I told him I could not spare the team, but if my son-in-law was disposed to take part of his mules and part of mine, I would let him have part of mine and he could take the cotton to Lagrange. He objected to it because, he said, he was not done bedding his cotton land. I told him when the wagon returned from Lagrange we would have time to finish bedding by the 6th of April, and that was as early as I would plant, even if I was then ready, and Monday was the 6th of April.

Q. Do you keep any book or memorandum of the time when you finish planting each crop and commence the next? *A.* Not every year, but frequently I do; I first mark in the almanac when I commenced planting and when I get through.
Q. Did you mark in your almanac this year when you finished planting corn? *A.* No, sir.
Q. Or when you commenced planting cotton? *A.* No, sir.
Q. Then you do not speak from any memorandum, do you? *A.* No memorandum; I just speak from positive knowledge of the facts; because I planted cotton earlier this year by several days than I had been in the habit of doing for several years, and have been regretting it ever since—when I think of it.
Q. Why sometimes keep a memorandum? is it not because you can not recollect facts without it? *A.* Sometimes; I merely do it for reference a long time afterwards; sometimes I want to know when I planted one year, and look over my almanac; sometimes I don't find it marked, and frequently I do; I have a bundle of almanacs I have kept for some time—some marked and some not.
Q. Can you easily recollect an incident three and a half months after its occurrence, and locate it on that day? *A.* No, sir, I can not; I could not have located these had it not been for these concurrent circumstances; I know that I commenced planting cotton the sixth day of April.
Q. What fact enables you to state distinctly that you commenced on the sixth of April, and to say that you know you are not mistaken? *A.* I just know it as well as anything I ever done, for I had the day set apart—Monday—that it would be the sixth April, and to commence planting cotton seed; we had finished planting corn and finished bedding our cotton land on Friday, and the boys that I had with me got a holiday until Monday.
Q. How often since that day have you thought of the fact that Duke was there at that interview? *A.* I don't know that I ever thought anything about it until I understood that he was arrested.
Q. When was he arrested? *A.* I can not call to mind; I know it was Wednesday or Thursday, two weeks ago; I remember the gentleman that came by asking where he lived; he came right by my patch; he inquired where Mr. Duke lived; I

pointed out to him, and then he passed in back by my house pretty soon after.

Q. Didn't the arrest of Duke create as much excitement in your neighborhood as the intelligence of Ashburn's death did? *A.* Well, sir, I was quite unwell for a few days afterwards; I was taken down to my bed and did not go out anywhere last week.

Q. Did not the arrest of Duke, being a near neighbor, make as much impression on your mind as the intelligence of the death of Ashburn did? *A.* I didn't know what to think of it.

Q. Please answer my question. Did not the arrest of Duke, being a near neighbor, make as much impression on your mind as the intelligence of Ashburn's death did. *A.* I did not know that it did, sir; they both made considerable impression on my mind; I thought it was a very unnecessary thing to kill the man.

Q. Did not the arrest make a decided impression on your mind? *A.* It did, sir, under the circumstances. I knew that Mr. Duke was at home at the time that the murder was committed, and if he was arrested innocently, I might be also, or any other man. I knew in my mind that on Monday night, at sunset, he was in his father's house, forty miles from Columbus, and I did not see how it was possible for him to go to Columbus and back before he was known to be in the neighborhood again.

Q. For these reasons then, you state that the arrest of Duke made a decided impression on your mind? *A.* Yes, sir.

Q. But still you can not tell what day of the week it was, and it was only two weeks since? *A.* I am not positive as to the day, only that it was Wednesday or Thursday.

Q. While you can not be positive about the day of the week of an occurrence that made a decided impression on your mind, about two weeks ago, you are positive about the day of the week of another occurrence that made a similar impression on your mind, three months and a half ago. *A.* Well, it was just the circumstances attending it. I should not have sent my wagon and part of my mules off my plantation at any other time.

Q. Is it your custom to send them off your plantation on that particular day of April each year? *A.* No, sir.

Q. Then how can you be so positive that you sent them that day? *A.* I think I have answered the question as plainly as I can do; because I had finished planting my corn, and was preparing my land to plant cotton, and between the finishing of the corn, and the planting of the cotton, I think I had time to spare two of my mules. That is what recalled that back to my mind. But this, there is no such thing to call it back.

Q. I have to repeat the question—why do you recollect so distinctly about the date of finishing the corn? *A.* I should never have thought about it again if these circumstances had not transpired.

Q. Do you remember which day you finished plowing over your corn the first time this year? *A.* I do not.

Q. Do you remember what day you finished planting cotton? *A.* I can't remember, without I was to count up how many days I was planting.

Q. Do you remember what day you finished plowing over the cotton the first time? *A.* I don't, sir.

Q. The second time? *A.* No, sir.

Q. Do you recollect when you finished plowing over the corn the third time? *A.* No, sir. I didn't charge my mind with it.

Q. Do you recollect the day you commenced planting corn? *A.* Yes, sir.

Q. What day? *A.* I commenced planting corn on the 16th, I think, of March.

Q. What circumstance enabled you to recollect that? *A.* Well, I just got ready to go to plant by the 16th, and commenced.

Q. Do you always commence on that day of the month? *A.* About from the 12th to the 16th, I do.

Q. What enables you to be certain that you got ready and commenced on the 16th? *A.* I know that I got my corn prepared, and commenced planting; that is all that enables me to do it, and I know that I marked the date in my mind, that it was the 16th of March when I commenced planting corn, but as to plowing it afterwards, I didn't charge my mind with that.

Q. Can you recollect any other incident connected with your crop, between the 30th March and 1st of July, so as to locate it positively on a particular day? *A.* I can, the day before 4th of July.

Q. I speak of 1st July. *A.* I recollect my people plowing in my cotton along the first days of July.

Q. I didn't ask about anything that occurred in July. *A.* Well, I remember the last time I plowed it before 1st July;

of course they were the last days of June; I was plowing my cotton then.

Q. Do you recollect any particular incident connected with your crop so as to locate it positively on a particular day between the 10th of April and 1st June? *A.* I don't know that I can, only that I was doing certain business at certain times; as to pointing out the particular days, I can't do it.

Q. What was the time of the moon on the 30th of March? *A.* I don't know, sir.

Q. Did you finish planting corn on dark nights or light nights? *A.* I don't know that, sir.

Q. Don't planters and farmers pay considerable attention to the moon? *A.* I do not pay much attention only in a few things.

Q. You have no recollection, then, whether you finish planting corn about full moon or about the change? *A.* No, sir.

Q. Have you any recollection of the condition of the moon when you commenced planting cotton? *A.* No, sir.

Q. When did you first hear that Mr. Duke was charged with any connection with the murder of Ashburn? *A.* I didn't hear it till may be the next day; I think I didn't hear it the day he was arrested; I don't think I heard it until the next day after he was arrested; I didn't go anywhere from home.

Q. Prior to that time did you ever suspect that he would be charged with any such connection? *A.* No, sir.

Q. Then there was nothing connected with that affair, was there, which called you to charge your mind particularly with the time you saw him at the blacksmith shop? *A.* No, sir, nothing that I know of that would require me to charge my mind particularly with it.

Q. If he had not been arrested do you think you would ever again have thought of having seen him there at that particular time? *A.* Well, I don't know that I should, sir.

Q. If he had been absent and not present on that occasion, would you have recollected that after you heard of his arrest? *A.* Yes, sir; I should have recollected it; he had been gone for may be two or more weeks from home, and if he had not been there I should not ever had any thought about it.

Q. Do you recollect every person you saw that day? *A.* On Monday?

Q. Yes; Monday, the 30th March. *A.* No, sir; I do not.

Q. Do you recollect every place you were at that day? *A.* Yes, sir; I think I do; I was at home until after I eat my dinner and then walked up to the shop and remained there until after sunset.

Q. Do you recollect what you were doing in the forenoon of that day? *A.* I don't think I was busy that day; only sitting in my house—reading, perhaps.

Q. Do you recollect what you were doing the day before? *A.* I was at church on Sunday and I recollect very distinctly what I was doing the day before that—on Saturday.

Q. Do you recollect where you were on Tuesday, all day? *A.* Yes, sir; I was part of the day down at my son-in-law's, and the balance of the day I was at home.

Q. What were you doing the portion of the day you were at home? *A.* I came home from my son-in-law's to get my son to prepare the wagon that night to take that cotton on next morning; it was that thing brought me home from my son-in-law's.

Q. Do you recollect where you were all day Wednesday? *A.* I was at home part of the day, and in the evening I went up to the workshop.

Q. Who did you see at the workshop that evening? *A.* I seen Mr. Woodward there, and there was some other person there, but I don't distinctly recollect who it was; I think myself that there was a relative of mine—I think James Crowther was there, but I am not positive.

Q. Then you can't be positive who was there on Wednesday? *A.* No, sir.

Q. Where were you all day Thursday? *A.* I think I was at home.

Q. What were you doing that day? *A.* Thursday afternoon I commenced trying to stock a double plow.

Q. Were you at the shop that day? *A.* No, sir, I think not.

Q. Where were you Friday all day? *A.* Well, I reckon I was working on this same double plow—it took me some time to make it, because I didn't know much about it.

Q. Were you at the shop any portion of that day? *A.* I don't think I was, sir.

Q. Who did you see that day? *A.* I don't recollect seeing any person but my own family; I was at home.

Q. Could you say that you did not see any other person? *A.* No, I could not.

Q. Where were you on Saturday? *A.* I can't tell for certain where I was Saturday—as like as not fishing—I go fishing frequently.

Q. Then you can't remember where you were Saturday? *A.* No, sir.

Q. Where were you on Sunday? *A.* I was at church.

Q. What church? *A.* The church I belong to, Trinity Church, Merriwether county.

Q. Who preached that day? *A.* We had no preaching.

Q. Where were you Monday? *A.* At home, I suppose.

Q. Were you at the shop any portion of Monday? *A.* I can't tell that.

Q. Any distinct recollection about Tuesday? *A.* None, sir.

Q. Or any other day of that week? *A.* None, sir.

Q. What were you doing on Monday after Monday, the 30th March? *A.* Planting cotton seed.

Q. What were you doing on Wednesday week after 30th March? *A.* I think I answered that I couldn't tell what I was doing about two weeks afterwards: my people were planting cotton; I can't say what I was doing myself.

Q. What were you doing the Tuesday week after 30th March? *A.* My people were planting cotton; I don't know whether I was planting with them or not; I expect in all probability I was about the field part of the day and part of the time in the house.

Q. Who did you see that day? *A.* I saw my people, I reckon, if I was in the field; if I was in the house I may have seen any one who came in, but I can't call to mind about that.

Q. What were you doing Wednesday before 30th March? *A.* My people were preparing the ground for planting cotton; I don't know what I was doing myself.

Q. Who did you see on that day? *A.* I don't know, sir; I don't keep a diary of what I do every day—I don't suppose many men do in this country.

Q. Do you remember who you saw on the Thursday before the 30th March? *A.* No, sir, I do not.

Q. Or the Friday before the 30th of March? *A.* I don't think I saw anybody that day but my son—we were out bird-hunting that day—shooting birds.

Q. Where were you on Saturday? *A.* I was home until dinner; I was home in the morning; my son went up in the morning to Mr. Duke's, and he said that the Duke boys intended to set the sedge field on fire that evening, and after dinner we walked up there with our guns; they attempted to burn off the sedge but it didn't burn but very poorly, and the balance of the evening me and my son spent shooting birds; while up at the sedge field I saw several of the Duke boys, and among them William Duke.

Q. Name every person you saw that day? *A.* I saw Norman, John Duke, Wayne Duke, and Joseph Jackson, and just before I left the field I saw William Duke. I was then about fifty yards to him, but I didn't speak to him; but I said to Norman, says I, "Has Willie got back?" Says he, " Yes."

Q. Can you state the names of all the persons you saw any day from the first day of January until the first day of June this year, except the three or four days about the 30th of March? *A.* I don't suppose I can, sir, when I saw any person at all.

Q. Did you see William Duke then on Saturday? *A.* I don't think I did, sir; I passed right to the field, and I did not go back about the house that evening any more.

Q. Is William Duke frequently down about Columbus? *A.* Well, sir, he has been backward and forward several times since his father lived there.

Q. Does he occasionally spend some time down there? *A.* Yes, sir.

Re-examined by Mr. Stephens.

Q. What is your age and occupation? *A.* I have been a farmer all my life almost. I am sixty-seven years old next October.

Recross-examined by Brown for Prosecution.

Q. Is your memory as good as when you were a younger man? *A.* No, sir, by no means.

Questions by Defense by permission of the Court—by Mr. Stephens.

Q. From the sensation produced at the time of the news of the assassination of Ashburn, are you positive as to the facts you have stated here? *A.* Yes, sir, I am; the leading facts.

Q. Do you hold any office in your county? *A.* Not now, sir.

Q. Have you held any? *A.* Yes, sir.

Q. What position? *A.* I acted as Judge of the inferior Court there for several years.

Question by the Prosecution by permission of the Commission.

Q. Was not the sensation produced on your mind by the arrest of Duke as great as that produced upon your mind when you heard of the death of Ashburn? *A.* suppose it was greater, sir.

The Commission then adjourned until Monday morning at ten o'clock.

McPHERSON BARRACKS, ATLANTA, GA.,
10 o'clock A. M., July 13, 1868.

The Commission met pursuant to adjournment.

Present, same members as yesterday, the Judge Advocate and his assistants, all the accused on trial, and their counsel.

The record of the previous day was then read and approved.

Witness Andrew Sheppard, whose testimony of the previous day had been read over to him by the Judge Advocate, asked and obtained leave of the Commission to make the following correction to his answer to question No. 18, viz: "My brother Eddie was one who was not present; he had the toothache."

Witness C. T. Arrington, whose testimony of the previous day was read over to him, asked and obtained the permission of the Commission to correct his answer to question No. —— in his testimony of the previous day, so as to make it read, "I think I was gone eight days."

Mr. Eugene Davis, having been granted by the Commission leave to retire as reporter, Mr. James O. Clephane was duly sworn as reporter in his stead.

Witness, ROBERT T. C. TUCKER was then recalled by Mr. Brown, of counsel for the prosecution, and by leave of the Commission, and interrogated as follows:

Q. To whom did the cotton belong that was carried to Lagrange, and who carried it? *A.* The cotton belonged to a young man by the name of Burke. Burke had bought it.

Q. Of whom? *A.* Thomas Parham.

Q. How many bales were there? *A.* I do not know how many he bought—my wagon carried six.

Q. Who drove your wagon? *A.* My son-in-law.

Q. What is his name? *A.* Blunor W. Williams.

Q. To whom did he deliver the cotton in Lagrange? *A.* I do not know, sir.

Q. Did you hear him say to whom he delivered it?. *A.* No, sir. The old man's son went up with the wagon, and disposed of the cotton at Lagrange.

Q. Is Burke a dealer in cotton in Lagrange? *A.* He was buying cotton at that time. I do not know whether for himself, or some one else.

Q. Was it Burke's son who went with the cotton? *A.* No, sir—Parkham's.

Q. Does Parham live in Lagrange? *A.* No, sir.

Q. Where does he live? *A.* Near me —about a mile and a half from me.

Q. Does Burke live in Lagrange? *A.* I suppose he does; I see him frequently when I go there.

Q. Has he a place of business in Lagrange? *A.* Not that I know of.

Q. In what business did you see him when you met him in Lagrange? *A.* I generally meet him in the street.

Q. How long has he been known there as a cotton buyer? *A.* I do not know, sir, that he ever bought a bale of cotton in Lagrange in his life.

Q. Did you hear no one who went with the wagons say on their return to whom they delivered the cotton in Lagrange? *A.* No, sir.

By leave of the Commission, the witness was re-examined by Mr. Stephens, as follows:

Q. In your testimony of yesterday, in reply to question No. ——, you state as follows: * * * *
* * * * * *

By that you mean you did not see him at the house? *A.* No, sir, I did not see him at the house, because I went on to the field.

Q. You said that you saw a man, you took to be him, some forty or fifty yards distant, and one that they told you was Duke. Did you mean to say that you did not see him on that evening? *A.* No, sir, I did not see him, as I went to the field.

Q. We understand you to state that you did see him, and they told you that it was William, and you said, "Has William come back?" *A.* Yes, sir; in the evening when he came into the field I saw him there, but I did not see him at the house as I went on; when I went by the house I did not know that he was at home.

Q. You stated that Mr. Joseph Burke bought this cotton; and you also stated that you never knew he bought a bale of cotton in Lagrange in your life; you mean by that that you never knew him to buy a bale of cotton in your life, of your own personal knowledge? A. Yes, sir, of my own personal knowledge, he bought this out in the country there, in the neighborhood where I lived; he bought of Mr. Thomas Parham.

Q. Do I understand you to state that you know, of your own knowledge, that he made that purchase, or that that is what you heard that he bought of Mr. Parham? A. Burke told me himself, and requested me to haul it for him.

By Mr. Stephens, of Counsel for Defense.

JOAB ABNEY, a witness for the defense, being duly sworn, testified as follows:

Q. State your name in full. A. Joab Abney.

Q. What is your occupation? A. I have been peddling for the last three or four years when I have been able to do anything; I have been sick for the biggest part of the time with rheumatic pains and smallpox; I never got over that.

Q. Have you a distinct recollection of where you were when you first heard of the death of Ashburn? A. I have.

Q. Where were you? A. I was in the porch of my own house, and heard it from neighbors passing around it.

Q. Where is your house? A. It is up above the railroad, in the neighborhood of the old city mill, as it is called, outside of the incorporation.

Q. What city? A. Columbus.

Q. What day of the week was that? A. That I heard this conversation?

Q. Yes, sir. A. It was Tuesday morning.

Q. Who were the persons you heard talking? A. I did not know them; they were black people passing.

Q. Where were you the Monday before the Tuesday you heard of Ashburn's death? A. I was at home.

Q. Where were you the day before? A. I was at home from eleven o'clock till night.

Q. State to the court if you were absent before that, when you left Columbus, where you went and when you got back, as you have stated you were there at home. A. I left home on Thursday morning to carry William Duke to his father's, in Merriwether county, Georgia; I got there with him that night, after sunset; I remained there all night; the next morning I went to my brother's fourteen miles further from Columbus, on Friday—Jas. Abney's; there I remained Friday night, and left for Columbus on Saturday; I went to within twenty miles of Columbus, stayed all night, and went home at eleven o'clock on Sunday.

Q. Are you positively certain—absolutely certain of these facts you have sworn to? A. I am, sir, certain of every word of it.

Cross-examined by Mr. Brown.

Q. How long have you lived where you now live? A. In the same house?

Q. Yes, sir. A. A month before Christmas.

Q. Where did you move from when you went into the house where you now live? A. Within fifty yards, sir.

Q. How long have you lived in Columbus? A. Eight years last December.

Q. Are you in the habit of carrying persons in your buggy for pay? A. No, sir.

Q. What induced you to carry Duke home? A. I wanted to go to my brother's and he was there sick, and asked me if I could take him to his father's so he could get shed of the chills.

Q. How long had he been in Columbus? A. Mr. Duke lived in Columbus when I moved there, I think. I first got acquainted with him when I moved there.

Q. Had he lived there all the time after you became acquainted with him? A. I knew him all the time when I seed him, and he remained there all the time until his father moved out there to Merriwether county.

Q. Where did he live when his father moved to Merriwether county? A. He always claimed his father's as his home when I talked with him; I saw him in Columbus boarding at Martin Beck's; Mr. Beck told me he boarded there.

Q. How long had he been in Columbus immediately prior to the time you carried him home? A. I can not answer—I do not know.

Q. How often had you seen him there the last two weeks? A. I saw him every two or three days, I think I might have seen him every day—I did not know he was sick having chills. He went out, but I was not able to go about much in town myself; I can not answer how often.

Q. How far did he board from your house? *A.* Six hundred yards I should think.

Q. How far is it from Columbus to his father's in Merriwether? *A.* Forty miles.

Q. Did you make the trip in one day? *A.* We did, sir.

Q. Did you both travel in the same buggy? *A.* We did, sir.

Q. Did you work one horse or two? *A.* Worked one horse, sir.

Q. Describe the horse? *A.* He was a large bay horse.

Q. About how old? *A.* Ten or twelve years old.

Q. Describe the buggy? *A.* It was a common ordinary buggy.

Q. Did they belong to you? *A.* Neither of them, sir.

Q. Whose property were they? *A.* The horse belonged to Christopher C. Abney, my son.

Q. To whom did the buggy belong? *A.* Abram Odum.

Q. How long had you the horse and buggy at your house before you started? *A.* I do not think they were there at all; yes, they were brought up there that morning for me to get in and ride.

Q. Who brought them? *A.* A small son of mine.

Q. Where did he get them? *A.* He got them from his brother down town.

Q. What month and what day of the month did you start. *A.* I started on the last Thursday in March.

Q. What enables you to recollect that fact distinctly? *A.* Because I knew it was the last days in March, and then when I got out to my brother's another circumstance; he was planting his corn and grumbling because they had not done planting in the very last days of March, and had not bedded up his land for cotton. We had considerable conversation about it, and I told him there was time enough.

Q. When did you first hear of Duke being accused of having been connected with the Ashburn murder? *A.* It has been some six or eight weeks ago, I reckon; two months after the occurrence, as well as I recollect.

Q. Whom did you hear speak of it? *A.* My son told me of it; that he heard it in town from a young man by the name of Pitman, at Cook's Hotel.

Q. Prior to that time had you any distinct recollection about the time when you went with Duke to his home? *A.* I had not thought anything of it at all.

Q. When was your attention first called particularly to the day when you went home with Duke, and by whom? *A.* Right then when my son told me that they were speaking of arresting him on the charge of being connected with this case. Says I, "That's all nonsense; Duke was in Merriwether, we all know;" that was the first thing that drawed my attention to it.

Q. Was not that about two months after you went home with Duke? *A.* I reckon it was, as well as I can recollect; I ain't positive.

Q. Do you always recollect the date of an occurrence two months ago? *A.* No, sir.

Q. Did you make any memorandum of the date when you went home with Duke? *A.* I did not.

Q. Are you in the habit of making memoranda of what occurs as you pass along? *A.* I am not.

Q. Are you not often mistaken about the particular day of an occurrence two or three months past? *A.* I would suppose, when there was not any thing very interesting in it, I would be liable to be mistaken.

Q. At the time you went with Duke did you then consider there was anything interesting connected with the transaction? *A.* I did not.

Q. Was it rainy weather or clear weather when you went with Duke? *A.* I think it rained; I got very wet; I was very cold when I got there; it rained on me ten miles that evening.

Q. Did you get there before dark or after dark? *A.* I got there before dark.

Q. Were the nights dark or moonlight? *A.* It was a very dark night, I think, as well as I can recollect.

Q. What time of the night did the moon shine? *A.* If it shone at all I do not recollect it; I have no recollection of seeing any moon.

Q. How long did you stay at Duke's? *A.* Until about 8 o'clock the next morning, as nigh as I can recollect.

Q. You say you then went to your brother's; how long did you stay there? *A.* I got there that evening about 1 o'clock and stayed there the next day until about the same time of day.

Q. Did it rain that day? *A.* It rained that morning before I started.

Q. What time did you leave your brother's? *A.* From 8 to 9 o'clock.

Q. What day of the week? *A.* Saturday.

Q. Do you mean 8 or 9 o'clock in the forenoon? *A.* Yes, sir.

Q. How far is it from your brother's to Columbus? *A.* Fifty-two miles.

Q. Did you drive 52 miles by 10 or 11 o'clock the next day? *A.* By 11 o'clock, sir.

Q. Where did you stay all night Saturday? *A.* I stayed all night in a mill of old man Whitehead's—I disremember the name of it—within twenty miles from Columbus.

Q. On what road does old man Whitehead live? *A.* He lives on the road leading from Columbus, at a forks that leads almost anywhere—it leads to Macon, Warm Springs, and anywhere you want to go.

Q. What is old man Whitehead's given name? *A.* Thomas.

Q. Do you say he lives twenty miles from Columbus? *A.* Twenty-one miles, he says it is—measured.

Q. Did you stop a mile before you got to his house, or a mile after you passed his house? *A.* I passed his house a mile.

Q. Describe the house in which you stayed. *A.* It was a log house, on the left-hand side of the road—a new log house.

Q. Do you mean the left-hand side of the road as you go toward Columbus? *A.* Yes, sir; the left-hand side as you go toward Columbus.

Q. Was it a double house, or what sort of a house was it? *A.* Only one room, I think.

Q. Can you recollect the name of the gentleman who lived there? *A.* I can not; I know his name well enough, but I can not bring it to mind.

Q. Describe his personal appearance. *A.* He is a tolerably small man, sir; he looks like he was about thirty years old.

Q. What is his complexion and color of his eyes? *A.* I disremember.

Q. Do you recollect the color of his hair. *A.* I do not.

Q. Has he a wife? *A.* He has, sir.

Q. How many children did you see? *A.* Two or three, as well as I can recollect.

Q. Do you recollect the appearance of his wife? *A.* I do not; she was complaining of being sick; I paid no attention to her; I was sick myself.

Q. Has he a lot and stables? *A.* He has a lot; whether there are any stables or not in it I can not answer.

Q. Did you see your horse fed? *A.* I did.

Q. Was he not in a stable? *A.* He was not.

Q. Where was he? *A.* In a lot.

Q. Was he loose in the lot or tied with a halter? *A.* Loose, I think.

Q. Is there any other house between old man Whitehead's and the house where you stayed all night? *A.* Yes, sir.

Q. How many? *A.* Two.

Q. Do you know who lives in either of them? *A.* I have heard both their names, but I disremember.

Q. Then the house in which you stayed all night is the third house after you passed the old man Whitehead's going towards Columbus, is it? *A.* It is sir.

Q. Have you been there since? *A.* I have.

Q. When were you there last. *A.* Some five or six weeks ago.

Q. Did the same man live there then? *A.* He did.

Q. Did you try to refresh his recollection as to the time you stayed with him before? *A.* I did; for I could not pay the bill; he could not change the money, and I stopped and paid him; I know he recollected it.

Q. Did you and he talk anything about the day of the week or month when you stayed there before; I mean this last time? *A.* The last time I was there I had frequently conversed with him; I was passing by as I was peddling through the country; I stopped for the purpose of paying the gentleman for the fare that I owed him that night.

Q. Was anything said between you and him about the day of the week or month when you last stayed all night with him? *A.* I do not recollect that there was, sir; he told me he was acquainted with my brother, and I told him I had been out.

Mr. Stephens—He does not understand the question. Was there anything at that time said about the day of the month when you first stayed there? *A.* When I went to pay him the bill?

Mr. Stephens—Yes, sir. *A.* No, sir.

Questions by the Prosecution.

Q. Have you and he at any time since talked about Duke or Ashburn? *A.* This gentleman that I paid the bill to?

Q. Yes. *A.* I never seen him.

Q. Was there any conversation between you and him about Duke or Ashburn at the time you paid him the bill? *A.* Not that I recollect.

Q. Was it not a dark night when you stayed with him on your return? *A.* I judge it was, sir; I did not go out.

Q. Do you recollect what time of the moon it was? *A.* I do not.

Q. You say you got home on Sunday; what did you do the balance of that day? *A.* I did not do anything; I laid down and rested until three o'clock, and then there was a prayer-meeting at my house, and I attended that.

Q. Was you at home on Monday? *A.* I was.

Q. What were you doing Monday? *A.* Nothing at all, sir.

Q. Were you in town that day? *A.* No, sir, I was at the upper end of the street at my son's; I was not in town; that was as far as I was able to get.

Q. How far is the upper end of the street where you were from the Perry House in Columbus? *A.* From where I was Monday?

Q. Yes, sir. *A.* About three hundred yards, I judge, sir.

Q. Whom did you see on the street? *A.* I have no recollection.

Q. Did you see any persons that day? *A.* I do not recollect of noticing a person; I saw a great many people; I could not name ne'er one; I saw a great many people passing, but I do not recollect any particular one.

Q. Did you converse with any of them? *A.* I expect I did, but I do not recollect anything that passed.

Q. Did you hear nothing of Ashburn's death on Monday? *A.* I did not.

Q. Whom did you first see on Tuesday? *A.* Black, colored people.

Q. What time of the day was it? *A.* Just at light.

Q. Do you recollect the names of any of them? *A.* I do not, I paid no attention to them; I just heard them talking and going on; I asked them what was the matter, and they told me Ashburn was killed.

Q. How many of them were there? *A.* That passed by my house with that conversation?

Q. Yes. *A.* I have no idea how many passed there.

Q. Can you mention no one who passed by your house and spoke of Ashburn's death that day? *A.* I do not know any of their names; I could go and put my finger on several of them.

Q. Did you hear any white persons speak of it that day? *A.* After I got down to my son's I heard several persons say that he was killed—white people.

Q. Can you name any of these persons other than your son? *A.* That I heard speak of it? I can not, sir, there were so many; I heard several speak of the occurrence of his being killed, but who they were I do not know at this time.

Q. Does not your memory serve you as to any of them? *A.* I think, as well as I recollect, I heard William Brooke speak of it, and my son; any further I do not know as I can name any.

Q. Where does Wm. Brooke live? *A.* He lives in Alabama—Girard.

Q. You state that you can remember no other person? *A.* I can not distinctly, sir, except my own family—my wife and daughter.

Q. Have you a good memory? *A.* Tolerably, sir, only.

Q. How old are you? *A.* I will be 63 the 12th day of next month.

Q. Is your memory as good as it formerly was? *A.* No, sir.

Q. Have you a good recollection of dates? *A.* Of anything that occurs particularly, I have, sir; but what I pay no attention to I never recollect.

Q. Was there any public meeting or particular occurrence that took place in Columbus three months ago, you can now mention the date of? *A.* There was not.

Q. Do you remember on what days the late election was held? *A.* I do not.

Q. Is there no particular occurrence in Columbus that you can mention, with the time, within the last three months? *A.* If there is I do not recollect it. I am hardly ever there.

Q. Is there any other occurrence that took place during the month of March that you can now mention, with the particular day on which it occurred? *A.* There is not, sir. I was sick all the time, with my knee out of place, lying in bed.

Q. Is there any particular occurrence that took place during the month of April that you can now mention, with the day on which it occurred. *A.* I don't know that there is.

Q. Is there any during the month of May? *A.* I do not recollect.

Q. Do you recollect any during the month of June? *A.* Yes, sir, some occurrences I recollect in the month of June.

Q. Do you recollect the exact day on which they took place? *A.* No, sir.

Re-direct—Questions by Mr. Stephens.

Q. Is there anything, Mr. Abney, that fixes it in your mind why you got back to Columbus at that time, when you went with Mr. Duke? *A.* Anything that I recollect as the cause of my coming at that hour?

Q. Yes, sir. *A.* There was a prayer-meeting appointed at my house before I left home. I told them I would be certain to be there. The meeting was appointed for half-past three o'clock, and I told them I woud be certain to be back. I left my brother's sooner than I intended to, and went on further than I should have that evening, in order to get there in time to comply with my promise, and got there at eleven o'clock.

Q. Whose buggy did you say it was? *A.* Abram Odum's.

Re-cross-examination by Mr. Brown.

Q. Did you have any more than one prayer-meeting at that house during the spring? *A.* A good many, sir.

Q. Were they on Sunday? *A.* They were, sir.

Q. Usually on Sunday afternoons? *A.* They were, sir.

Q. About the same time of the day that this one took place? *A.* Yes, sir.

Q. Do you recollect the day of the week and of the month when this one was appointed? *A.* It was appointed about a week beforehand, before it was attended to. It was noised about that at half-past three o'clock, at my house, on that Sunday, the last Sunday in March, there would be a prayer-meeting.

Q. Can you tell the exact day when it was appointed? *A.* I can not.

Q. Can you name the day of the month when any other one of the prayer-meetings was held there? *A.* I can not without referring back, sir.

Q. Referring back to what? *A.* I could get the almanac, and tell when they every one were.

Q. Look at this almanac and tell us, if you please, (handing witness almanac of 1868.) *A.* I can not see. Any one of you may look at the day of the month.

Q. Try my glasses, and see if you can see through them. *A.* I know I can not. I never seed any that I could see through. (putting on the glasses and looking at the almanac.) I can not see, sir, enough to make it out.

Q. Have you glasses of your own? *A.* I can not use them; none of them does me any good.

Q. Can you read without glasses? *A.* I have been so for the last five or six weeks that I can not read at all.

Q. Then how can you tell by the almanac when the prayer-meetings were held? *A.* I could get some one else to look, and I could count it back; there was the first Sunday in April; the second and third Sunday along; they could tell by the almanac what day of the month they came on, I suppose.

Q. Was there one held there every Sunday in the month? *A.* There was for four or five Sundays handrunning.

Q. Do you recollect any other particular occurrence connected with either of the other prayer-meetings? *A.* I do not, sir, of importance.

Q. Did you at the time attach any importance particularly to your trip with Duke? *A.* The prayer-meeting being appointed there, as it was the first one, and I was just coming home with Duke from the carrying of him, made me know the days and months more perfectly than I would in any conversation with my brother; that is what made me notice so very particularly.

Q. You say that you recollect the day when the prayer-meeting was held, but can not recollect any day when it was appointed? *A.* No, sir; I do not recollect any day when it was appointed.

Q. Are you sure this was the first one that was held at your house? *A.* I am, sir, in that house.

Q. Is that the house where you now live? *A.* It is.

Q. Now, please name some persons who were at that prayer-meeting. *A.* William Brooke, Abram Odum.

Q. Any others? *A.* I disremember

their names, certain; there was a dozen or two there.

Q. Can not you name somebody else besides Brooke and Odum who were there?
A. I can not for certain.

Q. Can you recollect anybody who was at either of the others? A. Yes, sir.

Q. Who? A. Mr. Brooke, Mr. Odum, Mr. Thomas Cochran.

Q. Now, on what day was the one held when Cochran attended? A. What day of the week, do you mean?

Q. No, of the month? A. I can not tell.

Q. Was it the first, second, third or fourth prayer-meeting that he attended? A. I think he was there pretty much at all of them.

Q. Was he at the first one? A. That I can not recollect.

Q. Can you say distinctly that he was at the second? A. I can not; I answered distinctly that he was at two or three of them afterwards, whether the second or third I can not say.

Re-direct by Mr Stephens.

Q. Mr. Abney, when did you first ever hear that your testimony would be required or desired in this case? A. Never until week before last.

Q. Where were you? A. I had just returned to Columbus; my son told me he expected I would have to come up here, and I told him I reckoned not.

Q. Where did you next hear it? Where were you when you next heard it? A. I stayed at home a day or two, and then I heard it from two or three different persons. The next I heard of it was last Thursday evening.

Q. Where were you, is my question? A. I was in the east corner of Marion County.

Q. How far from Chambers? A. Forty-seven miles.

Q. Was it there where you were subpœnaed? A. It was.

Q. What were you doing down there—on your business—peddling? A. I was.

Questions by the Court.

Q. On return from your brother's to Columbus, in March last, did you pass Duke's? A. No, sir, I did not.

Q. Was the first prayer-meeting in your house held on the first Sunday in April? A. It was held on the last Sunday in March.

By Mr. Stephens, Counsel for Defense.

STITH A. PARHAM, a witness for the defense, being duly sworn, testifies as follows:

Q. Where do you reside, Mr. Parham? A. In Merriwether County.

Q. Do you know Wm. Duke? Do you see him here in this line of gentlemen? (pointing to the prisoners.) A. Yes, sir.

Q. Which is he? A. That is the gentleman sitting by the window, (pointing to prisoner Duke.)

Q. How far is your place of residence from that of his father's in Merriwether County? A. About a mile and a half.

Q. Did you see him there at his father's the latter part of March of this year? A. I did.

Q. Was it the last week in March? A. Yes, sir.

Q. When did you see him there—the latter part of March? A. I saw him, I suppose, about the 30th.

Q. What day of the week was the 30th? A. On Monday.

Q. Where was he? A. He was at home.

Q. What hour of the day did you see him, and where was he? A. He was at his father's shop, and I suppose the sun was an hour high in the evening, or later.

Q. Did you see him there at any other time that week? A. I saw him the next morning.

Q. What hour of the day of the next morning did you see him? A. I suppose the sun was not more than two hours high.

Q. Is there anything that fixes it in your mind that you did see him at these particular times, on the Monday and Tuesday that you have mentioned? A. I think there was, sir.

Q. State what facts fix it in your mind? A. There was a gentleman bought some timber from me to saw up into lumber, and I went up there the next morning to see about it.

Q. What kind of timber was it? A. Pine timber.

Q. What land was the timber on that you sold? A. It belonged to me.

Q. What was it to be sawed into? A. Lumber.

Q. Was it the tract of land you were living on, or some other? A. It was not the tract I was living on.

Q. Who was living on the tract? A. Mr. Duke.

Q. The father, you mean, of William? *A.* Yes, sir.

Q. Who was it bought the lumber from you? *A.* James Oglethorpe.

Q. When did you begin delivering that lumber? *A.* It was stock lumber; timber to be sawed up into lumber.

Q. You sold the trees, then, and it was cut into stocks, but to be hauled to the sawmill? *A.* Yes, sir.

Q. When did they begin to haul away these stocks? *A.* I do not remember, sir.

Q. How many days were they hauling them away? *A.* They were some two or three days.

Q. Not longer than that? *A.* I don't remember whether they were any longer than that or not.

Q. Was there anything special that called you up there that Monday to see after the hauling of them? *A.* No, sir; nothing in particular.

Q. Was there anything Tuesday? *A.* Yes, sir.

Q. What was it? *A.* I went up there to see about it on Tuesday.

Q. What was it that called you up there? *A.* I do not recollect what caused me to go up there, but Mr. Oglethorpe wanted me to go up there, and see about the timber that was to be delivered.

Q. Who was hauling it? *A.* There was a young man whom we had hired to haul it for him.

Q. What was his name? *A.* Hanley.

Q. Where were you when you first heard of the death of Ashburn? *A.* I was in Lagrange?

Q. What day did you leave home? *A.* The first day of April.

Q. Do you know the day of the week? *A.* Wednesday or Thursday, I ain't certain which.

Q. Now are you certain that when you went up to see about these logs, was the Monday or Tuesday before you went to Lagrange. *A.* Yes, sir.

Q. State to the court what facts fixed that upon your mind? *A.* Well, that was the cause of it. After I got to Lagrange, hearing that Ashburn had been killed, caused me to reflect, to look about, as it made a great deal of noise in the neighborhood.

Q. What did you go to Lagrange for? *A.* To see some cotton.

Q. Whose cotton was it? *A.* It was my father's cotton and mine.

Q. Did you make any preparation for starting the cotton off at any day or any time previous to starting? *A.* Not that I remember.

Q. Where was the cotton? *A.* It was at my house, at my father's.

Q. What was it that called you up to the shop Tuesday morning? Was there anything connected with the hauling of the lumber that called you up there? *A.* No, sir, not that I know of, with the exception that when I got up there, Mr. Hanley, who was hauling the logs, had taken a large stock and had broken his ring, and I went up to the shop with him from the field where they were hauling, or the new ground, rather.

Q. You know the fact that that is what called you up there—that the ring of the ox-yoke broke? *A.* Yes, sir.

Q. Now from that fact and the number of days that he was hauling, and connecting the time when you went to Lagrange, are you certain that that is the evening that you saw Mr. Wm. Duke, the accused, there at his father's shop? *A.* Yes, sir.

Q. Are you positive of it? *A.* I am.

Cross-examined by Brown.

Q. Whose wagon hauled that cotton to Lagrange? *A.* Mr. Williams' wagons hauled my father's.

Q. Is Mr. Williams the son-in-law of Mr. Tucker, who testified here as a witness? *A.* He is.

Q. To whom was the cotton delivered in Lagrange? *A.* To Mr. Frost, I think.

Q. What is the christian name? *A.* Francis or Frank Frost is all the name I heard.

Q. Is he a cotton dealer? *A.* He is.

Q. Does he keep a warehouse? *A.* I don't know.

Q. Where was the cotton stored from the wagons? *A.* I think, perhaps, sir, it was carried to the depot, if I am not mistaken.

Q. Were you not with it? *A.* I was up in town.

Q. Did you not go up for the purpose of selling it? *A.* No, sir.

Q. Was it sold before you left home? *A.* Yes, sir.

Q. Did you not go up to deliver it? *A.* I did.

Q. Where did you deliver it? *A.* At

the depot, I suppose; didn't myself go down to the depot.

Q. Do you mean the railroad depot? *A.* Yes.

Q. In Lagrange? *A.* Yes sir.

Q. Who carried it down to the depot? *A.* Mr. Williams and the negro man.

Q. Do you know whether it was shipped from the depot? *A.* I do not.

Q. Who ordered it to the depot? *A.* Mr. Frost, perhaps; I don't recollect.

Q. To whom had the cotton been sold in Merriwether? *A.* It was sold to Mr. Frost.

Q. Are you sure of that? It was carried to him when it was sent to the depot.

Q. Is that the same that was carried on Williams' wagon? *A.* It was.

Q. How many bales did that wagon carry? *A.* Six, I think, sir.

Q. Who paid for it? *A.* I don't recollect, sir.

Q. Who received the money? *A.* I did.

Q. Where did you receive it? *A.* I received it from Mr. Abrams.

Q. Where? *A.* In Lagrange.

Q. At what place in Lagrange? *A.* In Mr. Wymbush & Abrams' house.

Q. Who sent you to them for the money? *A.* Well, sir, I don't know.

Q. How happened it that you received the money from them when you had sold the cotton to Frost? *A.* Mr. Abrams went up there to Frost's and brought it down there to the house.

Q. Is Mr. Abrams a merchant? *A.* Yes, sir.

Q. Did you receive it in his store-house? *A.* I did.

Q. Was there any memorandum given at the time, or any receipt? *A.* I think there was.

Q. Did you sign it? *A.* No, sir.

Q. Who did? *A.* I don't recollect.

Q. Did you receive the money without being required to give a receipt for it? *A.* I don't recollect, sir, whether I did or not.

Q. Do you recollect the amount you received? *A.* Not the exact amount.

Q. About how much? *A.* I suppose between eight and nine hundred dollars.

Q. What time of the day was it? *A.* About ten or eleven.

Q. What day of the week? *A.* Thursday, I think, sir.

Q. Are you certain of that? *A.* Yes, sir.

Q. What day of the month? *A.* Second day of April.

Q. How long did you stay in Lagrange? *A.* I stayed there until one or two o'clock in the evening.

Q. How far from your residence to Lagrange? *A.* About twenty miles they call it.

Q. When did you get home? *A.* I got home the same evening.

Q. What time of the evening? *A.* It was dusk I suppose, sir—about dark.

Q. Was it a dark night or a moonlight night? *A.* I can not recollect, sir.

Q. Was it cloudy or starlight? *A.* I don't recollect.

Q. Did it rain any that day? *A.* Not that I know of.

Q. Do you recollect whether it did or not? *A.* No, sir, I have no recollection whether it rained or not.

Q. What did you do the next day? *A.* I went down to my father's.

Q. What did you do there? *A.* I paid him over the amount of money his cotton brought.

Q. What did you do the next day? *A.* I don't recollect, sir.

Q. What did you do the day after. *A.* I don't know.

Q. Where were you on the Monday before the 30th of March? *A.* I don't remember.

Q. Where were you on the Wednesday before? *A.* I can not tell, sir.

Q. When did you first hear of Duke's arrest? *A.* Well, sir, I was not at home when he was arrested; I didn't hear of it till I was summoned to come up here; I was not about home.

Q. Where were you when you were summoned to come up here? *A.* I was at home.

Q. Did you state that you had never heard of Duke's arrest before you was summoned to come? *A.* I don't recollect whether I had or not, sir; if I had, it was only a few minutes before.

Q. When were you summoned to come up here? *A.* I don't recollect the day of the month, sir.

Q. Do you recollect the day of the week? *A.* It was Friday evening, sir, I believe.

Q. Are you certain of that? *A.* No, sir, I am not certain of that.

Q. About how long ago was it? *A.* some time last week.

Q. Did it not make a decided impression on your mind when you heard that Duke had been arrested? *A.* No, sir, not in particular, it didn't.

Q. Was there not some excitement in the neighborhood about it? *A.* His being arrested?

Q. Yes. *A.* I suppose there was, sir; I was not at home.

Q. Do you state that it made no impression an your mind?

* * * * * * *

Q. Which was regarded the more important event, the arrest of Duke or the hauling of the stock to the mill? *A.* The arrest of Mr. Duke.

Q. Then how is it that you can locate the particular day of the week on which the stocks were hauled there, and a half month ago, and can not locate the day of the week on which you heard of Duke's arrest, a little over a week ago? *A.* Well, sir, I don't know why it was.

Q. Can you locate any other particular event that took place on a particular day, about the time the stocks were hauled? *A.* Well, nothing more than going to Lagrange and something of that sort, sir.

Q. Has there been anything since that time, and prior to the time you heard Duke was arrested, that called your attention especially to the date when the stocks were hauled? *A.* Not that I recollect, sir.

Q. If Duke had never been arrested do you believe you would ever have located in your mind again the time the stocks were hauled? *A.* Yes, sir.

Q. What would have caused you to locate the time? *A.* In settling for the lumber.

Q. Have you settled for it? *A.* No, sir.

Q. Were there any books kept at the time of the transaction? *A.* I suppose there was.

Q. Do you know that fact? *A.* No, sir.

Q. To whom did you deliver the stocks? *A.* James Ogletree.

Q. Who hauled them? *A.* Hanley.

Q. Where's Ogletree's mill? *A.* In Merriwether county.

Q. How far from your house? *A.* Half a mile.

Q. Is it your opinion that he kept a book that shows the date of the delivery of those stocks? *A.* Well, I suppose he has a book; I don't know.

Q. Will his books show the date of the delivery? *A.* He was some two or three— I don't know how many days he was hauling the stocks from the field. I suppose he set it down though.

Q. How many stocks were there? *A.* I suppose some fifty. He hauled them out of the field—just outside the field, so that they could clear the ground. The stocks are there yet.

Q. Then the stocks are still on your premises are they? *A.* No, sir, they are on Jordan Reese's premises.

Q. How far are they from the mill? *A.* About a mile and a half, or nearly so—well, about a mile and a half.

Q. Have none of them been sawed up? *A.* I think they have, sir. I don't know; I think they have.

Q. Do you recollect how much he was to pay you for the stocks? *A.* Yes.

Q. When was the payment to be made? *A.* There was no time specified.

Q. If Duke had never been arrested, would you ever have regarded the date of the delivery of the stocks of any consequence? *A.* Yes, I think I would.

Q. As no time was fixed for the payment, why would the date of delivery have been a matter of any importance? *A.* We would have a settlement about it.

Q. Well, as no time was fixed for the payment, why would it, when they were delivered, have been a matter of any consequence in the settlement? *A.* I don't know, sir, why it is.

Q. Can you give any reason why it would have been? *A.* No.

Q. Can you name the persons you met on the Saturday before the 30th of March? *A.* In the evening when we were up at the shop, sir, I saw Robert Tucker, Jordan Reese, and Woodward, and another gentleman was there, and Mr. Norman was there.

Q. Can you name any other date when you were at that shop, about that time? *A.* I was there frequently. We met there frequently, every day or two, sir.

Q. You say Robert Tucker was there that day? *A.* Yes, sir.

Q. At the shop? *A.* Yes, sir.

Q. What time of the day did you see him there? *A.* Late in the evening.

Q. How long did he stay there? *A.* I left him there.

Q. Name some other day of that week when you was at the shop? *A.* I was there Tuesday morning.

Q. Name another day when you were there? *A.* Well, sir, I went up to

14

Lagrange, and I have not any recollection when I was there again at the shop.

Q. Without regard to the day of the week, state the next time you were at the shop, when you came back from Lagrange? A. Well, sir, I don't recollect.

Q. Who was there the next time you was at the shop? A. I have no recollection, sir.

Q. State the last time you were there before the Saturday before the 30th of March? A. I can't call to memory, sir, when I was.

Q. Can you locate another particular day during the months of March and April, when you were at the shop, except Saturday before the 30th of March? A. No, sir.

Q. Were you not there frequently during both these months? A. Yes, sir.

Q. Then, why is it that you can locate no other day, except those two days, when you were there? A. I don't recollect, sir.

Q. Can you tell how many persons were there on any other day when you was there in these two months, and give the names of these persons? A. No, sir.

Q. Do you know what time you commenced plowing over your corn? What day of the month? A. I suppose some time in May.

Q. No, I desire to know the particular day of the month? A. No, sir.

Q. Can you tell what day of the month you commenced planting corn? A. Yes, sir.

Q. What enables you to remember that? A. Circumstances of my planting corn; about the 10th day of March I generally plant corn. I commenced this year to plant corn then.

Q. Can you swear that positively? A. No, sir, I can't. It was about that time.

Q. Can you state the day positively on which you commenced planting cotton? A. No, sir.

Q. Is there no incident connected with your farming operations there that you can locate on a particular day, except the delivery of those stocks? A. Not that I recollect now.

Re-examined by Mr. Stephens.

Q. If your mind had been directed by any of these events, is it not highly probable that you could remember the particular days on which they occurred? A. It is probable that I could, sir.

Q. If you were to cast up and think as to the day of the week that you were summoned to appear here, thinking over where you had been when you left home, could you not, and would you not most probably be able to tell exactly what day of the week it was? A. It is likely that I could, sir.

Q. When you say then, in reply to the question asked you by Gov. Brown, that you can not now state any particular day on which any occurrence happened at your house, as the planting of cotton or corn, do you mean or not simply to say that you can not now answer the question presented to you, without reflection? A. Well, I was up there frequently, but I can not recollect the date.

Q. When you come to think and reflect upon the death of Ashburn, and your being in Lagrange, and where you were before, are you positive and distinct that these events occurred at the times you stated here to-day? A. Yes, sir.

Q. Have you or not ever had a subject mentioned, the date when something occurred, when you could not recollect it at once, but after thinking over other matters connected with it, become as positive and certain as to any event of your life? A. Yes, I have done it.

Q. After thinking over closely these events that you have testified about, are you or not certain and positive that they occurred in connection as you have stated them? A. Yes, sir, I am certain.

Re-cross-examined by Mr. Brown.

Q. I would ask if your mind was directed as distinctly to events to which I directed your attention, as it was directed to the event of the hauling of the stocks, whether you could not recollect them as well? A. Well, I don't have any recollections of any particular day when I was up at the shop, or whom I met, or anything at the shop.

Q. Now I desire to direct your mind positively and distinctly to the day on which you heard of the arrest of Duke and received the subpœna, and desire you to take time and answer what day of the week and what day of the month it was? A. I don't recollect the day of the month it was. I recollect the day of the week.

Q. Please take time to reflect, and then answer? A. (After short reflection, the witness says): I have no recollection of the day, sir.

Q. I ask you, if you desire it, to take longer time for reflection? A. No, sir.

Hereupon the Court gives the witness privilege to go into a room by himself and take time for reflection. The witness says, "I don't wish to retire."

Q. Do you believe, on an hour's reflection in a room, that you could answer with any more positiveness than you do now? A. No, sir.

Q. What has caused you to reflect so particularly on the date when the stocks were delivered? A. I don't recollect, sir.

Q. Has your attention never been called particularly to that subject? A. No, sir.

Q. Then how is it that you can be so positive as to that incident, and can't be positive as to any other that has occurred within the last six months? A. It made more impression on my mind I suppose, sir—the hauling of the stock.

Q. Can you mention any other incident that occurred between the first day of January and the first day of June, giving the precise date, of which you can be as positive as of the date of the hauling of the stock.

This question was objected to informally by Mr. Stephens, and withdrawn by Gov. Brown.

Q. Can you now state distinctly the day of the week and month on which they began to haul the stocks? A. No, sir, I can not. They were hauling on the days that I mentioned.

Q. Can you mention any particular day when you know they did haul stock? A. Yes.

Q. What day? A. The last day of March, sir.

Q. Is there any other incident that occurred between the first day of January and the first day of June, that you can recollect as distinctly, and locate as positively on a particular day, as you can that incident? A. Well, I suppose there is. I suppose I could do it.

Q. What is it? A. Well, I commenced planting cotton on the 15th day of April.

Q. Do you swear that positively? A. Yes, sir.

Q. What day of the week was it? A. I don't recollect the day of the week.

Q. Then how can you swear positively to the day of the month, and you can't recollect the day of the week? A. I don't recollect the day of the week. I recollect that that was the time. I set it down.

Q. You say you set it down? A. Yes, sir.

Q. Where did you set it down? A. In a book or on a piece of paper.

Q. Was it on a book or on a piece of paper? A. On paper.

Q. What sort of a piece of paper? A. White paper.

Q. What have you done with it? A. It's at home, I suppose, now, sir.

Q. Did you set down on a piece of paper the day the stocks were being hauled? A. No, sir.

Q. Well, now, can you locate any other particular incident between the 1st of January and 1st of June which you did not set down on a piece of paper, and give the particular day? A. I can give the day of the month, but I can't give the week.

Q. What is the incident to which you refer? A. I could look over and see, and I could refer to my almanac and see what day of the week it was, if I wanted to see.

Q. If you knew the day of the month, you could look at the almanac and find the day of the week, could you? A. Yes, sir.

Q. Can you give the day of the month now on which any other incident occurred that you did not reduce to writing? A. I commenced planting corn on the 10th of March.

Q. Did you not state a while ago, under oath, that you would not be positive about that? A. No, I would not be positive, but since reflection I commenced planting corn on the 10th of March and cotton on the 15th of April.

Q. Did you set down the day on which you commenced planting corn? A. I put down the day of the month, not the day of the week.

Q. Where did you put it down? A. On a piece of paper.

Q. I asked you if you could locate any other incident within the time I have mentioned, and give the precise day that it occurred, which you did not put down on a piece of paper. A. Yes, sir, the 31st of March; I supposed they commenced hauling stocks about that time—about the 31st of March.

Q. I said any other incident; you have already testified about that incident. A. Well, I don't remember, sir.

Q. Can you remember no other? A. No.

Examination by Mr. Stephens.

CLIFFORD A. STYLES was introduced as a witness by the defense and duly sworn, and testified as follows:

Q. Doctor, please give the Court your name in full—christian name and all to the Court. *A.* Clifford A. Styles.

Q. Are your a brother to the Hon. William H. Styles, Minister to Austria some time ago, and to the Rev. Dr. Joseph C. Styles, of Richmond, Va.? *A.* Yes, sir.

Q. Where do you reside now, Doctor? *A.* In Merriwether county.

Q. This State? *A.* State of Georgia.

Q. What is your profession? *A.* Physician.

Q. Do you know William Duke. *A.* I do.

Q. Do you see him in this row of gentlemen? *A.* I do.

Q. Will you point him out to the Court? *A.* I will. (Witness points out Mr. Duke, the accused.)

Q. How far do you reside from his father's? *A.* About three miles.

Q. Did you see him at his father's at any time during the latter part of March of this year? *A.* I did.

Q. What was the day of the week and of the month, and state the circumstances where you saw him? *A.* It was on Monday, the 30th of March, 1868, at his father's workshop, about forty miles east of north of Columbus.

Q. What time in the evening? *A.* Between five and six P. M.

Q. Has your attention been called specially to the time on which you saw him? *A.* Yes, sir.

Q. Do you recollect when Mr. Ashburn, of Columbus, was assassinated? *A.* I do, sir.

Q. Do you recollect where you were when you first heard of it? *A.* I do.

Q. Where were you? *A.* In Duke's workshop.

Q. Was Mr. Duke, the accused, present at the time you heard the news? *A.* He was.

Q. Do you recollect the day of the week it was when you were there and heard the news? *A.* I think it was about Thursday; I am not certain.

Q. Are you certain that it was the Monday evening before the news reached you that you saw him there? *A.* I am.

Cross-examined—Questions by Brown.

Q. What enables you to be so positive on that subject? *A.* In regard to having seen him there, sir?

Q. Yes, sir. *A.* From the fact that I was called in the neighborhood to see my patients on the 30th of March.

Q. Did you visit those patients more than once. *A.* I did sir.

Q. How often? *A.* I don't remember exactly, several times.

Q. On what days did you visit them? *A.* About twice a week I was in the habit of going to Greer's—then I stopped on the road to see those who were sick on the plantations.

Q. Give the precise days of the week and month on which you visited each of those patients each time? *A.* I can't do it; I have not my record with me.

Q. Why did you bring your record with you? *A.* Because I had no thought I would be called on to produce it.

Q. Did you not come under a subpœna, Doctor? *A.* I am not certain whether I have or not, sir; I was noticed by the gentleman who stopped at the house. He told me to come on.

Q. Have you received any written subpœna? *A.* I have not, sir.

Q. Did you pass by the shop more than once while you were visiting your patients in the neighborhood? *A.* I did.

Q. How often did you pass there? *A* I don't remember very exactly. I have been in the habit of passing there generally about twice a week.

Q. Can you locate with distinctness any other day in the week or month when you passed there? *A.* No, sir, I can not.

Q. How long have you been practicing in that neighborhood? *A.* I think about three years.

Q. Have you generally passed the shop twice a week during that time? *A.* Only for the last year, sir, have I been in the habit of passing there twice a week.

Q. Can you, upon your oath, locate any other distinct time, within the past year, when you passed that shop, giving the day of the week and month? *A.* I can not unless I have my record with me.

Q. This, then, is the only instance within the year when you can locate the precise day without your record? *A.* It is, sir.

MILITARY OUTRAGE IN GEORGIA. 141

Re-direct Examination—Questions by Mr. Stephens.

Q. Is this because you lately looked at the record and know it to be so?

This question was objected to by Gov. Brown, and withdrawn by consent of counsel.

Re-cross-examined—Questions by Governor Brown.

Q. Have you looked at your record in reference to this particular visit? A. I did, sir.

Q. After having examined the record for the purpose of refreshing your recollection, are you now able to state from memory and not from record, that it was on that particular day? A. Yes, sir, I am, from the fact that old Mr. Duke came from Columbus on Sunday.

Q. Is that on your record? A. No, sir; old Mr. Duke started from Columbus on Sunday with a little pair of steers—one gave out and he left them at King's Gap in the mountain, about ten miles from his house. We came on together to the shop; I saw William Duke then, and I expressed my surprise at seeing him there, for I had heard a short time before that he was going to Arkansas; whereupon he remarked that he had been home several days.

Q. Well, now, Doctor, what connection is there between that affair about the steers and your record. A. Only that I remember that it was on Monday, the 30th, that I passed there.

Q. Well, does your record have anything to do with that? A. Nothing to do with the steers.

Q. Does it have anything to do with the particular time that you passed Duke's? A. Yes, it has to do with that, it reminds me of the time that I passed by there.

Q. Nothing written in it about Duke or passing Duke's? A. Nothing.

Q. Does not your record relate simply to your visits in the neighborhood? A. It does simply.

Q. Well, now, if you find upon your record that you visited—passed there on the 27th, 28th, 29th, 30th, and 31st of March, and the 1st, 2d, and 3d of April, how can you tell, looking at the record, what particular day you passed Duke's and saw William at home? A. Because I remember a few days after I passed there, I returned, and he was there, and asked

me and his brother if I had heard of the assassination of Ashburn.

Q. Well, Doctor, what has your record to do with that? A. It has nothing to do with that; it only refreshed my mind that I passed there a few days after I returned, and he asked me if I had heard of the assassination of Ashburn.

Q. If your record shows that you are visiting patients in the neighborhood on a dozen different days, and you are in the habit of passing the shop twice a week, how can you say from the record that you passed there on this particular day and not on another day in the record? A. Because when I passed by Duke's it was on my way home, and by referring to it I could always tell what day I passed, because it was on my way home.

Q. State what other days about that time it appears from your record you were in the neighborhood seeing patients. A. I can't tell, sir, for I only examined my record in regard to this case.

Q. When did you make that examination of the record, Doctor, in reference to this case? A. About a week and a half ago, I think.

Q. How then did you connect the entry of the 30th of March with that particular incident, rather than the 29th of March?

Judge Benning—I object to the question on the ground that the witness has never said there was an entry of that day.

Hereupon the Court adjourned until Tuesday morning, 10 o'clock A. M.

McPherson Barracks, Atlanta, Ga. }
10 o'clock A. M. July 14, 1868. }

The Commission met pursuant to adjournment.

Present, the same members as yesterday, the Judge Advocate and his assistants, the prisoners on trial and their counsel.

The record of yesterday's proceedings was read as far up as to the evidence of Dr. Styles, and approved.

The evidence of Joab Abney was then read to him; he desired to make no corrections, and was discharged.

The evidence of Stith A. Parham was then read to him by the Judge Advocate in open court. The witness desired and obtained permission of the court to add the following to his testimony:

"Well, about the time I started from home—upon reflection I recollect the time

I left home; it was on the 7th of July, and I landed here on the 8th. This is all the correction I want to make."

Mr. Crawford, of counsel for the defense, presented the following to the Commission:

"Mr. Crawford, of counsel for the prisoners, begs leave to announce to the Commission the severe indisposition of Mr. Stephens, and his inability to be present to-day, and to ask an adjournment until to-morrow, at which time he expects to be in attendance."

The Commission granted the request, and adjourned to 10 o'clock A. M. to-morrow.

McPHERSON BARRACKS, ATLANTA, GA.,
10 A. M., July 15, 1868.

The Commission met pursuant to adjournment.

Present, same members as yesterday, the Judge Advocate and his assistants, the prisoners on trial, and their counsel.

The record of yesterday's proceedings was read and approved.

The examination of Dr. Clifford A. Styles, a witness for the defense, was continued.

Judge Benning, of counsel for defense, having on Monday objected to the question asked by Gov. Brown, "How then do you connect the entry of the 30th of March with particular incident rather than the 29th of March?" this morning withdrew his objection, and the witness answered:

A. From the fact that on referring to my memorandum I did not see that on the night of the 29th I had visited Mr. Greer; I did on the 30th; that was the day I passed the shop.

Q. On what other day about the 30th did you find by reference to your memorandum that you did visit Mr. Greer? *A.* I did not find any reference on my memorandum that I visited Greer on any other time near the 30th of March.

Q. When did you last visit him before the 30th of March? *A.* It had been some four or five—I don't remember exactly—some four or five days, I think.

Q. When did you next visit him after the 30th of March? *A.* I presume about five days after.

Q. What was the matter with him. *A.* Inflammation of the bowels.

Q. Is it usual to visit patients with that disease only once in five days? *A.* He had a chronic case; it was a chronic case, sir; in the country in chronic cases we can not get around, sir, oftener than in four or five days; I was visiting his wife also, I said, at the same time; she had a spinal irritation.

Q. In your examination on Monday afternoon did you not state that you visited several other patients on the same afternoon? *A.* Yes, sir; I did, sir.

Q. Then how can you now single out Greer's case from the balance, and remember that it was in connection with a visit to Greer that you saw him? *A.* From the fact that the sick on the other plantations were not on my memorandum, as I attended them by contract, and I was in the habit of attending them—of passing there twice a week, to see if anything was needed.

Q. Was there any connection in any way between Greer and Duke that caused you to charge your mind particularly with the presence of Duke that particular evening? *A.* From the fact that on referring to my record I found that it was the 30th of March that I attended Greer. I remember when I returned from Greer's on the 30th of March I met Wayne Duke, with a pair of steers, on his way home; I remember that was on Monday.

Q. Did anything occur at that time that caused you to suppose that you would be called upon to recollect the particular date of that visit? *A.* No, sir, nothing at all, sir; there *was* something that of course reminded me forcibly of it—not that I expected to be called as a witness here. A few days afterwards I was at the shop and heard that Ashburn was assassinated; of course I remembered having passed there, sir, a few days before, and on reference to my record I found it was the 30th of March; I remembered that I had just passed there a few days before; I refer to the death of Ashburn.

Q. What connection was there between the death of Ashburn and Duke that caused you to think of the place were you saw Duke when you heard of the death of Ashburn? *A.* From the fact that I was trying to locate myself, where I first heard of it; before then I mentioned it was there at the shop that I heard of it.

Q. Were you apprehensive that you would be accused of any connection with Ashburn's death? *A.* Not at all, sir.

Q. Then why was it necessary to locate yourself at the time you heard? *A.* As soon as I heard of the arrest of William Duke I felt certain that he was innocent of what he was accused, namely, the killing of Ashburn, and I remembered having first learnt from him of his having been assassinated.

Q. Doctor, had you ever thought of the necessity of locating Duke at the time Ashburn was killed until you heard of Duke's arrest? *A.* No, sir, I had not.

Q. When did you first hear of Duke's arrest? *A.* I don't remember precisely. I think it was about a month ago.

Q. What day of the month was it? *A.* I don't remember, sir. I didn't think it was necessary to remember it. There was nothing particular occurred on that day to remind me of it.

Q. Do you recollect the day of the week? *A.* I don't recollect. I think it was on Saturday.

Q. Did you hear of it the same day on which he was arrested? *A.* No sir. I heard it on the following morning.

Q. Are you satisfied that it has been as much as a month ago? *A.* I am not fully satisfied—I think it was.

Q. Did not the arrest of Duke make a decided impression on your mind? *A.* It did.

Q. As he was your neighbor, did it not make more impression on your mind than when you heard of the death of Ashburn? *A.* It did not, sir, from the fact that a notorious character, one who was well known in our county to both whites and blacks, more especially the latter, some of whom informed me that they knew him when he was an overseer; and that he was a remarkably cruel one—passed away on the 30th of March; and that this was the first masked assassination I ever heard of in the State. Of course, it made a great impression on my mind.

Q. As you traveled somewhat out of your way, Doctor, to state Ashburn's character as an overseer, will you state who gave you that information? *A.* I can, sir.

Q. Who was it? *A.* A freedman by the name of John Reese was one; another was named Sambo Elyeas; another by the name of Cooper, whose surname I don't remember—his christian name is Cooper.

Q. As they stated to you that he had been so cruel to the blacks, did they state to you how it was that he had such a desoon as I heard of the arrest of William cided influence over them? *A.* They did not.

Q. Who told you that this was a masked assassination? Did Duke tell you that? *A.* I don't remember his having told me so, but I heard it, and saw it in the papers that it was done with masks.

Q. Did you not state that you got your first information of the assassination from Duke? *A.* Yes, sir. I said nothing though in regard to its being a masked assassination. He merely asked me if I had heard of the assassination of Ashburn. That is all I remember. A few days afterwards I saw that it was a *masked* assassination.

Q. Who first told you that the assassination was a masked assassination? *A.* I heard it from common talk, and saw it in the papers.

Q. What papers? *A.* I think the Columbus Sun. I don't remember exactly. I think the Columbus Sun.

Q. Of what date? *A.* I don't remember the date—it was shortly after the occurrence.

Q. Do you take the Columbus Sun? *A.* I do not.

Q. Whose paper did you see it in?

By a *member of the Commission*—I object to the manner of conducting the cross-examination, on the ground that the questions asked are very irrelevant, and their answers will only encumber the proceedings.

Counsel for the prosecution answered the objection with the following:

"As the witness swears to a particular fact which occurred three and a half months since, with great positiveness, it is not only relevant, but necessary to the investigation of truth to test the accuracy of his memory on other incidents that occurred about the same time. If he can be positive about no other fact or date of that or another period, it is fair to argue that he may be mistaken when he swears so positively to the fact of the date of Ashburn's death, and Duke's location at the time.

"It is a question of the strength and accuracy of his memory, which can only be tested by interrogating him as to other incidents that occurred about the same time."

The court was cleared for deliberation and the objection overruled.

To the question "Whose paper did you see it in," witness answered:

A. I saw it in a paper at the Sulphur Springs; it was lying on a desk; I don't know whose it was; I presume it belonged to the proprietor there.

Q. Had you ever thought of the date of Ashburn's death after you had heard of it until you heard of Duke's arrest? *A.* When he told me that Ashburn had been assassinated I asked him when it was, and he told me when it was; he told me it was a few days before that he had been assassinated; I then read from the papers afterwards when it was.

Q. Didn't Duke tell you the day on which it occurred? *A.* He told me the day, but not the day of the month.

Q. Had you thought of the date of Ashburn's death at any time within the last two months before you heard of Duke's arrest? *A.* No, I had not.

Q. What caused you to look at your memorandum book when Duke was arrested? *A.* I didn't refer to it then; I did after I heard that I would be needed here, about a week and a half ago.

Q. Did you look at any entry except the entry of the 30th of March? *A.* I did, sir; I looked at the entries that were near the 30th of March; I saw at that time I had not passed in that direction, on my way home, coming from Greer's.

Q. Have you not stated that you passed the shop twice a week? *A.* I did, sir; it may have been the latter part of the week; it may have been Saturday; I was there on Monday; it may have been Saturday when I passed again; that was not near enough for me to refer to; I went to the shop about Thursday, I think, to see about having some work done; I hadn't passed; I didn't go on professional business from my house to the shop.

Q. How often did your memorandum book show that you passed there on the last week of March? *A.* I didn't take particular notice of that, from the fact that I saw that I had not been by there for some time before the 30th of March— some little time.

Q. After having refreshed your memory by referring to your memorandum book, how often do you say you were there the first week of April? *A.* I can not say, sir, how often; I didn't take any particular notice of the time, from the fact that I did not think it was near enough the assassination of Ashburn to have any thing to do with this case.

Q. Then when you referred to your memorandum book you simply looked for an entry that fitted the time of the assassination of Ashburn, did you not? *A.* I remembered that he was there when I was informed of the assassination of Ashburn; I remembered that I met Duke a few days before I heard of the assassination, when I was returning from Mr. Greer's; I remembered that it was on Monday, from the fact that the steers had been left at Kings Gap on Sunday.

Q. If the assassination had been on the 28th of March, and you had formed an entry on your book fitting that date, would you not have believed and so stated here that that was the date you saw Duke. *A.* I would not, from the fact that I remembered that it was on the 30th of March that Ashburn was assassinated; it was impressed on my mind.

Question by the Court.

Q. Why did you not bring your memorandum with you to read from and confirm your evidence? *A.* Because I had no idea that I would be called on to produce it; never having been on the stand before, I had no idea what questions would be propounded.

The evidence of this witness given on day before yesterday was then read to him, and upon agreement of counsel, permission of the Commission and the request of witness, the remainder of his evidence given in to-day was read over to him from the reporter's notes. He desired to make no corrections, and was discharged.

Questions by Mr. Stephens.

F. G. WILKINS, a witness for defense, was then introduced, and duly sworn. He testified as follows:

Q. Please state to the Court, Mr. Wilkins, your name in full, and where you reside. *A.* F. G. Wilkins. I reside in Columbus, Georgia.

Q. Where were you at the time of the death of Ashburn? *A.* I was at home, dwelling in the north-eastern portion of the city.

Q. Did you hold any official position at any time, and if so, what was it? *A.* I did, sir—Mayor of the city of Columbus.

Q. Who were the officers under you? *A.* The Treasurer was Robert H. Grain;

the Clerk was M. M. Moore; the Wharfinger was James Barber; the City Physician was Dr. Roper; Hospital Keeper, Mrs. Catherine Anderson; the Magazine Keeper was James Liner; Clerk of the Market was also James Liner; the Marshal, Chief Marshal, was M. M. Murphy; the Deputy Marshal and Chief of Police was Robert A. Wood; the Captain of Police was Captain A. W. Allen; the police officers—I think I had reduced them about one-half. I will name them over as near as I can: There's William Cash, Charley Bradey, James Wiggins, Edward Burns, (I think he was a policeman at the time, I disremember—my memory is at fault), A. C. Roper, David Stuart.

Q. What hour of the night were you first informed of the death of Ashburn? A. About ten minutes to 2 o'clock, I think. At least, somewhere in that neighborhood.

Q. Did you go immediately to the scene or not? A. I did, sir.

Q. What measures did you take in relation to it? A. The first steps that I took, after getting to the place was to get into the house; I found in the house (the policemen and Marshal went with me) only four persons, a negro woman, white woman, negro boy and a white man by the name of Bennett. I don't know his first name, and there was a negro man standing outside of the door.

Q. Do you know the names of these other persons that you saw there? A. Only two of them, Anna Flourney and this man Bennett. I knew his name was Bennett, having seen him when he was pointed out to me.

Q. What else did you do, Mr. Wilkins? A. I assembled the three persons together—the negro woman, white woman and Bennett (I at that time had lost sight of the boy)—and asked them if they could give any definite idea as to who were the perpetrators of the act. After talking with them a few moments and not learning anything from them, as they all appeared to be very much frightened, I then went into the room where Ashburn lay and looked at him, and had him straightened. I came out immediately and sent one of my policemen down after the coroner; I am not confident whether the coroner came back with him or not. I am very well satisfied that he did, and I told him what he should do; to immediately summon a jury of inquest, to hold the inquest over the body next morning, and in summoning the jury, to take none upon it but the most intelligent men in the city. After he came back, I then instructed my marshal; I only had, I think, about eight men and the deputy marshal and my captain. My instructions to my marshal was to distribute them to the best possible advantage, and to arrest all men they might find passing about between that hour and day. That time, I think, brought me up to near 3 o'clock. I instructed the marshal, also, to keep a man in the neighborhood of the house where Ashburn lay; and at that time I returned home. But previous to my return home, I also gave my instructions to my marshal as soon as he ate his breakfast to go round and summon the Board of Aldermen to meet me at the Council Chamber at 9 o'clock, which was done, and the Board met me, save two. We then introduced an ordinance, condemning the act, and offering a reward of five hundred dollars for the perpetrators of the murder—either one or more.

Q. What's the usual reward offered in cases of murder? A. I believe the Governor of the State usually offers from $250 to $500. I don't know that I ever knew a larger amount—i don't recollect now, though; he may have done it; I don't recollect having any occasion for offering a reward before that.

I then during the day increased the police force to sixty men—had them all appointed and on duty by night, with instructions to each one of them to be vigilant, and do everything they could to ferret out the perpetrators of the deed. I forget now whether I kept the whole number of those men on duty until after the election or not, but I kept a greater portion of them.

Q. How long was the election after that? A. Well, I would not have been able to tell the day he was killed, hadn't it been for the papers. I find that it was on the 30th of March. The election was on the 20th of April—on Monday.

Hereupon, owing to the sickness of one of the members of the Commission, the Commission adjourned until to-morrow morning at ten o'clock.

McPherson Barracks, Atlanta, Ga., }
10 o'clock a m., July 16, 1868. }

The Commission met pursuant to adjournment. Present, the same members as yesterday, the Judge Advocate and his assistants; also, the prisoners on trial and their counsel.

The record of yesterday's proceedings was read and approved.

The examination of the witness, F. G. Wilkins, was resumed by Mr. Stevens of counsel for defense.

Q. Mr. Wilkins, you yesterday mentioned names of certain parties under you as Mayor—Barber, Wood, Roper, Wiggins. Are these the parties on arraignment here? *A.* They are.

Q. Are you acquainted with all the parties on arraignment now? *A.* I am, with the exception of two. I know them all, but these two not so intimately as I know the most of them. There are two of them that I do not know so well, although I have known them several years.

Q. Which two are they? *A.* Mr. Duke and Mr. Hudson.

Q. State to the Court the character of these parties you know intimately and well? *A.* They are all gentlemen of good character.

Q. Do you know anything special about Mr. Chipley's habits at night—being out or not? *A.* I do.

Q. State it to the Court. *A.* I know something in reference to his habits. I myself am in the habit of being out at all hours of the night, and I do not recollect of ever having met Mr. Chipley out in the street after ten more than on one or two or three occasions.

Q. What is the occupation of Mr. Chipley? *A.* He is a merchant.

Q. Has he any family? *A.* He has.

Q. Of whom does his family consist? *A.* His wife, and I think one child, as far as I know.

Q. What is the occupation of Mr. Bedell? *A.* He is a clerk in an insurance office.

Q. Do you know his habits as to being out at night or not? *A.* I do.

Q. What are they? *A.* Mr. Bedell is in the habit of being near his place of business and sleeping apartments at night. There is where I have most frequently met him. I have met him on one or two occasions between the middle part of the city and my dwelling in returning home from a visit from some young ladies.

Q. As Mayor, were you frequently out at night yourself in different parts of the city? *A.* I was, sir.

Q. Do you know other persons in Columbus about the size and make of Mr. Chipley? *A.* I am a very poor hand to locate anything of that kind, but there are several in Columbus, though I can not locate them. I do not know that I could name them now.

Q. Do you know Capt. Tom Blanchard there? *A.* Very well.

Q. How does his size and general make compare with Mr. Chipley's? *A.* They are made very much alike—about the same height and breadth.

Q. Do you know Rory McNeil? *A.* I do.

Q. How does his size and general proportions of body compare with Mr. Chipley? *A.* Very much, with the exception of McNeil being somewhat taller—very little taller, however.

Q. Do you know John McNeal? *A.* I do.

Q. What do you say of his size—comparative size? *A.* His general make would correspond with Mr. Chipley's more than the others.

Q. Do you know Laurence Burroughs? *A.* I do.

Q. How does his size compare? *A.* He would come nearer filling the bill than either of the others.

Q. Do you know one Jake Burroughs? *A.* I do.

Q. What would you say of his size compared with Mr. Chipley's? *A.* Compare very well, sir.

Q. Are you acquainted with that man Bennett that you say you saw in that room that night? *A.* I know him.

Q. Are you acquainted with his general character for truth and veracity. *A.* I am.

Q. From that general character would you believe him on oath? *A.* I would not.

Q. Do you know Wade Stevens? *A.* I do.

Q. Do you know his character for truth and veracity? *A.* I do.

Q. From that character would you believe him on his oath? *A.* I would not.

Q. Do you know George Betz, the young man? *A.* I do.

Q. Are you acquainted with his general character for truth and veracity? *A.* I am.

Q. From that knowledge would you believe him on his oath? *A.* I would not.

Q. Do you know Charles Marshall, who has been a witness in this case? *A.* I do.

Q. Do you know anything of a present watch that was made to him at any time this year? *A.* I know there was a watch presented to him—a watch and chain.

Q. Do you know the circumstances under which it was, and why it was, presented to him? *A.* I do.

Q. Please state to the court. *A.* Do you want all the circumstances connected with it?

Q. In the first place, when was it? *A.* I think it was the latter part of the last week of the 20th of April.

Q. Do you mean to say it was a few days after the election? *A.* Yes, sir.

Q. Now state why it was presented to him? *A.* It was made up by the citizens—a few young men of the city—on account of his being reduced in consequence of his action during the election. The young men of the city, from his general deportment there, took a fancy to him, and thought at first they would make up a contribution sufficient to buy a handsome suit of clothes and present it to him. A few days after that Capt. McSpadden, of the Internal Revenue Department, then came to me and said that he thought the citizens ought to make him up a handsome present; that he was going away himself, but if they would get up such a present he would give $25 towards it. Well, they changed from the suit of clothes to a watch and chain. The money made up was, I think, some $300 or $350, and Capt. Harris, of the Internal Revenue Department, paid $50 toward it, after the watch was purchased and presented to Marshall. It was in consequence entirely of his action during the election—the part he took and the interest he exhibited.

Q. Do you know anything of his having received money otherwise? *A.* Yes, sir; I let him have $100.

Q. State the circumstances under which you let him have it, and why you let him have it. *A.* The Sunday night week previous to the election I was down town about ten o'clock at night. He met me near the side door of E. Bonnard & Co.'s store; I was then talking with Mr. Bonnard. He took me off to one side and remarked that he had applied for a furlough, and he was satisfied he would get it; that he was obliged to go to new York, and he desired to borrow $200, and wanted me to let him have it. I asked him when he expected to go; he told me he wanted to get off the following Thursday. I then told him, says I, "If you expect to go Thursday I will not loan you the money, but if you will promise me to remain until after the election I will let you have it. At the time he first mentioned it to me he proposed to put upon the note Capt. Mills and Capt. Harris. He then consented to remain till after the election. Nothing further was said between us in reference to the money until after the election. He came to me and told me he was going to leave on such a morning, and I told him I would let him have some money. I went to the Secretary of the Democratic Club there, who had charge of the moneys. That was after the election. I wanted to know how much funds they had—that I wanted some for this purpose. All that was left was $25; I got that, and a friend of mine made up, I think, $30. I paid him $45 myself, and gave it to him the night before. He left for New York in the morning.

Q. Was he active during that election? *A.* He was.

Q. In co-operating with what party? *A.* The Democratic party.

Cross-examined by Brown.

Q. Mr. Wilkins, how long have you been acquainted with Mr. Marshall? *A.* I think he came there in April or May, 1867, and I became acquainted with him two or three months after he got there.

Q. When did he first commence to co-operate with the Democratic party? *A.* Previous to the election.

Q. About how long previous? *A.* We did not conceive we had any use for him until about two or three weeks before the election.

Q. When did he first commence to take a stand in politics? *A.* A short time before the election; in fact I can not say he took a stand in politics, further than operating for our benefit during the election.

Q. When did you first learn he was a Democrat? *A.* Pretty soon after I got acquainted with him.

Q. Did he not at all times express himself very freely and favorably towards the Democratic party? *A.* I do not think I ever had any conversation with him as to his political position until a short time previous to the election; my first knowledge of his being a Democrat was previous to his being appointed Orderly Sergeant of his company; the former Orderly Sergeant was very much opposed to him in politics, and through my police officers I learned that Marshall was a strong Democrat, as his Orderly Sergeant and himself used to have some very sharp words upon politics.

Q. Was not his position in the city well known as a Democrat some months before the election? A. It was; at least I looked upon him as such; I do not know as I ever heard any one else say so.

Q. What were his associations there? Was he well received by gentlemen of the Democratic party? A. I do not know that I now recollect of ever seeing him in company with any of the citizens; he would frequently meet me upon the street of the city, and I would always treat him kindly and politely.

Q. Did you frequently stop and converse with him on politics? A. I never conversed with him on politics at all unless it might have been just previous to the election, and at the time he spoke to me about borrowing the money.

Q. You say a friend made up $30 of the $100 you loaned him; who was that friend? A. I received $25 from the Democratic purse, $5 from Gray, and $45 I gave myself, and $25 was given by Mr. Coleman.

Q. Do you know who contributed the $25 that was made up by Mr. Coleman? Did he say, when he gave it, who he got it from? A. No, sir; he did not.

Q. Did you demand any note or security from him when you gave him the money? A. I did not.

Q. Did you expect him to return it or pay it back? A. I had very little expectation of ever receiving it—would have been very glad if he had.

Q. As it was made up by contribution, did you not all really understand it to be a donation? A. No, sir; no one knew any thing about it, save myself and Mr. Bonnard, until after the election.

Q. Was it not after the election that it was made up and handed to him? A. It was; I had promised him to let him have the money, provided he would stay until after the election; and if there had not been a dollar contributed I should have furnished all of the $100 myself.

Q. You spoke of $200 being applied for by him. A. Yes, sir, he applied for $200.

Q. Did you promise him any definite amount if he would stay until after the election? A. I did not.

Q. Will you name the persons, as far as you know them, who contributed towards the purchase of the watch? A. I know of only two persons.

Q. Who were they? A. Capt. Harris, of the internal revenue department, and McSpadden of the same department.

Q. Have you no information as to the names of the other persons who contributed? A. I think Mr. Gray was the gentleman who raised the money, and, as well as I recollect, he mentioned the name of Mr. Saulsbury. As to the amount contributed, I know nothing.

Q. I believe you stated that Mr. Harris, of the internal revenue department, contributed $50. How much was contributed by the others mentioned? A. Twenty-five dollars Harris paid for himself, and $25 for McSpadden. He told me he paid that after the watch was presented. He told me that about two weeks ago.

Q. Then how much altogether can you account for? A. On the watch?

Q. Yes, sir. A. I can not account for any of the rest; $50 is all I can account for. I do not know how much Mr. Saulsbury contributed.

Q. Did you not hear the persons making up the money speak of any one of these gentlemen now on trial having contributed. A. No, sir, I did not.

Q. What do you understand to have been the value of the watch and chain? A. I think Mr. Speer told me, it was purchased of him; it was between $300 and $350.

Q. The watch and the money then amounted together to some $400 or $450, did it? A. Yes, sir.

Q. Do you know of any other person in Columbus who received anything like that amount for his services in aid of the Democratic party during the election? A. I do not.

Q. What is the highest amount that you know of any one else having received for his services? A. I do not know, sir. There was a great deal of money spent; I do not know of another person receiving a dollar except the few dollars that I put up myself.

Q. You state you would not believe Mr. Bennett on his oath. Why do you make that statement? A. From the simple fact that I am satisfied he has sworn to a lie in one instance particularly, or lied with me previous to his taking an oath to the fact.

Q. Had you been put upon the witness stand and asked the same questions prior to the death of Ashburn, would you have sworn that you would not believe him on oath. *A.* I can not tell that, because I would not recognize him as Bennett if I had met him previous to that time.

Q. Then all you have stated of your knowledge of his general character relates to a knowledge acquired since the death of Ashburn, does it not? *A.* It does.

Q. When your refer to a falsehood that he has sworn to, or false statement he has made to you, do you not refer to a statement on oath taken in reference to the death of Ashburn? *A.* I do.

Q. How long have you known George Betz, the witness you have testified about? *A.* I have know him from childhood, I might say.

Q. Had you been examined under oath as to his general character, prior to the death of Ashburn, would you have sworn that you would not believe him on oath? *A.* I would.

Q. Had you known him intimately? *A.* I have for the last two or three years.

Q. About the time he was arrested and imprisoned for the murder of Ashburn was he not generally spoken of by the citizens of Columbus as a man of good character? *A.* He was not.

Q. Did not the newspapers of Columbus speak very highly of him about that time, and of his family connections there? *A.* I do not recollect ever seeing his name in print until after his arrest, though it might have been.

Q. Why do you say you would have sworn, prior to the death of Ashburn, that you would not believe Betz on his oath? *A.* More particularly from the fact—in consequence of my friendship for his father; I tried to make something of the boy, and placed him upon my police; I found him to be very unreliable; he would frequently lie to me when he was reported for dereliction of duty; I kept him some time, trying to make something of him; finally I had to discharge him; I reappointed him once afterward; I found it was impossible to do anything with him; there was no confidence to be placed in him; none of the police liked to walk with him, because they disliked to report each other very much, and ascertaining that, finally I gave him up.

Q. How long prior to Ashburn's death had you finally discharged him from the police? *A.* I can not tell, but I think it must have been a year.

Q. How long have you known the witness, Stevens, about whom you testify? *A.* I have heard of the family there for several years, although I may have met him frequently; during the last two years that I knew him he was Wade Stevens.

Q. If you had been asked on your oath, in Court, prior to the death of Ashburn, would you have answered that you would not believe him on oath? *A.* I would.

Q. Why would you have made that answer? *A.* From his associations and the manner in which he and the family lived.

Q. I desire to separate the young man from his family and ask you whether, from any knowledge of his own conduct, you make this statement? *A.* Yes, sir.

Q. What conduct? *A.* His association with negroes and his habits generally, and even his white associates.

Q. Do you know anything outside of those associations that showed that his word could not be relied upon? *A.* Nothing in particular.

Q. Then your testimony relates to the low standing of his family and the fact that he associates with low people, does it not? *A.* Yes, sir.

Q. It does not relate, then, to your knowledge of his previous falsehood? *A.* No, sir.

Q. You spoke of the action of the Council the day after Ashburn's murder and the reward they bid for the murderers; what other acts were done to ferret out the guilty parties by the city authorities? *A.* Nothing further than the instructions given to the officers to be diligent—diligent in using every exertion to ascertain who the perpetrators of the act were; all that was done was what was usual in such cases.

Q. Did the officers of the city report any discoveries made? *A.* They did not.

Q. Were any arrests made by the civil authorities? *A.* There were none.

Q. Was not Mr. Bedell arrested the day after Ashburn's murder? *A.* If he was I was not aware of it.

Q. When were the first arrests made in the city after the death of Ashburn? *A.* I can not tell exactly the date; at the time the most of those young men were arrested and confined in the Court-house; that was the first arrest.

Q. When were they arrested and confined in the Court-house? *A.* I can not give the date; I do not know whether it was previous to the election or after.

Q. As it is a mere matter of opinion, give us your best judgment on that subject? *A.* There is one circumstance that satisfies me—it was previous to the election—the fact that Marshall was still the orderly sergeant of the company, which he was not after the election. It must have been previous to them. That is the only circumstance that I can now bring to my mind.

Q. Do you feel very confident that no arrests were made the next day after the death on account of the murder? *A.* None that I can now recollect.

Q. From your best opinion would you say that any were made within ten days after the murder? *A.* From the fact of their being arrested previous to the election, I should say those young were arrested ten or twelve days after the murder of Ashburn. That is, I would think so.

Q. Was it not just three weeks from the death of Ashburn to the election? *A.* Yes, sir.

Q. Will you name the persons who were arrested and confined in the court-house? *A.* I will name some of them; I do not know that I can name all of them. There was Mr. Roper, Dr. Kirksey. Mr. Barber, Mr. Bedell, Mr. Chipley, Mr. Wade Stevens, William Bedell, Bob Ennis, Thomas W. Grimes, John Stabler, and John Wells.

Q. Under what authority were these arrests made? *A.* I understood it was by military authority.

Q. Then there were no arrests made by the civil authorities? *A.* None, sir, that I heard of.

Q. How long were they confined before they were discharged, when arrested and confined in the court-house? *A.* I do not recollect.

Q. As it is a matter of opinion, just give us the best of your recollection as to whether it was a day or two, or a week? *A.* Several days. I do not know that they were there a week.

Q. Were they discharged? *A.* Yes, sir.

The examination of the witness having been concluded, and his testimony given yesterday and to-day having been read over to him, the Judge Advocate inquired if there were any corrections that he desired to make. He said:

"I do in my testimony of yesterday, in reference to the number of my police. I stated it was 12; it was 14. There were 12 on duty at night, but there were two others that I kept for duty in the day time. I want to make that correction—to have it 14 instead of 12.

"I also want to make a correction where I speak of their being raised. I stated that I raised them to sixty; upon reflection I find it was only thirty. I was in the habit when I raised my police to double the force. A short time previous to that I had been using thirty men, but I had reduced them down to 14. That is why I answered so promptly that I had raised the force from 30 to 60."

Question by the Court.

Q. As Mayor of Columbus did you receive any information as to who might have been implicated in the murder of Ashburn? *A.* Not that I recollect of.

Questions by Mr. Stephens.

THOMAS C. MILLER, witness for defense, was duly sworn and testified as follows:

Q. State your name in full and where you live? *A.* Thomas C. Miller. I live at Lagrange.

Q. What is your occupation? *A.* A farmer. I am also in the warehouse business.

Q. Please state to the Court whether these are the books kept in your warehouse, (handing witness two account books.) *A.* (Holding up one of the books.) This is the receipt book. It will be well enough for me to state that Mr. Frost is a partner of mine in the warehouse business. (Holding up the other book.) This is the cash book. The receipt book is the one I keep at the warehouse. My son usually attends to the weighing of the cotton, but it happens that this cotton was weighed by myself. The entry is in my handwriting.

Q. Do you know Mr. Stith Parham, of Merriwether county, Georgia. *A.* Very well, sir.

Q. Did he sell any cotton or deliver any cotton to your firm any time this spring? *A.* He delivered cotton there. The cotton was brought by a young man by the name of Burke, who was sent out in that neighborhood by Mr. Frost to purchase cotton.

Q. Did he deliver any there the 2d day of April of this year? *A.* Yes, sir, he was there with the cotton. I think the cotton was hauled there by a man by the name of Williams, who was hired to bring the cotton up there. He came up with the wagon.

Q. Do you know that man, Mr. Williams, who hauled it there? *A.* I know him when I see him; I frequently see him.

Q. Do you know Judge Fletcher, of Merriwether county. *A.* Very well.

Q. Is Mr. Williams any kin to him? *A.* I think perhaps he's a son-in-law of his; I have heard so, but I do not know.

Q. Will you show the Judge Advocate the entry of the cotton delivered there the 2d of April, which is in your handwriting? *A.* I will, sir. [The witness handed the receipt book containing such entry to the Judge Advocate, who exhibited it to the Commission, by the different members of which it was inspected.] It was as follows.

"No. 1,390—Received of Joseph Burke (11) eleven bales cotton.

"April 2d, 1868."

MARKS.	NOS.	WEIGHTS.	PRICE.
	1	445	
[4]	2	458	
	3	396	
	4	381	
Mending.	5	431	
	6	355	
Insurance.	7	437	
	8	410	
	9	464	
	10	436	
	11	436	

Q. I understand you to state that this entry is in your handwriting? *A.* Yes, sir.

Q. You state to the court distinctly and positively that that entry is correct as to dates and all that pertains to it? *A.* Yes, sir.

Q. What book is this? (holding up second book referred to previously by the witness.) *A.* That is the cash book of Mr. Frost, that he keeps in paying off cotton—the amount he pays for each lot.

Q. In whose handwriting is the entry in this book—cash book? *A.* In Mr. Blue Frost's handwriting.

Q. Is he of your firm? *A.* No, sir, I was not connected with him in the purchase of cotton; we were only connected together as warehousemen.

Q. You had no interest in this book? *A.* I had no interest in the cotton at all, only where this cotton was purchased by this young man. He asked me to look after that cotton particularly, because he was not a cotton buyer, and did not know much of this cotton.

Q. Do you know this to be the cash book of Frost? *A.* It is, to the best of my knowledge and belief. I received it from the young man, and he told me it was.

Q. Did you ever see him make entries in it? *A.* Yes, sir.

Q. This is the book you saw him make entries in? *A.* Yes, sir.

Q. Do you know in whose handwriting these entries are? *A.* In Mr. Blue Frost's; he was the cash clerk.

The Judge Advocate stated that he would admit that if Mr. Blue Frost were present he would testify that he kept the cash book presented to the court, and that he made the entry in the same of the date of April 2d, 1868, in the following words and figures, to-wit: "1868, April 2, S. A. Parham, 11 B. C., $863.05," and that he would testify that the entry was correct.

Question by Mr. Stephens.

Q. I understand you to say, Mr. Miller, that the cotton entered in your receipt book and that mentioned in the cash book is the same lot? *A.* Yes, sir, to the best of my knowledge that is the same lot of cotton.

Cross-examined by Mr. Brown.

Q. You say to the best of your knowledge it is the same cotton; have you any knowledge on the subject? *A.* I have no knowledge only from my entries and what I remember about the transaction.

The testimony of the witness was read over to him and he was asked if he had any corrections to make; he replied that he had none.

The Commission therefore adjourned till to-morrow (Friday) morning at 10 o'clock.

McPHERSON BARRACKS, ATLANTA, GA.,
10 A. M. July 17th, 1868.

The Commission met pursuant to adjournment.

Present, the same members as yesterday, the Judge Advocate, and John D. Pope, one of his assistants, the prisoners, and their counsel.

The record of yesterday's proceedings was read and approved.

The Judge Advocate submitted the following statement, requesting of the Commission that it might appear on record, which request was granted:

"The records of the Commission show that on the 9th instant the counsel for the prisoners asked that a *subpœna* be issued for H. C. Whitley, and that he be ordered by the Court not to leave Atlanta without the permission of the Court, and that the Commission decided to leave the matter in the hands of the Judge Advocate. The Judge Advocate states that he *subpœnaed* Mr. Whitley, as requested, and that the witness has since left Atlanta, with the consent of the counsel for the prisoners, upon showing that his services were needed elsewhere."

This statement has been submitted to the counsel of the prisoners and was not objected to.

Questions by Mr. Stephens, conducting the examination for defense.

JOHN PEABODY was introduced as a witness by defense, duly sworn, and testified as follows:

Q. Mr. Peabody, please give your name to the Court in full. *A.* John Peabody.
Q. Your residence? *A.* Columbus, Ga.
Q. Did you hold any official position in Columbus in March last? *A.* Yes, sir; I was Solicitor General of the circuit.
Q. By that you mean you was prosecuting officer under the penal laws of Georgia? *A.* I do.
Q. Did you attend, or not, the inquest over the body of Mr. Ashburn? *A.* I did.
Q. Did you, or not, conduct the examination there in your official capacity, and if so, how did you happen to be there? *A.* I was sent for by the Coroner and got there after some witnesses had been examined; I had those that had been examined re-examined, conducting the examination from that time.
Q. Do you recollect of any witness stating the position of the person that had the English coat, or any description of one of that sort?

Question by the Judge Advocate.

Q. I want to know of the witness first if the examination was reduced to writing?
A. Yes, sir; that is, not all of it; part of it was.

Questions by Mr. Stephens.

Q. Was there any writing taken down at all of the examination? *A.* Mr. Bostock, Justice of the Peace, was present, and he took down most of the testimony after I was there; he had some of the testimony written down before I got there, but I didn't read that; I don't know whether that was an official record or not; I only know that he took down some of the testimony.
Q. What position did Mr. Bostock occupy then? Did he hold any official position? *A.* He was a Justice of the Peace.
Q. By whom was the investigation had? Was it by the Coroner or by Mr. Bostock? *A.* It was by the Coroner; it was a Coroner's inquest.
Q. Mr. Bostock, then, simply attended it as Justice of the Peace? *A.* I don't think he attended it as Justice of the Peace; a Justice of the Peace has nothing to do with a Coroner's inquest when there is a Coroner.
Q. Was or not Mr. Bostock the military appointment, as Justice of the Peace? *A.* That was the common report. I never saw his commission. He must have been, for he has been appointed within the last two years.
Q. Is it within your knowledge whether there was any official record made and kept, or not? *A.* I know the coroner did not himself make a record, and there was none returned to the Clerk's office of the Superior Court, because I inquired there and found none had been returned. The proceedings at an inquest are to be returned to the Superior Court, and turned over to the Solicitor General. This is why I inquired if it had never been returned.
Q. Do you, or not, know whether it was returned to Capt. Mills, who was the military commander there at that time? *A.* I only know what the coroner told me about it.
Q. You can state what he told you? *A.* He told me he had returned it to Capt. Mills.
Q. Are you acquainted with Mr. Bennett who has been a witness in this case? *A.* I know him by sight and reputation— have no personal acquaintance with him.
Q. Did you see him there that day at

the examination by the coroner's inquest?
A. I did.

Q. Are you acquainted with his general character? A. I am.

Q. From your knowledge of his general character, would you believe him on his oath? A. I would not.

Q. Are you acquainted with the general character of Stevens, a witness in this case —Wade Stevens? A. I am.

Q. From your knowledge of his general character, would you believe him on his oath? A. I would not.

Cross-examined by Judge Advocate.

Q. Are you acquainted with Capt. Mills, Commander of the Post at Columbus, Ga.? A. I am, sir.

Q. Did you ever have any conversation with him as to the failure of the civil authorities to prosecute an investigation as to the murder of Ashburn? A. I had a conversation with him as to the failure of the city council only.

Q. Where did that conversation take place? A. In his office.

Q. Did you not in that conversation say that the city council made a mistake in not investigating Ashburn's murder, and that you supposed the reason they had not done so was because they didn't know where it would strike—or words to that effect? A. I made some such statement as that to Capt. Mills, but not exactly as you have asked the question.

Q. Can you state in your own way what you said to him on that subject? A. Capt. Mills asked me if the city council had done anything more than offer the reward for the apprehension of the murderers of Ashburn—if I knew they had done anything more. I told him I didn't think that they had; he asked me then why I thought they had not. I told him I did not think that they, as individuals, cared to know who were the murderers of Ashburn. I think I also told him it was not the part of the city council—I am very sure I did—to make such an investigation; it is not usual, nor is it their duty. That is about the substance of what I said on that subject.

Q. Did the civil authorities of that locality whose duty it was to make proper efforts to discover the murderers of Ashburn make any efforts at all in that direction? A. They did.

Q. Who were they who did, and what did they do? A. The Coroner held an inquest; we examined every person in or about the house where Ashburn was killed; we examined every person who pretended to know, or who we had heard knew anything about it, and after this investigation the jury returned their verdict, and nothing more was done. nor is anything more done in any case under such circumstances, unless afterwards other testimony is developed; that is the uniform practice, so far as I know, in the circuit in which I live.

Q. Is it the uniform practice in your locality, in cases of great crime, for the officers of justice to cease all efforts to ascertain who committed the crime upon the return of the Coroner's inquest that they are ignorant of the persons who committed the offense? A. I don't know any difference in practice, whether the crime is great or small. That is the uniform practice, within my knowledge, so far as the officers of justice are concerned. If any extraordinary efforts are made they are always made by persons who are interested as friends to the deceased, or by persons against whom the crime was committed; under the laws of this State it is made the duty of no officer to investigate a crime; it is left with the Coroner's inquest in the first place, and with the grand jury in the second; no officer is charged with the investigation of a crime in this State.

Q. Recurring to your conversation with Capt. Mills; did you not in that conversation state that the city authorities, or the civil, one of them, were not disposed to prosecute an investigation as to the murder of Ashburn, because they did not know where it would strike, or words to that effect? A. No, sir, I did not make that remark in reference to any authority at all, but in reference to the community as individuals. I have just stated what I said to him in reference to the City Council—that as individuals they did not seem disposed to investigate it. I stated also that in my opinion that was the feeling of the community; but I did not say that that was the reason that actuated any civil officer in the discharge of his duty, nor did I think it was. I don't know that that was the reason that actuated the members of the City Council; I told Capt. Mills I supposed so.

Q. I understand then from your statements that, among other things, you stated to Capt. Mills that in your opinion the community at Columbus were not disposed to press an investigation as to who committed the murder of Ashburn; am I correct? A. I didn't say "press an investigation;" I simply meant they did not care to find out who it was that did it—as individuals they didn't desire to know. I stated that as to myself I did not desire to know as an individual. In that same connection, too, I made this remark to Capt. Mills on that very same subject; I likened the community to himself. "Suppose," I asked him, "you had reason to believe that some of your soldiers had committed a great crime, for which they would deserve great punishment, while you as an officer would desire to punish the offender, you would not as an individual, outside of your official duty, desire to know who committed that crime;" simply this, that is the idea I conveyed, and he agreed with me exactly—he didn't differ with me in opinion, but coincided with me, that that was the natural feeling he would have in reference to his soldiers, and was not surprised to find that that was the feeling of the community in reference to its citizens. I did not state to him that the community desired to shield the murderers of Ashburn, but on the contrary I told him particularly they did not. He so understood me. But simply as individuals they did not desire to make extraordinary efforts to know who it was that did it.

Q. Then I understand from your statements the feeling of the community to be about this—they did not desire to shield the murderers of Ashburn, but were very anxious not to know who the murderers were? A. I didn't say they were very anxious not to know. I said I did not believe they wanted to know—that is, that they would not make any efforts to know who they were. That's the idea I wanted to convey.

Q. Was it not your duty as solicitor general of your judicial circuit that constitutes you the prosecuting attorney of all offenders of the criminal law, yourself to cause some investigation to be made into this murder? A. The law makes it my duty to prosecute on all indictments found by a grand jury. It makes it my duty also to examine the returns on inquests, and if any one has been charged by that inquest with the commission of a crime, it is my duty to present them to the grand jury for their action; but it is not my duty to hunt up any crime—to be an informer—to hunt up cases for the grand jury. I am simply to prosecute after they indict, and it is my invariable custom to have nothing to do with the getting up of any prosecution against any citizen—I leave that to the citizens themselves. I am not a public informer, nor do I expect to be. The reason I didn't bring it before the grand jury is that I was at the Coroner's inquest, and it was a very full investigation. Then there was nothing therefore for the grand jury after that inquest to examine. I never knew of any other testimony, never heard of any—no information has ever been given me from that day to this of any evidence against any one, nor has any one ever applied to me to prosecute any one for the murder of Ashburn. I stated to Capt. Mills in that same connection that I was ready to prosecute in this case; and that I had refused to have anything to do with this case or the defense of it, or give any advice or assistance, because I might be called upon, in my official capacity, to prosecute it, and I did not want to entangle myself with it.

Q. I understand you then that the Coroner's inquest not having developed who were the murderers of Ashburn, any further investigation that might take place would have to be a voluntary act on the part of some of the citizens or somebody else, for that purpose—that there was no person officially bound to make an investigation in regard to the murder? A. No, sir. Well, I may say you are right, unless the grand jury, who are generally charged to investigate any crime—they are generally charged with it—should do so.

Q. From your knowledge of the feeling of that community in regard to the murder of Ashburn, how long do you suppose it would have been before there would have been any voluntary act done towards bringing the murderers to trial and punishment? A. I can not say, sir. I heard of some effort being made by his son to ascertain who the murderers of his father were. I heard of a good deal of effort made by others, who are citizens of Columbus, to ascertain it. If you mean, however, by the community, simply those who dislike Ashburn.

Q. I meant the community at large. I didn't mean individuals. A. There were some individuals who have made effort to ascertain who the murderers of Ashburn were, and a more diligent effort, and a greater effort I have never known, to ascertain the perpetrators of a crime in that county, or any other county in this State;

but it was confined to persons who, I was satisfied, were actuated by a hope of the reward for the discovery of the murderers of Ashburn.

Q. Was there any effort on the part of any of the citizens, outside of Ashburn's family and immediate personal friends, to discover the perpetrators of his murder, until after a reward had been offered for the discovery of those perpetrators? A. Well, perhaps, I was mistaken in saying that the effort was confined entirely to those who were actuated by this desire to obtain the reward. There was an effort made the very morning Ashburn was killed, to discover who they were by some of his immediate friends, the very morning; and the city council offered a reward that same day for the discovery of the murderers of Ashburn. So there could not have been much effort before that reward was offered. There was some made that morning. I know.

Q. Did you not, in the conversation above referred to, which you had with Capt. Mills, state to him that the reason why no greater effort had been made by the community to ascertain who were the murderers of Ashburn, was that they did not know where the investigation might strike, or words to that effect? A. I did tell Capt. Mills that the community did not know, or they could not tell, who were the perpetrators of that affair, and because of the fact they were the less anxious to discover who they were. The idea that you want me to answer is this, whether I did not tell him that the community did not know who did it, and knew not whom it would fall upon. Yes, sir, I did tell him that. I told him in that connection that the community were perfectly astonished at hearing of the death of Ashburn—they were not prepared for it—they had not suspicioned it—they never dreamed of such a thing, and from the number who evidently were engaged in it, they were at a loss to know who had done it, where it would fall. That's one reason why they did not do it—they did not desire, as individuals I mean, to investigate it. The reason why they did not desire to do it was because they could not comprehend—they could not believe that any such number of persons in the city would have deliberately committed an assassination, and from the circumstances the only solution that they could give to it was that they had gone there for some other purpose, and that Ashburn had fired at them and he had been killed in that way; and that was my supposition, as I supposed the general feeling of the community was.

Q. Had you any knowledge of or acquaintance with Bennett prior to his examination before the coroner's inquest? A. I had only heard of him—heard very little about him—never saw him previous to that time?

Q. Then you had no knowledge of him, of his general character, before he testified at the inquest, had you? A. Very little, sir; what I had heard of him would not have been sufficient to form an opinion as to whether he was a credible witness or not.

Q. Have you now any such knowledge of his general character as to enable you to say whether or not he is worthy of credit under oath? Did you not form the opinion you have expressed here this morning, from a particular circumstance—that is, that he testified before the Coroner's inquest differently from what you have learnt he testified here? A. I think I have now sufficient knowledge of his character to testify as to whether I would believe him now under oath or not, and that knowledge was derived from anything growing out of his examination here at all, but from the facts developed on the trial of Bennett himself, before the Superior Court in May.

Q. You had personal knowledge, I suppose, of those facts? A. I heard the witness testify as to the facts, and others informed me of other facts which were not proved as to his character.

Q. Have you heard him generally spoken of among his acquaintances in that community? A. I have.

Q. Since the murder of Ashburn only? A. Only at that trial, and about that time.

Q. That was since? A. Yes, sir, that was in May.

Q. Have you not heard his general character more spoken of since it became known at Columbus that he was to be a witness against the prisoners on trial? A. No, sir, I have heard very little spoken of him since he was a witness in this trial.

Q. I didn't say since he was a witness, but since it became known that he would become a witness? A. Well, since then I have heard very little about Bennett since the trial in May; I have not heard his friends speak of him at all, since then; my judgment was formed from what his friends spoke of him on that trial, and the public generally; it was the testimony of his friends that formed my judgment.

Q. Then you formed your opinion mainly from the developments on that trial, I understand? A. I did, sir.

Q. How long have you known Wade Stephens? A. I first heard of Wade Stephens about a year ago; some time during last summer.

Q. Is he not quite an obscure man in that community? A. Well, he was obscure to me; I think he was.

Q. How then did you become acquainted with his general character? A. He came to me as solicitor general, to prosecute a freedman by the name of John Wells, and it was upon that trial that I found out—learnt what I know of his general character; I knew nothing about him before.

Q. Well, Mr. Solicitor, it seems to me you make up your opinions as to general character in the court-house? A. I frequently do, sir, but not always.

Q. Do you know anything in regard to Stephens' general character for truth and veracity? A. Yes, sir, the facts developed on that trial were such as to cause me to inquire at once of persons who knew him, as to who he was, and I then learnt who he was.

Q. How many persons did you ever hear speak of him as regards his character for truth and veracity, or his character in any respect? A. Well, sir, I have heard quite a number. I heard his mother speak of him, his aunt speak of him, John Wells speak of him, and then they spoke of him without my asking about him. I then went to others who I supposed would not be inimical to him, and asked them who he was. I think I asked the sheriff, who it is generally supposed knows everybody, and I asked others whom I don't know, just to inform myself as to whether these witnesses had been actuated by any feelings of hostility to him, and I found out that others who were indifferent to him had the same opinion. He was my witness and I was endeavoring to sustain his character, and went to other persons and found I could not do it.

Q. Was he not at that time engaged in a law suit with his mother, aunt, and this man Wells, or some of them? A. He was prosecuting Wells, and he told me that there was some contest between him and his mother about the property. That is why I went to other persons to inquire about him.

Q. The information that you received from his mother and Mr. Wells would of course have been more or less affected by their bitterness growing out of that controversy, would it not? A. That was the natural consequence, and this is why I did not feel disposed to rest on their testimony alone; I was not satisfied with their statements.

Q. Could you rest on their statement at all? Were they people of such character as to justify you to put any dependence upon their statement at all? A. I would have put no confidence in their statements at all if it hadn't been that a mother spoke of her own son, and an aunt of her own nephew. If they had discredited a stranger, I would have thought very little of their testimony, but I did not think the natural feelings of a mother—I thought she would say as much for her son as anybody else would.

Q. Was he a witness for or against the side on which his mother's feelings were enlisted? A. He was a witness against John Wells, and his mother's feelings were enlisted in favor of John Wells.

Q. Has not your experience as a lawyer taught you that of all feuds, family feuds are the most bitter and unrelenting? A. No, sir, it has not. They are sometimes as bitter as others. I don't think I have come to that general conclusion.

Q. Did you inquire among those with whom Stephens usually associates as to his character for truth and veracity? A. I didn't ask the persons that I inquired of whether they associated with him or not, and therefore I don't know. I simply asked them if they knew his character.

Q. Then you have not spoken except as to his own family and Wells—from information derived from his associates, but from information which other persons, not his associates, so for as you knew, gave? A. No, sir, I can not say that any associate of Stephens ever said anything to me about him. I don't know that they were his associates. They professed to know his character, however.

Direct examination by Mr. Stephens.

Q. Did his mother discredit him, Mr. Peabody? A. She did, sir.

Q. In Court? A. Yes, sir, and in his presence.

Q. Did his aunt discredit him in Court? *A.* She did.

Q. In his presence also? *A.* Yes, sir.

Q. Could you find a man in Columbus who would have sworn, from your investigations, that he would believe him on his oath? *A.* I never made so extensive an inquiry as that; as far as I went I could not.

Q. You gave it up as a bad chase? *A.* And more than that, he didn't suggest to me anybody by whom he could prove it.

Q. Did you ask him if he could point out anybody who could sustain him in his character? *A.* I don't recollect that I asked him that question; I spoke to him about the testimony of his mother and aunt—that it would be impossible to find a verdict on his testimony, and his was the only important testimony in the case; I took it for granted that he would make any suggestion, if that was not his character, and it was at that time that I made inquiry of persons standing around in the Court-house as to who he was.

Q. Was his aunt in antagonism—have any interest at all in the case? *A.* Not in that case; but the case I referred to in answer to Gen. Dunn was a contest between him and his mother about property; I don't know whether she was interested in that or not.

Q. In the case you say she discredited him, did she have any interest? *A.* No, sir, none at all; at least she had no such interest as the mother did.

Q. Did she have any interest? *A.* She might have felt an interest in sustaining the character of her sister, which was called in question on the trial.

Q. Mr. Peabody, did you ever know a community to prosecute anybody for any offense whatever? *A.* No, sir, not to prosecute, but I have known them to take great interest in prosecution.

Q. Did Mr. Ashburn have many strong political friends in Columbus? *A.* I cannot say of my own knowledge; there were several persons who were of the same politics as Mr. Ashburn, and he was generally regarded as a man of influence in his party; but I don't think that he had many strong friends, even amongst them.

Q. Did he have a wife? *A.* That is the common report.

Q. Did she ever say anything to you, or give any information, or take any part in the prosecution? *A.* I never saw her or had any intercourse with her whatever.

Q. Did he have any children? *A.* I have seen one son, and heard of another.

Q. Was one of his sons there that morning at the inquest? *A.* I did not see him—don't know that he was there.

Q. Has that or the other son ever consulted you as the prosecuting attorney, giving you any information touching the death of the father? *A.* No, sir.

Q. Has anybody else? *A.* No, sir.

Q. Did Capt. Mills tell you of any information whatever that he had, secret or otherwise? *A.* He did not. He spoke of the testimony of one of the witnesses before the inquest, and Capt. Mills stated to me that he was satisfied that the person had sworn to a lie.

Q. Who was that person? *A.* That witness was the only one who pretended to identify any individual as being connected with this affair. He was a negro named Tom Johnson; and he identified two persons on that inquest. Capt. Mills said that he had ascertained that one of them had not been in the city for over three months before; and as to the other, he was satisfied that Thomas Johnson did not recognize anybody, and could not—that he didn't see anybody. Thomas Johnson has not been examined at this trial.

Q. Did you or not inform Capt. Mills of your perfect readiness to prosecute in case any testimony should be found, discovered, or brought to your knowledge? *A.* I did, sir, and that I might be in a condition to prosecute, that I had refused to represent Mr. Bedell when he was first arrested, or anybody else.

Q. When was he first arrested, Mr. Peabody? *A.* It was shortly after breakfast the morning after Ashburn was killed.

Q. Did you during that investigation do everything as diligently as you ever did to find out the truth of that matter? *A.* I did, sir.

Re-cross-examined by Gen. Dunn.

Q. Did you prosecute Bennett on the trial you referred to? *A.* I did, sir.

Q. After he was sentenced did you go to Judge Worrall to have his sentence remitted? *A.* No, sir, I spoke to him upon the bench, in my place as Solicitor General in public.

Q. What did you say to him on this subject? *A.* It was the last day of the court, and the counsel of Bennett, Mr.

Thornton, had made an application to the court to remit a portion of the penalty; the penalty was thirty days imprisonment and fifty dollars fine. He gave as a reason for it, from the character of the testimony, that there was no doubt in his mind that it was a prosecution got up against Bennett by his enemies, who had fallen out with him, and asked the court to remit a portion of the penalty. I stated to the court that I had been informed that some of the attorneys had doubted whether, in view of the fact that the State's witnesses had been discredited, or an attempt made to discredit them, whether he ought to have been convicted; and in view of that fact, and because it might be said that the jury and the court were actuated by political hostility to Bennett, that I desired that the court should remit that portion of the penalty, although I was satisfied that the conviction was correct. Yet there was an effort made, and witnesses introduced to discredit every witness for the State—every important witness.

Q. Did you argue the case before the jury? *A.* I did, sir.

Q. Did you not in that argument tell the jury that Bennett was the first Radical they had got hold of, and to punish him severely? *A.* No, sir; I did not tell them that; I did not advise them to punish him at all. I might have said in course of the argument, that he was the first that had been before them. I might have said it; I don't remember to have said it; if I said it at all, it was in answer to the argument of Mr. Thornton; it was not said by me without being induced by the argument of his own counsel. Mr. Thornton's argument to the jury was that it was a falling out of the Radicals themselves, and that it did not make much difference what became of the case; and that the witnesses for the State and the prosecutor were as bad as Bennett; and by that course he wanted to excite a sympathy for Bennett and get him off. I endeavored to destroy that sympathy, and think I did it. I argued to the jury that it was no reason that because he was a Radical, and the others Radical, that they should acquit him because of the character of the witnesses for the prosecution.

Q. Do you know who paid the fine inflicted upon Bennett in that case? *A.* Yes, sir, Mr. Chipley paid it.

Q. You have said in your re-examination that Ashburn had strong political friends; had he not violent political enemies also at Columbus? *A.* He had.

Questions by Mr. Stephens.

Q. Was the prosecutor, in that case you speak of, of the same party with Mr. Bennett? *A.* Yes, sir, and the principal witness; Mr. Ashburn's son was the principal witness for the prosecution.

Q. Was Mr. Bostock a witness also against Mr. Bennett? *A.* Yes, sir, he took a great interest in the prosecution.

Q. Do you know the circumstances under which Mr. Chipley paid the fine you have alluded to? *A.* I only know that the sheriff, after the court adjourned, told me that Mr. Chipley would pay the fine, and he did so.

Q. Did the sheriff tell you of any consideration, or of any arrangement by which Mr. Chipley had entered into Bennett's bail? *A.* He did not tell me anything about it; I had had a conversation with Mr. Chipley beforehand.

Q. Did Mr. Chipley tell you beforehand that he was going to pay the fine? *A.* He told me after he was convicted, that in case Bennett would furnish him certain information that he would pay the fine.

Q. What was the character of that information, was it political information? *A.* It was partly political and partly individual; he thought that Bennett knew how he came to be arrested, and he told me that Bennett had told him that, and had agreed to furnish him political information; his remark to me was, that if he does furnish that information I will pay the money out of my own pocket, but he would notify me if that was the case, and he never did; I never heard of him afterwards until he paid the fine; it was several days afterwards.

Questions by the Judge Advocate.

Q. Did Chipley state whether or not Bennett would give him information as to what the negroes had said, or would testify about him? *A.* No, sir.

Q. Or any other person? *A.* No, sir; he simply said that Bennett had told him how he came to be arrested.

Questions by the Court.

Q. How many people of Columbus, besides his relations, have you asked if they would believe him (Stephens), under oath?

A. I can not say how many; I only recollect that at that trial I went amongst persons that I saw standing about, and made inquiry of his character until I was satisfied what it was, and stopped; I never thought to ask since then; I have heard his character spoken of frequently.

Q. In your inquiries did you find any who would believe him? *A.* I did not; if I had, I would have introduced them on that trial.

Q. How soon after the murder of Ashburn did the grand jury sit? *A.* The second Monday in May was the session of the court; the grand jury sat at that time.

Q. Did the grand jury take any notice of the murder? *A.* They did not.

The testimony of the witness having been read over to him, the Judge Advocate inquired of him if he had any corrections to make. He replied that he had not.

Questions by Mr. Stephens.

THOMAS P. CHAPIN, a witness for the defense, being duly sworn, testifies as follows:

Q. Please state to the Court your name and where you reside? *A.* My name is Thomas P. Chapin. I reside at Columbus, and I am a physician.

Q. Are you not acquainted with Columbus Bedell, of Columbus? *A.* I am.

Q. Do you see him in the room? *A.* I do.

Q. Please state to the Court which is him? *A.* (The witness points out the prisoner.)

Q. Did you see Mr. Bedell at any time the evening before the death of Ashburn? *A.* I did.

Q. What hour of the evening, and where? *A.* It was about sundown, at the steps that lead to my office door.

Q. State the circumstances under which you saw him there? *A.* He came to me, and told me that he was sick and wanted me to do something for him.

Q. What did you do—did you make any examination, and if so, what? Just state what occurred between you and him on the occasion. *A.* I examined his tongue and found it coated. He had considerable fever. I prescribed blue mass for him, and told him to take it at bed time; to bathe his feet in warm water, and the next morning to take a seidlitz powder.

Q. Did you see anything more of him that night? *A.* No, sir.

Q. Did you make any entry of that prescription? *A.* Yes, sir.

Q. Have you it with you? *A.* I have. (Producing a small memorandum book.)

Q. What is the character of that book? *A.* It is a regular memorandum book.

Q. Will you turn to the entry of that prescription? *A.* I will. (Witness turns to an entry of March 30th, of Lum Bedell's, and then handed the book to the Judge Advocate, who handed it to the members of the Commission, by whom it was inspected.)

Q. Will you explain the meaning of these letters "O. R." after the entry? *A.* Official prescription.

Q. Is that the general medical expression? It is explained in the back part of the book. I got it up myself.

Q. What is the "R" for? *A.* Recipe.

Q. Office recipe? *A.* Yes, sir; in the back part of the book you will see what all those marks mean.

Q. When did you next see Mr. Bedell? *A.* I saw him the next evening.

Q. Did you again prescribe for him? *A.* I did.

Q. And these entries as to prescriptions in this book you state to be correct? *A.* Yes, sir.

Q. The dates and all, just as they stand? *A.* Yes, sir.

No cross-examination.

The testimony of the witness having been read over to him, he was asked by the Judge Advocate if he desired to make any corrections. He replied that he did not.

Questions by Mr. Stephens.

JOHN W. BROOKS, a witness for the defense, being duly sworn, testified as follows:

Q. Please state to the Court your name in full, where you reside, and your business? *A.* John W. Brooks; reside in Columbus, Ga., and am a druggist.

Q. Do you know Columbus Bedell? *A.* I do.

Q. Do you see him in court? *A.* I do. That is the gentleman. (Pointing to prisoner Bedell.)

Q. Did you see him at any time, the evening or night of the murder of Ashburn? *A.* Yes, sir, about 10 o'clock.

Q. Under what circumstances did you see him? *A.* He was complaining of being sick, and was there for the purpose of having a prescription prepared.

Q. Did he go to your drugstore? *A.* Yes, sir.

Q. What did he ask for? *A.* He spoke of getting some blue mass. I suggested to him that he had better put a little calomel with it, which he consented to. Of those two things I made the prescription.

Q. Did you make any examination of him? *A.* He asked me to look at his tongue. I did so.

Q. What condition did you find it in? *A.* Very foul.

Q. When did you see him again? *A.* Almost immediately after his release the next day.

Q. What time was that? *A.* I am not certain as to the hour, I mean as to the time of his arrest. I would state that I do not mean to say that I saw him the next day; or at least that he was released the next day. I am not certain about that, but only say I am certain in regard to his arrest the next day, and I saw him after his release from that arrest. I do not remember the day.

Q. Are there any other persons in Columbus that you know of who would correspond in height and personal appearance with Mr. Bedell? *A.* Yes, sir, I think they are, but I do not know as I could designate them just now.

Q. Do you know William H. Brannon there? *A.* I do.

Q. How does he correspond in size. *A.* I think he is about the same height, he has a beard very much like Mr. Bedell's, only longer.

Q. Any moustache on the upper lip? *A.* Yes, sir.

Q. Do you know a Major Bradley? *A.* I do not.

Q. Do you know one Jesse Bradford? *A.* I know several Bradfords there, I am not certain as to the given name of the party.

Q. Do you know Mr. McAllister's son-in-law? *A.* Yes, sir.

Q. What is his appearance in height and beard compared with Mr. Bedell? *A.* I have no recollection as to the condition of his face, whether he had any beard or not. I have not seen him for a very long time; he is about the same height, however—may not be as high.

Q. Do you know William Fogle? *A.* Yes, sir.

Q. How does he compare in height, general appearance, face, and beard, with Mr. Bedell? *A.* I can not say anything about the condition of his face, I do not think he is quite as tall as Mr. Bedell.

Cross-examined—Questions by the Judge Advocate.

Q. Can you readily distinguish between Mr. Bedell and any of these persons whom you have named as in some respects resembling him? *A.* I could in the day time, very readily.

Q. Could not you in the night, if he was in a room where there was a lighted candle? *A.* I could, sir.

Q. Could not any person that had been in the habit of seeing him and these others in the street as readily distinguish one from the other as you probably could? *A.* Very likely, sir, if they know him as well as I do, under the same circumstances.

Q. Can you say now what is the height of Mr. Bedell? *A.* I should judge that he was about six feet—probably a little over.

Q. What would you judge as to his weight? *A.* About one hundred and forty-five.

Q. Was this a very unusual prescription that you made for the prisoner Bedell? *A.* Larger than I generally put up.

Q. Do you remember the time of month and day, etc., on account of the size of the prescription? *A.* I do not, sir.

Q. How do you remember these circumstances? *A.* From the fact that he was arrested next day, and the fact of my putting up a prescription occurred to my mind at once.

Q. Was it a prescription that would have put him to bed if he had taken it? *A.* Ordinarily it would have made him very sick.

Q. Suppose he had not taken it, but carried it in his pocket, do you think it would have put him to bed? *A.* I reckon not, sir.

Q. Do you know of your own knowledge whether he took it or not? *A.* I can not say positively.

Questions by Mr. Stephens.

Q. Have you any reason to believe that he took it? *A.* I have.

Q. State it? *A.* The fact that he called the next morning quite early for some seidlitz powders, which he was instructed to take, in case the medicine did not operate copiously that night.

Question by the Judge Advocate.

Q. Did you make any entry in any book of this prescription? A. I did not.

Question by the Court.

Q. Did you not state before that you did not see him after the 30th of March until he was released from arrest? A. I would not be positive of that; I would not be positive that I had or had not seen him.

Questions by the Judge Advocate.

Q. From the 30th of March until after he was released from arrest, is that what you mean? A. I am not positive whether I did see him before or after his arrest that night—whether I saw him subsequent to that night; I am not certain about it.

Q. Then you are not certain about his having taken seidlitz powders the next morning? A. I meant to make that correction in my testimony; I saw him the next morning when he came down, and got the seidlitz powders from me.

The question put by the Court is again read to the witness, when he answered as follows:

A. That is a correction that I desire to make, and was going to speak to Mr. Crawford about just now when General Benning motioned me not to speak; I did see him in the morning.

Questions by the Judge Advocate.

Q. You now wish to make a correction, and say that you did not see him after he took the seidlitz powders? A. I saw him in the morning; I am not certain when I saw him after that. He was arrested after that, and I am not certain when I saw him after that time—in the time of his arrest.

Questions by Mr. Stephens, (by permission of the Court.)

Q. Are you very distinct of Mr. Bedell's calling for the seidlitz powders early that morning? A. I am positive of it.

Q. When you answered then that you had not seen him until after his arrest, did you mean that you had no interview with him at all from the time of his arrest until after his discharge. A. I do not think I had any interview with him; that was my meaning. I do not think I had any interview with him at all, after letting him have the seidlitz powders in the morning. I am not certain whether I saw him after that at all; I mean after his release.

The testimony of the witness having been read over to him, he was asked if he had any corrections to make. He said he had not.

Thereupon the Court adjourned until to-morrow (Saturday) morning at 10 o'clock.

McPHERSON BARRACKS, ATLANTA, GA.
10 o'clock A. M. July 18, 1868.

The Commission met pursuant to adjournment.

Present, the same members as yesterday, the Judge Advocate and his assistants, the prisoners on trial and their counsel.

The record of the previous day was read and approved.

Questions by Mr. Stephens.

ZACK T. KING, a witness for the defense, being duly sworn, testifies as follows:

Q. State your name in full and where you reside? A. Zack T. King, Columbus, Georgia.

Q. Your age? A. Nineteen.

Q. What is your business? A. I am a clerk in a bank.

Q. Do you know Mr. Columbus Bedell, of Columbus? A. I do.

Q. Do you see him here amongst these gentlemen? A. I do.

Q. Can you point him out to the Court? A. I can. (The witness pointed to prisoner, Bedell.)

Q. What is the business occupation of Mr. Bedell? A. He is a book-keeper for L. G. Bowers.

Q. In what business is Mr. Bowers engaged? A. I believe he is engaged in the cotton business; also in the insurance business.

Q. How far is your office from his? A. They are together.

Q. Same room? A. Same room.

Q. Do you know where Mr. Bedell was the night of Ashburn's assassination? A. Until 10 o'clock at night I do.

Q. Where was he? A. He was in the office.

Q. What was he doing? A. I suppose he was at work.

Q. Were you at work? A. I was.

17

Q. Do you know anything of him after that? *A.* I do not.

Q. What occurred at the time of his leaving the office? *A.* In what way do you mean?

Q. Did he say anything to you or you to him? *A.* He remarked that he was feeling unusually unwell that night, that he intended retiring early.

Q. You have said it was about 10 o'clock. What is your reason for stating so? *A.* When my brother opened the office he left, and was gone unusually long that night. When the bell struck 10 I counted it and also looked at the clock at the same time— at the same hour.

Q. How long after that did Mr. Bedell leave? *A.* Few minutes.

Cross-examination.

The testimony of the witness having been read over to him, he was asked by the Judge Advocate if there were any corrections that he desired to make. He replied that there were none.

Questions by Mr. Stephens.

HOMER H. STARR, a witness for the defense, being duly sworn, testifies as follows:

Q. State your name in full and where you reside? *A.* Homer H. Starr. I reside in Columbus, Georgia.

Q. Your age? *A.* I am in my twenty-sixth year.

Q. Your occupation? *A.* I am a shipper at a cotton house.

Q. Are you acquainted with Mr. Columbus Bedell, of Columbus? *A.* I am, by sight, but have no personal acquaintance with him, except in business transactions.

Q. Do you see him in Court? *A.* Yes, sir.

Q. Will you designate him to the Court? (The witness points to the prisoner, Bedell).

Q. Did you see him any part of the night on which Ashburn was assassinated? *A.* I did, sir.

Q. What time, and how did you come to see him? *A.* I was sitting in my room with the door open, and he passed there a little after 10 o'clock.

Q. How far apart are your sleeping apartments—yours and his? *A.* About twelve feet I should judge. I would not be positive.

Q. Are they or not opposite a hall of the house or passage? *A.* Yes, sir.

Q. What house is that? *A.* It is known as the McGea house.

Q. When he passed your door, was he going to his sleeping apartments? *A.* He was, sir.

Q. What time did you go to bed that night? *A.* I suppose it must have been 12 o'clock before I got into bed. I looked at the clock and found it was half-past eleven? I then prepared to retire.

Q. Was your door or not open until you retired? *A.* It was, sir.

Q. Could Mr. Bedell have left his room without your seeing him before you retired? *A.* He could not.

Q. Did you hear his door open after you had retired. *A.* I did not.

Q. Are these rooms that you and he occupied on the first or second floor of the building? *A.* Second floor.

Q. Do any other persons occupy rooms on the same floor? *A.* Yes, sir, several.

Q. State the names of the persons. *A.* Mr. Ellis, Mr. Duck, Dr. Urquhart. and Mr. Harris of the Internal Revenue office, whose sleeping apartments were there before he was married.

Cross-examined by Mr. Brown.

Q. Upon what street is this house? *A.* Broad street.

Q. Is it kept as a hotel? *A.* It is not, sir.

Q. Is it a boarding house? *A.* No, sir.

Q. Are there offices in it? *A.* Well, some time ago the Doctor had an office in there; and the Alabama Internal Revenue office is in that building also. Dr. Urquhart also had an office in the building.

Q. Whom do you mean by the Alabama Internal Revenue officers? *A.* I mean the collectors that keep their office in Columbus to collect the taxes on cotton and other taxes.

Q. Are they Alabama officers? *A.* They are.

Q. Do they keep their office out of the State? *A.* They did so to accommodate the cotton-shippers there.

Q. Who keeps this house? *A.* It is not kept by any person.

Q. What is under the sleeping apartment you speak of—it is in the second story as I understand you? *A.* Stores, sir; they are vacant though.

Q. To whom do the stores belong? *A.*

MILITARY OUTRAGE IN GEORGIA. 163

They belong to Mr. McGea; he has charge of the estate; I think, he has charge of the renting of the rooms; I don't know who the building belongs to; he is interested in them.

Q. What time did you go to your room that night? A. About 9 o'clock.

Q. Where had you been before you went to your room? A. I had been in my office.

Q. How far is your office from your sleeping room? A. About one hundred yards.

Q. What were you doing in your office? A. I was attending to my usual business there.

Q. What is your usual business in your office at night? A. To enter up the receipts of the cotton that was bought during the day.

Q. What persons were in your office that night? A. Henry H. Epping and Richard B. Watson.

Q. What were they doing in your office? A. I do not know that I can exactly tell what Mr. Watson was doing. Mr. Epping was writing letters, as is his usual habit. I never watched Mr. Watson's movements to see what he was doing.

Q. Where are they now? A. One is in Columbus; the other is in Abington, Va.

Q. Which one is in Columbus? A. Mr. Epping.

Q. What is his business in Columbus? A. He is a banker and a cotton factor.

Q. Are you sure there were no other persons present in your office that night? A. I will not be positive of it, sir?

Q. What time do you usually close your office and go to your sleeping room? A. As soon as we get through attending to what business we have to attend to during the night. We have no particular hour.

Q. Was there any body with you in your sleeping room that night? A. There was.

Q. Who? A. A gentleman by the name of J. M. Tomlinson.

Q. What is his age? A. I do not know, sir?

Q. Give your opinion? A. I should suppose about thirty or thirty-five.

Q. Did he go to the room with you? A. He did not.

Q. Did he come after you got to the room? A. He did not.

Q. Was he in the room when you got there? A. He was.

Q. Does he usually sit with you in the room? A. He was my room-mate at the time.

Q. Where is he now? A. I can not tell. I have not heard from him in six weeks.

Q. Where was he when you last heard from him? A. He was in Chambers county, Alabama.

Q. Had he gone to bed when you got to the room? A. He had not.

Q. Was there no one else in the room any portion of the night? A. In my room, did you mean?

Q. Yes, sir? A. No, sir, there was not.

Q. Who retired to bed first, you or Mr. Tomlinson? A. I do not exactly remember. I think I did. There were very few minutes interval between the time of both of us getting into bed.

Q. Did you sleep in the small bed? A. We did.

Q. What is your usual time of going to bed? A. It had been up to about middle of March about 12 o'clock. From 11 to 2 was my usual hour during the winter months.

Q. What were you and he doing from nine o'clock until you retired to bed? A. We were talking over some business matters that we had between us.

Q. Did you converse on nothing else? A. No, sir.

Q. Did it take you three hours to talk over the business matter? A. If it had not taken us that long we would not have been up. There was a general run of conversation—it was not confined solely to business.

Q. Upon what other subjects did you converse? A. Personal topics of the day—different things.

Q. Do you recollect any topic you conversed about, other than your business matters? A. I do not, because I never impressed it on my mind.

Q. Was there anything unusual to impress passing events upon your mind that night? A. There was.

Q. What was it? A. The arrest the next morning of Mr. Bedell.

Q. You say that you never impressed topics of conversation upon your mind. Why did you not if this arrest impressed passing events the next day upon your mind? A. Because I did not think that it was necessary.

Q. Can you mention any other event that was impressed on your mind that night, except what you said of Mr. Bedell? A. I do not think that I can, except the conversation that Mr. Tomlinson and myself had that night.

Q. Have not you just stated that you can not remember the topics of conversation that night. A. I said I could not remember the general topics of conversation, but I do the business conversation.

Counsel for defense objects to the line of interrogatories by the prosecution, upon the ground that none of the answers, if made, would elucidate the issue involved before the Court. The witness has already stated that the arrest of Mr. Bedell next morning impressed upon his mind the facts connected with what he has testified as to him; and whether the witness can or can not recollect any other incident of the night not connected in any way with Bedell, can not affect this testimony in this particular.

To which objection Mr. Brown presented the following answer: "As the witness swears with positiveness to the fact that he saw Bedell pass to his room at a certain hour, it is legitimate and proper to test the strength of his memory by asking him about all that transpired in his room about the same time, that the Court may be able to see whether it is safe to trust his recollection on this one particular point. The best, and almost the only test of the strength and accuracy of the memory of the witness as to the particular point, is to inquire as to his recollection of other facts that occurred at the same time."

The Court was cleared for deliberation. In a few minutes the doors were re-opened, when the Judge Advocate announced that the objection had been overruled.

Questions by Mr. Brown.

Q. What business were you conversing about? A. Have I a right to object to that question?

Q. I do not ask what was said. I simply want to know the character of that business. A. The reason I object to the question is because it was a private conversation on some private business, and I do not care to make it public. If necessary, however, I can do so.

Q. I do not ask you to go into any detail, but just to give the general nature of the business? A. It was in regard to some dissatisfaction that he had with a partner in Columbus.

Q. Was there anything unusual about Mr. Bedell's appearance that night when you saw him pass the door? A. Nothing that I noticed.

Q. How many stairways are there into the story where the bed-rooms are? A. Do you mean flights of steps, or number of steps?

Q. I mean the different flights of steps. A. There is only one, sir.

Q. How far is your room from the head of the stair steps? A. I do not know the distance. It is the last room. It is as far as from here (witness-stand, south end of room) to that wall, (north end of room.) I do not think it is quite that far—to about that first window beyond the door would be about the distance from the head of the steps to my first door. I would not, however, be positive about the distance.

Q. Is there a passage from the head of the stair steps to the back end of the house, with sleeping apartments on both sides? A. There is.

Q. You say yours was the last room. On which side is it—I mean now going from the stair steps? A. The left-hand side.

Q. Whose room was next to yours on the left-hand side? A. There is no room at all on the left-hand side. How am I standing?

Q. Whose room was next to yours on the same side? A. There is no room. There is a little passage about three or four feet intervening between my room and the next room, which is vacant.

Q. Were there any other rooms on the same side of the passage occupied at that time? A. There was.

Q. How many? A. Two.

Q. Who occupied the one nearest yourself? A. Mr. Harris. It was a bed-room.

Q. Who occupied the other? A. That was the office; it was used as his office.

Q. Where was Mr. Bedell's room? A. Opposite mine.

Q. Do you mean the last room on the right-hand side as you went down the passage? A. I do not.

Q. Was there one between him and the end of the passage? A. There was.

Q. Was not that then the one immediately opposite yours? A. Both rooms were opposite mine; mine is a large room that occupies the space of the two rooms— the one occupied by Mr. Ellis and the one occupied by Mr. Bedell—so both rooms are opposite mine.

Q. How many doors were in your room opening into the passage. *A.* Two.

Q. Did any door open from the end of your room into this little passage, across the passage you speak of? *A.* No, sir.

Q. Is there any partition through your room? *A.* In the room, do you mean?

Q. Yes, sir. *A.* There is not.

Q. Which door was open that night? *A.* The door opposite Mr. Bedell's room.

Q. In what part of the room were you? *A.* Pretty nearly the center; more towards the last end than in the center—not far from the center of the room, where the table sets.

Q. Which do you call the last end? *A.* The lower end of the passage—towards the fire place.

Q. How many feet do you say it was from the place where you sat to Mr. Bedell's door? *A.* That I could not answer, as I never measured it.

Q. I ask for your best opinion? *A.* I suppose about twelve feet from door to door; the passage is about twelve feet wide; I suppose from where I was sitting to the door that I had opened, was ten or twelve feet—may not be quite so far.

Q. Then you would say it was from twenty to twenty-five feet from where you sat to Bedell's door, would you not? *A.* No, sir, because I am not positive of the distance, either of the passages, or the distance from where I was sitting to the door.

Q. Is it not your opinion that that is about the distance? *A.* It is, from the present idea I have of the distance.

Q. Was there any light burning in the passage-way that night? *A.* There was not; the passage is usually very dark when none of the doors are open.

Q. Was there any door opened but yours? *A.* Not in my portion of the building; I do not know what occurred in the front part; I could not see whether it was open or not; Harris might have had his door open and I not see it.

Q. Did you remain all the time after you entered your room, and until you went to bed, in the same seat? *A.* No, sir, I do not suppose I did; I got up once or twice, I reckon, to get matches to light a pipe as I was smoking, but I occupied the same position probably during the whole time I was there, but I did not occupy the same seat all the time.

Q. Where did you go to get the matches? *A.* I went to the mantlepiece.

Q. Where is it? *A.* In the west part of the room; the situation of the building is east and west.

Q. Are the steps at the east or west end of the passage? *A.* They are at the east end.

Q. Then your room is in the west end of the building? *A.* It is.

Q. You went to the west end of your room when you went to get the matches? *A.* Yes, sir.

Q. Can you stand at the mantlepiece at the west end of the room and see out of the door furthest from you, and see Bedell's door across the passage from your door? *A.* I can not see Bedell's door, but I could see any person passing to and from Bedell's door, going towards the steps from the mantlepiece.

Q. Do not persons often pass through that passage of a night who are occupying rooms there without attracting your attention every time you move? *A.* Yes, sir, they frequently do.

Q. When they pass without attracting your attention, it would be impossible even the next day to say whether they had passed or not, would it not? *A.* Some persons could pass there without attracting my attention, but Mr. Bedell never came to his room without attracting my attention, if I was awake. He had a peculiar habit of wiping his feet on a mat before he opened his door, which always attracted my attention whether my door was open or shut.

Q. You have not answered my question. I will repeat it. When they pass without attracting your attention it would be impossible even the next day to say whether they had passed or not, would it not? *A.* It would if something unusual did not take place the next day in regard to them.

Q. If they did not attract your attention at the time, how could you swear the next day that they passed, no matter how unusual the occurrences that transpired the next? *A.* I could not swear to anything that did not attract my attention.

Q. Do you swear that Mr. Bedell never passed in and out of his room, when you were in your room, without especially attracting your attention? *A.* No, sir, I do not.

Q. Were not you and the room-mate with you that night very seriously engaged a portion of the time in conversation? *A.*

I do not know that we had anything very serious to converse about. He was relating and I was listening.

Q. As it was a matter of personal business that you thought should not be spoken of here, was it not a matter at the time that attracted your attention? A. Of course, I was interested in it and paid attention to what he was relating.

Q. Did you not feel for him a decided interest in the matter? A. I did.

Q. While earnestly engaged with him in conversation, would you as probably have noticed persons passing through the passage way as you would had you been less engaged? A. Upon hearing a person pass in the passage way when my door room is open, it is my usual habit to glance up and see who it is—just as almost any other person would do.

Q. Is it not probable that you might not have done that when you were very seriously engaged in conversation? A. It is.

Q. Then will you pretend to answer positively that Mr. Bedell could not have gone out there without attracting your attention? A. He might have gone out there, but it is not probable that he could have done so without attracting my attention.

Q. Is it not possible that he could? A. Well, yes, sir, he might.

Questions by the Court.

Q. Which way does your door open, to the right or to the left? A. To the left—the one I had open.

Q. Was it swung entirely back against the wall, or was it only partially open? A. I considered it only partially open. It was not against the wall.

Q. At what time did you close your door? A. At half past eleven o'clock.

Q. Was it when you looked at your watch or clock, or was it when you went to bed? A. Just before I retired to bed.

Q. At what time of night? A. It was after half past eleven o'clock.

Q. Where does the small passage lead to? A. It is just an open passage. There is nothing at all in it. It doesn't lead to any place.

Q. Was the floor of the hall covered by any carpet or matting. A. It was not.

Q. Where were the water-closets attached to the building? A. In the rear, to the west side.

Q. How did the occupants get to the water-closet? A. By a back step.

Q. How long have you lived in Columbus? A. I have been there about a year. I lived there previous to the war nearly all my life.

Q. Was there any one in Columbus who resembled Mr. Bedell in size and general appearance? A. Not that I can remember.

By Brown (with permission of the Commission.)

Q. What do you mean by the back way to the water-closet? A. I mean the back steps. The building has back steps and front steps. The back stairs lead down to an inclosed lot, where there were water-closets.

Q. Do you mean that there are back stairs from this passage up in the second story that go down to the water-closet? A. I do.

Q. Then were you not incorrect when you said there was but one stairway that went up into that sleeping apartment? A. If I remember correctly, I did not state there was but one stairway leading up there.

Q. You say you did not so state? I will ask the reporter to read the question put to you on that point and the answer.

The reporter read as follows:

Q. How many stairways are there into the story where the bed-rooms are? A. Do you mean flights of steps or number of steps?

Q. I mean different flights of steps. A. There is only one, sir.

Q. Is that correct? A. I misunderstood the question when I gave that answer.

Q. You now state there is a flight of stairs leading into this passage way between the bed-rooms, going up from each end of the passage way. A. There is a main entrance on the east side. Then there are steps leading down to the water-closets on the west end; but it is closed in, and there is no way of getting out into the streets. The back steps are only used to go down to the water-closets.

Q. What sort of an inclosure is it. A. It is a small yard; the back of it is part of the warehouse; there is a little space intervening, where there is a fence.

Q. How high is that fence? A. I do not remember; I do not know whether I noticed it or not; I could not tell.

Q. Could not a person get over it? *A.* I presume so, sir.

Q. Do you not know that a person could? *A.* That would depend altogether upon a person's activity; some might, and some might not.

Q. Could a person of Mr. Bedell's activity get over it? *A.* I know nothing of Mr. Bedell's activity; I do not know whether he could or not.

Q. Is it not an ordinary fence? *A.* I do not remember the fence; I know there is a fence; I could not tell whether it was an ordinary fence or what kind of a fence it was; all I know is that there is a little space between the water-closet and the warehouse.

Q. Do you pretend to say that a person of ordinary activity in that back lot can not get out without going back through the passage between the sleeping apartments? *A.* I did not; I did not say they could or could not.

Q. What do you now say about that? Can they or can they not? *A.* I am not positive: I do not know anything about Mr. Bedell's activity; I could not get over; they might or they might not; I would not be positive one way or the other.

Q. I only want to know what your opinion is about that? *A.* I have stated I could not be positive about a person getting over it.

Q. What is your opinion about it? *A.* I have no opinion in regard to it, because I do not remember the fence.

Q. How long have you roomed there? *A.* From September.

Q. Until now? *A.* Yes, sir.

Q. You do not recollect anything about the fence in the back yard of the building where you roomed? *A.* I do not.

Q. Have you ever been in it? *A.* Been in what?

Q. Been in that back yard? *A.* Yes, sir, I have been in the water-closet.

Q. Have you not been there almost every day since you have roomed where you do? *A.* I have not.

Q. How often have you been there? *A.* I have been there very frequently.

Q. As much as every other day? *A.* No, sir, sometimes I have not been there for a month or months.

Q. Are there not one or more windows from the west end of your room overlooking that lot? *A.* There are two that a person looks at in looking against the wall of the warehouse.

Q. Can you not see into that lot from those windows? *A.* Yes, sir, I can see in the back lot, but I can not see the water-closet; I can see the top of it, not the ground.

Q. Can not the fence be seen from your window? *A.* It can not.

Q. Then do you intend to be understood as stating under oath, that you recollect nothing about the fence there, and that you can give no opinion whether a person of ordinary activity could get over it? *A.* Yes, sir, I do, for I never measured the fence; I know there is a fence there.

Q. What is it made of? *A.* I presume it is made of wood.

Q. Don't you know? *A.* No, sir, I would not swear to its being made of wood.

Q. May it not be of brick? *A.* It may.

Q. May it be of stone? *A.* It is not likely to be of stone, as we do not use many stones in Columbus for fences; it may be of brick or wood, but not of stone; I do not think, I would not be positive about its not being stone.

Q. Are you positive it is not iron? *A.* I am not positive of what material the fence is.

Q. Do you swear positively that there is a fence there at all? *A.* Well, I am not positive there is, but to the best of my belief, knowing the place would not be left open, I swear positively there ought to be a fence there, if there is not; I would not swear point-blank that there is, for I do not remember ever seeing it; it is not usual for a person to leave a portion of a lot open, so I presume there is a fence there.

Q. This is a serious matter, and you are under oath. Please state the size of the lot. *A.* I can not state the size of it, as I never measured it; I have no idea; I can draw it off on paper—the form of the building and everything connected with it, but as to stating distances, I can not do it.

Q. Give us your opinion as to the size of the lot? *A.* I have none.

Q. Does it contain as much as an acre of ground? *A.* It does not.

Q. Does it contain a quarter of an acre? *A.* It might or it might not; I do not know.

Q. In your opinion, is there more or less than a quarter of an acre in that lot? *A.* There might be possibly a quarter of an acre, but there is more likely to be less than a quarter of an acre.

Q. Can you state there is no gate or door leading out on that back lot? *A.* None that I have any knowledge of.

Q. Will you state that there is none? *A.* To the best of my knowledge and belief I will.

Q. When you recollect so little about the fence, how do you remember that there is no gate through it? *A.* From the position of the building surrounding it; but I am not positive about there not being a gate; I have not said there was no gate.

Q. Am I now to understand you that you mean to say there was no gate? *A.* I said to the best of my belief there was no gate leading out from the back part.

Q. I will ask you if you will swear positively there is none? *A.* I will not swear positively one way or the other, because I do not know whether there is or not. I swear that to the best of my knowledge and belief there is none.

Q. Then as you do not know whether there is one or not, you can not swear there is not one, can you? *A.* I can swear to the best of my knowledge and belief there is not one.

Q. Please answer my question. Then as you do not know whether there is one or not, you can not swear there is not one, can you? *A.* No, I can not.

Questions by Mr. Stephens, (with permission of the Court.)

Q. Did you ever know any person to enter that building from that side of the house? *A.* No—never.

Q. Suppose there be a fence there, or a gate there, and a person should make egress from the lot, where would they go to? Do you know anything of the premises immediately on the outside of it? *A.* Dr. Urquhart lives next.

Q. Is his the adjoining house? *A.* Yes, sir.

Q. Does Dr. Urquhart's yard face right along by that dividing line between the lot that you occupied rooms on and his lot? *A.* It does.

Q. Do you know of any possible way of escaping from or getting out of your apartment from that end of the building at all to get on the street. *A.* No, sir, there is no way to get on the street at *all* from the lot.

Q. Were your apartments rented as sleeping apartments alone? *A.* Yes, sir.

Q. Do you know whether the occupants of the other rooms occupied theirs in the same way you did? *A.* Some did, and some did not.

Q. Did any of them live in the house—take their meals in the house? *A.* No, sir, not as a usual thing. At that time I had a room-mate that stayed there and he used to have his meals sent to his room.

Q. What was the business of that room-mate of yours? *A.* Portrait painter.

Questions by Mr. Brown, (with permission of the Court.)

Q. You stated you never knew any one to enter the building through the back part. Do you intend to state that no one ever did so enter? *A.* I do.

Q. You replied to Mr. Stephens' question that it was not possible for any one to go out through the back lot. In case of a fire in front, could not you make your escape through the back lot? *A.* I could by going through other lots.

Q. How would you get into the other lots? *A.* I would probably get over the water-closet, or the kitchen that is down there.

Q. Could you not probably get over the fence in case a fire was pursuing you? *A.* By breaking it down I could.

Q. Don't you think you could get over it without breaking it down if there were a fire in your rear? *A.* I would make a pretty desperate effort.

Q. I ask again if you could not get over the fence if there was a fire in your rear? *A.* I could try—I do not say I could get over it.

The examination of the witness having been concluded, the court thereupon adjourned until Monday morning at ten o'clock.

McPHERSON BARRACKS, ATLANTA, GA., }
10 A. M., July 20, 1868. }

The Commission met pursuant to adjournment.

Present, same members as yesterday, the Judge Advocate and his assistants, the prisoners and their counsel.

The record of Saturday's proceedings was read and approved.

The evidence of Mr. Homer H. Starr being read over to him, he desired and obtained permission of the Commission to make the following correction: "I am only a clerk in the cotton house; I am shipping clerk in the cotton house."

Mr. Stephens, for defense, by permission of the Court, asked this witness the following additional question:

Q. What do you mean by you door "opening to your left?" Will you show the Court what you mean? *A.* I mean that in going into my room from the hall, it opens to the left.

Whereupon the witness, desiring to make no further corrections, was discharged.

Mr. Stephens conducts the examination for the defense.

Mr. Roswell Ellis was then introduced as a witness for the defense, duly sworn, and testified as follows:

Q. Please state to the Court your name in full, and residence—christian name and all. *A.* Roswell Ellis; Columbus, Ga.

Q. Where were you the night that Ashburn was killed? *A.* I was confined to my bed with sickness.

Q. Where were your apartments at that time? *A.* My sleeping apartments were up stairs in the northwest corner of what is known as "McGehee's Building," on the west of Broad Street, north of Randolph Street.

Q. Did any other persons have sleeping apartments in the same building on the same floor? *A.* Yes, sir; several persons occupied rooms up there at the time.

Q. Who were they, to the best of your remembrance and belief? *A.* Mr. Bedell occupied the room immediately east of me. The adjoining one to him was occupied by a Mr. Reed, cotton merchant, or cotton buyer. The one adjoining that was occupied, I think, by Dr. Urquhart as his office. I don't think it was occupied at that time as a sleeping apartment. The corner room, the last one on that side of the hall, was occupied by Mr. Duck as a sleeping room. That is the north row of rooms. On the south side of the hall, the two first rooms next to Broad Street were occupied as a revenue office by Mr. McSpadden and a Mr. Harris, who were revenue collectors.

Q. Who in the next? *A.* The next, I think, sir, was a vacant room. It was not well ventilated, and is not fit for a sleeping room, or any other purpose. Between that room and the one occupied by Mr. Starr is a passage that was not occupied at all. The next room to it, that was occupied by Mr. Starr, and Mr. Tomlinson was in the room with him.

Q. When you say Mr. Bedell, whom do you mean? *A.* I speak of Mr. Columbus C. Bedell whom I recognize among the prisoners there.

Q. Did you hear Mr. Bedell when he came to his room that night? *A.* I did not, sir.

Q. Did you usually hear him when he came in or went out of his room? *A.* Almost invariably, sir, while I am in my own room.

Q. What was your own condition that evening, Mr. Ellis? *A.* I had been sick, sir, confined to my bed a week or ten days with severe illness. On Monday noon, I imprudently got up and walked down to my boarding-house. I remained up during that afternoon, retired to my bed about eight o'clock very much exhausted. I fell immediately to sleep under the exhaustion of the exercise and the influence of opiates. I slept unnaturally sound in the early part of the night.

Q. What time of night did you wake? *A.* It was between the hours of twelve and one, I recollect, and how far before that I can not say, I woke; I heard Mr. Bedell's clock strike one—the clock in his room he keeps running; I have no clock in my room; I would state that I was waked by the paroxysms of pain returning, and from that time I did not shut my eyes; I was in a great deal of pain.

Q. Did you go to sleep before day? and if so, at what time? *A.* I did not, sir.

Q. Do you think if Mr. Bedell had come in his room or gone out of his room, after you woke, that you would have heard him? *A.* I think so, sir; for I can always hear while everything is quiet, and even an ordinary conversation in his room.

Q. Is there a door or not between your room and his, opening into each other? *A.* It is unlocked, sir; my wardrobe stands against it—that is, as near against it as the knob of the door will admit, shutting out entirely the sounds.

Q. Do you usually hear Mr. Bedell when he comes in or goes out? *A.* Yes, sir, I do, sir, when I am in my own room first, or while I am in my room, and very often I am woke from my sleeping by his coming there; it is not an unusual occurrence.

Q. Are you acquainted with the habits of Mr. Bedell, of being in or out at night? *A.* I know his habits, sir, during the time that he has been rooming there; he has been very much engaged at night attending to his business, and to my knowledge he has been kept up during the cotton season to a very late hour; his hour of retirement varied, I suppose, sir, from ten until one—sometimes as late as two; I have occasion to know that he has been confined to his office on business on many occasions of his retiring late.

Q. Did you ever know him to attend any party meetings? *A.* I don't think I ever knew him to attend a public meeting of a political character; I don't recollect of ever having seen him at one.

Q. What was the usual mode of wearing his hair? *A.* Well, sir, I don't think it varied materially from the style he now wears it, sir; I think I should observe the difference, if any material one.

Q. Did you ever see it long, hanging down about the shoulders? *A.* Well, sir. I can't recollect that I have; I don't think it is his customary style.

Q. Was there a carpet or not in his room? *A.* No carpet in his room; there may be a piece of carpet near his bed, but he has no carpet to walk upon.

Q. Can you and do you distinctly hear any person walking in his room? *A.* Very distinctly, yes, sir, while in my room.

Q. Do you know or not his walk from other people's? *A.* Yes, sir; he has a peculiar walk, and I have heard it so often I can easily recognize it as his.

Q. Do you have a very distinct impression as to the facts you have testified about—the time you awoke up, and the pain, and the striking of the clock; and if so, state the reasons why they were impressed upon your mind? *A.* I have a very distinct recollection of waking before the hour of one, and hearing his clock strike one. Mr. Bedell, about, I think, between eight and nine o'clock the next morning, came into my room and inquired if I had heard him come in last night. I told him I did not, and in reply to me he told me he came in at some early hour of the night; I can not recollect now definitely. Mr. Bedell stated to me that he had learned that he was suspected of having been engaged in the assassination, and I replied to him that if he had came in after one o'clock, I should most certainly have heard it I thought; but having slept so very soundly during the early part of the night, I doubted very much whether his coming in would have disturbed me.

Q. Was there anybody about Columbus who was taken for Mr. Bedell sometimes? *A.* I know of none to my personal knowledge that I should at any time mistake for him. I have heard—(Judge Advocate objects to the witness stating what he has heard). Witness continues: I have seen a party—(will that statement do?)—who was afterwards represented to me, and I recognized, as bearing a resemblance to Mr. Bedell.

Q. What was the name of that person? *A.* His name was given to me as Hudson; no personal acquaintance with him.

Q. How did he wear his hair—long, over the shoulders? *A.* His hair was worn long, over the shoulders, with long beard; my recollection of him.

Q. How did his general size and height correspond with Mr. Bedell's? *A.* I think it corresponded with Mr. Bedell's.

Q. Do you know Mr. William H. Brannon? *A.* I do, sir.

Q. How would you say his height and appearance accord with Mr. Bedell's, including his beard? *A.* His appearance corresponds, sir, very much; I think his height would not; he is not quite so tall as Mr. Bedell.

Q. How does his beard correspond? *A.* His beard is worn in the same style, and very long.

Q. Do you know a Mr. Bradley, Major Bradley, there, who is a bar-keeper? *A.* I do, sir.

Q. How does his size and appearance correspond with Mr. Bedell's? *A.* He is a stouter man than Mr. Bedell; not so tall; wears a long black beard.

Q. Was there no way of getting in or out of that house to your apartments except through the front entrance on Broad street? *A.* Not at night, sir; they could not get out except by jumping fences or climbing.

Q. Where is the water-closet there? *A.* The water-closet belonging to that tenement is in the north-west corner of the lot.

Q. How is that back space, including the water-closet, inclosed? *A.* It is inclosed by a plank fence, within the inclosure within the yard.

Q. State to the Court how you would go—how you would pass from your room to the water-closet? *A.* I should pass out of a hall on to a platform, and from thence by a flight of stairs into a back yard.

Q. What is the distance; how far would you walk on the platform before getting on to the flight of steps that went down to the little inclosure in which the water closet is? *A.* Twenty-five or thirty feet, I think.

Q. How high is that platform from the ground? *A.* I think about fifteen feet, sir; I am not positive as to the height of the upper floor from the ground.

Q. You descend the space going down into the water-closet; what is the space included, as well as you can recollect—that inclosed space in which the water-closet is? *A.* Well, sir, about thirty or forty feet one way by probably between forty or fifty the other; I may be inaccurate in my recollection about it.

Q. How is that space inclosed? *A.* It is inclosed by an upright plank fence.

Q. Which side are the planks nailed on? Do they make the smooth side in the inclosure or on the outside of the inclosure? *A.* I have never had occasion to observe which side they are nailed on.

Q. How high is that fence, to the best of your knowledge and belief? *A.* Between six and seven feet. I think, sir.

Q. What does this fence separate? *A.* Explain which fence you mean.

Q. The fence that incloses. *A.* It separates the water-closet and a vacant kitchen from the main yard of the stores of the lot.

Q. What else does it separate, on the north side? *A.* Separates the yard of Dr. Urquhart from this lot.

Q. And what is on the west side of this space? *A.* The west side is a warehouse wall of Grey, Bedell & Hughes—extends north as far as Dr. Urquhart's yard.

Q. And what is to the south side of this space? *A.* There is a very high fence, which nearly protects the south side ; the balance is protected by walls of the houses; it was a fence originally built round a negro mart; the house it incloses was once used as a negro mart.

Q. You mean this high fence you speak about incloses what was the negro mart, still south of this building? *A.* Yes, sir.

Q. That fence that incloses the building south of the McGehee building is higher than this fence I am talking about to Dr. Urquhart's lot? *A.* Oh, yes, sir; that is fifteen feet high, I reckon.

Q. That incloses another space south of it? *A.* It incloses one that is occupied by Mr. Sykes.

Q. Who was the architect who constructed the plan for the McGehee house? *A.* I have understood it was Mr. Morton.

Q. Will you look upon this diagram and see whether it is a correct representation of the premises? I mean the inclosed space in which the water-closet is? (A diagram is here exhibited the witness; it is appended to the record and marked —. *A.* Yes, sir; I recognize that as a correct diagram.

Questions by Mr. Stephens.

Q. (Holding up a diagram representing the premises upon which the McGehee building is situated.) I will ask the witness where the water-closet to his apartment is? *A.* Letter B represents it.

Q. What does the letter E represent? *A.* It represents a vacant and unoccupied kitchen.

Q. What does G represent? *A.* It represents the fence dividing that lot from Dr. Urquhart's lot.

Q. What is the height of that fence? *A.* I presume about seven feet ordinary height.

Q. What does F represent? *A.* The yard of Dr. Urquhart.

Q. What does letter J represent? *A.* I represents the gateway between the inner lot and the main inclosure—main yard.

Q. What does H represent? *A.* A water-closet in the rear of J. K. Reed & Co.

Q. What does L represent? *A.* It represents the fence of the inclosure within the yard.

Q. What was the object of this fence represented by L? *A.* I think it was arranged to accommodate a family who formerly occupied these two room.

Q. Was it to make the water-closet for the stores below separate from these family water-closets? *A.* Yes, sir, that was the intention I presume.

Q. You say I represents a gateway. Could not a person going down the stair steps B, pass out at the gate I, and down the alley C to Broad street? *A.* No, sir.

Q. Why not? *A.* Because the stairway ascends to a platform on the second story and closes up entirely that passage—the little alley-way.

Q. Which way does it start from? *A.* It starts from Broad street, from the east.

Q. What does M represent? *A.* That represents a stairway between Mr. Sykes, and J. K. Reed & Co's.

Q. How high from the foot to the top of the stairway? *A.* About fifteen feet. I can not answer those measurements accurately. It is in the second story.

Q. So you say it is impossible for any person to pass through the gate I, and come down the alley C, and pass out to Broad street that way? *A.* Impossible, sir.

Q. What does K represent? *A.* K represents a very tall fence which incloses what was once used as a negro mart.

Q. Is that negro mart south of the McGehee building? *A.* Yes, sir.

Q. Does that high fence separate the negro mart from the McGehee lot? *A.* Yes, sir.

Cross-examined—Questions by the Judge Advocate.

Q. Several names were suggested to you of persons in Columbus, and you were asked to state whether or not those persons resembled the prisoner, Bedell. Could you not readily distinguish Bedell from any of the persons named? *A.* From my long acquaintance with Bedell I could, sir. At night I might be mistaken. I presume you do not ask the question with regard to night time?

Q. Whether you would mistake them at night or not, would depend whether you saw them in a light or not, I presume? *A.* Yes, sir, it would depend upon where I saw them.

Q. You might at night not be able to distinguish persons with whom you were very well acquainted, although they did not resemble each other, I presume? *A.* Yes, sir.

Q. You stated that you could hear Mr. Bedell go in and out of his room. *A.* I did, sir.

Q. You mean, I suppose, when he went in and out of his room as men ordinarily do, with his boots and shoes on? *A.* Yes, sir.

Q. Do you pretend to say that Mr. Bedell could not, by taking off his boots and shoes, pass in and out of his room without attracting your attention when you were shut up in your room? *A.* I do not think it is impossible.

Q. Is it at all impossible that he could not go in or out of his room in his stocking feet without attracting your attention? *A.* I think it is improbable, for the reason that from using his key to open the door, I should be very apt to hear him.

Q. Suppose his door were unlocked, could he not then pass in or out in his stocking feet if he chose to do so, secretly and privately, without attracting your attention? *A.* It is possible.

Q. Is it not altogether practicable? *A.* When the door is left open you mean?

Q. I mean when it is left unlocked? *A.* Yes, sir; I think it is probable that it could be done.

Q. Do you know whether the clock in his room struck the hours correctly or not? *A.* I think it does so, for I have often set my watch by it.

Q. By the striking? *A.* Yes, sir.

Q. Did you attend any party political meetings at Columbus, some time prior to Ashburn's death? *Q.* I am trying to refresh my mind whether it was before or after that the young men's Democratic Club was organized. I think the Democratic Club was organized after the death of Ashburn.

Q. That is not an answer to my question—I will repeat it: Did you attend any party political meetings at Columbus, some time prior to Ashburn's death? *A.* I do not remember, sir, of having attended any immediately before or within a short time previous to it.

Q. Then if you do not remember of having attended any political meetings a short time before Ashburn's death, you can not state positively whether or not Bedell attended such meeting. *A.* I stated from a knowledge of his general habit of not attending political meetings.

Q. You do not then of your own knowledge know whether he attended political meetings or not previous to Ashburn's death? *A.* I can not state positively whether he did or not.

Q. During the severe pain which you say you were suffering when you woke up that night, and which I understood you to say continued to be severe for some time afterward, would you be likely to notice as particularly a person entering or going out of an adjoining room? *A.* I was particularly wakeful, and should have heard everything that passed within the hall; that I could have heard, or would have heard anything passing through the hall.

Q. You could have heard, but would not the fact that you were then suffering severe pain have prevented you from remembering matters of indifference? *A.* If this important event had not been made known to me the next morning, and my memory refreshed, I would probably not have noticed anything that passed.

Q. How far were your sleeping apartments from the place where Ashburn was killed? *A.* I do not know precisely the locality of the house that he was killed in; from the description given me, I should judge it was about five hundred yards.

Q. It seems that he was killed in a house on Oglethorpe street, diagonally across from the Perry House; how far were your sleeping apartments from that locality? *A.* Between four and five hundred yards, I reckon; my measurements can not be very accurate, because I have never seen the building to know it.

Q. Could you not, in a still night, hear the firing of ten or fifteen pistol shots, at that locality where Ashburn is said to have been killed, from your sleeping apartments? *A.* Well, sir, I do not know; I could hardly answer that question; I have thought of the firing that night, and accounted for my not having heard it from the fact of that being in the house and my own room being closely shut up—entirely closed; if it had been in the street it is possible I might have heard it.

Q. You say that prisoner Bedell came into your room between eight and nine o'clock the next morning after Ashburn was killed? *A.* I thought it was about nine o'clock.

Q. Do you know whether he had been out of the house that morning previously? *A.* I can not state; the usual noise that I hear in his room I heard that morning; that is, walking about.

Q. You mean that you heard him walking about in his room that morning as usual? *A.* Yes, sir, that is probably a better shape to put it in.

Q. Did he come into your room apparently from his own room? *A.* I think he came from his room into mine.

Q. Did you hear the usual noises in his room that morning which indicated he had left his room and gone off for the day, before he was in your room? *A.* Yes, sir.

Q. Do you mean he had been out, you suppose, and returned before he was in your room? *A.* That is what I presume.

Q. What time did he leave the room that morning? *A.* I think about the usual hour; about 8 o'clock was his usual hour for leaving the room; I will not be positive as to the precise time.

Q. Do you mean you will not be positive as to his usual time of leaving his room, or as to the time he left his room that morning? *A.* As to either the usual time or as to the time that morning, I mean I can not be positive as to the precise hour he leaves his room, but habitually, I think, about 8 o'clock.

Q. Why do you suppose he had been out that morning on the street before he came in to visit you? *A.* Because I heard the usual noise in his room, the same as I hear any morning, and presumed, as a matter of course, that he had been out before the hour that he came into my room; he never remained in his room later than nine o'clock that I observed.

Q. Can you say now that you distinctly remember of having heard him lock up his room and leave it, and walk out on the front stairs that morning? *A.* I can not. I did not think it was necessary—consequently did not charge my mind with the importance of noticing these things.

Q. Then it seems that he could leave his room and walk down stairs and you not observe it? *A.* He might have done it by taking a great deal of care, or going out in an unusually quiet manner.

Q. Didn't he do it that morning? You do not remember of hearing him go out of his room down stairs do you? *A.* I do not remember. I may have heard him, but I would not probably have noticed it particularly. I did refresh my memory though with regard to his being in his room at the usual hour in the morning—the time he usually got up.

Q. You refreshed your memory about his being there the usual hour in the morning in consequence of Ashburn's death, and his asking you some questions in regard to where he was that morning? *A.* Yes, sir.

Q. As all matters relating to his whereabouts that night were thus so early brought to your attention, after their occurrence, how does it happen that you can not remember whether or not he left his room to go upon the street that morning? *A.* I can not tell how it happens. It was just neglect on my part, I suppose, to think at the time. I am sorry I did not impress the facts more on my mind.

Q. Then as he walked out of his room without your being able to recollect it, might he not have walked into his room without your recollecting it, even if you had heard it? *A.* It is possible.

Q. What was Mr. Bedell's appearance that morning when you first saw him. *A.* I did not remark any thing unusual.

Cross-examination continued by Mr. Brown.

Q. Who kept the store-rooms under the sleeping apartments at the time of Ashburn's death? A. They had been unoccupied for several months previous to that.

Q. Are you able to state of your own knowledge that the doors might not have been open that night? A. Do you mean the doors of the stores below?

Q. Yes, sir. A. I think they could not possibly have been open, for the keys were in the possession of Mr. Jack R. Reed, I think, or the owner, McGehee. If they had been forced open, it would have been evident the next morning.

Q. When did you see the keys in the possession of either of those gentlemen? A. I have not seen them myself, but as a near neighbor, I have known others to go there for the keys to enter to look into the premises; they were for rent.

Q. Do you know of your own knowledge who had the keys of those store-rooms on that night? A. I do not.

Q. Could you swear that they were not in Mr. Bedell's possession? A. No, sir, I could not swear that.

Q. If they had been in his possession, could he not have gone down the back stairway and opened the door, and gone through the store-room into the street? A. If he had not the back door key, I think it is impossible that he would go through that way, for they opened only with the front door key, and the back door keys are left ordinarily in the door. That is the habit in all vacant houses. So I presume he would have some difficulty in getting through that way even with the front door keys.

Questions by Brown.

Q. Do you know that that is the habit in all vacant houses? A. Yes, sir, vacant stores, I think it is.

Q. Do you know that the keys were in the back doors of the store-rooms that night? A. I do not.

Q. Do you know that Mr. Bedell did not have the front and back door keys of the store-rooms that night? A. I do not.

Q. Is it not possible that he may have had them and gone through there that night? A. I hardly know; I suppose it is possible.

Q. I see by the diagram that the fence marked "G," which divides the back lot from Urquhart's lot, is six feet eight inches high; is it not possible for a man of Mr. Bedell's height and age to cross a fence of that height? A. By climbing over? I presume it is; I have seen an active negro climb over by several motions.

Q. Can not any man of ordinary activity cross a fence six feet eight inches high? A. Not without some effort; I should not think he could; it requires effort to do it.

Q. Can a man do anything without some effort? A. There are some things which do not require as much as others.

Q. Can not a man of ordinary activity, desiring to cross a fence, make some effort? A. Well, if there was not an easier mode of getting to the point wanted, I suppose he would make some effort to get over the fence.

Q. Suppose a man had desired to go down that flight of steps and go out that way, that being the mode selected by him, would he not have made some effort? A. I presume he would.

Q. Then you do not pretend to say that it took any very great effort to get over that fence, do you? A. Having never tried it, sir, I can not tell what effort it required; it appears to me to require some effort and some activity.

Q. Is Mr. Bedell able to exert some effort and some activity? A. I should suppose; but whether sufficient to climb that fence I am not able to tell.

Q. If he had a motive in going that way, do you not believe he could get across it? A. I do not think it is insurmountable; I think he might have gotten over it.

Q. When over that fence, was it not possible for him to have gotten into the street? A. By crossing another fence—the dividing fence between the yard of Dr. Urquhart's and the street.

Q. What sort of a fence was that? A. I think it is what is called a picket fence; it consists of pieces of wood some two inches in diameter, upright, about four inches apart, I think, with sharpened points; I judge it is about five or six feet high.

Q. Do you feel certain that your description is correct as to that fence? A. I think so; I do not think I am incorrect about that.

Q. Is there no gate through it or other way to get from Dr. Urquhart's lot into the street without scaling the fence? A. There is a gate through his front yard into the street.

Q. Is there not a gate from Dr. Urquhart's lot into the street? *A.* Yes, sir.

Q. Suppose Mr. Bedell had desired to go out of his room that night without your knowledge, could he not have opened his door, with his shoes off, and gone down the front way into the street? *A.* In the early part of the night he might have done so, and with a great deal of care he might have done it in the after part of the night, but I in all probability would have heard his key, and the door shut.

Q. Suppose he had gone into his room with the intent to do that, could he not when he entered have simply closed his door without fastening either the lock or the latch, and let it stand so until he desired to go out, and have gone out making very little noise. *A.* Possibly he might have done so.

Q. Well, you pretend then to swear that he did not go out that night? *A.* I only pretend to swear that I believe he did not go out.

Q. You can not state that he did not go of your own knowledge, can you? *A.* No, sir.

Q. Did anybody else enter Mr. Bedell's room the next morning before he went into the street? *A.* I do not know.

Q. Would you not probably have heard them if any one had gone in? *A.* I might have heard them.

Q. Is it not as probable that you would have heard any one else going in his room as it is that you would have heard him going out? *A.* I think it is quite as probable, except, if you will allow me to add, that I can distinguish Mr. Bedell's walk in the hall and in his room generally from any one else, and I should probably have distinguished his walk.

Q. As you are accustomed to hear him pass there daily, is it not less probable that you would notice his walk than the walk of some one not accustomed to going through there? *A.* No, sir.

Q. Don't sounds that we are accustomed to hear daily and hourly in our rooms frequently attract little attention on our part? *A.* Yes, sir. I think so.

Q. As an illustration, we get so used to the striking of a clock that we may often be in the room, and it strikes, and we never notice it, may we not? *A.* It is sometimes the case.

Q. Is it not less probable then that we would notice a sound that we are so familiar with, than it is that we would notice one we are less familiar with? *A.* Well, I do not know that that would be an invariable rule, or conclusion. It depends on the character of that sound—what it is that attracts us.

Q. Suppose it to be a sound that we are not accustomed to hear, would it not be more likely to attract our attention? *A.* I think an unusual sound is more likely probably to attract.

Q. Then it is more probable that the sound of feet to which our ear is unaccustomed, would attract our attention than the sound of feet which we are accustomed to hear daily and hourly? *A.* You are speaking now with regard to general sounds. In my room I hear very little, except the walking—the sound of persons walking up and down; and Mr. Bedell's walk is so very different from any one else who occupies that room that I generally remarked it, and noticed that they were his footsteps. It was the same way with the other occupants. When I hear them come up stairs I very often listen and can tell from their steps who it is.

Q. When there is nothing to attract attention to Bedell's walk or cause you to take notice of his presence, how long do you usually remember when he comes and goes out of his room? *A.* Well, if there is nothing to attract my attention to him, I should probably not remember it five minutes or pay any attention to it.

Q. Did you consider on that night that there was anything special to attract your attention to his movements or to cause you to recollect? *A.* No, sir.

Questions by Mr. Stephens, (with permission of the Court.)

Q. Who occupied Dr. Urquhart's house at that time? *A.* Dr. Urquhart and family, I think, who was keeping boarders. There were quite a number of families occupying the house.

Q. Would not a person passing through that yard that night, from the number of occupants in the house, have been more exposed to observation than he would even in Broad street? *A.* Yes, sir, I think so, or quite as much so.

Q. Would the passing out of Mr. Bedell in the morning to breakfast have been likely to have made as much impression on your mind as the passing in or out at that late hour of the night would? *A.* No, sir, I think not.

Questions by Mr. Brown, (with permission of the Court.)

Q. As you went to sleep at eight or nine o'clock that night and did not wake until about one, could Mr. Bedell not have come in from the streets with his shoes off, and gone into his room without waking you? A. Yes, sir.

Questions by the Court.

Q. When and how did you hear of Ashburn's murder? A. I heard it between eight and nine o'clock, I think, the next morning. It was told me by Mr. Ingmire, who came in to see after my condition.

Q. You state that you are awakened by Mr. Bedell's coming in or going out. Are you positive that you were never awakened between twelve and one o'clock that night by pain and not by Mr. Bedell's coming in? A. I was awakened that night by pain and not by Mr. Bedell's coming in.

Q. About how many minutes before the striking of one did you wake? A. I can not tell. I thought of it frequently since the time; I have endeavored to refresh my mind and I can not determine the precise time that I awoke, but I know it was some time before the clock struck one. It might have been half after twelve or quarter to one.

Q. When was the person who was represented as appearing like Bedell pointed out to you? before or after the murder of Ashburn? A. It was subsequent.

The examination of the witness having been concluded, Mr. Stephens presented the following:

"The credit of the witnesses Underwood, Reese, Tucker and Parham examined on behalf of the prisoner Duke, having been attacked on cross-examination, counsel for the defense now propose to offer the testimony of Hon. Hiram Warner, Chief Justice of the Supreme Court of Georgia, to support the credit of the impeached witnesses."

To which the counsel for the prosecution replied as follows:

"The counsel for the prosecution object to the admission of the testimony proposed, on the ground that the credibility of the witnesses named has not been attacked. They were carried through a sifting cross-examination with the view of testing the strength and accuracy of their memory. The counsel for the prosecution distinctly state that they make no charge that the witnesses named are not gentlemen of veracity."

Upon this statement of the counsel for the prosecution, Mr. Stephens, withdraws his request.

Thereupon, at the request of Mr. Stephens, who was feeling very much indisposed, the Commission adjourned until to-morrow (Tuesday) morning at ten o'clock.

McPHERSON BARRACKS, ATLANTA, GA.,
10 o'clock A. M., July 21, 1868.

The Commission met pursuant to adjournment. Present, the same members as yesterday, the Judge Advocate and his assistants, all the accused on trial, and their counsel.

The record of the proceedings of the previous day was read and approved.

The testimony of Roswell Ellis having been read over to him, he was asked by the Judge Advocate if he desired to make any corrections. He said: "There is only one, probably two, important inaccuracies. In speaking of the location of my wardrobe and the door of my room, it makes me say that it shut out the sound. Not shutting out the sound it should be. The other is in regard to the height of the platform; that is unimportant, I think. It may be that high or it may not. I think probably it is not."

Mr. Stephens, by permission of the Court, proceeded to examine the witness with regard to another of the defendants, Mr. Chipley.

Questions by Mr. Stephens.

Q. Are you acquainted with Mr. Chipley, one of the accused? A. I know him very well, and recognize him among the prisoners.

Q. Will you state to the Court what are his habits as to being out at night? A. I have never known him to be out at night except at the meetings of our reading and chess club.

Q. Who is President of that club? A. I was, sir, for several months; I presume six months, or longer.

Q. How often does it meet? A. The business meetings are about once a month —on the first Monday of each month. The club-rooms are open both night and day for the visit of its members, and such guests as may be invited.

Q. How many months, or how long

about before the death of Ashburn, had he been married? *A.* I do not recollect the date of his marriage, but several months previous to that.

Q. You have stated that he was not so regular in his attendance afterwards. Will you be more specific, or can you be? *A.* His irregularity was remarked by other members of the club after his marriage—his irregular attendance upon the meetings. He seems to have lost that interest he formerly took in the club.

Q. Was there any notice taken in the club, or suggestion made in regard to his absence? *A.* I think there were some jocular proceedings, threats to expel him, or something of that kind. Your inquiry brings to my mind something of that kind that did occur.

Q. Was there any gaming or drinking at that club? *A.* The innocent games at cards were permitted, and chess and backgammon. No betting was permitted, and drinking prohibited. By a rule of the club, no spirits were allowed to be brought into the club-room.

Q. When you speak of the proposed action in regard of his absence, do you refer to the regular evening meetings, or to the monthly business meetings, or to both? *A.* I refer to all the meetings.

Q. Did he neglect attending even the monthly meetings? *A.* Very often.

Q. What is the character of Mr. Chipley in Columbus? *A.* He is regarded as one of the best citizens; his character is unexceptional, unimpeachable.

Q. Did you ever hear or know of his being engaged in broils, or difficulties of any sort? *A.* Never, sir.

Q. Do you know of any persons about Columbus of the same size and form of body as Mr. Chipley? Do you know Mr. Thomas Hogan? *A.* I do, sir.

Q. How would he correspond with Mr. Chipley in size of body? *A.* I think he would correspond very closely.

Q. In the night and masked, would you undertake to swear as to which was which between those men—if they were masked? Mr. Hogan and Mr. Chipley were masked at night, do you think you could possibly tell which was which—which was Mr. Chipley? *A.* Do I understand you to ask me if their faces were only covered by mask, or do you mean disguised otherwise?

Q. If their faces were covered, I mean, and in the dark? *A.* No, sir, not if they were masked and in the dark.

Q. Do you know Marion Estis? *A.* I do.

Q. How does he correspond in size with Mr. Chipley? *A.* His size resembles Mr. Chipley's.

Q. Do you know the Reverend Mr. Devotee? *A.* Yes, sir.

Q. How does his size correspond with Mr. Chipley's? *A.* I think he is a little taller than Mr. Chipley, but otherwise I think his size, his form resembles Mr. Chipley's, but not quite as heavy.

Q. Do you know Rhodes Brown? *A.* I do.

Q. How does he correspond? *A.* His form resembles that of Mr. Chipley.

Q. Do you know Capt. Bevins? *A.* I do.

Q. If Mr. Chipley and Mr. Bevins were walking, in the night, a few steps before you, could you tell which is which at night? *A.* If it was so dark that I could not distinguish their carriage, their step, I might not be able to distinguish them.

Q. Did you ever hear a person speak through a mask? *A.* I have.

Q. Is there a change of voice or not? *A.* It does, sir, obstruct the natural tone very much.

Q. Were you ever at a masquerade ball? *A.* The only masquerade party I ever attended was at Mr. Chipley's house last winter.

Q. Was that a fashionable party? *A.* It was not a ball, sir, but a collection of his most intimate friends—a select party.

Q. Ladies and gentlemen? *A.* Yes, sir.

Q. Could you recognize any of the parties, even your most intimate friends, at that party? *A.* I could not, sir, and that fact created a great deal of merriment on the occasion. Some of my most intimate friends came to me, and would recognize me, talk with me, and shake hands with me. I endeavored to scrutinize and ascertain who they were, but was unable to recognize a solitary individual until they were unmasked.

Q. Were you masked? *A.* No, sir.

Q. When did they remove the covering from their faces—before or after supper? *A.* It was before supper, after the dancing was concluded.

Q. Do you know the amount of rewards that were offered for the discovery of the murderers of Ashburn? *A.* My knowl-

19

edge of those rewards was derived altogether from newspapers and what I heard others say.

Q. What was the amount of rewards published in the papers? A. The City Council of Columbus offered a reward of $500 for the proof of conviction of the assassin.

Q. What was the reward offered by the provisional government? A. That I understand to be $2,000 for the conviction of the just party.

Cross-examined by Judge Advocate.

Q. Were you in the habit of attending regularly at the club of which you have spoken? A. Being president of the club, it was made my duty to be present, and that is the reason I was there regularly. I attended regularly on the occasion of the monthly meetings, and it was because of that I resigned the presidency, because it was not convenient for me to be always on hand.

Q. How many evenings in the week did you usually spend at the club? A. I can not say how often, because I was not very regular, except at the monthly meetings; sometimes two or three times a week, sometimes oftener, and sometimes not so often.

Q. How do you happen to know then, as you were not there often yourself, that Chipley was not there? A. It was generally remarked by members of the club.

Q. Were the evenings that you did not spend at the club-house, spent by you generally in your own room—by evenings I mean the early hours of the night? A. I spent very few evenings in my own room until my ordinary bed time.

Q. Were you in the habit of meeting Mr. Chipley when you spent your evenings elsewhere than at the club-room? A. Yes, sir.

Q. How often in a week did you probably meet him, the evenings you spent elsewhere than at the club? A. For several months I passed immediately by his residence to my boarding-house, and met him very often on my way to tea and back; saw him at his house, and would frequently stop and spend a few moments with him.

Q. Can you state where he spent the balance of the evening after the few moments you spent with him in the early part, going to and returning from tea? A. I can not; I presume with his family.

Q. It was then merely presumption with you that he spent most of the evenings at home with his family? A. It is presumption with me altogether; he has the character of being a home man, going out but little from home at night.

Q. Can you not, in an ordinary starlight night, distinguish readily between your acquaintances when your are near to them? A. Yes, sir; I might not be able to distinguish all of them, but it is not improbable that I would distinguish him.

Q. Why distinguish him? A. There are some acquaintances I would not be able to distinguish by starlight, but those with whom I am more intimate and familiar I would be able to distinguish.

Q. Then if you could not see the faces of those persons with whose appearance you are familiar, could you not distinguish them by their movement, their carriage, their step? A. Yes, I often distinguish acquaintances by their carriage and step, without recognizing their features.

Q. Did you not testify that you could recognize Bedell, the prisoner, by the sound of his foot-step? A. Yes, sir.

Q. Could you not recognize other acquaintances in the same way? A. Those whose step I am as familiar with as his. If the Court will allow me in speaking of the masked party, the masks only were spoken of, I desire to put in that evidence that the reason why they could not be recognized was not simply because they were masked, but that they were otherwise disguised by fancy costumes.

Questions by Mr. Stephens—with permission of the Commission.

Q. Did any of them have on calico pants? A. Yes, sir, of every variety; I could not mention the different styles.

Question by the Court.

Q. What is your occupation? A. I am a commission merchant.

The testimony of the witness having been read over to him, he was asked by the Judge Advocate if he desired to make any corrections: he replied that he did not.

Questions by Mr. Stephens.

CICERO JOHNSON, witness for the defense being duly sworn, testifies as follows:

Q. State your name in full? A. Cicero Johnson.

Q. What is your age? *A.* I was twenty-four years on the first day of last July.

Q. Where do you live? *A.* In the city of Columbus, Georgia.

Q. Do you know a gentleman of that place by the name of Columbus C. Bedell? *A.* I do.

Q. Do you see him in the court room? *A.* I do.

Q. Can you point him out to the court? *A.* I can. (Witness points to prisoner Bedell).

Q. Were you in his service at any time in the early part of this year? *A.* I was.

Q. At what time? *A.* I had been in his service about a year up to the time he left Columbus—was arrested.

Q. What was the character of your service? *A.* I attended his room.

Q. Where was his room? *A.* On Broad street.

Q. What building? *A.* The building called McGehee building.

Questions by Defense.

Q. Were you attending his room at the time of the death of Mr. Ashburn—I mean during that week, at that time of the month? *A.* I was.

Q. What were your usual habits of business in attending to it? How did you attend to it? *A.* In making up beds, making fires, bringing water, cleaning boots.

Q. What time of the day did you this? *A.* I went there of evenings after I knocked off work; I usually knocked off work at six o'clock; at that time I used to go there in the morning just before I went to work.

Q. What other work were you engaged in—what other business? *A.* Gin carpenter.

Q. Did you attend to Mr. Bedell's room the evening of the death of Ashburn—that night? *A.* I did.

Q. Did you attend the morning after the death of Ashburn? *A.* I did.

Q. Did you attend earlier that morning than usual or not? *A.* Yes, sir, I was there a little earlier that morning.

Q. Please state to the court why you went there earlier than usual, and what you noticed on going to his room? *A.* My reason was that I awoke that morning a little earlier than I generally get up; I woke up and I was told that Col. Ashburn was dead; I went round, and when I got where he was dead at, I stayed a few minutes and then I went round earlier than I commonly do to Mr. Bedell's room; I went round there earlier than common as I had woke up earlier than usual.

Q. Did you hear anything up there of Mr. Bedell's being supposed to be one of the parties who killed Ashburn—by "up there" I mean the house where Ashburn was killed? *A.* Yes, sir. I heard that some such looking man was seen there as Mr. Bedell; that was the talk; they were talking round when I went up there that morning.

Q. In going down to Mr. Bedell's room did you have any motive to satisfy yourself whether it was so or not? *A.* Well, I remarked to some people who were standing round there talking that I waited on him in his room, and if there was anything of it perhaps I could see something by going there.

Q. What time did you go to his room? *A.* It was about sunrise.

Q. What state of things did you find when you got there? Was Mr. Bedell in his room? Tell the Court what you found. *A.* Yes, sir; I found him in his room in bed; I found him in his room as I usually found him every morning.

Q. Was he asleep or awake? *A.* He was asleep, I would suppose; I found him as I usually found him every morning.

Q. Did you satisfy yourself that he was not there, and if so state the facts? *A.* Well, when I went into his room and looked round I thought to myself it was a mistake about his being there; I could not see any thing to give me any evidence to think he was there, because I could not see any sign or any thing of the kind; but I found everything as usual, as I generally found it—his clothes and everything—and for that reason I thought it must have been a mistake.

Q. Was there any other reason besides the position of his clothes and other things upon his table? *A.* Yes, sir; every thing was on the table just as I left it that night; I could not discover any thing at all changed.

Q. What things do you speak of? How did you leave them? *A.* I speak of his books, his lamp, his papers, his pistol, and his two goblets, that set on the table.

Q. Do you recollect distinctly how you left that pistol when you arranged the table the evening before? *A.* I do.

Q. Was it or not just exactly as you left it? *A.* Yes, sir; it was lying just as I left it.

Q. Did you say any thing to Mr. Bedell, while you were there in his room, about the death of Ashburn? *A.* Yes, sir; after I got through with his room, my usual business, I woke him up and told him that Colonel Ashburn was dead.

Q. What did he say? *A.* He said it could not be impossible.

Q. What else did he say? Did he make any other remarks? *A.* He said it was a very bad piece of business ; it could make it only worse for the city.

Q. Did you tell him then of what you had heard of his being connected with it? *A.* No, sir; I did not.

Q. Why didn't you ? *A.* Because I didn't know whether it was so or not, and I did not like to have any thing to say to him about it.

Q. How did you enter the room? *A.* I have a key and he has a key.

Q. Are there any other keys? Where does Mr. Bedell keep his bank key? *A.* I find it on the table of mornings when I go in there.

Q. How far is the table from his bed? *A.* It is about four feet from the foot of his bed.

Q. Was the bank key in the usual place? *A.* I disremember now whether I saw the bank key that morning or not.

Q. Was the pistol in the usual place? *A.* Yes, sir.

Q. I believe you have stated you had arranged the pistol the evening before ; put the pistol down the evening before on cleaning off the table. Am I correct in stating that? *A.* Yes, sir.

Q. Did you examine the pistol before you woke him up? *A.* Yes, sir; I picked it up and looked at it.

Q. Did you examine it to see if it had been recently shot off? *A.* Yes, sir; there was no load shot out of it at all.

Q. Did you examine his bowl of water? *A.* I washed his bowl out that morning, as I usually do.

Q. Did you see any colored water, smutty water, or any thing of that kind about it? *A.* No, sir, I did not.

Q. Did you at any time that morning, or at any other time, see a waste of any sort in Mr. Bedell's room? *A.* No, sir, I did not.

Cross-examined by Judge Advocate.

Q. Did you observe whether the lamp had been lighted the night previous? *A.* I light the lamp every night and leave it burning, turning it down very low.

Q. Did you observe whether the oil had burned low that night? *A.* No, sir.

Q. It was about sunrise when you first went into his room, was it? *A.* Yes, sir.

Q. Was it before or after sunrise, do you think? *A.* It was about sunrise.

Q. You found Mr. Bedell apparently asleep? *A.* Yes, sir, I found him asleep. He appeared to be as I usually found him.

Q. How long did you remain in his room? *A.* I could not say exactly the time, for I did not notice the clock when I went in to see what time it was, nor when I came out; but I remained there long enough to attend to my business as I usually did.

Q. How long did it usually take you to attend to your business in that room? *A.* I could not say positively, for I never timed myself.

Q. You have some idea of how long it took you, for you have some idea of time? *A.* I could not say positively what time it was.

Q. Did it take you an hour? Did it usually take you an hour to attend to your ordinary duties in his room in the mornings? *A.* I do not suppose it took me an hour, but I could not say exactly what time.

Q. Did it take you a half an hour? *A.* Well, I would suppose it was somewhere along about that time; sometimes it takes me a little longer than common. I don't hurry so much sometimes as I do at others; sometimes I am a little late when I come.

Q. How was it that particular morning —did you get through your work sooner than usual, or were you longer about it? *A.* Well, I could not say—I do not remember whether I was longer or not that morning, because there was a great deal of excitement then.

Q. Had you finished your work before you woke up Bedell? *A.* I had.

Q. How long did you remain there after you woke him up? *A.* I do not suppose that I was in there over five or six minutes after I woke him up.

Q. Had he arisen from his bed before you left? *A.* No, sir.

Q. He was still in bed when you left the room? *A.* Yes, sir.

Q. Did he seem to be sick? *A.* I do not know whether he was or not; he didn't say anything to me that morning about being sick.

Q. Do you know how long it usually takes Mr. Bedell, after he gets up, to dress himself and make ready for the day's duties? *A.* No, sir, I did not—I never was in there when he dressed himself to go out.

Q. Did you unlock the door that morning when you went in, or was it unlocked when you went to it? *A.* I unlocked the door.

Q. Did it make any noise when you unlocked it? *A.* Yes, sir.

Q. Pretty loud noise? *A.* It makes only a tolerable noise. It is a spring lock, and you have heard about what noise that makes.

Q. Would it make noise enough for a person in the next room—the room of Mr. Ellis—to hear it, do you think? *A.* If he were awake it would.

Q. Would it wake him up, do you think, if he were asleep? *A.* I think not, without he is a very easy waker.

Q. How did you go to that room—did you walk heavily or lightly, as you went about your work there? *A.* I walked as heavily as I usually walk; I naturally walk heavily.

Q. Did you not, while you were at your work that morning, have occasion to go out and return before you completed your work? *A.* I did.

Q. How many times? *A.* Twice.

Q. You went out of the room and returned to it twice that morning? *A.* I did.

Q. Did you shut the door after you each time you went out? *A.* No, sir, I only pulled it as I usually do.

Q. You shut the door without locking it each time then, as I understand? *A.* Yes, sir, just pulled it to.

Q. At what time did Mr. Bedell usually go to his breakfast? Do you know? *A.* No, sir, I do not know his breakfast hour.

Q. Do you know whether he went to his breakfast at all that morning? *A.* No, sir, I don't.

Q. Did you pass Mr. Ellis' room as you went in and out of Bedell's room on business that morning? *A.* Yes, sir.

Q. How many times did you pass his door? *A.* I passed it going and coming.

Q. That was four times wasn't it? *A.* That was twice; I passed it to go to throw out the slop-water at the back end of the house and passed it coming back.

Q. Did you go out the back way but once that morning? *A.* Once, only.

Q. You say that you went in and out twice during the performances of your duties that morning. Where did you go to the other time? *A.* I went to the cistern to get a bucket of water.

Q. In going to the cistern after a bucket of water did you pass Mr. Ellis' room? *A.* I did not.

Q. But each time that you went out you opened and shut the door, didn't you? *A.* I only pulled the door to when I was passing out; after I unlocked it I closed it.

Q. How many times did you open and close the door that morning? *A.* I opened it when I went out to throw out some slop-water.

Q. That is once. *A.* When I opened the door to throw out some slop-water of course I was compelled to shut it after me.

Q. Exactly, that is opening and shutting it at once. *A.* When I went after the bucket of water to the cistern I did the same.

Q. That is twice. *A.* When I first went into his room that morning I unlocked the door and pushed it to after me.

Q. That is three times. Now how did you get out when you left there? *A.* Of course I had to open the door, and coming out pull it to after me.

Q. That is four times you had to shut and open the door that morning, wasn't it? *A.* Yes, sir, that would be four times.

Q. Did you lock it the last time you came out? *A.* No, sir, I never locked it when I came out and he was in there.

Q. Did you see Mr. Ellis when you first went to Mr. Bedell's room? *A.* No, sir, I did not.

Q. Did Mr. Ellis know that you were in Mr. Bedell's room that morning? *A.* That is more than I am able to say.

Q. Did you see him that morning? *A.* I did not.

Q. Do you know how and when the prisoner Bedell first learned that he was suspected of connection with the assassination of Ashburn? *A.* No, sir.

Questions by Mr. Stephens, (with permission of the Commission.)

Q. In pulling the door to, the latch, does it make as much noise as unlocking it or closing it? *A.* Closing it would make twice the noise I suppose, for it is a spring lock.

Questions by the Judge Advocate, (with permission of the Commission.)

Q. Could not the door be left nearly closed without shutting it tight? A. Yes, sir.

Q. Could you not be using the key in closing the door so as to let the bolt come in slowly, lock it from the outside without making much noise from the movement of the lock. A. No, sir, I think not.

Q. What makes you think not? A. My reasons for thinking not are because it was made very hard, the spring lock-work, many times I thought I had fastened the door, when on going back and trying it I found it was unlocked.

Q. You could shut the door then entirely without locking it? A. Allow me to show you the way (witness illustrates his meaning by means of a lock on a door of the room.)

Q. Has the door of Mr. Bedell's room no fastening but the bolt of the lock? A. The lock on Mr. Bedell's door is a spring lock and it has a fastening on the inside, and when it is fastened on the inside, of course you can not get it open from the outside, because there is a catch that comes down when the opening goes in and shuts the door. When that catch comes down from that spring, of course you can not open the door.

Q. Is the bolt of the door connected with the knob of the door? A. There is no knob to it.

Q. It has no other fastening then than simply the bolt of the lock—the bolt of the lock and that catch that works? A. I made a mistake there; it is opened by the spring lock above the bolt. It is a bolt the same as on this door here, but the spring is above that.

Q. You could not then move the knob without the use of the key? Is that the way of it? A. No, sir, you could not unlock it by working this knob without using the key.

Q. And if you did not choose to lock it, you could fasten the door just as you fasten the one here without locking it? A. No, sir, for this reason: the catch on Mr. Bedell's was taken off from the lock and put up alone and used for the spring lock.

Questions by the Court.

Q. Do you know how many pistols or revolvers Mr. Bedell owns or has in his possession? A. I never knew him to have but one during the time I waited upon him.

Q. Does he keep a pistol or revolver at the bank? A. I am not able to say.

Q. Are you certain the pistol had not been discharged and reloaded? A. Yes, sir, I am certain of that, because I picked it up and looked at it. I did so for the reason that I heard that such a looking man as him was seen there, and the first thing that popped into my mind, was that if there was any thing of it, I could tell something by looking at the pistol—the pistol being misplaced or anything of the kind.

Q. Was the pistol always kept loaded? A. I have never known it to be any other way during the whole time I waited on him. The pistol was rather rusty round where it was loaded; it had been lying on one place and was a little rusty. I do not think it had been shot off the whole time I waited on him. I used to have it in my hand almost every morning.

Q. Was it your business to load and to keep the pistol in order? A. It was not.

Q. Where was the ammunition for the pistol kept? A. I never saw any at all.

Q. Was the pistol always kept in the same place? A. It was.

Q. Was it in a holster, in a case, or naked on the table? A. It was naked on the table, on the top of a book.

Q. Can not the bolt of the spring lock of Mr. Bedell's room be caught so as not to slip out? A. Yes, sir, the spring lock, by putting that catch down as I have before said, can be fixed so that the bolt can not spring out without you raise the latch.

Q. On what part of the pistol was the rust? A. I could show you very easily if I had one. It is on the part where the cartridge enters into the barrel.

Q. Can you always tell that a pistol has not been discharged by looking at it, and that it has not been reloaded? A. Yes, sir, I can tell when it has not been discharged and reloaded when it has been lying a long time, but if it has often been reloaded I could not tell.

Questions by Mr. Stephens, (by permission of the Court.)

Q. Were those white or colored people you heard talking about the murder of Ashburn at the house where he was lying dead; and to whom you made the remark you did about Mr. Bedell? A. Colored people.

MILITARY OUTRAGE IN GEORGIA. 183

The testimony of the witness having been read over to him, he was asked by the Judge Advocate if he had any corrections to make. He replied that he had not.

Thereupon the Court adjourned until to-morrow (Wednesday) morning at ten o'clock.

McPherson Barracks, Atlanta, Ga.,
10 o'clock A. M., July 22, 1868.

The Commission met pursuant to adjournment.

Present, the same members as yesterday, the Judge Advocate and his assistants, the prisoners and their counsel.

The record of yesterday's proceedings was read and approved.

The following communication received by the President of the Commission from Major General George G. Meade, commanding Third Military District, was read by the Judge Advocate to the Court:

Headquarters Third Military District,
(Department of Georgia, Florida and Alabama,)
Atlanta, Ga., July 21, 1868.

Bvt. Brig. Gen. C. C. Sibley, U. S. A.,
President of Military Commission.

GENERAL—In view of the action of the Legislature to-day, and the probable immediate admission of the State of Georgia, and consequent cessation of military authority, the Commanding General directs that the Commission, of which you are President, will suspend all further proceedings in the trial of the prisoners charged with the murder of Ashburn. The prisoners, however, will be retained in custody until further orders.

Very respectfully,
Your obedient servant,
[Signed.]   R. C. Drum, A. A. G.

The Commission then adjourned until Friday morning, ten o'clock.

McPherson Barracks, Atlanta, Ga.,
10 A. M., July 24, 1868.

The Commission met pursuant to adjournment.

Present, the same members of the Commission as at the last meeting, and the Judge Advocate.

The record of the proceedings of the last meeting was read and approved.

The Judge Advocate announced to the Commission that he had no further business to bring before them, and thereupon the the Commission adjourned *sine die.*

APPENDIX.

From the Columbus (Ga.) Sun, April 12, 1868.

COLUMBUS, April 7, 1868.

General William Dunn:

DEAR SIR—I represent Mr. Chipley, Dr. Kirksey, William and Columbus Bedell, and some others who have been arrested, they know not upon what charge, but suppose that information may have been given at headquarters charging them with complicity in the brutal (and, for our town, unfortunate) assassination of George W. Ashburn.

In this, as in all cases of gross outrage, the innocent are apt to suffer for the wrongs of the guilty. The gentlemen whom I have named are above suspicion as being in any way connected with the transaction; several of them are men of family, and if public justice can be satisfied, as I trust it can, by an examination here without taking them from their families, it is very desirable that it should be done.

An examination, I am sure, would acquit them of any participation in the assassination. They can give *any bonds* that may be required for their appearance, and if you can influence this matter, I hope you will consider it advisable to allow these gentlemen to be bailed, until such time as their appearance may be required.

Your ob't serv't,

R. J. MOSES.

To Gen. Wm. Dunn, Advocate General.

HEADQUARTERS THIRD MILITARY DISTRICT, Department of Georgia, Florida, and Alabama, Office of Judge Advocate, Atlanta, Ga., April 9, 1868.

Major R. J. Moses, Columbus, Ga:

DEAR SIR—Yours of the 7th inst. was received this morning.

I am directed by Gen. Meade to reply that he does not deem it advisable to interfere with the action of Capt. Mills.

While there is a determination here that the parties who murdered Mr. Ashburn shall, if possible, be arrested and punished, it is hoped this may be accomplished without any serious inconvenience to the innocent.

Major Smythe, of this office, is now in Columbus, and I suggest that you confer with him fully and freely.

Your ob't serv't,

WM. DUNN.

GEORGIA, }
MUSCOGEE COUNTY. }

Know all men by these presents that we, whose names are hereunder signed, are held and bound unto Gen'l Geo. G. Meade, or his successor in office, in the penal sum of fifty thousand dollars, for the payment whereof well and truly to be made to the said Gen'l Geo. G. Meade, or his successor in office, we hereby bind ourselves, our heirs, executors and administrators, firmly by these presents.

Witness our hands and seals, this 10th day of April, 1868.

The condition of the above obligation is such that, whereas, Gen'l Geo. G. Meade has arrested and confined Wm. R. Bedell, Christopher C. Bedell, Jas. W. Barber, Alva C. Roper, Wm. L. Cash, Wm. D. Chipley, Rob't A. Ennis, Elisha J. Kirksey, Thos. W. Grimes, Wade H. Stevens, John Wells (col'd), John Stapler (col'd), and James McHenry (col'd), who have this day been released by order of Gen'l Geo. G. Meade, on condition that they would each give security, in the sum of twenty-five hundred dollars, that they would each report and appear before the military authorities of the United States, at such time and place as the commanding officer of the Third Military District may direct. Now, then, if any of the said parties, so released, shall fail to appear and report to the military authorities of the United States, at such time and place as the commanding officer of the Third Military District may direct, and the parties

APPENDIX.

to this bond shall pay the sum of twenty-five hundred dollars for each and every one of said persons so released who may fail to appear and report as aforesaid, then this bond to be null and void; else, to remain in full force and virtue.

Witnessed by R. J. MOSES, Notary Public.

Christopher C Bedell	J E Denton	Geo R Flourney	W H Crane
Elisha J Kirksey	Wm Fee	A M Brannan	W S Lloyd
Thos W Grimes, jr	Aug Davis	H Middlebrook	L D Lester
Wm Dudley Chipley	J Affleck	J N Ramsay	G M Williams
Wm R Bedell	E Kurniker	C R Russell	N J Bussey
Alva C Roper	Jacob Greenwood	T Markham	G B Young
Robt A Ennis	J H DeVotie	Sam Meyer	Wm M Snow
Jas W Barber	A Pond	S W McMichael	W P Ramsay
Wash H Stephens	W K Wright	R C Roper	Joe Norris (col)
W L Cash	C G Holmes	S E Lawhon	Jack Brooks (col)
John Wells (col)	Mont J Moses	Aaron Hurt (col)	R W Milford
John Stapler (col)	J T Coleman	G Delaunay	R Hugh Nesbit
Jas McHenry (col)	C E Booher	J L Dozier	J T Daniel
R J Moses	G Laudon	J D Stewart	J B Stewart
James M Smith	H W Chandler	J Chaffin	J G Thweatt
Lloyd G Bowers	J W Williams	J G DeVotie	A J Welch
Wm A Bedell	T T Moore	W C Coart	T C Carmichael
Robt A Ware	W H Perry	E W Terry	Jno W Murphey
J Ennis	Wm F Hall	T F Ridenhour	Thos Sweet
L M Biggers	J T Blount	L P Aenchbacker	O C Howe
John Munn	Wm C Cherry	F G Wilkins	H Moseley
George G Rucker	Jas A Cody	M Joseph	Alfred Holmes (col)
R F Sankey	J H Sikes	R W Milford	Van Marcus
Thos Gilbert	S M Dixon	E F DeGraffenreid	Richard Scott (col)
Alvah Trowbridge	John Swed	N N Curtis	Jas Kivlin
Wm N Jones	John King	H J Thornton	D L Booher
J T Lokey	S H Hill	N L Redd	D F Grant
W M Jepson	Jos F Pou	Jno McIlhenny	J L Dunham
W S Freeman	W J Chaffin	Thos W Grimes	C C Cody
Jno N Barnett	W K Banks	W W Garrard	W A Barden
Thos G Pond	Wm Mchaffy	R J Moses jr	T S Fontaine
Geo W Dillingham	J M Hughes	Adolphus A Coleman	A A Dozier
Chas T Crowder	Jno Cargill	Jno Johnson	W P Turner
J W H Ramsay	Robt W Ledsinger	M M Moore	W L Tillman
J W Barden	R C Pierce	H H Starr	A G Bedell
J T Colbert	R W Coleman	W H Young	J J Clapp
Wash Roberts	J A McNeil	Ben May	Thomas, Redd&Hatcher
Moses Bell	J M Bussey	J F Bozeman	R M Gunby
Milton Martin	J A McNeil	B F Malone	Jno E Bacon
F M Brooks	Jno Fitzgibbons	F C Johnson	A C Flewellen
G W Gafford	F W Acee	S A Billing	Thos Harris
M Connor & Co	R M Gray	T J DeVore	C S Harrison
Thos S Young	Thos J Chaffin	L I Harvey	Jno W King
Wm J Watt	Oscar Lee	O M Stone	R B Lockhart
Jas Meeler	Henry C Pope	Cliff B Grimes	J J Bradford
J G Burrus	Sam Cherry	Jas E Roper	Henry McCauley
B B Fontaine	P H Alston	Wm Perry	Jos Kyle
G W Radcliff	F K Donnelly	L Harris	Thos Ragland
J S Pemberton	J W Pease	Peter Preer	W W Flewellen
C B Taliaferro	John McCarthy	F Reich	Jno Quin
C A Klink	Jas K Redd	R M Gunby	E F Colzey
D B Thompson	Lawrence Rooney	Alex Stanford (col)	Wm B Hudson
F S Chapman	T J Word	J A Corbally	C T Johnson
F J Abbott	C E Johnson	Jno A Frazer	F Meyer
J W Ryan	Zac Mayo	Robt B McKay	A G Redd
W H Jackson	J R Clapp	J P Illges	Toney Fuller (col)
J L Mustian	A F Johnson	F M Thomas	Thos Rhodes (col)
A V Boatrite	W B Jones	H M Jeter	Chas Gwinnett (col)
E S Swift	O C Dibble	Milo Booher	D F Wilcox
P A Clayton	M D Hood	A W Allen	Jas Britton
		Jno Peabody	F Landon
		W H Brannon	E A Fisher
		W H Wells	J W Brooks
		G J Peacock	L G Schuessler
		Chas J Moffett	Wm Snow
		Jeff Taylor (col)	Chas E Estes
		Sydney Smith (col)	Wm H Robarts
		Elb Cunningham (col)	L P Warner
		Willey Milburn (col)	Jno L Hogan
		M Woodruff	Perry Spencer

Dav Armstrong (col)	Arch Crane	Wm Lane (col)	Jas J Slade
Chas A Green	Jno Johnson	N Rosenthal	G W L Mathis
R J Hunter	Jno McDuffie	G E Andrews	O S Acee
Homer M Howard	V H Taliaferro		
L Meyer	E E Yonge		
B H Crawford	C Northrup jr		
A M Allen	J A Sellers		
C D McGehee	D Wolfson		
J H Whittlesey	N Crown		
W H Chambers	J A Kirvin		
R C Jones	A Illges		
Reese Crawford	E G Stewart		
J H Bramhall	Jno D W Rindenhour		
Wm Munday	W R Kent		
T M Barnard	S B Papy		
Oliver Cromwell	B A Thornton		
Frank Gunby	D P Ellis		
W E Barnard	W C Gray		
R G Mitchell	R B Murdock		
T W Bradley	R Carter		
G W Bates	J J McKendree		
Chas Rogers	Jery Reed (col)		
S B Cleghorn	W Fleming		
Francis H Ellis	T S Spear		
Seaborn Benning	Geo Hargraves		
W B Langdon	I Joseph		
L Gutowsky	J A Bradford		
J D Johnston	B H Mathis		
A Gammel	W A Drufus		
J S Roper	J L Howell		
W J Pike	L F Watkins		
D E Williams	J D Clarke		
Dr E B Schley	W C Bellamy		
Hal Mitchel (col)	E Barnard		
C Shepperson	L R Hoopes		
Thos Chapman	J F Iverson		
J S Acee	J J Grant		
Geo P Swift	A C McGehee		
Wm L Matthews	Carlisle Terry		
J C Andrews	C Y Holmes		
Wm L Afflict	R B Murdock, jr		
Wm H Mims	H H Epping		
Chas E Dexter	G H Betz		
Wm E Pond	J A Morgan		
J H Smith	S B Warnock		
W Rynchard	J J Whittle		
W L Salisbury	J B Collier		
R M Norman	J W Barden		
C H Law	Arthur Ingmire		
J T Langford	Jas A Bacon		
W L Robinson	Jno W Aven		
J F Burrus	R H England		
T A Cantrell	D W Champagne		
Robt Knowles	Jno F Howard		
J L Morton	H W Blair		
Thos Names	Jno H Connor		
B T McKee	E G Woolfolk		
Wm A James	R H Estes		
J E King	C H Jones		
J J Wood	Barney Hawkins (col)		
W H Williams	Jas Aven		
J B Hogue	Jno A Johnson		
J Kuruiker	Jno R Ivey		
Jno Foran	Wm Stringfield		
W C Hodges	Jas E Cargill		
Sandy Alexander (col)	P E Bedell		
D Y Ridenhour	D. F Cargill		
F McArdle	Francis Fontaine		
Rich'd Porter (col)	E S Roberts		
Wm Pane (col)	M Pleasant		

COLUMBUS, GA., April 10, 1868.

CAPT. WM. MILLS—

Dear Sir: I would have returned the bond sooner, but the citizens of Columbus, confident of the innocence of the parties in confinement of any offense against either the civil or military authorities, insist on going on the bond, as an assurance to the parties arrested that they have the entire confidence of their fellow-citizens, and are above any well-founded suspicion of criminal conduct. It is with difficulty that I am enabled to close the signatures, even at this point.

With thanks for your courtesy in my intercourse with you in this unpleasant business, I remain,

Your obedient servant,

R. J. MOSES,

From the Congressional Globe.

MR. BECK. I submit the following preamble and resolution:

The Clerk read as follows:

"Whereas, it is asserted by William D. Chipley and others, citizens and residents of Columbus, Georgia, that they have been arrested and imprisoned without cause by order of General Meade, commanding the third military district, and that the cause of their arrest and imprisonment has been withheld and refused, as shown by the following letter:"

"OFFICE OF BLOUNT & CHIPLEY,
Grocery and Commission Merchants,
Columbus, Ga., May 18, 1868.

"*Dear Sir:* I may be presuming in troubling you with the facts which I will herein relate, and if so, can only offer our utter want of representation as my apology; and yet it may be that you will think that outrages concern every citizen of the country whether he lives North or South. As long as such can be committed with impunity, no man can feel safe. It will not do for one to expect his character to protect him from such attacks, for virtue is the favorite target of such marksmen. On the 9th of March, ten white citizens of this place, and three colored, were arrested by order of one Capt. Mills, commanding this post, and placed in confinement at the court-house, where they were detained under guard until dusk on the evening of the 13th ultimo. At the expiration of that time we were released under bond, the amount and conditions of which are fully stated in the printed slips which I inclose. From these clippings you will find that I was numbered among the prisoners. Were I writing to a stranger it might be proper to offer some testimonial of character, but you have known me from my earliest youth, and on that fact I rest my case. My companions in this arrest, so far as my personal knowledge goes, are as far above the suspicion of any implication in crime as any citizen in this or any other community. What I want is to arrive at the cause of my arrest. During the arrest, nor upon our release under bond, could we obtain any information concerning the evidence which led to our incarceration. It was entirely *ex parte*, and no clue to its character or the names of our accusers has been given us. If you consider it proper, I would like for you to offer a resolution calling for the facts in the case. Regretting the circumstances which force me to trouble you in this matter.

I remain, sir,
Yours very truly,
W. D. CHIPLEY.

* * * * * *

During the reading of the preamble and resolution,

MR. DRIGGS said: Mr. Speaker, I rise to a question of order.

THE SPEAKER *pro tempore* (Mr. Ashley, of Ohio, in the Chair.) The gentleman will state his point of order.

MR. DRIGGS. I understand that debate is not in order on this resolution, and that being so, I wish to ask whether it is in order for the gentleman to make an argument in favor of the resolution in the preamble with no opportunity on our part to reply to it.

THE SPEAKER, *pro tempore*. It is in order to recite papers as part of the resolution.

The reading of the preamble and resolution was then concluded.

MR. BECK. I demand the previous question.

THE SPEAKER. Resolutions calling for executive information, under the rules, must lie over for one day unless there be unanimous consent.

MR. KELLEY and MR. UPSON objected.

So the preamble and resolution were laid over.

DR. CHIPLEY'S PETITION TO CONGRESS.

To the Honorable Senate and House of Representatives of the United States:

Your petitioner, Wm. S. Chipley, respectfully states that he is a citizen of the United States, and a resident of the city of Lexington, in the State of Kentucky; that he is the father of Wm. Dudley Chipley, a citizen of Columbus, Georgia, who has been arrested and imprisoned by order of the military authorities of the United States, without cause and in disregard of the provisions of the Constitution of the United States, and carried out of the district in which any offense charged against him was committed, to Atlanta, Georgia, some two hundred miles distant from his home, and is now confined there in a cell which is wholly unfit for the confinement, even as punishment, of a criminal. He is denied the privilege of seeing or consulting with either his family, his friends, or his counsel, and deprived of all information as to the nature of the charge against him, without power to summon or procure the attendance of witnesses in his defense. In short, he is utterly at the mercy of his persecutors, and deprived of every right which the Constitution and laws secure to the citizen. He is not, and has not been, either in the naval or military service of the United States. He is a commission merchant in Columbus, a married man, and a good citizen, as all who know him will testify. Your petitioner does not know certainly what the charges against his son are, and can only surmise, from the statements of discharged negro witnesses, who were arrested, confined, and examined touching his connection therewith, that he is imprisoned for complicity in the murder of one G. W. Ashburn, who was killed in a house of ill-fame kept by a negress, in Columbus, on the night of the 31st of March, 1868. These negroes, since their release, have voluntarily given affidavits as to the mode of examination resorted to—the torture, starvation, and threats against their liberty and lives, to which they were subjected in order to extort false testimony against his son and others, which affidavits are filed herewith, and made part hereof as fully as is copied *verbatim* herein.

Comment on the facts stated in said affidavits is unnecessary—indeed, can only be fitly made under the right of discussion in your honorable bodies. Your petitioner will not venture to make any. The enormous rewards—over $25,000—offered for the conviction of some person or persons as the murderers of Ashburn, have induced spies, informers, detectives, and suborners of ignorant and corrupt witnesses to embark in the scheme of procuring conviction, and with the military assistance afforded them, probably by arrangement for division of the spoils, it will be wonderful if they do not buy or coerce some testimony on which they can procure a conviction in a military court organized to convict.

But whatever means may have been or may hereafter be resorted to to procure conviction, your petitioner, conscious of the entire innocence of his son, does not desire to elude or evade, but on the contrary desires the fullest, freest, and promptest investigation of his conduct, either in regard to Ashburn's murder or anything else. All he asks is that he be tried before the organized courts of the country, in accordance with the principles and rights guaranteed to him by the Constitution and laws of the land; that he be treated as a citizen and protected by the presumption of innocence till his guilt is established; that the spies, informers, suborners, and perjurers who are seeking his life may be required to swear to such facts as they may state before a court competent and willing to punish perjury. The courts of the State of Georgia and of the United States are open and uninterrupted in the district in which Columbus, Georgia, is situated, and impartial justice can be administered therein without sale, denial, or delay. Such a trial can be obtained through the intervention of your honorable bodies, and your petitioner prays for such orders or resolutions as will procure it for his son and the other persons similarly charged and imprisoned.

Very respectfully, your ob't serv't,
W. S. CHIPLEY.

From the Atlanta Constitution
THE INQUISITION REVIVED.

If Innocent III, who instituted the punishment of the Albigenses and Waldenses in the twelfth century, or Gregory IX who in the Council of Tolouse, in 1229, gave final form to the inquisition, and committed to his Bishops the management thereof, could awake from their graves and revisit the haunts of men, they would recoil with horror at the relation of the atrocities perpetrated upon free born citizens in District III.

Gregory thought his Bishops too indulgent, and gave to the Dominicans the direction of the inquisition. Grant, in 1868, concludes that his soldiery is too indulgent, and to a set of spies, pimps and detectives transfers the offices of infamy and the responsibility of torture.

Atlanta, to-day, has within her limits, a bastile wherein tyranny revels and riots in wanton punishment of innocence; prisons where liberty is scoffed and laws are perverted to the tastes of blood-hounds and brutes; dungeons whose bars and bolts are proof 'gainst *Magna Charta*, and cells that bid defiance to the last appeal for personal liberty. O, what a shame upon civilization! What a deep, damning blot upon the American soldier! What a stigma upon the escutcheon of "the people's" government! General Meade, do you know the extent of the misery inflicted on the inmates of McPherson prisons? Can it be possible that you knowingly permit the inhuman severity there practiced by your subordinates? You, a brave soldier, a gallant representative of a proud and powerful government—is history to write you down "the tyrant," and transmit your name to posterity blackened with crime and besmeared with infamy? We are informed that you are not the author of these infernal atrocities; but you are in command, and can prevent them; and refusing to do so, when you have the power, is a crime but a grade below that of positive action. It is said, we know, that the prisoners are under the control and management of detectives, and that they, acting under orders from the head of the army, are responsible for the fiendish malignity and racking tortures visited upon the victims who have fallen into their hands.

It matters not, just now, where the responsibility rests—a great crime is being committed, a burning, blistering shame is fastening itself upon the military of the Third District, and the commanding General must answer to the country and to his God for the outrage. In the name of humanity, of christian civilization, of common sense and common justice, of the power and glory of the American flag, we enter our solemn protest against the wanton, wicked, revengeful treatment of the young men confined in the cells of McPherson

Barracks. The rack may come, and the hari-kari may drink the blood of the innocent: but martyrdom is not always the worst alternative in the final catastrophe of liberty.

STATEMENT OF JOHN WELLS, FREEDMAN, MADE JUNE 11, 1868, AT COLUMBUS, GA.

I was taken, with the other prisoners arrested at the same time with myself, to Fort Pulaski. We were all stripped and examined for weapons and money. All money was taken from the prisoners, and has not yet been returned so far as I know; nor has the clothing been given back to them. Each prisoner was put into a cell by himself; the cells are four feet by six feet, with a very narrow opening above for ventilation; one vacant cell was left between those occupied by prisoners, so that no two prisoners occupied adjoining cells. Soon after our arrival persons apparently in authority inquired, in the hearing of witness, whether "the razors" were ready to shave the heads of prisoners. Being answered affirmatively, witness was blindfolded and taken off to another part of the fort; his head was lathered; two men held him, while others, standing around, prepared to shave his head, and spoke of what was to be done. They drew his head back, and in an effort to put himself in a more comfortable position, the bandage was pushed from his eyes, when witness discovered he was in a casemate or other large room, and that a cannon had been trained upon him, and that a man seemed to be in the act of firing it directly at him. Witness was very much alarmed; supposed they were about to kill him, and begged for a little time to make a statement, and meet his fate. They replied that there was but little time then, but they would give him fifteen minutes. Witness stated all he knew of the occurrences on the night of Ashburn's murder; where he was at various hours of the night; how and when and where he heard of the killing; and affirmed most positively his own innocence, and his entire ignorance of any fact or circumstance going to implicate others. He spoke of his own previous character as a citizen and member of the church, saying he had told them the truth; that he could not utter a falsehood to implicate innocent persons, and that if for this they still persisted in taking his life, they must do it.

Witness was finally taken back to his cell; was left there for some days longer—during which he was repeatedly interrogated—and was finally permitted to walk out, and, at length, was allowed the freedom of the fort. This privilege was granted, as he was informed, because the parties examining him believed that he was innocent, and knew nothing against others. Witness was put to work about the fort.

The persons who blindfolded witness and interrogated him, he understood, were detectives, perhaps officers in the detective force.

John Stapler, another prisoner, witness learned, was put through the same process as himself. One of the detectives subsequently said to witness that Stapler had told two tales which contradicted each other. He (Stapler) was finally put into the "sweat-box," and kept there from Saturday morning until Sunday night. Does not know whether the answers finally extorted from him were satisfactory to the inquisitors or not. Heard, however, that Stapler stuck to the last tale he told, which, witness was informed, referred to Barber, another prisoner, and amounted to but little.

Witness was told that if he divulged anything he saw or heard while at Fort Pulaski, they would put him in there for five years. There was some lumber at the fort, which, the prisoners of the garrison told witness, had been brought there to erect a gallows to hang the prisoners from Columbus.

Ex-provisional Governor James Johnson, the present Collector of the port of Savannah, visited the fort while the prisoners were there. Heard him ask Barber who killed Ashburn; said he [Johnson] knew every one of the damned rascals, and so did he [Barber]. He denounced Dudley, Chipley, and Dr. Kirksey, and other prisoners, as damned scoundrels and assassins, and said they were the leaders of it. Johnson was very violent and denunciatory. Barber made no reply that witness, who was standing above, could hear.

It was reported at the fort that Alex. Stanford, an emigrant to Liberia from Columbus, while detained two weeks in Savannah waiting for the ship to sail, made several visits to Jas. Johnson, and for the sake of money, was induced to make statements, the object of which was to implicate others; and it was even said by many, if not all, that the recent arrests had been made in consequence of his pretended disclosures. Heard Johnson talking to Stephens the same day he talked with Barber, but some work was going on in the neighborhood, and could not distinguish what was said.

The white prisoners, at least Daniel and Betz, were taken off and examined also, but what was said and done witness did not learn.

A soldier prisoner, or one who appeared to be such, told witness that the authorities intended to hang five or six of the principal prisoners, and send the others to prison for ten or twelve years.

For nine days witness had no meat to eat, and supposes the other prisoners fared no better. His breakfast consisted of bread and coffee, without sugar; his dinner was rice soup. Supper same as breakfast. After the nine days meat was given to the prisoners.

Some of the soldiers of the garrison were kind, others were not. Of the latter class were two who used to gather up the food for prisoners, and throw it to them as if they had been dogs.

When the prisoners were taken to Atlanta from Fort Pulaski, witness was brought along with them, though in a separate car, as far as Macon, when he was told he could return to his home in Columbus.

The two detectives, who seemed to have chief control in the examination of prisoners, said they had come from Washington.

Prisoners had no bedding or blankets.

JOHN WELLS.

Witness:
P. W. ALEXANDER.
E. T. SHEPHERD.
WM. KING.
JOHN MCKENDREE.

STAPLER'S AFFIDAVIT.

STATE OF GEORGIA, }
MUSCOGEE COUNTY. }

John Stapler, being duly sworn, says, on the 14th of May, 1868, he was driving a wagon in the peaceful pursuit of his business, when a United States soldier came up to him and seized him, leaving his wagon and horses in the street, without anybody in charge but a boy, who he (Stapler) induced to mind them while he was under arrest. He was then taken to the military guard-house in Columbus, detained there about one hour, and then carried under guard to the Muscogee depot, and taken thence to Savannah in company with John Wells, James Barber and Wade Stevens. Remained at Savannah in the guard-house about an hour and a half; we were taken thence to the steamer and carried to Fort Pulaski. After some delay we were carried in, one at a time. Deponent was carried to a cell, and there confined. After being in the cell about one hour and a half, Whitley, a government detective, (the same man who has since frequently visited us at McPherson Barracks, Atlanta,) and Capt. Cook, who commands at Fort Pulaski, came to the cell and unlocked it and made deponent come to the door, when Capt. Cook directed his orderly to search thoroughly the person and pockets of deponent. Whitley and Capt. Cook then spoke together, and Capt. Cook ordered the barber sent for to shave deponent's head in one hour! Deponent was then put back in the cell. In about an hour he was brought out blindfolded, carried down into a room, seated in a chair, and the bandage taken from his eyes. Then he was asked by Whitley "if he ever was discoursed by a minister before he was put through," and he said he had an order from Gen. Meade "to put him through," and then asked Capt. Cook to allow him a little while before he put deponent through, to which Capt. Cook replied he would not do it. Whitley insisted, and at last Capt. Cook consented to give Whitley fifteen minutes by his watch "to put deponent through."

When the bandage was taken from deponent's eyes, he saw a soldier standing near a brass cannon with a string from the cannon to his hand, and wherever deponent turned the cannon was ranged upon him. Deponent's head was then lathered with two scrubbing brushes; there were two or three razors lying on the table. Deponent was made to stand up and be measured against the wall. During this time he was asked by Whitley if he knew, or had ever heard the people say anything about the

Ashburn murder. He said he did not know anything and had not heard anything about it. Whitley replied, you need not tell me a lie, the rebels have been posting you, but it is no use. Whitley then gave deponent till the next day to consult and study, and see if it would not bring some good. Deponent was then put back in his cell and there remained in solitary confinement, never seeing Whitley again for four or five days, when he came there, took him out of his cell, carried him to another part of the fort, and showed "the sweat-box," and told him if he didn't up and tell all he knowed about it, he would put deponent in that sweat-box and keep him there thirty days. Deponent told him he didn't know nothing, and could'nt tell anything without it was a lie; but he must tell him all he knew! He then put deponent in the sweat-box, which is a closet in the walls of the fort, a little wider than deponent's body, the door closes within three or four inches of the breast, the only air admitted is through a few auger holes in the door. He was left in this condition under the belief that he was to remain there thirty days, unless he told about the Ashburn murder. He remained in this position about thirty-three hours, when Mr. Reed and Capt. Cook came and took him out. Whitley came up and said he allowed they had taken deponent out too soon, and he would have deponent back unless he told what he knew. When deponent was taken out his limbs were swollen and painful, and to this day he suffers from the confinement. He was then turned loose and allowed to walk about the fort, where he remained until the 9th of June, he was then put under guard and carried to Atlanta. During all this time he was strictly forbid to talk to any one. About the 10th of June he was put in McPherson Barracks, where he was very well treated, except that he was under orders not to talk to any one without permission. On Saturday, the 11th of July, in the afternoon, Whitley came to deponent and other colored persons who had been detained in prison, and told us to go to Maj. Smythe's office. When he got there Maj. Smythe gave him an order for $146, which he supposed was for witness fees and transportation. Deponent further says that he was never used as a witness, and never knew anything to witness about. Deponent further says that Stevens and Barber both knew that he had been put in the sweat-box, and how he had been treated.

his
JOHN ⋈ STAPLER,
mark.

Sworn to and subscribed before me, July 13, 1868.
JOHN KING,
Notary Public.

SANDY NELSON'S AFFIDAVIT.

MUSCOGEE COUNTY, }
STATE OF GEORGIA. }

Personally appeared before me, this 6th day of June, 1868, Sandy Nelson, a colored man, who, being duly sworn, deposes and says that on Monday, June 1, 1868, about eleven A. M., deponent was arrested on the streets of Columbus by one Thomas Grier and a Federal soldier, and carried to headquarters of this post, and delivered over to Capt. Mills, commanding post; that in the room were three other United States officers, names not known, besides Capt, Mills; that he was first accused of being a *Democratic negro*, and a *book* was produced and referred to, in which were written names, among which deponent saw and read his own name. Deponent at once protested against this arrest, and told one of the officers: "Captain, I am not a free man;" to which the officer replied that "Yes, he was; but he was trying to make himself a slave again by his vote;" that questions and remarks were rapidly addressed to him by all these officers, not giving deponent time, if he could have so done, to have answered them. Finally Capt. Mills asked deponent, "When did you wait on Cliff Grimes?" to which he answered "Two years ago."

Mills—You need not be lying; tell me where Cliff Grimes was on the night Ashburn was killed?

Deponent—I do not know, as I was not here.

Mills—Where were you, sir?

Deponent—I was on the steamer C. D. Fry as a boat hand—Abe Fry, master—on the river. We were coming up to Columbus, and were met by the steamboat Shamrock near Bellevue, and by her were told of Ashburn's death.

One of the officers then asked him about Cliff Grimes' character. Deponent said: "He was a perfect gentleman; did not know anything else about him. He treated deponent very kindly."

After several questions and cross-questions to same effect by said officers, Capt. Mills told deponent that "all this lying would do no good;" that he (Mills) knew all about the matter, and was determined to get the truth out of deponent, and he might as well own up.

Deponent again asserted he knew no more than he had stated, when Mills asked him if he could write his name. Answer: "I can." Mills: "Here! write your name on this sheet of paper, so I can know you tell 'e truth;" at the same time giving him pen, ink and paper. Deponent said he was too sharp to write his name to a blank paper; but taking the pen wrote Capt. Mills' name. Mills: "You are sharp, Mr. Nelson." Deponent: "I am not sharp, but I am honest." Mills: "I'll have the truth out of you, sir." That deponent was kept in a guard-room under the court-house, all that night with nothing to eat; that on Tuesday Capt. Mills and the same three officers visited him in his cell and propounded substantially the same questions as before, with same results as before. This was about ten A. M. They left him again; he was locked up, and kept without one mouthful of food, and none was offered him by the guards. An old negro woman, Mary, brought him some food, but it was not allowed him by the soldiers. That he was so guarded and kept till Thursday morning, when Capt. Mills came again to see him, and asked about the same questions, with result as above, and as he was about to leave, deponent asked leave to go to see his sister, Nancy Nelson; he was allowed to go under promise of returning again that afternoon. He went, and reported back at about five P. M. same day. The food he got at his sister's was the first and only he received during his said confinement from June 1st to June 4th.

That he was again questioned by Mills same as before—same results—when Mills said "he would have the truth out of him?" Again he was put in the guard-house, where he stayed till Friday morning, 5th instant, at about 7 A. M., when he was released, Mills saying: "Mr. Nelson, you may go; I believe you are an honest man."

SANDY NELSON.

Sworn and subscribed before us, this 6th day of June, 1868.

WM. A. GUERARD,
D. P. ELLIS,
R. J. MOSES, Jr., Notary Public.

GEORGIA, }
MUSCOGEE COUNTY, }

Before me personally appeared Abner Griffin, who, being duly sworn, deposes and says that on the Wednesday, the third day of June, 1868, in the county and State aforesaid, being then in the employ of Colonel E. T. Shepherd, on his place in Wynton, Georgia, he was arrested by two Federal soldiers and taken under guard to Captain Mills' headquarters; that he was kept a prisoner there from 11 A. M. to 6 P. M.; that he was examined by two men, one in the uniform of the United States, and the other in citizens' clothes, with a military cap; that he was asked what time Dr. Kirksey came home on the night of the murder of George W. Ashburn, and he replied, between seven and eight, and that then one of the officers called him a damned liar, and said that they would send him to Fort Pulaski, with a shaved head and a ball and chain on him; that he was greatly frightened, and in exceeding fear of his life. Deponent testified that he got the Doctor's horse the next morning; did not notice anything different about the horse. The harness and buggy were in their place, where they had been put by deponent the night before; and that he was not then allowed to go out of the room; he was kept there all day, and before leaving he was again called in and asked the same questions over again, to which he gave the same answers. He was then told he might go, if he would be at his place when they sent for him again. Deponent promised, and was then permitted to go home. Deponent further says that he did not know any cause why he should be arrested, and asked, but no information was given.

his
ABNER ✕ GRIFFIN.
mark

Sworn to and subscribed before us, this 6th June, 1868.

R. J. MOSES, JR.,
Notary Public.
W. A. GUERARD,
RYMER O. MOSES.

Clara Brooks, a colored girl, ten or twelve years of age, employed on the plantation of Col. Edward Shepherd, testifies that she, in company with several other negroes, was arrested by Federal soldiers, taken to headquarters, and confined for a short time, and was questioned, under threats by the officers conducting the examination, as to the whereabouts of Dr. Kirksey, one of the parties arrested on the night of the killing of Ashburn.

Charlotte Hall, a negro woman employed as a servant in the house in which Grimes, one of the parties arrested, lives, testifies under oath that she was arrested, taken to military headquarters, placed in close confinement, not allowed communication with any one. She was kept in close custody for three days, and during this time was subjected to repeated long and severe examinations by the military officers; was cursed and threatened by the officers. She testifies under oath as follows: "Just before leaving, one of the officers told me I was lying all round, and that I would rather rot in the fort for three or six years than to tell the truth on my damned Democratic friends; that I might as well tell the truth, for Frederick (a Frenchman who waited on Mr. Wright) had told all about it, and that when I went to Atlanta and met Frederick he would catch me in a lie. One of the officers then took a piece of rope and put it under my chin, and said that when they got me to Fort Pulaski they would do me that way until I told the truth on my Democratic friends. Was re-imprisoned, taken out again, and re-examined in the same way. One of the officers was writing at a table when I was being examined. I do not know what he wrote. Before being discharged I was asked if I was not the mistress of some of the young men. One of the officers proposed to send me to Fort Pulaski, but the others objected, and, after being warned not to let my Democratic friends run me off, I was discharged."

Cicero Johnson, a colored man, testified that he was arrested, taken to military headquarters, and was examined by Major Leonard, of the Freedmen's Bureau, Capt. Mills, and another officer. Had several long and severe examinations, and was repeatedly cursed and threatened; was put in prison without food, bedding, or lights, and was taken out from time to time and examined and re-imprisoned; one of the officers said to me, "We are tired of your lying and will have to send you to Fort Pulaski, where you will have your head shaved and wear a ball and chain." The same officer asked me if I knew how long I would be alive; was accused of being a Democratic negro and was questioned as to my reasons for quitting the Loyal League; the officers told me they knew all about the matter, and their questions and threats were to make me implicate the young gentlemen arrested for the killing of Ashburn.

From the National Intelligencer.
PUTTING NEGROES TO TORTURE.

We have conversed with several intelligent gentlemen from Georgia, delegates to the New York Convention, in reference to the extraordinary cruelties perpetrated by the military commander, Meade, in that State, and his infamous satellites and co-workers. Two men were assassinated on the same day, not long since, in Georgia. One was a southern citizen, prominent, respectable, but no Radical. He was assassinated in open daylight, on the public highway. The military authorities offered a reward of two hundred dollars for the apprehension of his murderers. The murder of this citizen, from whatever motive, did not move these officials from their equipoise. But that night, in a low negro brothel, at Columbus, there fell, also by the hands of assassins, (most probably of his own party,) a low Radical tool, Ashburn by name. Ashburn was an inmate of this degraded haunt of vice, and had his own feuds with his own low personal and party associates, whose path he had crossed. It was a murder like the other, however, to be duly investigated by the appropriate and ordinary modes of civil tribunals. Yet it suited the purposes of the Radical faction and carpet-baggers in Georgia, who thrive upon whatever of malignity and prejudice they may excite against the southern people, to ascribe this assassination to prominent citizens, men of good repute as orderly and quiet citizens, and enjoying the entire respect and esteem of the community. All of a sudden, numbers of these were thrown into prisons—small, narrow cells, destitute of proper light and ventilation—denied the privilege of seeing relatives, or counsel, or of meeting or learning by an open preliminary investigation what were the crimes actually laid to their door. Whilst thus cut off from all human intercourse except that of their cruel captors, still greater barbarities were practiced upon negroes, in order to make them accuse and criminate these gentlemen. We omitted to state that in contrast to the reward of two hundred dollars offered in the first case of a prominent citizen slain, there was offered the unusual and extraordinary reward of forty thousand dollars by the military for the discovery of the assassins of Ashburn. We need not say that such rewards as these may always procure bad men who are ready to commit any perjury essential to the earning of such a reward. Those who, thousands of years ago, offered thirty pieces of silver for false testimony, wanted their case proved up, and proved it was. Give a radical military "detective" forty thousand dollars and the use of the torture upon witnesses in order to fabricate his testimony, and he will hang any number of victims that may be needed to appease the malice of tyrants.

Two infamous "detectives," of the Baker-Stanton sort, were summoned, coming, it is said, from this city, and went down to Georgia. They were told that they could earn this forty thousand dollars if they succeeded, and then the military gave them *carte blanche* to arrest any citizen of Georgia, and full power over the unfortunate negroes, to bribe, threaten, starve, imprison, and torture these wretched creatures, who swore in the presence of Almighty God that they knew nothing about the matter, until they should, *to save themselves from further suffering* consent to tell whatever stories foul monsters put in their mouths. That they have done these things can be proved by the testimony of the released negroes, who have been subjected to these infernal cruelties. We have published the affidavits of some of those, but they leave much to be stated.

Among the methods of torture employed by these wretches upon the negroes, to make them swear away human lives, was the instrument known as the "*sweat-box*." This, we understand to be a box of wood, inside of which the victim is made to stand. The wooden side of this box, by means of a screw, are compressed closer and closer, until the individual can scarcely breathe; then a stream of hot air or steam is thrown upon the victim; he is almost stifled; a pressure put upon his heart and lungs, until the agony of his position is such that human nature sinks under the infliction, and the poor creature cries out that he is ready to testify to anything desired. *We assert that our information is positive and reliable, that these infernal cruelties have been practiced by the Federal military in Georgia upon black men, in order to make them swear away the lives of innocent white men and respectable citizens before a military commission, "organized to convict," and with murder in their hearts.*

From the Columbus Enquirer.

A MISERABLE PRETENSE.

It is reported here that the military authorities deny their agency in the cruel statement of the Columbus prisoners, and the foul means used to extort testimony against them, saying that the whole matter is in the hands of detectives or agents sent from Washington! Who commands in this "district?" Who takes jurisdiction from the civil courts and assumes it for the military power? How could detectives or agents from Washington do such deeds here without the co-operation of the military authorities? The military being the ready executors of the orders of the agents from Washington, and military authority being supreme in this State, it is hardly credible that such a pretense has really been set up.

It is not, however, at all surprising if the instigation of these outrages upon the rights of citizens can be traced to Gen. Grant. To disobey his commands would be insubordination, and for this reason the chief responsibility may devolve upon him. But this does not relieve the military power of the agency in the matter. It only aggravates the case by showing that its highest officer approves the acts done, and that therefore one avenue of relief may be considered as closed. Can the people of the North feel secure against similar treatment of themselves, should Gen. Grant be elected President, with a Radical Congress to sustain him?

From the Columbus (Ga.) Enquirer, September 17, 1868.

GEN. MEADE'S "VINDICATION."

Gen. Meade's statement concerning the prisoners arrested and tried for the murder of Ashburn (from the National Intelligencer) does not exculpate him, or clear up some suspicious acts with which he must have had connection. That he needed such exculpation is virtually admitted by his declaration that he wanted the trial "for his own vindication." In what respect did its developments or its results vindicate him? Did it disprove the charges of the arbitrary arrest of citizens without any evidence whatever against them, and the refusal to them of a speedy investigation and an honorable discharge if innocent? Did it clear up the mysterious outrage by which men were, for a number of days, held in torturing and loathsome confinement, without being informed of the character of the charges alleged against them, and at last discharged without reparation or even apology for the outrages inflicted upon them? Did it disprove the affidavits as to "sweat-boxes" and other means of torture to which prisoners were long subjected in a military prison within the district under his command? Instead of disproving these charges, the trial tended to confirm them, and they have since been exposed by a detective, and confessed by Gen. Meade.

It appears from this report that Gen. Meade was, before the trial commenced, anxious for it to be by military commission (for "his own vindication"), and that he then claimed the right to carry on the trial to its conclusion, even if civil authority should be restored while it was pending. What produced the change that afterwards caused him to drop the trial as quickly as possible? It was evident before the "restoration" furnished a pretext for dropping it, that the military authorities were quite tired of it. The evidence for the defense was most overwhelming in its proofs of a conspiracy, of perjury, and its strong suggestions of subordination of perjury. There was to be no "vindication" of the Commanding General, or of any one else who had been active in the prosecution, by the continuation of the trial. That was plainly to be seen. At this stage of its progress, Gen. Meade's claim of authority to carry on the trial to its conclusion was abandoned; the trial was abruptly closed; those witnesses who had perjured themselves were sent far out of the State and beyond the reach of the civil authorities; the party unmistakably indicated as the chief suborner, was permitted, like the militia captain who was a "little lame," to start in advance and put himself far out of the way of civil authority or process. Was there any "vindication" of General Meade in all this?

What followed? One of the detectives "employed by *Gen. Grant* and Gen. Meade to work up the case," made a public confession of the infamous means resorted to to intimidate and corrupt the witnesses. Then Gen. Meade found it advisable to try another mode of "vindication," and the mode was the publication which we are considering. To use a very common and homely phrase, he has "jumped from the frying-pan into the fire." He has only involved himself in new difficulties and perplexities.

It will be remembered that when the Macon Telegraph, on the authority of a citizen of Macon, stated, a few weeks ago, that Gen. Meade had admitted the resort to the "sweat-box" and described the instrument, the General demanded the name of the author of the report, and made him state publicly that his (Gen. Meade's) allusion to the matter was made to a little child, and was probably only a piece of pleasantry. Now he has admitted the use of the sweat-box, and his description of the instrument corresponds with that which he gave to the child. Why, then, was he so indignant when his remarks to the child were made public? Why solicitous that he should be understood as speaking to her only in jest? The "vindication" evidently does not cover this inconsistency.

The laurels of Gettysburg! Have they not been ingloriously bedraggled in the politics of Georgia?

NOTE.

At the time Gen. Meade dissolved his military commission, convened to try the Ashburn prisoners, he remarked to the counsel for the defense that he would be compelled to publish a statement in his own vindication. Knowing that any report which would vindicate him in his deep and damning guilt must necessarily be replete with falsehood, this publication was postponed several weeks that his misrepresentations might be exposed. After it was put into the publisher's hands, the press dispatches of the 10th of September announced that Gen. Meade had at last been delivered. This work was at once suspended, and after ten days' delay the abortion has been placed before the country in the shape of a synopsis in the National Intelligencer of the 10th, and Gen. Meade's official communication accompanying his exhibits, and of date — July, 1868. The review of the synopsis from the Columbus (Ga.) Enquirer, which has been made a part of this publication, fully exposes Gen. Meade's false positions. A brief notice of a few points in his official report may be proper before he is consigned to the grave of infamy which he has prepared for himself. Gen. Meade says in his report:

"On the 30th of March last, a little after midnight. G. W. Ashburn, ex-member of the Constitutional Convention of Georgia, was assassinated at a house where he was boarding in the town of Columbus."

He does not add the fact that he was killed in a low negro brothel, where crime ran riot, and where, at least, two violent personal enemies had visited that night; men who had threatened to kill him. although members of the Radical party.

Gen. Meade goes on to state that "subsequently Capt. Mills reporting that the energy of the civil authorities was all show and merely assumed, and that he could place no reliance on them, I removed the Mayor and Board of Aldermen, together with the Marshal and his Deputy—appointing others, and appointing Capt. Mills Mayor. About the 6th of April, nearly a week after the assassination, Capt. Mills having obtained sufficient evidence to warrant his action, arrested, by my order, some ten citizens of Columbus. either as participators, accessories, or for having some knowledge of the facts of the case. These persons were subsequently released on bonds to appear and stand their trial."

Capt. Mills told the citizens that he did not know why the arrests of the 6th of April were made, and that he had no hand or part in it except to make the arrests by order from superior officers. He assured several of the gentlemen arrested that if the Ashburn affair caused it, they need not be troubled, as "he knew they were not guilty." When released on bond to stand trial, Mills declined to tell them what the charge was, or the names of their accusers. This portion of the report involves a question of veracity between Gen. Meade and Capt. Mills.

Gen. Meade further adds:

"Soon after his arrival at Columbus. Mr. Whitley reported he was satisfied Capt. Mills was on the track of the criminals, and had arrested some of the principals, but that it was utterly impracticable to obtain any testimony from any party in Columbus, as their lives would be forfeited if they dared to disclose what they knew, and he recommended that certain parties, whom he believed had a knowledge of the affair, should be removed to some secure place, where, being protected, they could without fear disclose such facts as were in their possession."

This is simply stuff. With the military power of Third Military Kingdom at his back, Whitley pretends that he was not safe in Columbus. The whole matter lies in a nut-shell. Fort Pulaski, with its cannon, sweat-boxes, loathsome cells, and depressing climate, offered better facilities for "operating upon the fears" of prisoners than Columbus, hence the removal.

The nursery-rhyme General, the man who told the little child in Atlanta such very funny stories, rose even above his colleagues Smythe, Whitley, and Brown, when he penned the following:

"All these reports are herewith submitted, and it will be seen from them, and from the affidavit of the prisoners themselves attached to Mr. Whitley's report, that the exaggerated statements which, for political purposes, the press have given circulation to are false, and have no foundation beyond the fact admitted by Mr. Whitley that he did operate *on the fears of two negroes*. Wells and Stapler, whom he believed knew something; but soon finding they knew nothing, they were released."

Gen. Meade basely, maliciously, and deliberately lies when he states that the prisoners ever made such an affidavit as is represented above. He boasted some weeks ago that John Wells had made an affidavit that he had never made any prior affidavit concerning his treatment at Fort Pulaski. It will be noticed that this man's account, as contained in this book, is in the shape of a statement, witnessed by four of the most respectable citizens of Columbus. Of his suborned wretches no one can speak, but that such an affidavit was ever signed by Bedell, Barber, Hudson, Kirksey, Duke, Wood, Chipley, Wiggins, or Roper, is false. Dr. Kirksey did write a statement addressed to "whom it may concern," and intended for the agent sent out by the Secretary of War to investigate the outrage, which was signed by the other prisoners. This statement spoke of the personal bearing of the garrison officers as kind, and of Whitley as respectful. Not being such men as he could suborn, he dared not be otherwise. That statement protested against arrest without warrant—imprisonment without examination in cells two feet ten inches wide—the restriction on visits from friends, relatives, and counsel, and other outrages. Any other statement purporting to be from the prisoners is a forgery. The original paper, as written by Dr. Kirksey, was not intended as a retraction of any charge made against the authors of the outrage, but designed to nail the guilt where it belonged—to Gen. George G. Meade. Wells was detained nearly a month, and Stapler a longer time. This is what Meade calls *soon*. The funny man thinks that Daniel, who laid in a cell at Pulaski for weeks. and Grimes, who was imprisoned at Atlanta, and others, were well compensated for their suffering when he paid them three dollars per day of the money of the United States. He says:

"The character of the crime, the social *status* of parties implicated in its commission, and the doubts as to the guilt of of the several parties, had no influence on me except to increase my determination to bring the facts out, even at the risk of for a time putting persons to inconvenience who might subsequently prove innocent. Hence many arrests were made of parties who were subsequently released, on its being proved that they were neither participators or had any knowledge of the case. In all these cases these parties were well treated, and on being discharged were paid the usual witness fees for the period they were removed from their business.

Gen. Meade deprives his peers in everything, and his superiors in many attributes that mark a gentleman, of their personal liberty, and then insults them with such statements as the above. Grimes, Daniel Cash, Marks, Lawrence, Wm. Bedell, Eunis, and others, whose names there is not time to obtain, never received a dollar, but refused their contemptible offer with scorn. Great stress is placed upon the *animus* of the Columbus people and the *status* of the parties arrested. Consider the Duke *alibi*. He proved by the man he boards with that he was not in town. The man who carried him to the country swore to it; another acquaintance saw him going; one man slept with him, the night of the assassination, forty miles from the scene of the murder; a dozen others swore he was at the same place at dusk the evening Ashburn was killed, and early the following morning; one witness, a physician, knew he was correct concerning the time by the date in his record; another located it by a log sale which involved entries in the books of the mill-man and a blacksmith, who mended a link broken while hauling logs; several others were interested in a cotton transaction, and their recollection was fully confirmed by the books of the cotton dealers in Lagrange. Thus was an unequaled *alibi* established, and *not by Columbus witnesses*. Yet Duke was sworn to more positively by the witnesses for the prosecution than any other prisoner.

"The trial has been in progress now some twenty days, and the evidence for the prosecution made public. It is for the Department and the people of the country to judge whether with the evidence as adduced on the trial, I was not only justified but compelled to arrest and bring to trial the parties implicated."

He claimed that this trial was necessary for his vindication. Why was it interrupted? While the suborned witnesses were trying to swear the lives of innocent men away, the Commission held long sessions, but when the defense commenced introducing their overwhelming testimony the Court held very short sessions. It was Gen. Meade's idea to place the evidence for the prosecution before the country and then turn the prisoners over to the civil authorities, but a dilatory Legislature disappointed him, and caused a portion of the evidence for the defense to be produced notwithstanding the short sessions of the Commission.

A few days after the trial commenced, General Meade declared to many persons that he would give his head for a foot-ball if he did not convict all or a part of the prisoners. This fact shows that he, Meade, was in possession of the whole secret of the manipulating of the perjured testimony manufactured by Whitley.

Very soon after the rebutting testimony had been gone into, Meade saw that everybody was convinced that the whole batch of testimony against the prisoners was a mess of perjured villainy, very blunderingly gotten up. Meade then at once determined to get the case off his hands. About the time Meade commenced this trial there were two resolutions before Congress, to-wit: "Arming the negroes," and the continuance of all trials began by military commissions by the same court, even after Georgia had been admitted into the Union by the adoption of the 14th Amendment.

Congress had been impressed, by Gen.

Meade, that he would convict the Columbus prisoners, and it would afford capital enough to drive through Congress the bill for arming the negroes; and they were determined that Meade should have the pleasure of convicting the prisoners; hence the resolution that the trial should not be taken out of his hands after Georgia's admission.

When the rascalities of Howard and Meade, in regard to this trial, began to be exposed, how quick the Jacobins of Congress dropped these two measures, because the point they expected to make out of this thing against the Southern people was lost. The Georgia Legislature was slow in adopting the 14th Amendment, but Meade was in haste in getting the Columbus prisoners out of his hands. To expedite the passage of the 14th Amendment he manipulated the Legislature, and endeavored to have some of the Democratic members expelled. He failed in that. In the mean time the trial was progressing, and the further it progressed the more damning the guilt of Meade became apparent. Every means was resorted to to induce the Legislature to pass the Amendment, and relieve Gen. Meade.

One, or probably two, of the lady friends of Meade approached Mrs. B., a friend of Gen. Meade and a Southern lady, and appealed to her to do all she could with her Democratic friends to get this measure passed by the Legislature.

One of the counsel for the prisoners, against the expressed wish of the prisoners, absented himself from the trial for one whole week. The cause of this absence, as he stated to Major E., was to operate with Democratic friends to get the measure passed. Nothing was left untried to relieve Meade in this way, but the Legislature was dilatory. Meade finally, desperate at the continued exposure of his guilt by the developments of the trial, resolved to adjourn the Military Court, which everybody knew was a final dissolution.

The part that Grant, Meade, Howard, and Congress took in the trial of the Columbus prisoners gave it an importance that can hardly be appreciated. The villainy of the whole thing should be freely ventilated to the people.

Smythe, Whitley, and the perjured witnesses have been sent away from justice by Gen. Meade, and it will not be long before an outraged public will make Meade and Brown regret that they are not with their brother suborners.

www.ingramcontent.com/pod-product-compliance
Lightning Source LLC
Chambersburg PA
CBHW020035240426
43666CB00041B/1634